Architectural Framework for Web Development and Micro Distributed Applications

Guillermo Rodriguez
QuantiLogic, USA

A volume in the Advances in Web Technologies
and Engineering (AWTE) Book Series

Published in the United States of America by
    IGI Global
    Engineering Science Reference (an imprint of IGI Global)
    701 E. Chocolate Avenue
    Hershey PA, USA 17033
    Tel: 717-533-8845
    Fax: 717-533-8661
    E-mail: cust@igi-global.com
    Web site: http://www.igi-global.com

                    Library of Congress Cataloging-in-Publication Data

Names: Rodriguez, Guillermo, 1975- author.
Title: Architectural framework for web development and micro distributed
  applications / authored by Guillermo Rodriguez.
Description: Hershey, PA : Engineering Science Reference, an imprint of IGI
  Global, [2023] | Includes bibliographical references and index. |
  Summary: "With Micro Distributed Applications (MDAs) becoming the new
  frontier of web development where components will be created to
  distribute to clients, this book is for those involved in the software
  development domain to assist in understanding the new wave of
  applications to come, and the creation of search systems"-- Provided by
  publisher.
Identifiers: LCCN 2022028316 (print) | LCCN 2022028317 (ebook) | ISBN
  9781668448496 (h/c) | ISBN 9781668448502 (s/c) | ISBN 9781668448519
  (ebook)
Subjects: LCSH: Software frameworks. | Software architecture. | Web site
  development. | Computer file sharing.
Classification: LCC QA76.76.S63 R63 2022 (print) | LCC QA76.76.S63
  (ebook) | DDC 006.7/6--dc23/eng/20220815
LC record available at https://lccn.loc.gov/2022028316
LC ebook record available at https://lccn.loc.gov/2022028317

This book is published in the IGI Global book series Advances in Web Technologies and Engineering (AWTE) (ISSN: 2328-2762; eISSN: 2328-2754)

British Cataloguing in Publication Data
A Cataloguing in Publication record for this book is available from the British Library.

For electronic access to this publication, please contact: eresources@igi-global.com.

Advances in Web Technologies and Engineering (AWTE) Book Series

Ghazi I. Alkhatib
The Hashemite University, Jordan
David C. Rine
George Mason University, USA

ISSN:2328-2762
EISSN:2328-2754

MISSION

The **Advances in Web Technologies and Engineering (AWTE) Book Series** aims to provide a platform for research in the area of Information Technology (IT) concepts, tools, methodologies, and ethnography, in the contexts of global communication systems and Web engineered applications. Organizations are continuously overwhelmed by a variety of new information technologies, many are Web based. These new technologies are capitalizing on the widespread use of network and communication technologies for seamless integration of various issues in information and knowledge sharing within and among organizations. This emphasis on integrated approaches is unique to this book series and dictates cross platform and multidisciplinary strategy to research and practice.

The **Advances in Web Technologies and Engineering (AWTE) Book Series** seeks to create a stage where comprehensive publications are distributed for the objective of bettering and expanding the field of web systems, knowledge capture, and communication technologies. The series will provide researchers and practitioners with solutions for improving how technology is utilized for the purpose of a growing awareness of the importance of web applications and engineering.

COVERAGE

- Human factors and cultural impact of IT-based systems
- Quality of service and service level agreement issues among integrated systems
- Integrated Heterogeneous and Homogeneous Workflows and Databases within and Across Organizations and with Suppliers and Customers
- Web Systems Architectures, Including Distributed, Grid Computer, and Communication Systems Processing
- Strategies for linking business needs and IT
- Web systems performance engineering studies
- Software agent-based applications
- Mobile, location-aware, and ubiquitous computing
- Case studies validating Web-based IT solutions
- Information filtering and display adaptation techniques for wireless devices

IGI Global is currently accepting manuscripts for publication within this series. To submit a proposal for a volume in this series, please contact our Acquisition Editors at acquisitions@igi-global.com or visit: https://www.igi-global.com/publish/.

Titles in this Series

For a list of additional titles in this series, please visit: www.igi-global.com/book-series

Trends, Applications, and Challenges of Chatbot Technology
Mohammad Amin Kuhail (Zayed University, UAE) Bayan Abu Shawar (Al-Ain University, UAE) and Rawad Hammad (University of East Londo, UK)
Engineering Science Reference • © 2023 • 373pp • H/C (ISBN: 9781668462348) • US $270.00

Strategies and Opportunities for Technology in the Metaverse World
P.C. Lai (University of Malaya, Malysia)
Engineering Science Reference • © 2023 • 390pp • H/C (ISBN: 9781668457320) • US $270.00

3D Modeling Using Autodesk 3ds Max With Rendering View
Debabrata Samanta (CHRIST University, India)
Engineering Science Reference • © 2022 • 291pp • H/C (ISBN: 9781668441398) • US $270.00

Handbook of Research on Gamification Dynamics and User Experience Design
Oscar Bernardes (ISCAP, ISEP, Polytechnic Institute of Porto, Portugal & University of Aveiro, Portugal) Vanessa Amorim (ISCAP, Polytechnic Institute of Porto, Portugal) and Antonio Carrizo Moreira (University of Aveiro, Portugal)
Engineering Science Reference • © 2022 • 516pp • H/C (ISBN: 9781668442913) • US $380.00

Advanced Practical Approaches to Web Mining Techniques and Application
Ahmed J. Obaid (University of Kufa, Iraq) Zdzislaw Polkowski (Wroclaw University of Economics, Poland) and Bharat Bhushan (Sharda University, India)
Engineering Science Reference • © 2022 • 357pp • H/C (ISBN: 9781799894261) • US $270.00

Handbook of Research on Opinion Mining and Text Analytics on Literary Works and Social Media
Pantea Keikhosrokiani (School of Computer Sciences, Universiti Sains Malaysia, Malaysia) and Moussa Pourya Asl (School of Humanities, Universiti Sains Malaysia, Malaysia)
Engineering Science Reference • © 2022 • 462pp • H/C (ISBN: 9781799895947) • US $380.00

Security, Data Analytics, and Energy-Aware Solutions in the IoT
Xiali Hei (University of Louisiana at Lafayette, USA)
Engineering Science Reference • © 2022 • 218pp • H/C (ISBN: 9781799873235) • US $250.00

Emerging Trends in IoT and Integration with Data Science, Cloud Computing, and Big Data Analytics
Pelin Yildirim Taser (Izmir Bakircay University, Turkey)
Information Science Reference • © 2022 • 334pp • H/C (ISBN: 9781799841869) • US $250.00

701 East Chocolate Avenue, Hershey, PA 17033, USA
Tel: 717-533-8845 x100 • Fax: 717-533-8661
E-Mail: cust@igi-global.com • www.igi-global.com

Table of Contents

Preface

The text that you find before you fits a void in the technological space that prior to this body of work was un-addressed. There has been an evolution in the development space that has been such because of the flux that has been created by solutions that have preceded. At one point in history teams use to build software systems such that they would be bought at retail outlets and be physically carried to computers to be installed on and utilized. Humanity has migrated from this paradigm to one where the software that is needed sits in the cloud and may be purchased at the whim of the customer without the need to have to leave the comfort of their homes. Society has become indoctrinated into this paradigm where what it wants is before them when they want it as long as the internet connection functions. Society has migrated from the world of patience to a world of intolerance for anything but immediate satisfaction because such is the urgency that mankind all subscribes to. This evolutionary process that society has been under has ushered in the world that it now finds itself in and has ushered in the domain of the companies that have more clout than some governments around the world. This dynamic has created institutions that rival governments which have a seat at the United Nations because such is the power that technological organizations have had bestowed upon them by the masses. Only the future generations will be able to determine if progress was made or if society regressed but nevertheless, the status quo is as such because of the decisions that have been made collectively and the power that technology has come to have with each and every one. Today is a time when the FAANG stocks can largely determine how markets move because this is the reverence humanity pays them and the clout that they hold over everyone and apparently the capital they hold. This clout that they have placed on society has manifested in the technological landscape and the solutions that are now viable. Physical products have changed because of the momentum of influence that technology has had on the very essence of commerce. It is because of this clout that technology mandates that development teams must now alter the mode by which they develop those solutions that the masses will become loyal to. Society has conceded much to technology and has done so to the point that it now mandates what products will become the winners and which products will remain in obscurity. The evolution of the technological landscape has been such that it now means that organizations must play by the rules of engagement that it mandates. The products that teams are to build and that their customers will buy will be such not because of the shiny shrink wrapped box that they come in but because they may be found firsthand by any suitor. It is a new game that organizations must play where the stakes are high and the winners will take the lion's share of the spoils. This text is about this dance that organizations are all subject to and must partake in to have their products take root with customers. This text is about the evolutionary journey that humanity has been on and yet never recalls buying a ticket for. There is a just reason why organizations find themselves where they are now and it is because of the dynamic that is change and the momentum that search has had.

The law of unintended consequences mandates that there are ramifications to decisions taken that on the onset may not have been considered but nevertheless will present themselves to have flux on the domain. Each time a search is performed on one of the platforms of the search providers has led to feeding the monster that has become that entity that governs much of the experience of society in general. Society in essence helped to build these organizations that fuel much of humanities drive literally and figuratively today. Where would society be for example without Google maps? Where would society find itself if it could not answer the most obscure of questions from children that have proven to be just a little brighter than the parents perhaps? Daddy, can you tell me how photosynthesis happens? A question that has plagued more than a single parent on a given occasion. Humanity has come to depend on these businesses that it in turn has helped to create with the endless amount of time and interest that it has bestowed upon them. When this did occur, these businesses evolved and they changed much like an organism evolves over time. These businesses changed to become larger and have more clout in society because after all they were the preferred organism by the environment. Whether it happened knowingly or unknowingly is inconsequential because society finds itself at a point and time where the reality of these decisions have come home to roost. Collectively society has to now live with the reality of what it has created. These entities in turn have created a flux upon society whereby now development teams need to change the manner by which they create those solutions that the masses consume. This is where the doctrine of Micro Distributed Applications (MDAs) comes in, they are points of leverage that rely on the same entities that force society to function in this particular mode. This mode of operandi has in turn become the protocol by which understanding in the landscape occurs. It is the means by which the winners and losers are selected, it is done by popularity. It is this leverage that development teams will need utilize to help their applications communicate relevance and in turn viability. This mechanism by which relevance is now determined is such because of man's choices and the state of technology being what it is currently. It is because of this marrying between implicit and explicit choice that the tone by which the future will be dictated and this dictation will occur through distributed JavaScript applications that the masses will vote upon to elect the winner, but now it will be done through utility, function, and as a result the landscape will become the domain of MDAs.

Just as the days when society use to have to drive to the retail store to purchase that needed software are gone so too will be gone the days when development teams will build large monolithic applications that sit on servers in the cloud and consumer the profit of business to the benefit of the large public cloud organizations. Society has now come to usher a new age, where applications will be smaller, distributed, JavaScript laden, microservices infused, and that utilize the hardware of the client to operate. Society is ushering a new paradigm that has been forced upon everyone by the large search providers and because of which development teams can now leverage them to help their applications obtain clout where these applications become the voice of authority on the internet and consequently help organizations reap the benefits of mass adoption. To get to this understanding however entails that development must first part on this journey that has taken society to where it now finds itself. In order to understand how society has arrived where it finds itself at present entails that the primer must first be understood as it is the underpinnings that dictate system homeostasis. This change that is spoken of did not happen overnight, but rather occurred over a prolonged period of time and it occurred with societies consensus. This journey is detailed in the early chapters, and it is used to help define the doctrine of development that has arrived and that development teams must now subscribe to in order to create SaaS applications that are relevant and have clout with the populous.

The introductory chapter of the text lays the grounding for what the reader needs to expect from the text. The introductory chapter serves as a mechanism by which the content of the text can be given a theme, and which helps to set the stage for the understanding of where the domain now finds itself. The chapter discusses how relevance has come to dictate the mode by which industry must now adhere to in building web applications. The subject matter of distributed systems is discussed where the reader is introduced to how the distributed nature of MDAs will come to dominate the landscape given their reliance on the physical hardware of the client lessening the burden of the MDA provider on their own hardware to execute functionality. The reader is introduced in the chapter to the notion of why indexing data has been the driver to derive the new system homeostasis where functionality on the web will be driven by the ability of it to be indexed and categorized by the search providers based upon the mass adoption of the community at large. This chapter helps to put the focus of the text into a better light with the reader so that you can come to understand how the profession has arrived at the junction it finds itself at and why it matters for development of applications to come.

The chapter on the ruins walks the reader through the history of indexing and how the landscape evolved over time to its current state. The chapter discusses the mathematical foundations that envelopes the indexing domain so that the reader can become privy to the underpinnings of what constitutes search. The chapter introduces the reader to the notion of system variables as they are the basis for the derivation of the search engine formulas that are derived in a later chapter. By understanding the roots of the paradigm, it will become feasible to help the reader find the new datum point where the profession now finds itself at and help the reader understand the significance of the new development construct that is brought forth here with MDAs.

The chapter on system variables discusses the indexing domain and the particular attributes of the domain that influence page relevance. By understanding the components that have flux on the system it becomes easier to have influence over the domain and this is the reason why this chapter has significance. The chapter is discussed under the guise of the systems engineering doctrine whereby it becomes easier to understand why system state is such, it is because of the attributes of the landscape that create flux. This flux that is alluded to here is because of the relevance that the search engine providers have placed on the attributes that are defined here and which come to play later in not only the modeling effort that is undertaken but also with the creation of the physical MDAs. The system attributes are the specific components of relevance that are utilized by the search providers to determine worth and as such it mandates that they are not only understood but they are woven into the fabric of MDAs that are built. This chapter helps to set the stage for later content whereby the attributes identified here are later discussed under the guise of creating relevance.

The chapter on prescriptions walks the reader through a physical artifact that is provided by the largest search provider and discusses the content under the systems perspective that was addressed previously. This chapter helps to create that alignment between the theoretical and the practical so that the story that is to come can come to have meaning with what may be seen in practice. This chapter highlights for the reader the gaps that are present between what is outwardly conveyed by the index provider with the reality that unfolds itself when search does occur. There is a reason why a delta is determined between the system variables and what is outwardly expressed by the search provider, given that the magic formula can never be disclosed for fear of capitalization by the populous. It is nevertheless interesting to note that a parallel does exist between what is discovered to show worth in the indexing space and what is outwardly expressed by one of the major search engine purveyors. This should be the case however given the narrow scope of the page, assuming of course that the system boundary is deemed to be the page, which is at times not the case as can be seen with studies that focus on query logs for example.

Search is an activity that the masses all perform to have their questions answered by the powers that be and as such it is important to understand what exactly it entails with regards to the system variables that have been identified. The chapter on search delves into the physical Python algorithm that was created in order to determine system variable worth with both the Yahoo and Bing search engines. The chapter introduces the reader to not only the code that was created to data mine the search providers but also sets the stage for the defining of the metrics that will later be used to create the approximation formulas to the search providers. The algorithm created in Python does not simply function as a data mining utility but also fits the purpose of extracting the indexing results from the search providers that later may be used to validate the supervised learning model that is created. This chapter is a direct example of what may be accomplished through a supervised learning model and shear computational effort. The reader should also note that the code written in the Python programming language could have been extended to utilize the data science functions that are readily available in Python, but an alternative approach was implemented. The text specifically utilizes the R programming language to conduct the mathematical work effort to divide the labor and show the reader that the two domains do not necessarily need to be comingled. An alternative approach to tabulation can be taken whereby programming and computation can be divided, and a clear handoff can be obtained between one domain and the other. This leads to the creation of files that may be ingested by the mathematical package of choice of the reader and leads to options for further tabulation because after all discover should not have a burden placed upon it to function in a set manner. Discovery should be malleable to the audience whereby they can be empowered to fish for themselves, which is the primary premise here. You are free to take the data extracted and utilize the data as you see fit because it has been made available to you.

Through the aid of the search activity that is performed in Chapter 5 it became feasible to utilize a statistical software package to begin to decipher the information that the data held. Chapter 6 takes the reader on this journey where the R statistical software is utilized to ingest the data files created through the Python data mining algorithm and uses them to create approximation formulas for both of the search engines. Through the use of the system variables and their corresponding indices it became feasible to inject the information into a logistic regression that was used to derive a predictive formula for each of the search providers. This process was followed here and done such that an approximation formula to the Yahoo search engine was determined that proves to be 77.78% accurate. It can happen, truth can be deciphered by understanding the paradigm under the guise of the systems domain. You can take the systems perspective and apply shear computational power to the problem frame to determine the formula that a major search engine provider holds near and dear, this body of work proves this fact. In doing such it was possible to undeniably state the manner by which relevance could be quantified and consequently to surmise the manner by which future applications need to be crafted to show relevance with the search engine purveyors. If the reader stops for a moment to embrace this reality it becomes empowering because this entails that the reader as an individual with no investment at least on the scale of Yahoo, is able to adopt this mathematical paradigm and in turn provide similar results to those of the Yahoo search engine. This is the power that is afforded to all now through computational work effort and software development. And yet even more profound is the realization that because of the disclosure of this paradigm it becomes feasible to understand exactly how that message must be crafted for the audience in order to receive favor.

With a direct case in hand of what constitute relevance the text next takes the reader on another statistical journey through a random forest study whereby the specific attributes in the data mining exercise can further be analyzed and consequently have their worth on the total system flux be determined. This exercise allows for the determination of the impact factors for each of the system attributes for each of the search providers and thus helps to further clarify the picture that MDAs need to paint for their captive audience. The physical determination of the worth of the system variables allows developers to state for example that when creating content via MDAs and the search engine crawling the content is Bing then header two content should be emphasized in lieu of header one content, which deviates from the narrative of the W3C and the style guide coincidently. This is the power that being metrics driven affords the one who wields this sword. Through this mode of operandi, it becomes feasible to state without qualm the course of action that needs to be taken as unequivocally the data always points to true north. It is by following this compass that teams have an opportunity to be correct in their execution and their mandate to create worth for the business because navigation of the business domain without such is but simply an expensive gamble. This is a benefit that this text provides, it provides for the reader the succinct determinants of worth that may be leveraged upon when creating this new breed of applications that businesses are to rely upon. Development teams can now feel empowered to leave the qualified argument and migrate to the quantified argument because after all they hold the compass in hand that points to true north.

The discourse up to now helps to clarify the picture of what constitutes worth with online content and consequently the makeup of the web applications that are to be created. This leads the discussion to a formal discourse of a new modern web architecture that will be the manner by which Micro Distributed Applications or MDAs will come to be created. Chapter 8 leads the reader through the formal definition of the architectural framework for MDAs and helps to clarify the blueprint that may be used by the reader to create their own MDAs. The chapter brings to light the enablement that may occur through JavaScript when implemented in a dynamic runtime loading framework whereby the needed dependencies are harnessed as needed which diverges from current doctrine whereby dependencies are formally defined statically in web documents. The chapter also covers the security mechanisms that may be implemented in order to secure these micro pieces of functionality so that they become obfuscated from prying eyes and facilitate the securing of code fragments. The chapter also provides for the reader the physical process flow that needs to be adhered to when creating MDAs and which may be used in a practical implementation.

Chapter 9 is the first of four chapters that provide for the reader a practical context surrounding the nature of MDAs. Chapter 9 presents a formal case study for a Micro Distributed Application for a mortgage broker. The chapter dives into the requirements that would be needed by the business in order to be able to leverage the clout that is tied to link equity through MDAs. The chapter sets out to define the base use case and the sequence diagrams for the application so that the reader may become familiar with how business requirements can subsequently be tied to functionality through MDAs. The chapter also highlights how MDA content may be tied to search relevance through the identification of relevant terms and their binding to page attributes as identified in the random forest study in Chapter 7.

Chapter 10 builds on the requirements from Chapter 9 and proceeds to take the reader on the journey of creating the application whose requirements were defined in Chapter 9 prior. This chapter provides a hands on approach to the creation of MDAs for the reader where specific code fragments are discussed and whereby the reader is provided with the visual output that is created through the MDA. In this chapter the reader is physically able to see the individual user interface elements that are created through

MDAs and thus helps the reader to fill in the picture of the capability of MDAs. In this chapter the code required to create the functionality is divided into the frontend part and the server side components, both of which are discussed in detail in this chapter so that the reader is able to get a complete picture of how the complete system is to function given the architectural outline that was provided prior.

Chapter 11 is a second use case that is presented to the reader whereby the requirements of the business entail the creation of an MDA within the confines of the WordPress content management system. As was done previously in Chapter 9, this chapter guides the reader through the requirements needed from the MDA in UML format whereby the physical use case and sequence diagrams are created. The requirements outlined in this chapter are more extensive than the previous requirements outlined in Chapter 9 which allows the reader to understand the complex problem frames that may be solved through the use of MDAs. The requirements from this chapter become more aligned with what would be found in practice and thus allows the reader to experience a case where parity is present between the theoretical and the practical.

Chapter 12 creates the solution that was outlined in the requirements in the previous chapter. This chapter walks the reader through the creation of a WordPress plugin whereby the functionality that is required from the bootstrap process of the MDA is physically embedded within the confines of the WordPress plugin allowing the reader to understand how MDAs may be leveraged in existing content management frameworks with little accommodation needing to be made for the framework that MDAs require. Once the WordPress plugin is implemented then the reader is taken on the physical journey of creating the MDA. The creation of the Micro Distributed Application is done in incremental fashion whereby each requirement outlined is addressed sequentially so that the reader can experience the manner by which functionality may be created in a layered approach. The user interface screens are provided for the reader in conjunction with the code fragments that create the displays, thus giving the reader concrete examples of how MDAs translate to web applications that may interact with an API. The examples in this chapter include the server side code that was created as an API whereby the physical endpoints are called under POST, GET, and DELETE modes. The MDA created in this chapter logs data to flat files whose data may later be retrieved and altered, all of which occurs through the MDA and the API of which the complete code to do such is provided for the reader. This chapter serves the function of helping the reader firmly understand how MDAs may be created and integrated with existing frameworks that interact with an API for state management. After reading this chapter the reader will be able to go forth and create their own applications by using the code provided in part and extending it for their particular needs and objectives.

Chapter 13 presents to the user a framework that may be leveraged in order to index structured, semistructured, and unstructured data. The concept of a composite inverted index is introduced to the reader whereby indexed content across the three different repository types may be indexed in such a manner that it becomes feasible to create search systems that fall under the guise of constant time and all without the need to have to leverage big data constructs such as Hadoop. The content from this chapter will allow the reader to create their search systems to fit their particular needs in their own web applications. The content of this chapter extends the search paradigm context that was discussed prior and helps the reader come to understand how the search paradigm may be applied to leverage their existing data across repository types such as what may already exist in a data lake for their particular business. After reading this chapter the reader will be able to create their own search systems to meet their search needs not simply for web applications but for their enterprise in general.

The conclusion brings together the content that was described previously and outlines leverage points that may be utilized in an enterprise to spearhead business objectives. The chapter serves as a summary of the work done and how it may be viewed from a business perspective so that a practical outlook may be derived from the reading of the text. It is the hope that after reading the final chapter of the text the reader is able to understand the bigger picture of the endeavor undertaken and is better able to understand the business ramifications of the solutions that were depicted. A primary objective of the text has been to help to serve multiple purposes and cease to be binary as the text addresses a technical challenge, but does so from a business leverage point because after all, if technological endeavors do not help to build capital, then they are but simply a novelty for the playground. This book has endeavored to cease to be part of that abstract argument and has sought to help the reader understand the development domain by first helping the reader understand why homeostasis is such and it is because of this argument that true north can be determined and followed to a desired objective for the betterment of the business.

This text is for a technical audience whose function in a business setting revolves around the creation of applications that help to drive revenue for the business. The book helps the reader to come to an understanding of how the indexing domain may be leveraged by this new wave of JavaScript applications that have been termed Micro Distributed Applications and by whose creation and implementation will allow the enterprise to reap the benefit of clout by the existing search systems that the masses utilize. This book helps to fill in the picture of the evolution that has occurred and will continue to occur in web development whereby the new breed of applications will become JavaScript laden highly distributed, and whereby the businesses that implement them will stand a chance to win the indexing race. It is because of this clout and attention that the winners will be determined, and it will be these winners that will be able to reap the benefit of that much capital injection from the masses because such is the game that all businesses have come to be subjected to. This book helps to drive that discussion that will be had regarding the manner by which web development will reposition to and this repositioning will only be feasible through a firm understanding of how indexing relates to the development landscape. Given the sophistication that the search purveyors have evolved to it mandates that organizations cease to stuff links into the background of the page and play fairly. This fair play notion is the domain of Micro Distributed Applications because it is the means by which the masses will vote for the prom king. In the end it turns out that it has all been but simply a popularity game that all have played in their youth. It just so happens that now this game has high stakes with large spoils that will determine which businesses survive and which businesses will become extinct. This is the extent that search relevance has come to have on the development domain, that it not only determines the winners and the losers, but it also determines the manner by which the engagement is to occur. This engagement as may be validated by the data derived in this body of work points to the MDA camp.

Guillermo Rodriguez
QuantiLogic, USA

Acknowledgment

To those that are clandestine but yet whose voice was nevertheless heard

This text needs to acknowledge those that came prior and laid the groundwork for what became the discourse here. No names will be provided here as those that contributed to what is found in this body of work would entail a volume larger than this book. Individuals do not accomplish their goals in a vacuum but rather accomplish them because of the work that others have laid bare before them, which is what happened here. If you are reading this and are an academic, then you can take assurance in knowing that you have contributed to someone's body of work that would not have been possible without your labor. The writer of this passage is but simply a voiceless entity that may find a voice through the work of someone else because of what was written here. This is the legacy of an individual's labor; it is the sweat from their brows that provides subsistence to that seed that may just one day sprout and provide that rich fruit that all crave. Only time will tell if this body of work will find such embrace, but let it be known that this body of work, this fruit only came to be because of the toil and the work of all those who have no voice here, but yet may be heard clearly. Nothing would have been possible without their toil and their effort and this needs to be acknowledged for what it is, a gift that can never be repaid. Thank you for what you have done, your efforts were not in vain, and your efforts have made a difference as is evident by the words written here. This tribute will only ever be repaid if at some point the author of this passage can one day come to be themselves voiceless but yet heard in the work of another. This after all is the ultimate privilege to anyone, to find acclaim without being referred to by name specifically but rather to find clout because of a small contribution that in turn elevated the work of another.

Introduction

The text introduces the concept of Micro Distributed Applications (MDAs) and their relevance in current software engineering endeavors. In order to understand why the profession has arrived at its current junction and why web development must fundamentally change to encompass the doctrine of distributed JavaScript applications the reader is introduced to the evolutionary factors that have come bear on the profession. These factors have pushed the software engineering domain slowly but surely to the realm of MDAs. Micro Distributed Applications have come to be because they offer the following benefits:

1.   Alignment with search engine indexing
2.   Leveraging of the hardware of clients
3.   Provide plug and play functionality
4.   Can be integrated with content management systems such as WordPress
5.   Offset the economic expense of SaaS products in the public cloud
6.   Can be built with a layering architecture to facilitate modularity
7.   Segregate the interface with the data layer via APIs
8.   May be implemented to facilitate a subscription model
9.   Facilitate continuous deployment
10. Allow for the creators of which to become the voices of authority on the internet

Software engineer has changed how humanity interacts with their software systems and MDAs have become but the fat clients of days gone by with additional benefits to their creators. MDAs are but the manifestation of the evolution of the space and as such represent a momentum for development that will force teams to rethink their software engineering initiatives. Software has changed because the focal point is now the customer and the utility that may be provided to them first and foremost. Teams have to subsequently rethink the mission of the product and must do so because organizations that do not have a voice in the digital age are but those same storefronts in malls throughout the country that have little or no foot traffic. To prevent this dire existence teams must come to leverage the architectural pattern of MDAs as they have become the gateway to relevance given their direct alignment with the search purveyors. This degree of influence that needs to be derived happens because the masses come to agree with the message conveyed by the MDA author and to receive this nod of authority entails that teams will need to provide that degree of functionality that is desired by the audience. The argument has changed from one of what can be sold to one of where all that matters is what is best for the audience because it is through them that traction occurs with the stewards of the web, the search purveyors.

The software domain has progressed to current state by moving from bigger to smaller. Teams build micro services now in lieu of web services. Teams for years have written classes and extended them as a means to always have a base layer to reference and build upon. Applications moved from being installed on the hardware of the user to being accessed via a website where no license key could be forged. The user interface was partitioned from the business rules to facilitate the work effort for teams. The introduction of HTML 5 and the canvas object meant that drawing in real time became feasible in JavaScript, which in other programming languages requires the installation of modules. The phase shift that the profession is continuously on has led the discussion to MDAs as they are the current leverage point for teams and business. To support this argument the text derives the metrics to show the reader why MDAs are the mode by which development needs to migrate towards. It is the data after all that tells the story of what needs to be done and this is brought to bear in the text so the reader can come to understand why change is mandated and why organizations will need to rethink their development efforts going forward because if they do not they will be left without a voice and in current times business viability is directly proportional to degree of influence, which is an inherent component of MDAs.

Chapter 1
Micro–Distributed Applications

ABSTRACT

The disappointment that organizations find themselves in with regards to viability is a direct result of reality being less than their expectations. Organizations have become accustomed to trying to set objectives that are just simply out of reach at times and this dynamic has played itself out to the dismay of many in the online marketing domain in part because true north has been elusive. This is the hallmark of arguments that are qualified because qualification is the domain of ambiguity. It is through this ambiguity that disappointment has been able to make a permanent abode in all too many businesses. It is only by migrating the organization to a metrics driven enterprise that a business stands a chance to cease to find disappointment because after all it is the numbers that always reveal truth.

INTRODUCTION

To be digitally relevant in current times has become as important as ever given the dependence of electronic commerce and the quantity of alternatives that users have at their disposal to spend their funds. To become digitally relevant entails to become significant to the masses, it means to be able to leverage those systems that are currently in place that can help the organization move from the depths of obscurity to relevance. This degree of relevance in the digital age has taken on more of a significance given the quantity of digital natives that make up the population. In recent times the name of a company has been elevated to a verb to denote searching on the internet. Being digitally relevant has surpassed basic business as it fulfills a central need of the masses to find what they need. Businesses need to be digitally relevant to remain afloat as their subsistence is directly tied to their notoriety with the populous. These organizations need to be able to have a larger marketing presence than their competitors, the probability of their survival demands it. Being digitally relevant means that the potential to make a sale is increased. In the days of the phonebook there were companies that had a name that began with the letter 'A' for the simple fact that it would facilitate their finding when individuals looked through a list of companies. Those physical references are now long gone and the name of a business matters little as it is now the notoriety of the business domain that plays a pivotal role in the branding of the business, as one can attest to by noting of the popularity of domains such as Google.com and Uber.com. The search for notoriety

DOI: 10.4018/978-1-6684-4849-6.ch001

is a central theme of all businesses as their survival demands it, in the digital age however the playbook has changed, the need to leverage technology has been enhanced and it will be those businesses that excel at its execution that will succeed independently of the first letter in their name. To take a business to the realm of digital relevance means that the business has a chance to survive and to survive digitally has never taken on as a heightened level of importance than it did during the COVID pandemic. Mall foot traffic was replaced by traffic on the digital highway, it no longer matters if the business is a large department store as it only matters if potential customers are able to find the store front. To be digitally relevant means to have that breath of fresh air after being underwater for a prolonged period, it is the differentiator between life and death to business. To be digitally relevant means to lessen the magnitude of disappointment by elevating the reality component to meet the expectation component or better yet to have reality exceed expectations and thus to upend disappointment all together. The reality that is proposed here has been in the making for quite some time as technological advances do not happen in a vacuum or are the result of a cosmic bang. Technological advances occur because of the constant flux that technology brings to the forefront and lays bare at the feet of those that dare to take hold of it. Those businesses that adapt and change will benefit and find the pot of gold at the end of the rainbow much as has been the case for Amazon. Amazon was founded in a garage and the inventory in that garage was sold over the internet. The storefront that is available to each customer is such because of the information highway, it masks the obscurity of the reality that humanity find itself under at times and has consequently levelled the playing field for all would be entrepreneurs. The story of Amazon is a story of a dream being at the right place at the right time in history at least in part and this is where the profession finds itself now. Technologists find themselves at a junction in time that mandates a paradigm shift and those businesses that are able to capitalize on the new breed of Micro Distributed Applications (MDAs) will stand to win the indexing race and be propelled to the winner's circle and those businesses that do not capitalize on the opportunity that exists will become irrelevant and much like that garage that was the warehouse for Amazon at one time will simply become faceless structures in the landscape.

Web developers have all been drilled with how relevance on search engine rankings translates to utility and have been exposed to the subjective arguments over what is relevant and what is simply noise, but that argument has failed miserably in taking this qualitative treatise and moving it forward to one that is quantitative in nature and affords the visibility to see the forest for the trees. In this text this premise of obscurity is tackled from a data science perspective, which leads the discussion into what relevance in the digital domain entails and why it is significant to the development effort in general from a quantitative perspective. The argument made here seeks to help the reader capitalize on their web presence by presenting the hard data to support the argument. When the argument physically parts from the numbers the purview changes to one in which relevance ceases to be a binary proposition and migrates to one where relevance and its corresponding attributes can be quantified. This journey will take the reader to a new realization because development teams will need to rethink how software is built for the masses, how it is packaged, and how it needs to be distributed because of the leverage that must be harnessed. It is by taking this step forward and embracing this change that the fruit that is relevance stands a chance to be tasted, after all it is only those organisms that are able to feed that have a chance to be embraced by the morning sun of a new day. If a business is able to create online content and organically be driven to the top of the search heap, then this business stands to reap the benefits that can only be afforded by the masses. This business stands to gain significantly financially because of the prowess that can only come by way of the digital age. This much needed input is what all businesses crave and in the digital age there is no more pressing need than to be able to capitalize on the traffic of the internet because after all the traffic of the mall is but a semblance of what it once was.

By shedding light on the intricacies of search systems and their relevance to content classification will also facilitate the introduction to the process of creating these search systems for your own specific needs and all without the need to implement large NoSQL data stores as is often found in corporate America. By taking the supervised learning model that is developed in chapters five and six for example you could create a similar system as that of the Yahoo search engine. Given the nature of language and its ability to function as an index in a dictionary where the definition of the term could simply be a series of resources in some UNC path or the World Wide Web would allow for the creation of a search system that would function in constant time - $O(1)$. Constant time represents the optimum performance of an algorithm and as such it entails that you could create your own search systems that would function at a maximum efficiency. This topic is discussed here because search surpasses the web and has become an instrumental aspect of the enterprise especially in an age when the volume of data being produced by organizations has increased and will only continue to accumulate. This is where part of the power of computer science resides, in the translation of mere data to information because once information is obtained from the bowls of obscurity then and only then does it become feasible for the organization to make good decisions. Search systems have surpassed being merely components that litter the landscape and have become artifacts of leverage. This text is about this leverage that is at the disposal of all businesses if they simply understand how the tool may be wielded to their benefit. To be perfectly frank, corporations today have little choice but to arm themselves with this weapon because if they do not then it will be their direct competitors that will win the information race and relegate the slow to act businesses to the bottom of the pile and after all, how often does anyone click to the end of the search results?

RELEVANCE

In theory one should simply be able to turn to the Google style guide and let that help drive the argument forward and let the customers magically appear. But to be clear that is the same document that the internet community at large has been privy to for years as of this writing and still the argument lingers in the realm of the qualified. The argument presented in this text brings the argument forth void of that ambiguity because it is a quantified study whereby the influence of the system variables are identified and classified. This discourse sets the argument that a new dynamic will come to dominate the landscape, one whereby it will be the utility provided by domain that will stand to become the differentiator of the business. If there is a law that can be upheld with technology it is that innovation is the driver of capital wealth, it is the key to winning in this constant tug of war between rivals. This study marks the bellowing of a call to action that will become a race between organizations because development and the creation of digital content has now just changed. Industry speaks of SaaS applications as if it is a given that products are to be built this way, the public cloud, well that too is a given, how else are you supposed to get all this to work? And yet, the profession has lost sight of the prize, of the thousand pound gorilla in the room. Development teams can build the greatest products, but if nobody can find them then it means that they will be lost in obscurity and void of the needed injection of users that they must have. This junction that is spoken of is part of the evolutionary process that is software development of the web that in actuality has been in the making since Google first indexed those pages for the masses and this is what this text is dedicated to. This text seeks to define this new paradigm and aid development teams in creating these search relevant systems so that they can be leveraged to expedite the general search effort for endeavors undertaken. Through these factors of leverage it will be possible to build those applications that will find the embrace of the masses because after all they will be readily available.

This text represents a paradigm shift in the landscape of technology, but it also denotes a paradigm shift in the human capital domain as well because the driver for this added value is in the development teams that make the web applications that are consumed by the masses. It will be the technical resources that are the driver for this change and as such it represents a paradigm shift in the business landscape that has been dominated by the marketing group with pay per click campaigns and search engine advertisements. This technological change that is presented here is such that it has now changed the dynamic of business and has empowered computer scientists to take a seat at the table because it is these individuals that will be able to create value for the business by propelling the business forward in this digital race for customers. The intertwining between technology and marketing has taken on a binary relationship in the new wave of web applications that are to be built as indexing and search relevance is directly tied to the development effort. The conditions for engagement that have been defined by the large search engine providers such as Google, Bing, and Yahoo and they have inherently created a system constraint that has led to the evolution of software development. The reason why development is where it is at now is because of the decisions the masses have made as they have voted for the winner implicitly through each search that has been performed by way of the search purveyors. As a consequence of this paradigm shift it will be by understanding the metrics surrounding search that will allow development teams to create those applications to show relevance. It is this understanding that now takes software teams to the frontier of development that is aligned with marketing and the age of the Micro Distributed Application (MDA). The marketing doctrine will change to be infused with the understanding of the metrics behind relevance and become empowered with those applications that implement it. It will be those individuals that create this leverage for the business that will consequently find new relevance in the same businesses that they have been employed by. This will all be accomplished through MDAs and their alignment with the objectives of the business along with the marketing context which prior did not see such correlation.

In this text the argument is laid to bare for a framework for the leveraging of those inherent underpinnings that must be capitalized on for the creation of content for the masses and whether this is in the form of a website or a SaaS application, the underpinnings remain the same, the essence of the argument is about a new architectural framework by which the new generation of web content and search systems will be created. This new web architecture is a movement towards distributed software that is available by way of a common web programming language – JavaScript. The movement is not new, but it represents a shift from current doctrine. Gone will be the days when web applications will reside on some server and execute exclusively by way of it. Modern web architecture will execute in the browser and will execute on each node that leverages the code base. Society was exposed to the power of the new browser-based applications with the advent of Angular and React. These JavaScript frameworks are enabling developers to create complex web solutions through a browser-based programing language context and core APIs for data transfer. The indexing context of the search engines dictates that relevance is tied to a voting share from fellow peers, which implies that in order to be relevant in the modern web you must obtain a bigger share than your competition. This share will be obtained organically by proxy from each domain user that deems the content to be relevant and significant enough to place on their domain, thus creating a vote for the target domain and/or product implicitly. It will no longer be that the domain with the best content will win the search engine relevance race, but it will be the domain with the best application or utilities that will win. The shift has already happened and now the question begs to be posed, where is your organization in this race? The text also presents this argument from a quantitative stance, void of the subjective mindset that plagues humanity all too often which only functions to turn the protagonist to the victim. In this text the search engine formula for one of the major search purveyors is identified with an almost 80% accuracy and the endeavor was accomplished with the consent of the search purveyor as they made their data freely available. The process proves that prediction can be made if the journey first parts by first identifying the system attributes that are at play.

DISTRIBUTED SYSTEMS

The gravitation towards distributed software is a necessity for the creation of indexable online content as so much of what is done online first parts from search. This indexing effort is of the utmost importance because if worth is measured by popularity, then it means that the most popular distributable applications will see its proprietors' win the indexing race. This competition is not exclusive to software vendors either as it is open to all. Any online retailer or web page for that matter can create a distributable component that could be consumed by the masses. Take for example the case of a mortgage broker that creates an online mortgage calculator. If this calculator is distributed to third parties for free, then it represents an external link to the source. Linkage to source from external references is what drives a significant portion of worth or relevance. This paradigm is not new, it is an old paradigm that has its roots in the HITS and the PageRank algorithms, but it is a different paradigm now; this new course is evolutionary in the progress of web content. The creation of jQuery was revolutionary to creating web content as has been recent developments with cross platform user interface libraries such as bootstrap. What is being seen now is the marrying of indexing relevance with web development in what can only be called a modern web dynamic. This dynamic will drive how applications of the future will be developed and consumed by clients on subscribing websites. Take for example the case of reserving a table for dinner where a patron must first find the restaurant closest to them and then they are taken to the external link that their table reservation provider has given to make the reservation there. In this whole process a risk is undertaken by the proprietor where the customer has left the original restaurant website where a much cleaner solution would have been to have taken the reservation directly on the restauranteurs' website. By building such applications creators are embedding their work product directly into the workflow of the current subscribing client and cease to intervene in the process flow. In this scenario the subscribing website consumes needed functionality and incorporates it into the play seamlessly and effortlessly. This scenario represents an optimization to current doctrine and a much needed flux that needs to be imposed upon the landscape, which simply leads to further synergies. External to the user experience of performing some needed body of work in one location, MDAs can facilitate the complete process of not simply table reservation, but of also food ordering for example. This scenario represents the commingling of MDAs through an SDK or local API. It would entail the interfacing of components so that each could feed into the next one. So, this scenario would be much like making a table reservation on OpenTable (www.OpenTable.com) and then having the meal order processed through DoorDash (www.DoorDash.com). Disbursed silos of applications are simply what is being highlighted here and much to the chagrin of those that have been in the technical field for decades for sure. This synergy parallels the migration of applications from console-based entities to web artifacts and which ushered the way for the DOTCOM tidal wave. This is history repeating itself once again in a flavor that is not much different than what was seen in the past. Technological momentum is moving towards Micro Distributed Applications

(MDAs), which are JavaScript applications that may be handed off to clients and function directly on the client node and consequently could facilitate the integration of Micro Distributed Applications by diverse vendors. The ability to plug and play directly by dropping references to external code directly on the client web application is not new, it is done now with widgets, but this has not been done for the benefit of application integrations, nor has this been done for the sake of obtaining a digital presence benefit, which invertedly leads the discussion to a common place, a place where efficiencies prevail, a place where simplicity reaches a peak maturation state, which only leads to the embrace by customers. The race has changed, it has migrated to a new paradigm where the beneficiaries are the populous at large as this shift represents a benefit to the application developers, the consuming clients, and most importantly to the visitors to the page (application rather now). So, profound has been the need to classify and index online content that it has fundamentally changed the way the industry will create digital content and the software that is web applications.

In current practice the service providers simply give an external link for the dedicated page of the customer, but in the case of a physically distributed component (MDA) that lives on the website of the client it has a greater degree of utility as the application can now control the complete message presented to an audience. While a simple link per say could provide the offeror with link equity it could also be stripped away given the link attributes that are afforded through HTML, in actuality the service provider does not control their own destiny, the customer does. If the customer however physically places the MDA on their page, then the balance of power alters and favors the creator of the utility. In this case the service provider can control the quality of the link equity as well as the quantity of link equity to name but two impact factors. If you were to take some current service provider and their link equity and overnight be able to multiply it by a factor of 2 it means that the providers' website would naturally be more visible to a search enquiry. The need to be digitally relevant mandates that MDAs take root as their utility presents a tangible benefit to those creators. From a business perspective this represents a huge upside to the business as well because of the quantity of funds that can be saved by not having to invest as heavily on pay per click advertisements. In the mode that marketing teams currently operate by they invest a tremendous amount of capital on online advertisements with the search providers and social networking platforms where they hope that their investment will lead to some tangible benefit but are not guaranteed such by any of the businesses that all too willingly take these marketing dollars. According to Graham (2021) of CNBC, Google's advertisement platform that is known as their search engine generated $147 billion in 2020 and accounted for 80% of Alphabet's revenue. The market share for Google in online advertisement was determined to be 29% of digital spending globally for 2021. Graham (2021) also reported that Alphabet's market capitalization was over $1.5 trillion in 2021, which put it only behind Apple, Microsoft, and Amazon. So, a company through a digital service was able to generate comparable worth to businesses such as Apple, Microsoft, and Amazon and was able to do so through a webpage that has one image, a textbox and a submit button. A search service that simply marries query strings to possible advertisement interest is so lucrative that it generates the majority of the corporation's revenue, this is the degree of importance that search systems have shown to have. The ability to be able to take a business from the bowls of obscurity on the web to prominence through MDAs entails that a business can forgo that extraordinary expense that has simply functioned to line the pocket of the investors of Google and consequently use that money for an alternative purpose such as employee salaries, innovation, or computer equipment. The stakes are large for what Micro Distributed Applications (MDAs) represent and what they mean for the bottom line of a business. Please do note that the argument that is being made here is not that online marketing will cease to exist but is rather that it will evolve where part of the focus will need to be on the creation of micro applications that can be utilized across the web. Technology can either be a faithful spouse or alternatively can turn into your staunchest enemy and it is for every business to decide what type of relationship they wish to have, there are no middle of the road arguments, a business will need to make a choice and it will be to either the benefit or detriment of the organization.

METRICS DRIVEN

In this body of work, a concentrated effort was undertaken to migrate the argument from a qualitative stance to a quantitative one where it was sought to remove the subjectivity from the landscape and thus allow for the argument to take an alternative focal point, where it became the metrics that became the drivers for the momentum of the discussion. Taking this stance allows to differentiate between the noise in the domain and consequently determine mathematically what is pertinent to search. To void your argument of the quantitative aspect means that it is simply an argument that is subjective in nature and arbitrary. You can for example take a look at the documentation that Google currently publishes on search relevance and thus come to understand at a high level what is pertinent to them which is a positive, but still leaves a void as to where the significance lay and in what proportions it is bundled. You cannot in this type of argument for example determine how much significance is credited towards a link structure as opposed to title tags. Up to now the indexing space has been laden with the subjective and the hearsay where it is the opinions of the individuals that is taken for truth. In this paradigm there is a component that is lacking which is the metrics component and as such it leaves the audience in a state of paralysis for which the only recourse becomes experimentation through trial and error. Humanity seems to have regressed in this form of being and has consequently arrived at a junction where truth alludes and where only the semblance of truth persists. This reality is but a farce and a tragic comedy as it leaves the protagonist not simply in a room with the lights off, but it also leaves them also blindfolded as well. The business needs a greater degree of assurance than is currently afforded as this mask upon the eyes serves to only present silhouettes and the semblance of truth. These shadows that become apparent through these appendages and that fade into the stillness of the dark landscape seep through at times which simply lead to exaltations of jubilation since truth must be present even though it is hard to see. But what is before the actor cannot be claimed because it cannot be seen with assurance, as the shadow is but simply just that the silhouette of the person, but never the actual person. The protagonists in this play have come to be alchemist in a world where the laws of chemistry allude them, which happens because they fail to become metrics centric first and foremost. While the style guide provided by Google is a benefit it still lacks that substance that the audience so desperately craves to understand as the style guide for lack of a better moniker is lacking substance and is but that silhouette. Of course, they will not disclose it you may be saying, it is the secrete sauce after all. As brief of an attempt as there can be in the way of the style guide by Google it is far more than is afforded by its counterparts at Bing or Yahoo which coincidently enough is zero. The suggestion being made by Google for indexing relevance amounts to a faint-hearted attempt at keeping the masses at bay with their questions, it is a way of saying - hey we did something but amounts to nothing more than what may be deemed common knowledge today over the indexing space. What is interesting however is that the findings of this text are consistent with the style guide by Google and help to support the central theme here. The argument that has been conveyed was relevant, but it was conveyed in a manner of half truths and innuendoes that leave the reader with an obscure focal point that can never be fully obtained. As is often the case in consulting it is the little things in the discourse that reveal the greatest insight and so too is the case here, and now the data has been harnessed to reveal the metrics of relevance to back up the claim of what truth is, an alternative plot can be crafted. The profession at large can now come to understand the reason why change must occur and also have a course of action to get to a state of relevance, the question simply remaining is who will get there first.

It is paramount to take a metrics laden approach when undertaking any investigative study because all too often the argument can become obfuscated and lead to a perception of truth that is all but and whereby preconceived notions of right and wrong are but general rules of thumb that lack impact across time. Society to some extend has been indoctrinated into this mode of being through education and life experiences and because of which the protagonists are burdened, and it is this load upon their shoulders that keeps them from seeing the truth that is before them. There have been many a study for example that has been invested in to understand query logs to better understand the search domain, but query logs are simply manifestations of an individuals' interaction with a search engine. Query logs are cross pollinated with data from disbursed systems, the individuals whose labor was invested in to conduct the query. Investigators in their understanding of truth have gone forth and conducted studies to understand the system when in actuality they have been looking at several systems all at once. It is amazing at times how humanity is able to progress in life when it seems to stumble at the onset of the race. Systems theory dictates that the understanding of a system begin by first understanding the base attributes of the system and to do so you must first define the boundary constraint of the system under study. This boundary constraint is defined here to be the page, it is within the page that you are able to determine the base attributes of the individual component under study. It is by making this first assertion that the argument is able to proceed forward on solid footing as this perspective allows the removal of the noise in the argument and lets the investigative process concentrate on what is actually pertinent in the discussion. And if there are any doubts at hand then look no further than the argument that is posed by Google in their style guide, which puts forth the assertion that what is pertinent are in fact the components of the page. Much like that consulting scenario that was discussed earlier, it is the little things that tell you quite a bit, but you must be aware enough to be able to pick up on the subtleties of how truth is being conveyed by the source. You have to understand the protocol in the communication stream to be able to decipher the message and without which the audience is but only able to make out the silhouette of truth through the appendages that are but the misconceptions of the protagonist.

In current times there are vast amounts of data within reach, and there also exists the ability to reflect on this data through libraires and utilities. This plethora of data can also be exposed through the use of shear computational effort to do the heavy lifting, which serves as the enabler to the determination of truth. With these assets within arms reach, it facilitates matters for the investigator to migrate towards a metrics driven view of the world as the argument can let the numbers fall where they may and let the derived metrics tell the investigator what truth is in its purest and simplest form. It is truly amazing that investigators can turn an algorithm upon some data source such as the search engines themselves and extract the needed data from them and use that same data to validate the computational formulas that are derived. The tools that are at the disposal of the investigator facilitate matters to derive new truths for the particular domain under scrutiny by using the systems that are already at hand and ready to be leveraged. While reading the text you may wonder why this same system was not used to derive a supervised learning model for the Google search engine, the answer of which is that Google limits the amount of queries to their search engine by IP address and as such the same system was not able to be used to extract the same quantity of data from Google as was extracted from Bing and Yahoo. What could be stated however is that the data extracted from the Yahoo search system did show a high degree of consistency with the Google search engine results collected, in their limited quantity. The magic sauce has therefore to a certain degree already been leaked by way of the supervised learning model that was created for the Yahoo search engine could very well be argued. This is the power that computational effort and a data driven approach affords, it gives humanity the ability to decipher what is before it and at times to the astonishment of all. The moral of the story here being that there is no need to live in a folklore as there is another story that may be embraced that is richer, more fulfilling, and better able to move society forward. It is a story where truth becomes the central them, and it is such because of the compass that points to true north, which is data laden.

EVOLUTION

The formal discussion in the journey that is outlined here departs by understanding the historical context of search engine architecture and the foundational arguments that have driven the discourse for the domain. Life is much as the old adage says, if you do not know your history you are bound to repeat it. The indexing domain is an ever evolving paradigm that has been in the making for over fifty years as of this writing; it is no wonder that wrapping ones hands around the paradigm is a challenge in of itself. The historical context is extremely important from a systems perspective as it allows for the understanding of the base argument and its evolution as well as to physically see how the argument fits into the base unit of measure in the model – the attributes. The historical context of web content along with the trends that have come about also aid in understanding the manifestation of what can only be called the modern web architecture of the applications that are to come. The search paradigm is still in the infancy stage of its life, take for example the case of mobile devices and their search market share over the last ten years. There are definitely some questions that will still need to be answered in the years to come such as securing of JavaScript software, Cross-Origin Resource Sharing (CORS), authorization, and authentication to new just a few. The domain is still nevertheless in exciting times as the process of creating online content is constantly evolving, thus ensuring of keeping of the interest of the audience. This interest is warranted because it is this system flux and its base underpinnings that are bound to show influence in the momentum of web development. Given this dynamic it is of the utmost importance then to understand the system at hand and to do so you must first frame the argument so whether you are dealing with people or artifacts the parallel does exist in the model, base components drive value. You could be looking at a mechanical system, an information technology system or a person centric system and the parallel holds; modeling behavior boils down to the fundamental unit of measure. The chapter titled 'The Ruins' takes the reader through the historical context that lay bare to those current base units of measure that drive value in search system architecture and the fundamental lens through which the problem frame needs to be understood. When you study the historical context and bring to light the system dynamic to frame the message going forward an awakening occurs because it is through this understanding that the systems perspective places the lens upon the reader to bring into focus what lay ahead. This understanding however can only occur if the protagonist awakes from their slumber to come to appreciate the landscape for what it is, a horizon that captivates and holds all those that care to peak captivated by what it unfolds. This is what truth is, an awakening of the soul that leaves all those that care to peak over the edge of obscurity to a new realization of reality that are simple, beautiful, captivating, and changing.

The systems perspective is an important facet in any study for the sole reason that without it the foundation of investigation has a significant higher probability of failure. The Economist magazine has defined an index termed the 'BIG MAC' index. Under this paradigm the economics authority has determined that inflation may be gauged between countries by looking at the comparable price difference between 'Big Macs'. Well, a Big Mac in Milpitas, California has a fundamental difference from a Big Mac in India as the product in the Asian country is not even made of the same substance. So, does the price disparity allude to inflation or a fundamental difference in the supply chain or something even more complex? It may be contended that the index does coincide with the flux in inflation, but then the argument could be made that what is truly unfolding before the individual is not a systems variable, but rather a proxy to the system variable. System variables are those components that can be measured directly from the model's behavior or combined from the base measurements to derive an amalgamated index such as velocity in a physical system. When dealing with large systems the complexity of the problem domain is further enhanced or complicated. How then can one deal with this complexity to derive truth? Systems that are termed complex systems are systems of systems such as climate change and exhibit the characteristic of being difficult to decipher, the current audience reading this text is fortunate in this case because the challenge before it is factors smaller and actually quite simple, comparatively speaking, as in this case the focal point is but simply a page. There are have been countless arguments however that have complicated the problem frame because of the comingling of separate systems with the page attributes such as the query logs that were spoken of previously, but for truth to bear good fruit there can be no compromise and the investigator must function within the confines of the domain and to do so he/she need to first understand the landscape and the parameters that affect system homeostasis. It is these variables that must be represented in the discourse as it is those factors that affect flux and yield to predictability and understanding of the landscape because without such the gyrations in the data would be but simply noise before the audience and the domain of chaos. This perspective is where this body of work begins to differentiate itself from previous bodies of work in that the systems perspective is taken as the central theme of inquiry. It is simply too easy to get lost in an investigative study when confounding relevance with prevalence. The 'Big Mac' index theme is prevalent throughout existing bodies of work in this domain area and countless other domains. To the specific point take for example the searching of server query logs to determine a direct association between query and preference; it was reported by Smyth (2004) that in current research 90% of all selected links are in the top five positions. So, analysis of query logs is skewed and ever so biasedly so towards the first five links in a result set from a given search engine. Truth cannot be the realm of simply the top five in ninety percent of all cases; yet research continues in this domain almost aimlessly grasping at truth when there is only the promise of an empty hand at each swipe. The search for value by drawing conclusions from what is prevalent must be excluded from the investigative process if progress is to be made. The systems perspective is ever so important for this specific reason; it is the means by which humanity can decipher the roadmap by which the road to discovery is paved. It is ever so interesting to study systems theory and discover that the base premise of it is found in biology just as it is found in business; the argument that lay bare here is by no means new it is simply focused on the paradigms of web and search engine architecture and in the end what you will find is that the truth holds across domains because system theory is domain agnostic.

The search engine providers while different businesses share a central commonality with regards to search and indexing and this being that there are some fundamental constraints that all must play by.

The football field is the web page, and the markup language tags are the players. The business that can maneuverer through the playing field best will win and what is at stake is nothing less than an extra ordinary amount of capital. The best search systems will attract the most visitors and the greatest amount of revenue dollars, so the stakes are high as is the reward. They all play the same game on the same field with the same cast of characters, so the differentiator is a part of the architecture and one reason why this subject matter is an important focus. Each of the search providers unwilling has told a story that is absolutely 100% qualified through an architectural framework and quantified through an equation. This discourse brings two such equations or at least their approximations to light in this text to help quantify the domain at hand. What will be revealed in the end is that there is one index factor that while much like its brethren is a little different and the reason why the development domain stands on the cusp of change. Digital relevance mandates that development teams take this special child and capitalize on it for the benefit of notoriety and as such the profession has inadvertently sailed to a new land, and while it resembles where departure occurred from it does stand apart from it; much as Columbus found upon landing on the American continent. The realization that this special attribute brings forth allows the development community to further understand and clarify how the web programming landscape needs to change as this change is mandated by the need to be relevant. Much like the geese that head south for winter to find greener pastures so too must current applications migrate to new fields where they stand a chance to thrive and prosper in an environment that is conducive to their wellbeing. This is the hallmark of technology; it is the constant change of the landscape that causes the profession to change how business is conducted. Teams have to adapt to the landscape or risk finding themselves in a field where there is no more grass or customers for that matter that can help keep the organization alive. Take the case where some shoe vendor takes it upon themselves to create an MDA that allows individuals to determine their correct shoe size for any given pair of shoes. Now imagine this MDA physically residing on countless websites throughout the internet where each website would point to this vendor's website where the particular shoe could be purchased. It would entail a windfall for the shoe vendor that could occur within a short period of time and all of which would happen without investing capital on pay per click advertisements with the search engine providers as they would be gracious enough to afford this business the top rank spot because of the link equity that it would acquire. It seems to be almost an Italian tragic opera at play between the entrepreneurial shoe vendor and its competitors where in the end there would certainly be a death and it would be all those that turned their back to the technological advances that are before them in the form of MDAs. It will be those businesses that will drink from the spiked punchbowl that will find death before intermission because they refused to see the truth that was before them.

In order to create the supervised learning model for the search providers an algorithm was created that you will find in the index section of the text in its entirety. The algorithm is provided freely and openly without guarantees and you are free to take it and use it as you see fit. The algorithm was created with the Python programming language which would also allow you to further investigate the models created through Pandas (https://pandas.pydata.org) and Scikit (https://scikit-learn.org/stable/). The Python programming language is a dynamic language and for which the framework may be downloaded here https://www.python.org/. The code to extract information from the search engine providers has been uploaded to GitHub and which may be downloaded from the following repository https://github.com/guillermorodriguez/Dissertation. The code has been added to the appendix in part for the interested few to read over without the need to refer to the repository. Please feel free to download the code base and experiment with the code; you are free to use any and all parts of the code for your own purposes. One of the reasons why the data and the codebase is available to the reader is that the problem frame will change and as it does this current body of work may evolve with this change. With the code and the mathematical model defined any change to the algorithms by the search engine providers can be modelled with what has been made available to you with some modifications of course. Can you hear that? It is the sound of the race gun going off. The race is on, the search engine providers are off and running as they will undoubtedly change the way they do business to adjust for the new dynamic and of course development teams will be right behind them; well at least now they will try. The reality of the matter however is that the indexing domain serves to help the profession understand the significance of search and thus helps it to leverage this paradigm in the MDAs that can be created. If the search paradigm for example changed whereby the search providers began to place an emphasis on some other facet of the domain, then development teams could adjust their applications to fit this mold and thus work to keep their point of relevance in the digital realm.

The application of decision science to create predictive models has proven to be an increased area of focus currently, in this endeavor supervised learning was used to derive the predictive models given the search algorithm, which resulted in a tangible result. There was an underlying premise in the argument however and that was that you needed to understand the process at hand to control it. Well, you cannot control what the search engine providers do with their algorithms, but what can be done is to understand the process and the underpinnings of the process or the system attributes as has been stated previously. Even if the search engine providers introduce a new system variable into the equation it does not mean that the result is chaos once again, but rather it entails a new understanding of the problem frame and of the underpinnings. You do not need to discard the foundation but will need to build upon it – enhance it to keep moving forward with the process and the understanding of the problem frame. In the early days of the internet the argument was made by search engine providers that page ranking was based upon how many keywords the search engine found on the page. This particular indexing methodology is currently common in practice and is referred to term frequency – inverse document frequency (TF-IDF). To circumvent the constraint some eager willed website owners took this to mean that they could add as many keywords as they wanted in order to create a higher index and in order to keep the users on the page they hid the keywords in the background of the page by masking the keywords with the same foreground color as the background color of the website. The result of this whole endeavor was that web site visitors would still see the same website, but the website crawlers would deem the content more relevant based upon the keyword(s) masked within the background of the website content. To be digitally relevant in today's world means that you have a voice where others do not, and the volume of that voice is directly tied to the monetary gain that it affords. This book seeks to help you decipher that elusiveness that is prominent with online content that if solved correctly could propel your organization to have a larger voice in the world. Given the evolution of the indexing domain it has also become pertinent for all members to play fairly by the rules and where circumventing of the rules could result in the blacklisting of your particular website or application. Micro Distributed Applications (MDAs) allow for fair play because these applications adhere to the rules set forth by the search engine providers. MDAs give businesses the ability to become digitally relevant by creating micro systems that other website owners may take and utilize for their benefit and by doing so allow these small and dedicated applications to live within their confines. It is this dynamic that allows development teams to capitalize on the rules that are at play and allows businesses to achieve a greater voice and thus help the organizations take their message to the masses.

PERCEPTION

In a discussion with a colleague once they proclaimed that the search engine Google did a bad job of classifying website content. The argument was then made to the colleague if that was actually the case or whether website owners did a poor job of fitting website content to meet the requirements of the search engines? After all, if the protocol differs from what the sink node expects in the communication stream then all will be lost in the transmission. When this argument was made to the individual it altered the world view that they prescribed to as they proclaimed that they did not know where the hurdle lay. If the problem was with the search engine providers such as Google, then they would not be as profitable as they are. Google certainly would not be able to afford the multi acre campus in one of the highest priced real estate markets in the continental United States and they certainly would not have a stock price hovering around $2000 per share as of the summer of 2021. The current revenue model that is utilized by Google is so lucrative that even Facebook implemented the same revenue type model, ads by user interest. Building and creating systems that can properly classify and create content is a domain with much interest. But it is definitely a matter of playing a game and to play this game it is fundamentally paramount to be able to weed out the noise in the landscape and focus on what is truly important, the system variables. To fail to understand the systems perspective means certain death or worse a dire existence until the proverbial end. The manifestations that become humanities reality are complex – systems made up of subsystems each with its own model that when combined produce erratic behavior that is construed as chaos, but in actuality can be understood when you drill down to the base components that drive value. This value metric on the web has evolved from its infancy of linked memos to a diverse content of distributed web nodes of semi-structured data that must be classified to be indexed. The understanding of this indexing effort by the search engines entails that you can capitalize on the domain and consequently reap the benefits that the web exposes to all and this being ultimately a share of a user base. Whether you choose to use this leverage to create wealth or to help an audience meet some desired objective will not be feasible until the framework for the creation of your desired body of work is understood. This book will provide one such framework that will allow you to create content that leverages a modern web architecture that will ultimately help guide your online efforts to a positive place.

There has been much said about indexing and search in the past, but this body of work is the first that takes the argument forward and places numbers to the argument so that you can see firsthand what is truly relevant with concrete examples from two of the major search providers. It is so easy to get lost in an argument by being subjective, but it is quite another matter altogether to state that you believe premise 'A' is true because the data mandates it. Subjectivity when analyzed from a qualified point of view can amount to nothing more than a fool's errand. It is harsh to realize this, it is hard to come to the conclusion that you have fallen into this trap, but the reality of the matter is that we have all fallen into this trap, it is difficult to admit when you are wrong, but if you are is it not better to leave the burden behind and move towards a new world view, one that does not require a constant uphill climb to defend? So, let the argument move forward and not claim that that search systems do a bad job of classification, but rather come to an understanding of what constitutes a good search system and what development teams can do to leverage this constant tug a war between the protagonists, at least until the scene changes. Development teams can then take this doctrine and utilize it to create the new breed of web applications that have been termed Micro Distributed Applications (MDAs) and use it to create digital relevance for business. Development teams stand at the cuff of a paradigm shift in the landscape that is web programming and in this text this paradigm shift is presented with the data to backup the claim. It is not a new construct entirely that is presented here as what is disclosed in the text here is but simply the evolution that lay before an industry. Development teams are already creating JavaScript applications for websites and using these browser based applications to perform some needed function, but development teams have not yet made the transition to create these applications for distribution whereby they can then be used to help businesses achieve digital relevance. Development teams have simply stopped short in the discourse and have not made the leap just yet, this book is here to help teams make that leap and help them create this new paradigm that could propel an organization to a different station from where it finds itself now. This argument is made first and foremost by first understanding the metrics behind what constitutes relevance in the search domain with the search engine providers. It is this truth that helps to drive the discussion of the influence of the system attributes over the web development space because after all the two domains are inextricably linked. To be digitally relevant means to have a web presence that fits the protocol expected by the search engines and to be such means to have a solution the leverages the underpinnings of worth, i.e., the system attributes. Web solutions have poor traction not because the search engine providers do a poor job of indexing, but it is because the message transmitted and disseminated by the search purveyors is in fact out of sync with the expected tone of the receiver. Current web applications lack the correct prescription and are therefore not indexed favorably, they are in a state of discord with expectations. This text is here to facilitate the harmonizing of the work effort of the reader with the indexing domain to help these applications find that much needed voice that applications need in order to find that much needed injection of digital prowess.

Two practical experiences affirm what mandates digital relevance, the first was meeting a gentleman that owned an online index and the second was interviewing at a business that helped online retailers capitalize on their electronic presence. In the first case the gentleman admitted that he was helping businesses reach the top of the search engine rankings by listing them in a proprietary online index. The creation of the external links which could number in the hundreds, or thousands was the mechanism by which the target node was being transferred link equity and thus obtain a higher degree of digital relevance. In the second case it was during an interview that one of the interviewers chuckled and said that one of their customers a large retail chain was contacted by Google and was told that they were not quite sure what they were doing but acknowledged that whatever they were doing was working to increase their digital relevance. In the second case they admitted that they were sitting in front of the incoming traffic to the customers website and were consequently creating content that was "tailored" to the audience. The stakes for relevance are high and there has been a constant tug of war between the actors in the past, but this farce that has been lived has come to an end because digital relevance is now tied to an architectural framework that is open to all and it will be the best applications that will succeed to catapult their corresponding businesses to a state of notoriety. It is amazing to see the extent to which businesses have gone to in order to obtain a voice on the internet and have done so at times in a manner that has been unethical or deceptive, as the gloves seem to come off when it comes to the all mighty dollar. Businesses seem to do whatever is necessary in order to succeed even if it means to hide keywords in the background of the website to skew their keyword index ratio. The evolution of the web has taken the development community at large to a new paradigm however that is a distant relative of the world that was once known. This new world has evolved through the use of ECMAScript, Cascading Style Sheets (CSS) and network topology to a new level of dimensionality that forces upon its audience to view the landscape through a different lens. The web development landscape has changed tremendously over the years and development teams have seen the migration of the JavaScript language to become a server side construct thus giving web developers the ability to manage frontend and backend development with a single programming language and by doing so the profession has created an ubiquitous construct for development. It is because of the evolution of the front end development language that development teams are now able to dynamically circumvent the user interface and create applications much like was done for standalone Windows systems of the past. The paradigm shifted over time from the personal computer to the web and now the domain sees a shift once again. This time however the shift has created a greater degree of homogeneity on the web because development teams can now place their applications on any given node and let it run on the resources of the target machine all without the need to run on dedicated and expensive hardware.

It is the hope of this text that it will help you create digitally relevant content and shed the shackles of digital obscurity. Secondly, it is the hope that your teams will be able to create their own search systems that function in constant time. It is with this aim in mind that value is created for diverse organizations and consequently it will be these businesses that will help shape the landscape of the world that is surely to come. There are times in life when paralysis occurs because of a fear to move as many a soldier has been told prior to battle, it is those poor souls that refuse to move that are usually the cause for grief. Business amounts to nothing short of war and you will either take your competitors' customers or they will take yours, it is a harsh reality, but it is the truth of business. It is a question of survival, and you will either be able to create relevance for your business or risk seeing the doors close at some point. The obscurity of your business on the internet is directly proportional to the obscurity of your business in general, the two are tied at the hip.

ECOSYSTEM

Given the migration to the public cloud and the inherent expense in running web applications in the environment of the public cloud providers such as Azure, GCP, and AWS it stands to reason that there be a change to help organizations offset the financial burden of these systems and there is no better way to do this than to offload the work effort to the same computer that is running these applications. The change that this body of work proposes does not simply matter because of the indexing domain, but it also matters because of the economics of the domain. Novet (2021) reported in October of 2021 that revenue in the quarter for Amazon Web Services totaled $16.11 billion. It was also reported by Novet (2021) that almost 15% of the revenue for Amazon came by way of AWS. The expense that businesses are going through is tremendous and there appears to be no end in sight given the demand for computational power. Businesses have physically done away with the servers in the cold storage closets and now connect to them via an internet connection, they have become abstractions that can be spun up when needed and turned down when they are not. The migration to the public cloud has been a change that has been adopted by corporate America as a necessity for scalability and it would be hard to argue that point given the flexibility that is afforded to start a server as needed. In the past organizations would have had to have ordered the hardware and then would have had to physically have mounted the hardware in the server room all before seeing a tangible benefit to the team. This latency is now lost in the paradigm as teams are able to create resources just in time and thus help organizations stay productive. This evolutionary step in the process however has subsequently delineated its demise because these resources that are but abstractions to developers could just as easily be located on the laptop of some individual down the street from the organization's office. It is but the Airbnb model all over again where housing or computation effort in this case can be provided by anyone that has room to accommodate the patron, i.e., a willing piece of software. There physically is no reason why computational effort could not be offloaded to some client instance and have the client instance interact directly with some API. This paradigm shift that is spoken of is a hedge to the challenge because it allows teams to leverage an existing resource that is free to them and which has plenty of computational power given the advances in processing resources. Moore's law mandates that the quantity of transistors that can be placed on a chip double every 18 months and as such the computational effort that customers' computers present is a hedge that is freely available to all development teams if they simply capitalize on the matter, which they can with MDAs, and for which the expectation is that performance will only improve every 18 months more or less. Businesses can offset the burden of the expense from the cloud providers by simply having the applications they develop run on the browser of their audience all without the need to execute on the server. The challenge that development teams currently face with this dynamic is that currently there does not exist a mechanism by which JavaScript code can be compiled and distributed and thus leaves it susceptible to theft by anyone that can manage to obtain a copy of it. In the traditional sense of web development this would be true, but in the case of MDAs you can physically encrypt the code fragment between client and server and on the client side decrypt the code fragment and then physically delete the fragment dynamically after execution. The use cases that are presented later in the text bring forth this dynamic for the reader whereby you can see this dichotomy play itself out where code fragments are loaded dynamically and consequently removed from temporary memory thus removing the footprint of the actor in the play. This paradigm is distinct from how development teams currently conduct business because currently developers load code segments statically from resources on the internet. In this configuration the code segments could just as easily be downloaded and viewed entirely by a third party. This configuration does afford the ability to create content in a distributed manner by leveraging the resources of the client thus alleviating software from the burden of the expense of performing some needed body of work on some leased piece of hardware. This new breed of applications that are presented in this text make sense not simply from a capitalization perspective but also from cost reduction perspective as well. It represents the best possible type of argument that can be made to the business it is a positive on multiple fronts and it also goes without saying that you actually do not have a choice because either your business will seek to take advantage of the construct or your competition will and consequently they will stand to win the indexing race as well. This entails that you may be that actor in the Italian opera that finds themselves drinking from the spiked punchbowl just prior to intermission, an unsavory place to find oneself to say the least.

The current state of the World Wide Web would have been unconceivable some 10 years prior, but such is humanities unquenchable thirst to create bigger and better that society has forced the landscape to evolve. No longer do individuals have to type some query string into the browser as they can now simply speak to Siri their questions and have an answer returned to them. The search domain has changed the way the masses interact with their devices it has not simply changed in form, but it has evolved to accommodate humanities mode of being. This change that is seen has caused organizations to have to change how they conduct business because after all it is the customer that dictates to the business, and it is the business that must adapt or risk losing their patronage. It is for this reason that offerings must conform and provide the best possible experience to their customers. This positive experience that is sought to provide some clientele will only be feasible if teams are able to extend some sort of olive branch towards them before they decide to become a customer and organizations can accomplish this through the creation of functions that may be distributed via the internet. This olive branch becomes nothing less than the means by which engagement happens as it will be these same users that will come to depend on this functionality much as is the case with map applications for example. Individuals will become patrons because organizations will provided them with a positive experience that wields them towards the business in a positive and mutually beneficial manner. The benefits of capturing the attention of users to then capitalize on this potential resource has been shown to produce good fruit in recent years with products such as the Robinhood mobile application (www.Robinhood.com). The Robinhood's of the world have shown the development community at large that by being able to provide a tangible benefit to some user base they can be converted to customers, it becomes a simple numbers game where some of the populous is bound to convert to paying customers. Micro Distributed Applications fit this mold of providing some utility to a user base where this user base will undoubtedly yield some percentage that will convert to customers. Outside of the direct benefit that linking structure provides organizations, it is the nature of the message that is created through MDAs that makes the persuasion to adopt the paradigm. It is an argument that has its roots in the past but is nevertheless all too familiar, it is about engagement and utility. It is an argument that places the customer first and which leverages the inherent structure of relevance that has been imposed on the masses by the search providers themselves.

Industry obfuscates the problem frame of indexing with the use of big data constructs such as MongoDB and they do so while losing sight of the economies of scale that may be achieved through proper algorithm design. In computer science efficiency is spoken of in terms of Big O notation where the optimum design pattern is always $O(1)$ compliant, i.e. constant time such as in the case where there exists a dictionary and a definition can be found by way of the word. This key to value association allows developers to implement a paradigm by which a classification of a series of documents could be created using TF-IDF for example and classify them based upon the term's mode of importance. You could then sort this list in incremental fashion so that the more relevant resources are based at the top of the stack. This artifact could then be leveraged to return a response to a query and respond with the file UNC path or better yet the URL of the document indexed, much like the search engine providers do. You could also alternatively replace the TF-IDF function in the process with the supervised regression model that was created for the Yahoo search engine and create your own equivalent search engine to theirs. Think about the significance of the statement that was just made, it means that without having to have made the capital investment that Yahoo made in creating their search system you are able to implement a similar system. This is the power that computational muscle with data science provides, it gives developers the power to discover truths that are before them with ease and a little brain matter.

You are invited on this journey, to discover what is before you and what you may be able to accomplish by understanding Micro Distributed Applications (MDAs), supervised learning models for search indexing, and search systems. It is the hope that by reading this text you will be able to create search relevant applications as well as be able to implement your own search systems without the need to invest in big data systems. The mode of operandi of web development has changed and it will be those organizations that implement relevant systems that stand a chance to win the race for the proverbial customer. It will also be those organizations that are best able to create economies of scale that will best be able to create value for their clients. The web development paradigm has changed and consequently industry is experiencing a new architectural framework that must be abided by to create value in the ever evolving and dynamic world that is the World Wide Web. It is up to each individual to evolve and adapt to the system flux that is before them because if you do not then you will find yourself much like the software vendors of years gone by, developing console applications when businesses migrated to the cloud. Those that fail to adapt will find that the degree of disappointment before them to be directly proportional to the delta between their reality and their expectations.

REFERENCES

Graham, M. (2021). *How Google's $150 Billion Advertising Business Works*. CNBC. https://www.cnbc.com/2021/05/18/how-does-google-make-money-advertising-business-breakdown-.html

Novet, J. (2021). *Amazon Web Services Tops Analysts' Estimates on Profit and Revenue*. CNBC. https://www.cnbc.com/2021/10/28/aws-earnings-q3-2021.html

Smyth, B., Balfe, E., Freyne, J., Briggs, P., Coyle, M., & Boydell, O. (2004). Exploiting Query Repetition and Regularity in an Adaptive Community-Based Web Search Engine. *User Modelling and User-Adaptive Interaction.*, *14*(5), 383–423. doi:10.100711257-004-5270-4

Chapter 2
The Ruins

ABSTRACT

The journey to current state is layered with the remnants of the past. The architectural framework that has become the fingerprint of Micro-Distributed Applications (MDAs) has its roots in the remnants of legacy applications that evolved over time from backend systems to front-end systems through the enrichment of the programming language of JavaScript. The evolution of the development profession saw its marrying with the indexing domain whereby current state has become a semblance of the past but at the same time something different. Success in the medium that is the web has become not simply a factor of feasibility, but it has also become a matter of relevance. Relevance has taken on a new prescription that has created a flux upon the datum point that had once been known; this new junction has become the realm of MDAs.

INTRODUCTION

The history that has unfolded to provide what is the current World Wide Web and all of its benefits has its roots in networking and the child of government research. An interesting point of the internet and the World Wide Web is that the creator of the internet is Sir Timothy John Berners-Lee and much unlike the founders of Google is not a man of vast riches. The schematic for what is known as the web comes by way of a proposal that Berners-Lee made in March of 1989 under which he was able to successfully implement a communication stream between an HTTP (Hypertext Transfer Protocol) client and a server in November of 1989. This simple protocol that is the root of electronic commerce, i.e., Secure Hypertext Transfer Protocol (HTTPS) has also given way to the mobile revolution that is currently underway. While it may have been the application of networking topology that has led humanity to where it is today and the foundation for what is part of the content of this book it is something slightly different that has created the mechanism that drives the architecture of indexing. The current indexing paradigm is driven by mathematics and the proposition that value or indexing prominence can be directly derived by way of a fundamental truth, which is tied to the node under inspection.

DOI: 10.4018/978-1-6684-4849-6.ch002

In this text a discourse is undertaken as to what drives relevance on the web and specially how these factors of worth lead to the realization of a fundamental architectural footprint for web development that has its roots in the remnants of the past. The HITS algorithm is one component from the past that brought forth a mechanism to model search relevance by looking at the link structure and assigning an authority value to the graph edges in the link network. The most famous of the algorithms that have laid the path to where the community at large stands is the PageRank algorithm. The PageRank algorithm is a mechanism by which sink relevance is determined by way of the link structure. The relevance of a sink node is determined due to the quantity of links that point to this destination – a metric that can be determined directly by way of the appendages of a network architecture. The central premise in each of the algorithms is to assign worth based upon how many times a particular node is referenced. The doctrine prescribed to here is quite rudimentary if you think about it and quite common in everyday life. Kids in school are popular because of the quantity of friends that they have. Journal publications are deemed to be relevant by the quantity of peer journals that reference it. So, whether the discussion is in reference to a network structure, a social construct, or academic prominence the central tenant remains the same and this being that popularity or relevance rather is tied to points of reference. If this argument is allowed to take a pragmatic stance for a minute whereby a mathematical context is translated to plain simple English, it would resemble something as follows.

A particular site is relevant if a series of sites point to it. The site pointed to is called the authority and the sites pointing to the authority are called the hubs. The degree of relevance to a site is directly proportional to its appendages.

In a similar manner the PageRank algorithm could also be translated and for which the translation of the mathematical context to plain English would result in verbiage such as the following.

An index that resolves to number of inbound links to a page divided by the number of outbound links from the page whereby the relevance of a node is directly proportional to its index value.

There is an event in the life of seniors in high school that many attend called prom and for which a prom king and prom queen are elected. During an election year the country selects the president of the country by way of a vote for which the cumulative sum of shares decides the winner, given some weight by state. Is there a difference between the paradigms at a high level that society has all come to know and accept and the ruins that have laid the groundwork for the current state of the World Wide Web? To a large extent what is seen with page indexing and the current architectural state of search engines is the manifestation of a solution to a problem frame that society embraces and what it has come to accept as truth. The algorithms that have created tremendous wealth are based upon common notions of better and worse and have simply been abstracted to apply to some desired domain. Popular people, businesses, kids or whatever you want to put here have influence because of the attention received. Degree of clout can take on variant forms in the physical world such as kids to friends, people to followers on Twitter or businesses to yelp positive reviews. The argument posed by the search engines to evaluate significance are as such because it is based upon a commonality that humanity adheres to and understands. While the measurement of popularity on the web has taken on an abstraction by the search engines to what is embraced by the masses in pop-culture the argument still holds to a central tenant and this being that popularity is but a measurement of influence. It is this degree of influence that they equate to worth in their algorithms and it is the measuring stick by which they evaluate the relevance of every website that is indexed and as such it is the burden of all that care to have influence to understand the dynamic. One could very well make that argument that developers do not need to understand their algorithm in minute detail as long as they can understand what factors provide their applications with a positive flux and consequently which factors affect their rank negatively. The writer of these pages take a slightly different perspective in this body of work however and as a consequence derives the approximation formula in minute detail for the search engine providers – Yahoo and Bing and in the case of Yahoo it is found that through a supervised learning model an approximation is feasible that shows an almost 80% degree of similitude with the search engine provider's search results. By performing this work effort what is determined is quantitively how each of the factors of the system compare to one another and consequently which factors bare the greatest degree of importance over the landscape. The result of this process is significant as it allows for a narrative to take root whereby it becomes feasible to state objectively and without subjectivity how the algorithm determines degree of influence when inspecting a particular node on the World Wide Web. It is the migration of the argument from a qualitative context to a quantitative context and whereby the ambiguity of the story is shed and what lay to bare are the facts. It is important to understand in detail because if the problem frame is not afforded this courtesy than it simply entails that what is known is less probable to be true and have the proverbial compass point to somewhere other than true north.

The indexing paradigm and its degree of influence over the World Wide Web has resulted in paradigm shifts in development teams in how they build and manage software. The paradigm shifts that pods have undergone has also been dynamic and evolutionary in nature given the availability of technologies over time and given the adoption of mobility by the masses. The roots of web development have been rudimentary from the onset but have evolved and have helped to shape the reality that is before the masses. There was a point in time when developers would embed functionality from disparate locations into their web applications through the use of iframes. The issue with doing such however is that it gives the beneficiary no control over the content of the frame as the consuming node simply accepts what is provided to use without objection. The iframe paradigm entailed a progression in the process by which applications could reuse the physical work product of another entity and capitalize on it; at a significant price however as it entailed complete loss of control over the message to the consuming clients. What was needed in the discourse was a refinement to the prescription whereby developers could reuse some body of functionality but at the same time retain control over the message and ideally be able to enhance or modify the prescription as needed so that it would fit the theme being conveyed to the customer. To meet this objective the community at large came up with a solution in the form of widgets or utilities such as jQuery (www.jquery.com), Vue.js (www.vuejs.org), Bootstrap (www.getbootstrap.com), Angular (www.angular.io), and D3.js (www.d3js.org) to name but a few. The historical timeline for the creation of each of the utilities mentioned is given below in table 1. It is worth mentioning that at times it has been corporations such as Twitter and Facebook that have led to the state of the web as it is found today. It has been through this direct effort by many private citizens and corporations that progress has been made and where the development community at large finds itself now, which is on the cusp of the next wave of applications. Web applications have progressed from plain unaltered content to customizable widgets and will next transition to what will be Micro Distributed Applications (MDAs). This wave of utilities will be plug and play whereby websites will simply be able to embed needed functionality directly into their pages and for which their customization will occur directly through a web interface. This effort is proven necessary because of the significance that the search engine indexing domain has become. This argument also leaves out the general momentum of the discipline whereby applications have become smaller and distributed, which are factors that will also force the hand of development teams to migrate to MDAs outside of the indexing domain benefit. It just so happens to be that the evolution of the web development domain has brought these factors to bare at a junction point in time where indexing relevance and development methodology find a common synergy. MDAs as such represent an evolutionary step in the web development domain that cannot be deterred because the masses have dictated so and as such MDAs will become the new mode by which business will be conducted on the web given that indexing clout and development ideology are in sync through their utility.

Table 1. Framework Release Dates

Framework	Release Date
jQuery	August 2006
Vue.js	February 2014
Bootstrap	August 2011
Angular	October 2010
D3.js	February 2011

The past which are the ruins of web development and indexing has had an influence with the current state that the profession finds itself in, but this current state is nevertheless in transition. It becomes imperative therefore to understand the blueprint that has been left behind because it is upon this foundation that teams will build the new structures that will weather the burden of the users to come. While development pods are free to create their own reality, collectively this occurs through a bounding constraint from whence once departure occurred from and this is a proposition that cannot be overcome and as a matter of fact it should be embraced because it represents a line of progression that will help take the profession to a new datum point. This progress that is spoken of is also a collective dynamic that everyone has had a hand in shaping much as the masses collectively decide which pages are to receive attention so too do the masses collectively decide where the momentum of the profession is to venture to. This is why progress has been made by not simply the labor of the public sector but by the capital investments of the private sector as well with the tools and frameworks that they make available to all. There is a reason why as of September 2021 GitHub.com had 56 million users, individuals want to contribute and want to have a voice. The masses want to help shape the new reality that all are to live by and this is why they upload their own code to GitHub and make it available to all to consume, and enhance. The discourse of this text is simply the explicit state of where development teams are and where they are going and for which there has been a great many that have helped to create this story. This is the reason why it is a great time to be in technology, everyone has a voice into the reality that the next generation will see, feel, and then themselves contribute to. This is why the story does not end here, it is because the story of humanity is to continue and as any evolutionary process will dictate the forthcoming sequence will surely surpass the previous version. This is the law of humanity and for which technology will never be able to find an escape velocity from. For proof of these assertions the reader could simply turn to the GitHub repository that has been made available as part of this endeavor. It is public and freely available for any and all who care to take it upon themselves to want to make their voice heard.

SEARCH

If you take an abstractionist view of the domain of search for a minute, it reveals an interesting aspect about humanity and this being that people in general seek to find relevance. Individuals rush to the mall to buy the jersey of their favorite teams in order to link a sense of identity with that of something that is bigger than themselves. Individuals buy large homes because they have become the new form of a modern day castle and what better way to assert power and clout than to reside in a place that resembles such. Individuals buy large vehicles because it gives them clout on the road and it makes people in smaller vehicles fear them because after all it is the biggest bull that must be brandished the most space. It's much like the American adage, bigger is better and it is better because it gives relevance. The domain of search is about finding relevance in the landscape and thus classify for humanity what is important and what well is less relevant, it fits into the notion of right and wrong because it is a meaning that all are intimately familiar with, winners and losers. The technological panorama has become but simply a manifestation of humanities inherent truths. This truth that is spoken of is relevance and it is found in humanities notion of importance because it is ingrained in the hardwiring of mankind, there is no escaping it. The cup that is sought is not bound to simply individuals, but it is also sought by businesses, its demand can be found everywhere and the reason why the search purveyors attract the attention of millions in marketing dollars and the influx of the masses. Everyone wants to be relevant, and everyone seeks to be the king, the bull, or the winner. The search purveyors have but simply provided this summary for all to bear witness to in the first ten links of the search results. The search results have become the modern day newspaper for all to view and to comment on.

This component of influence that is at the core of the indexing domain is the primary reason why the journey parts from here. It is by understanding the innerworkings of where search comes from that it allows for a better understanding where current state resides. The journey undertaken also dives into detail over the systems perspective to help clarify the discussion that is to come, and this is done by defining what system variables are and why they are pertinent when understanding a domain. To lose sight of what is pertinent simply entails a groping along the wall to find a way when it would have been a much simpler endeavor to turn the lights on. Humanity often times struggles to find clarity because much is lost when the landscape is obfuscated with the haze of noise confounding the problem frame, such as with the use of proxy variables that only show a semblance of truth and yet hide truth beneath the cover of haze. It is because of these components that reside outside of the landscape under investigation that are prevalent but lack relevance. Prevalence is the domain of chaos and the root of much consternation as these proxy variables can show great congruency with actual system variables as is the case with the 'BIG MAC' index, but yet fail to meet the boundary constraint component that would regulate them to other than distortions. It is for this purpose that the discussion dives into understanding what is before the investigator from the systems perspective and consequently what must lay outside the boundaries of the discussion because in doing so it allows the protagonist to turn the lights on and forgo having to grope the wall to find the way. In the end the story turns into yet another search endeavor, but for which in this case no query result will be returned by the search purveyors because after all it is their secrete to keep and for the rest to decipher.

THE HITS ALGORITHM

The HITS algorithm is the brainchild of Jon Kleinberg of Cornell University. The algorithm takes relevance as an underlying theme in the evaluation of link structures between source and sink. The sources that link to a destination are deemed to be the hubs and the hubs point to the authorities as depicted in figure 1 below. The HITS algorithm depicts the notion of relevance that has been spoken about previously because it is the points of interest that has clout and it is the member nodes which acquiesce to this notion that affirm the point of authority.

Figure 1. HITS Algorithm Sample Node Structure

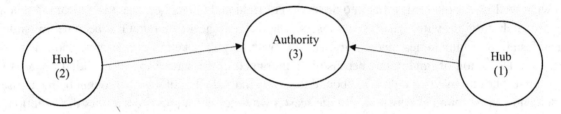

According to Berry (2005) the HITS algorithm keeps track of the index value of each authority by calculating the authority score by way of the equation depicted in Eq. 1.

$$a_i^{(k)} = \sum_j h_j^{(k-1)} \quad \text{Where } e_{ij} \in \varepsilon \tag{1}$$

It is reported by Berry (2005) that in the equation from above the authority score is the sum of the scores across the web landscape and subsequently the hub score may be defined by equation Eq. 2.

$$h_i^{(k)} = \sum_j a_j^{(k-1)} \quad \text{Where } e_{ij} \in \varepsilon \tag{2}$$

In both of the equations given above the value of 'k' is across the web links encountered to be either pointed to or pointing away from some designated node. The hub score from above represents the score for a source to a series of sinks. The above equations can be converted to matrix notation such that the matrix derivative simply designates a node as having a link value (1) or not (0), which can be expressed as follows.

$$L_{ij} = \begin{cases} 1 & \textit{if there exists i and j such that } e_{ij} \in \epsilon \\ 0 & \textit{otherwise} \end{cases}$$

The linear constraint defined for 'L' above entails that figure 1 may be represented as the following matrix, whereby the source node is represented by the row and the sink node is represented by the column.

$$L = \begin{matrix} 0 & 0 & 1 \\ 0 & 0 & 1 \\ 0 & 0 & 0 \end{matrix}$$

The transpose of L becomes as follows by definition.

$$L^T = \begin{matrix} 0 & 0 & 0 \\ 0 & 0 & 0 \\ 1 & 1 & 0 \end{matrix}$$

Given the equality definition below and that each hub node has equal weight at initialization and defined to be vector i then the following relationships can be stated.

$$L * L^T = I$$

$$i = \begin{matrix} 1 \\ 1 \\ 1 \end{matrix}$$

The authoritative vector j can then be computed as follows.

$$j = L^T * i = \begin{matrix} 0 & 0 & 0 \\ 0 & 0 & 0 \\ 1 & 1 & 0 \end{matrix} * \begin{matrix} 1 \\ 1 \\ 1 \end{matrix}$$

$$j = \begin{matrix} 0 \\ 0 \\ 2 \end{matrix}$$

The resulting hub vector ii that is then derived using the authoritative vector (j) is then defined to be as follows.

$$ii = L * j = \begin{matrix} 0 & 0 & 1 \\ 0 & 0 & 1 \\ 0 & 0 & 0 \end{matrix} * \begin{matrix} 0 \\ 0 \\ 2 \end{matrix} = \begin{matrix} 2 \\ 2 \\ 0 \end{matrix}$$

To much the chagrin of the systems engineer it was the system attributes of the system that defined homeostasis with the HITS algorithm. The terminal weight of the nodes in the case of the authoritative vector or the weight of the hubs proves to validate by inspection. In the case of the authoritative matrix only node three has significance as nodes one and two point to it. In the case of the hub matrix both nodes one and two prove to have the same weight. By physical inspection of the derived matrices the reader can note that node three has zero hub weight, no external links are found from this node and in the case of the authoritative matrix nodes one and two have zero significance as no node points to these entries.

The HITS algorithm brings to light the relationship that exists between relevance and obscurity on the World Wide Web. Just as is the case for the popular kid and their friends or a celebrity and their followers on Twitter; popularity is a derived matrix of the network structure present and completely verifiable through the linkages of the nodes. Significance or degree of authority much like the reality humanity finds itself in is such because of the interest that is taken between source and sink.

A PRACTIAL IMPLEMENTAION OF THE HITS ALGORITHM IN PYTHON

The HITS algorithm was implemented in the Python programming language given the availability of modules rather easily. One such Python package is NetworkX (https://networkx.org/), which has the direct purpose of facilitating the analysis of complex network structures. For the purposes of this exercise however the Python code will be constructed to tabulate the authoritative vector j given a network topology that is defined as matrix L and by equating the authoritative vector j to the product of the transpose of L and the initialization vector i as was tabulated above.

Matrix tabulations in the Python programming language are facilitated through the NumPy package (https://numpy.org/), which is the component that is used in this exercise to illustrate the calculation of the authoritative vector j with the least amount of code possible. Each of the modules referenced here may be installed through the pip command lines as given below.

```
pip install networkx
pip install numpy
```

In each of the command lines given above, the latest version of the package would be installed for the particular version of the Python framework being utilized.

```
import numpy as np

# Network Map
data = np.array([[0,0,1], [0,0,1], [0,0,0]])

# Network Map Transpose
data_transposed = data.transpose()

# Initialization Vector
initialized_weights = np.array([[1],[1],[1]])

# Vector Product
result = data_transposed.dot(initialized_weights)
```

```
# Output
print(result)
```

As the reader would imagine the output of the Python code written above is in unison to what was tabulated previously. The agility to which code may now be written cannot be understated as the code fragment from above could be extrapolated for example to function in a generic mode by way of a function and which could also be enhanced to output the network topology graph with other Python packages that could be installed by way of the pip command line as was demonstrated previously for the NumPy and NetowrkX Python packages. This exercise highlights the benefits that may be afforded by way of a development construct to solve problems. This was in fact the process that was followed to data mine from the search engine purveyors and the manner by which the content of this text came to be, it was through the use of built in packages and their leveraging to harness the strength of shear computation effort to do the heavy lifting. This would not have been feasible in not a too distant past, but such is the benefit that computational power affords today that now it can be leveraged for the mundane and for the not so mundane and all of which may be used to help the business obtain a leverage point that can help propel the business forward. It has become the age of the computer in a manner, but it will only yield to those that are able to hit the keyboard in just the right sequence so as to harness that leverage point. This is in part what this text is about, the leverage of the computational context to create those solutions that can help propel the business forward to build a wedge between obscurity and relevance and at times it can be as simple as rethinking how an old problem was solved and exchange the tools previously used for new ones that are better equipped to solve the challenges that lay before the business.

PAGERANK

The precursor to the paradigm of indexing content on the web and the query search window is the brainchild of two Stanford University computer science students Larry Page and Sergey Brin who were collaborating on a research project called BackRub. Larry and Sergey moved their research project to a physical domain on September 15th, 1997 and registered the domain name Google.com. The actual physical credit for defining the algorithm that was used as the primary indexing protocol by Google is attributed to Larry Page.

The PageRank algorithm has a simple premise at heart and can be viewed as a counterpart to the HITS algorithm; PageRank is interested in determining the balance between inbound and outbound links to derive an index for a page. The PageRank algorithm is defined as follows by Berry (2005).

$$r_j\left(P_i\right) = \sum_{Q \in \tau_{P_i}} \frac{r_{j-1}(Q)}{|Q|} \quad \text{for } j = 1, 2, 3, \ldots\ldots \tag{3}$$

In the above formula the variable 'P' represents the individual page or sink, $r_j(P_i)$ represents the PageRank for a given sink, the denominator of the right hand side of the equation represents the outbound links from the sink, and the numerator represents the inbound links to the sink from a series of sources. The PageRank formula is a simple summation ratio between inbound and outbound links. The PageRank algorithm has been a victim of link stuffing by search engine optimizers in the past as certain sites allow individuals to create dynamic content which can be linked directly back to the desired page for which link equity is desired. To counterbalance this tactic by the search engine optimizers the search engines specifically Google will ignore back links to sinks for which the anchor tag contains the 'nofollow' value to the attribute 'rel' as depicted below.

```
<a href=http://www.SomeURL.com/Destination rel="nofollow">Link</>
```

The essential benefit of the above being that it keeps the source page from losing part of its link equity to content posters such as bloggers or general content creators. This example represents the dynamic that is ever so present in the world of the web and its indexing and also represents the evolution of the search engine's architectural framework that has been created and refined by each search engine provider.

The PageRank formula denotes the just cause for the migration to MDAs as the content creator of the MDA, or the sink node would be linked to by each source node that decides to place the application on their corresponding website. This forces the PageRank algorithm to tabulate a higher quotient for the sink nodes and if there exist enough subscribing clients to the application it would entail a greater degree of clout for the sink node since PageRank and clout, i.e., network appendages are intrinsically linked. It becomes a similar case for the HITS algorithm as each additional source node to some sink forces an additional row to be appended to the matrix known as L transpose. The very essence of the computational nature of relevance as it was determined to be from the onset would entail that the course of action has been set. The rules of engagement as they were defined from the beginning mandated from the onset that application development for the web would change at some point and become distributed, smaller, and client centric. It had to be so because the equations mandated it.

A PAGERANK ALGORIMTH IMPLEMENTATION IN PYTHON

The PageRank algorithm can be implemented in the Python programming language similarly to what was done previously with the HITS algorithm. The code segment that is provided next defines two dictionaries whereby the first dictionary lists the associations for the sink node of inbound links and the second dictionary lists the associations for its outbound links. Once these datasets are traversed it becomes a trivial case of computing the ratio of PageRank. The result that is printed on the last line of the code segment is the PageRank value that is tabulated from the dictionary references. The algorithm ensures that in the case where there are no outbound links from the sink node the denominator be set to 1 to avoid a division by 0r exception. The algorithm provided defines each URL as a simple letter, but in a commercial setting these values would contain each domain or specific URL that is being evaluated.

This exercise highlights the parallel that exists between two distinct paradigms that are fundamentally different, but yet similar enough so that their resultant can be compared and understood under a similar light. The argument was made previously that while each of the search engine purveyors is free to define their own reality the fact of the matter is that they are playing on the same field with the same cast of characters and for which they all share a common goal. And while their direct models may differ in subtleties what cannot be altered is the fact that the boundary constraint is but the page. In the case of Larry and Sergey they as much as confessed this truth with the name of their original treaties. This is in part why the systems argument cannot be escaped, it is because the confines of the game are finite and while their permutations may be many in theory, the reality of the matter is that feasibility and conjecture can be polar opposites.

```
denominator = 0
inbound_links = {'A': 2, 'B': 1, 'C': 5}

numerator = 0
outbound_links = {'Z': 1, 'ZZ': 1}

for key, value in inbound_links.items():
numerator += value

for key, value in outbound_links.items():
denominator += value

if denominator == 0:
denominator = 1

result = numerator / denominator

print(result)
```

SEARCH ENGINE MARKET INFLUENCE

Before Google made the transition to an English language verb it was but simply a search utility which made it one of several that were available in the market. The official launch of Google search was made in 1998 and before it there existed the likes of MSN Search, Ask Jeeves, Webcrawler, Lycos, Excite, and several others. Over time the majority of the search providers lost their market share and have either become regulated to a slice of the market or ended being put out of business altogether. Johnson (2021) reported global market share of search engine traffic to be as noted in table 2 as given below for the month of September of 2021. The market share shows that the top three search engines account for 96.18% of the total global search engine traffic.

The ability to be able to make an appreciable impact of an organization's internet presence on each of the search engine providers noted below entails that visibility globally is increased. In the case of the Google search engine the impact could be such that it enables the business to derive differentiation. The relevance of this text is significant not merely from an academic perspective but also from a business perspective because it means that search engine leverage can increase the physical bottom line of the business. The ability to create this leverage by way of Micro Distributed Applications entails that a team can create this benefit for the business independent of its size and consequently grease the wheels of competition for the organization. This is the classic case of a technological paradigm having a direct and positive impact on the bottom line due to the significance of search and what search entails for each business by way of their web presence and for which the proverbial hedge has become Micro Distributed Applications. This degree of influence that the search purveyors have imposed on the development community at large is not a burden, but it is rather a lever that levels the playing field between businesses since an online presence knows not the actual size of the storefront. It is a leverage that allows all businesses to compete in an open and fair environment whereby it becomes but the creativity and degree of innovation of the pod that determines viability of the business. Search influence has become but the democratization of the capitalist system in a way that has not been seen prior. No longer does an organization need to invest in a production line as Henry Ford once did to create a product, but rather businesses can create products from coffee houses and a laptop. The search domain has leveled the playing field for all businesses and people alike as has never been seen prior. This is the reason why venture capital funds flow throughout the world and are not centralized in any given region. The conditions of engagement have altered because of this democratization that is being witnessed and because of which it can be that David that can take on that Goliath and win because after all that slingshot, that weapon for competition has been exchanged for that keyboard whereby that pebble that may be hurdled forth to stake some claim are but the applications that teams can build. And it is because of this leverage that has been afforded that teams can now compete, but competition will be skewed to those businesses that understand the underpinnings for engagement to yield leverage which will yield the argument to the domain of MDAs eventually.

Table 2. Search Purveyor Capitalization

Search Engine	Market Share (%)
Google	86.64
Bing	6.79
Yahoo	2.75

QUERY LOGS

The page index proposition has been studied from the perspective of the search engine query logs to try to derive the symbiotic relationship between query terms and user preference. The rational for the study being that given a search term and a series of user link preferences it can allow the investigator to create a correlation between the link selected and the query term(s). From the systems perspective this represents a grave issue as the example highlights the cross pollination of data points across system boundaries. The study boundary also highlights another issue at the systems level and this being that an individual user is also utilized as a proxy variable to a system variable. It is amazing to see how much effort and funding has gone to this specific mode of study with search engines and their underpinnings to have the base argument fail due to a fundamental issue at the systems level that directly implies that only an inconclusive termination point can be arrived at in the argument.

The utilization of the individual users to assess value across the playing field is a biased proposition because users and all of their specific preferences are being used to gauge value in general. If the argument for data mining of the query logs was to derive a specific user centric customizable search experience, then the argument for the utilization of the query logs would make complete sense. Each user is specific in their preferences and as such what may be relevant content for user 'A' could be completely irrelevant to user 'B'; how then could the search result experience come to terms with this disparity? Take for example two users that are searching for the query term 'China', the first user is searching for information that is relevant to their upcoming travel plans to the country while the second user is searching on the query term for dinnerware. In this specific example can the search experience be cross user relevant? Do you think that the AdWords marketing strategy by the search engine providers would work in this case? The answer to the question of course is no. Now let's take this example one step further and for the sake of argument say that the two users are a husband and wife sitting in bed on their tablets searching the internet on the home Wi-Fi. The query logs in this case which track query by IP address would show the exact same user with divergent selection options, i.e., the mapping between query term and link selection. In systems theory when you move away from the specific and move into the domain of the proxy the whole world view starts to come apart. Before closing here though let one more factoid be brought to bear; in 90% of all cases the link selection in a result set returned by the search engine provider was in the top five of the links presented as reported by Smyth et al. (2004). Truth cannot be derived when only 5 of say 60 records are used in a stochastic model. The data for query logs is heavily skewed and by definition of statistics represents a non-normalized set which entails that the data construct falls into the domain of the non-considerable.

The second major issue with using a data store such as the query logs to analyze the preference to link rank of a data set is that the encompassing model is void of the fundamental attributes that may be derived directly by way of the base system model. If a variable is utilized to measure an index across the model, then this variable must be directly derived by way of the model and not through a proxy variable that may or may not show parity with the actual system variables much like the 'Big Mac' index of the Economist magazine. The physical sciences have functioned around the system specific attributes from their very inception such as in physics with force, acceleration, and mass. When the discussion has moved away from the physical sciences is when humanity has seen a real propensity to link affect to the nonspecific system attributes or to proxy variables thus leading the argument astray, away from the root of truth. The discussion next proceeds to the system level and to the defining of the base systems theory formulations that will allow the discussion to proceed through sound methodology and good science.

SYSTEM THEORY

The derivation of cause and effect can be an obscure paradigm given the lack of understanding of what constitutes system variables. This discourse moves the discussion forward in this section by placing the boundary around the generic problem frame so that the problem frame can find delineation between a valid component and a non-system component. This is the first step that must be undertaken when studying a system because to set course without doing such entails a misalignment between truth and data collected. The system boundary becomes that catalyst by which the landscape can be better understood and thus help the investigator be better able to find comfort in knowing that a sound anchor point can be counted on independent of the cross winds that are to blow to try to veer off center the plumb line.

System variables have degrees of states, this state is driven by the degrees of separation that the variable exhibits between the direct measurement from the source. In the physical sciences motion is understood by the use of variables such as velocity, which is defined as the distance travelled by some object in a specific period of time. The base components that drive the definition of the variable equate to distance and time. Since the specific distance that an object travels can be directly measured by its direct behavior and the time that this takes is specifically tied to the behavior of motion then the components of distance and time are deemed to be variables of the first order. The formal definition for system variables of the first order is as follows.

System variables of the first order are those components that can be directly measured from the base system under study through either direct measurement or quantified through the behavior of the base system.

In the example given previously distance and time are system variables of the first order while velocity is not. Velocity is a system variable of the second order since its definition is the composite of variables of the first order. This leads the discussion to system variables of the second order and for which the formal definition is as follows.

System variables of the second order are those components that are derived by the amalgamation of system variables of the first order and thus yield a differentiating unit of measure from those system attributes that were combined and are of the first order.

From the example from above it can be seen that while the units of measure for distance (i.e., meter) and time (i.e., seconds), velocity on the other hand is in the form of distance over time (i.e., m/s). This leads the discussion to a junction point at which scientific inquiry finds itself at times and at the root cause of why much discord comes about. There are times when the investigative study parts from the road that the physical sciences have paved in the form of system variables of the first or second order and the investigative study finds itself in the domain of something else, proxy variables if you will. The definition for a proxy variable now follows.

Proxy variables are components that cannot be classified as being of the first or second order and while these variables may approximate the model behavior cannot be tied to the direct system constraint boundary that model's homeostasis for the individual element.

Two examples have already been provided for proxy variables in system modeling, the first being the 'Big Mac' index and the second being the clickthrough rate given some query term. The manifestation of the reality humanity experiences is the domain of system variables of the first or second order. Society however seems to be inclined to forgo the comfort and assurance that anchor points of the first and second order provide and instead gravitates to what is plausible and for which its assertation can be bound often times to that proxy variable. The hard sciences have taught all a lesson however and this is that empiricism will always bare good fruit because cause and effect can be explained without equivocation. Take the case of force being equal to mass times acceleration; the combination of two system variables, but nevertheless together in one equation and for which the current state of life would be elusive if not understood. The conjecture is true because it can be proven, but it is only such because it is a private party where only citizens of the first and second class are allowed to partake.

Governance of truth is the realm of the academic and the station of men and women with righteous pedigrees, or is it? Truth is in fact the right of all to bare hold to and to be able to press to a breast pocket much as a keepsake. But this truth that is sought will never find the inner lining of that tweed jacket if it is not preserved like the finest heirloom. It is the burden of all to maintain this mode of prejudice over truth because it is the purest form of the best quality of mankind. With truth there can never be any compromise because a mother will never compromise over her child. Truth must be seen as that innocence of that baby that has just left its mother's womb and it is for everyone to protect and to do such the arguments set forth must part from what can be measured from the subject under study because anything but is nothing short of treason, the irony of it all is however that the offence is to the only actor in the play, to the investigator. It is a case of the transgressor becoming the victim.

SYSTEM STATE

The HITS and the PageRank equations were a utility to the specific domain at a specific point in time. From a systems perspective the HITS and PageRank algorithms define a model that has its roots in a facet of the attributes of the system – i.e., the link structure of the web. In an academic setting one metric to determine value of a publication and consequently an author is the amount of literature that references the source publications for the target author. Do you see the parallel that can be created here between the physical and virtual document? Current state of search has become but the manifestation of the reality that humanity holds for relevance in its own notion of significance. The internet has simply become a reality of an abstraction. Humanity has projected its world view to the physical digits and bytes that is the internet and have consequently structured the relevance of the abstract with what it knows to be good and true. In this body of work, what is sought is to understand this dynamic further but do so by moving the discussion past the simple network structures and move the discourse to an attribute parity mapping. Each page – sink or source tells a story with regards to the attributes that define its utility to the search goer. To validate the premise simply head over to a Google, Bing or Yahoo search page and enter a query term, any search will do, do you notice something? Certain aspects of the results are brought forth to your attention immediately; these points of interest are highlighted or put in bold font for you to view by some of the search providers to click on of course. It is those tidbits of information that come to you from sources that are in the weeds that convey a great worth of detail for you. Sometimes in life it is not those entities that make the loudest sound that convey the most significance, but it is rather those that make the smallest wave that are the most profound. It is the burden of each however to be attentive enough to be able to listen and decipher what is before you or you risk losing the full intent of the message that is being transmitted.

In the following chapter the story is expanded whereby the discussion proceeds to those specific points that the system conveys to anyone that cares to listen intently enough to forgo the expense of what is the sunk cost of bias. Every system has a specific set of characteristics that define its behavior – you could make the argument that this may even extend into the nonphysical or qualified driven domains. Behavior can absolutely be modeled under any circumstance you simply need to understand the underlying attributes of the system and the methods that act upon those attributes much as is found with the functionality of class structures in software engineering. The class – the container to the functional node encompasses the attributes and methods that drive behavior for which at times it inherits its behavior from a parent or encompassing class thus making function extensible through the concept of inheritance, but always by way of the attributes as they define the parameterized boundary constraints of behavior. When taking the systems perspective in mind you can extend the discussion even further and define those class attributes to be the specific primary base attributes or the system variables of the first order. This super class now can have child classes that extends from the base class and define those system variables of the second order that are based very simply from the base attributes of the inheriting class and being of the first order.

Systems theory and architecture go hand in hand as the two domains focus on the classification over some construct that can be modelled by way of the class structure with attributes being of the first or second order and for which base attributes of the second order are derived from those inherited classes that contain the first order primary components. In the end it all fits together like a glove where each finger defines a class to model the individual nodes and when all are brought together, what is apparent is a clear image of the hand before your very eyes. This notion of system variable order is fundamental to understanding behavior and a primary reason why the material found herein was able to obtain traction and in fact it may be the only means by which the empiricist in anyone may be satisfied.

SYSTEMS REFLECTION

The discourse from the literature in this chapter has discussed the landscape from the network level perspective but has yet left the discussion void of the system and its inherent attributes. Yet the rumblings of truth about system level factors of influence are present as the style guide that will be analyzed later in the text reveals. The PageRank and HITS algorithms addressed the discourse in part as they address the appendages of the node in question, the external forces upon the face of the object in a manner, but yet the potential of the document or object in question has been left from the discussion. The document or node if you will has relevance not simply because of these external factors but has such because of its inherent attributes. To leave these factors out of the discussion is to view the problem fame under the guise of those eye coverings that were discussed prior. It would be equivalent to taking a football team and using their win to loss ratio and utilizing it as the conclusive factor of prominence, without taking into account the players on the field. Past performance is not necessarily tied to future performance as the factors at play must be considered. To be able to predict behavior it becomes paramount to understand the attributes of the system that dictate outcome, it is about understanding cause and effect.

Metal fatigues over time and at some point, is bound to fail, engineers have come to understand that system homeostasis is a direct function of stress and time. It is the reason society is continually upgrading infrastructure. Much as the bonds of the atoms in metal change over time so too must equal consideration be given to the components of the system that are subject to flux over time or otherwise it leaves the argument susceptible to sudden and catastrophic collapse. The HITS and PageRank algorithms make sense because of the degree of clout that they encompass, but what is needed to be able to understand the indexing domain is to understand the elements that are encompassed by the boundary constraint, the page elements. This body of work initiates the investigative process from the boundary constraint and proceeds forward from this reference point, which facilitates the process of discovery since the landscape does not become crosspollinated from external systems and it also allows for the capturing of the factors that function to create homeostasis. When this process is followed what is found is that future state can be determined, and it can be deciphered because of the nature of progress in the space which is embodied in the process. Network linkages are important when understanding worth on the World Wide Web as are the characteristics of the body under study. It is in part however by understanding what the ruins convey that it allows for a better understanding of current state and the reason why the chapter was named as such. This process of understanding the past under the guise of the systems perspective facilitates the understanding of the ramifications of what it unfolds. What unfolds is a story that has evolved over time and yet is tied to the past. What unfolds is a trajectory of what software development will need to be because of where the journey parted from. What results is the understanding that the journey that the profession is on is dynamic, evolving, and has only helped to create opportunities where they once did not exist. This level of understanding can only be brought forth by taking that journey that is lit by the lantern that is systems theory.

WEB DEVELOPMENT

The web development paradigm has changed in mode from being a concentrated effort where code physically runs on a server and rendered with minor user interface interaction to be quite the contrary. The frameworks noted in table 1 have facilitated part of this endeavor for teams and have helped developers to change their focus. To facilitate matters further industry has seen the once client side only language of JavaScript migrate to become a server side paradigm as well through Node.js (www.nodejs.org). The skillset that use to be separate, the server side development from the client side development has become skewed and as a consequence organizations have seen development become ubiquitous across the membrane that is the fiber cable. The profession has also seen once prevalent roles such as graphics designers become more obtuse given that the frameworks facilitate the development of the user experience for developers without the need to employee a graphics person in the complete process. It is because of these changes that the paradigm of web development finds itself where it is now. Teams can now create full applications that sit on the client side and run on their browser instead of completely on servers, thus migrating the work effort from server side to client side. Moore's law has further contributed to this paradigm shift as teams can now leverage the physical hardware of the client to perform their needed body of work and consequently offload part of the labor from the servers. Even the cellphone browsers have become more sophisticated and capable of running micro applications, rendering a homogeneous landscape for applications.

Teams are now able to create these client side applications in the browser window for their audience and allow them to interact with the mobile friendly software from anywhere that they wish to connect from. The GET request that Berners-Lee made in March of 1989 is the same request that browsers make to physically download the libraries that client side applications depend on to function. In reality nothing has changed and yet everything has changed all at the same time. The difference between today and years gone by is that now web applications perform a multitude of GET requests to retrieve each of the dependencies that applications require in order to execute on the clients' browser. One need to simply turn on debug mode in the browser of choice and view all the network requests that are occurring in real time. Each request being a dependency for these outwardly exposed applications to function correctly. The increase in traffic of Content Delivery Networks (CDN) over time is highlighted by Clement (2020) when it is shown that traffic in exabytes per month has increased from 54 in 2017 to 252 in 2022, an almost 4-fold increase in a matter of just over five years. The reader should note that this does not simply imply quantity of users, but the data may also refer to size of applications that those users are building and subsequently placing on CDNs. Current applications are leveraging the construct because it facilitates the sharing of resources across the World Wide Web. It entails that these applications can become available for anyone to consume given an internet connection and a willing subscriber to the utility. Content delivery networks also provide these applications with the ability to become resilient because of the redundancy of the availability of the software artifacts as relevant content can be uploaded to distinct servers all over the world. CDNs also facilitate the distribution of the software to locals that are more central to demand, so a client in south Asia for example could download the software directly from a public cloud provider server in Australia without the need to have to deal with the latency that it would entail by placing the software in say New York.

One facet of the discussion that has been left void is the programming language, as the JavaScript interpreters are built in directly into the internet browser software and alleviate teams from having to configure such on each subscribing clients' machine, The ubiquitous of the domain has facilitated the communication across the medium that is the network of distributed computers. In days gone past teams would not only have to install the software on the physical machine running the application, but they would also have to ensure that the runtime environment or the interpreter was installed in order to execute the code. One of the reasons why the Java programming language has been such a success is because of the Java Virtual Machine (JVM) where the high degree of adoption of the JVM has facilitated the adoption of the programming construct and has thus meant a greater market share for the programming language. In particular with the Java programming language industry saw this adoption extend past the personal computer and see it prosper for mobile devices where it become the language of choice for Android development. With regards to JavaScript industry has seen a similar evolution as it has not only become a server side development construct but it is also a development language for mobile development. Reactive Native (https://reactnative.dev) for example is a mobile development framework that leverages the JavaScript programming language which has enabled it to become a viable option for mobile applications there once again showing the portability that the language construct affords the implementor.

Table 3 as given below shows the release or development date of some popular programming languages. The year that the PHP programming language was released also witnessed the release of the client side construct of JavaScript. Unlike PHP however the JavaScript programming language has become much more popular with the development community and in part it may be attributed to its ability to modify the user interface. It has meant that the development community has been able to create rich user interfaces because of it and as a result this has led further to the adoption of the language construct. This inherent need to create these rich interfaces has also led to the development of frameworks as was noted in table 1. This migration and this enablement that has resulted because of adoption has entailed that a new breed of applications has resulted. MDAs represent this migration path that the development community at large has been on irrespective of the indexing domain. It just so happens however that the two roads have crossed, and the junction point has consequently become more prominent because of it. MDAs leverage the same constructs that JavaScript applications are infused with and expand on it. MDAs are but simply the next wave of JavaScript applications that will be smaller and more distributed, which is the path that development has been on.

The development space as it is known today has been in the making for more than 20 years just from a programming language construct and teams have been creating languages to support the paradigm for decades now as noted in table 3. The reality that is seen today in the form of dynamic web applications is because a great many people have been working in the space and have created tools for teams to utilize, each utility building upon the next and finding refinement along the way to create the experience that is the leverage that teams are currently using. Given the ubiquitous nature of the programming construct of choice - JavaScript where developers can use the language to write frontend, backend, and mobile applications entails that industry is seeing the culmination of the doctrine into what can only be called an ubiquitous ecosystem that will become the next reality. The argument that is set out in this text is that it is because of this evolutionary journey that teams now find themselves at a fork in the road. This fork in the road that is spoken of is a change that is to come because of a time and place. It is because of the influence that search engines have on the products that are available over the internet and it is because of the paradigm that exists for development that the time is here for these two dichotomies to merge to bring forth the new wave of application development. This tidal wave of development that is to come will be so because businesses mandate that they stay viable in the quest for the attention of the customer. At heart it is but an economics argument since it is the economics of the dynamic that mandate where teams are to place their labor. It is because of this need that teams will see these types of applications take on a greater degree of relevance and focus. There simply is no escape from the pull that is being imposed on teams to build these new breed of applications because after all if they do not then survival in the ever so competitive environment that is the internet will become less probable.

Table 3. Programming Language Historical Release Dates

Language	Year
Perl	1987
Ruby	1995
Ada 95	1995
Java	1995
Delphi	1995
JavaScript	1995
PHP	1995

WEB SERVICES

Webservices are the mechanisms by which data is transferred from databases over the wire to the welcoming recipients that are the web and mobile applications that consume it. The argument has been made that webservices were spawned from the remote procedure calls (RPC) paradigm, which on the surface does make sense, but when you dive a little deeper into the history of the web you find the work of Berners-Lee from March of 1989, which predates remote procedure calls or the XML-RPC specification. The work of Berners-Lee which evolved to web traffic is what gave way to the transfer of data by way of the GET method of webservices, it was the precursor for the communication protocol. From these rudimentary beginnings is how much of what facilitates our lives today has come about, such as online banking, Internet of Things (IoT), mobile applications, and video conferencing. Complexity over the domain that is before mankind has been tamed because of simple data structures that facilitate the communication between disparate systems. Humanity has consequently become more connected whereby individuals do not need to be physically next to one another to be able to feel connected, distance has become but a reality that can be circumvented at a whim because of the power of technology.

In June of 1998, XML-RPC was released which defined the SOAP protocol, the specification is an acronym for Simple Object Access Protocol. The specification outlines the mode by which communication occurs between disparate machines and for which the protocol was to transmit data through the use of XML. The specification was to use the Hypertext Transfer Protocol (HTTP) as the mechanism for bridging the gap of communication between the disparate nodes. SOAP allowed developers to find comfort and an already familiar state whereby functionality on a disparate machine could be invoked across the World Wide Web and thus provide teams with functionality across the ubiquitous layer that had become the internet. SOAP defined three particular tenants, and these are:

1. An envelope which would contain the detail that was to be communicated between source and sink.
2. Encoding rules that would dictate how objects were to be represented.
3. A convention that dictated the method in which endpoints could be invoked.

This paradigm that became SOAP is what allowed teams to usher in formally the generation of web-services and distributed computing for the World Wide Web. It was because of the ability to reuse and recycle functionality across applications and more importantly to offer said functionality to customers that teams were able to create a leverage for web development. This leverage that was created allowed for progress and the movement forward because it meant that users could leverage the functionality of others without the need of having to create their own dependencies from scratch. Industry progressed because teams were able to share their products and services with the masses and as a consequence of the paradigm shift teams in turn were able to leverage the work of others, thus facilitating the work effort.

In April of 2002, the World Wide Web Consortium (W3C) made public the working draft of the Web Service Description Requirements, which outlined how disparate nodes on a network could communicate with one another. While the XML-RPC provided a formal definition of how communication over the internet could occur, it was the standardization of the paradigm that facilitated the adoption of the construct. Part of the requirements that were outlined in the specification that set the tone for the future of webservices were as follows.

- Processors of the description language had to support XML Schema.
- Description language had to describe end points using URIs
- Interface binding had to occur over HTTP/1.1

It was in part because of the initial specification requirements that industry now finds itself in its current state of openness and data availability. The standardization over a model has always lent itself to interchange because the rules governing the domain become fixed and better understood. By creating this common doctrine or protocol over the subject it became feasible for developers to develop to the specification and consequently for consumers of the data to utilize the endpoints that exposed the much needed functionality.

Once industry came to an agreement over the rules of engagement it became corporate America that placed their full weight behind the endeavor with programable structures that were infused with the technology. Microsoft introduced ASMX webservices to capitalize on the protocol that had been defined and consequently went on to develop WCF webservices. The introduction of webservices into the programming structure that become .NET allowed for developers to change the nature of their applications. Webservices allowed teams to separate the core business logic from the physical pages that generated the content for the users. To facilitate matters further the introduction of the Model View Controller (MVC) design pattern into .NET projects allowed for developers to structure their projects with this separation of control directly and easily. The consequence of the paradigm shift was that the physical web pages become easier to manage because they were simply views of the application, they represented a particular state of matters, such as a physical account of a customer. This evolution has helped to usher the paradigm that teams subscribe to now were JavaScript utilities have the burden of performing all the needed user interface actions and the webservices layer function to keep the integrity of the data. The backend and the frontend function together with clear lines of segregation that also allows for the segregation of work for teams were some team members are strictly dedicated to the application aesthetics and others dedicate their time to the core business functionality.

The advent of representational state transfer (REST) webservices has worked to lay the architectural layout of how teams are to maintain state within their applications through the ubiquitous layer that is the World Wide Web. REST represents an additional affirmation by the development community at large that the course of action that it has been on is correct and warranted. Industry has doubled down on the paradigm that teams have subscribed to and as a consequence it has left teams on a path where there is no turning back. Teams need to be able to expose their needed functionality to the development community, it is one reason why APIs have seen such an explosion in their growth. Looking at the utility of Postman (www.postman.com) you find that they reported in February of 2020 that their API platform was used by more than 17 million developers in over 800 thousand organizations worldwide. Webservices are driving in part the digitalization of businesses because they allow for distinct business units to share information between one another. This digitalization of corporations is needed because it allows for information interchange and the creation of economies of scale, thus helping businesses become more productive. Webservices are not simply a technological advancement at an abstract level, but they are the grease that facilitates communication and whether this is for external or internal use is simply inconsequential as the benefits are what is sought.

This benefit that is spoken of here is bound to the subject matter of this text because it leads to the creation of entities that can interact across the landscape given that the only constraint is the Hypertext Transfer Protocol (HTTP). It entails that client side applications can become dynamic and can conform to what was once known to be the domain of thick clients. It also entails that the same webservices that are invoked for data transfer can be utilized to manage the dynamic loading of the MDAs that can be developed as will be seen in further chapters. This is yet another reason why the age of MDAs has arrived, it is because the technological necessities are in place that facilitate the development effort and the leveraging of which leads to search relevance, economies of scale, and the digitalization of the business.

SUMMARY

The development landscape has progressed and grown with the advancement in technology to meet the demand of the populous. The masses have experienced the growth of the online search engines to the point that they have influenced how products are marketed. This degree of influence has resulted in the redefinition of online content creation where the naming structure of the URLs for example must now be considered in order to facilitate search relevance. Such has been the influence of indexing that it has come to affect the profession and the manner in which organizations structure their physical products online. Software businesses have migrated their products from the hardware of their clients to exist in the cloud so that their same clients can access the physical products and by doing so alleviated organizations from having to package, distribute, and manage licenses individually. Businesses did so eagerly and willingly because they understood that being able to outwardly expose the products to the clients was a positive and a necessity to be able to get the message across to be able to obtain as large a share of the available customers as possible. When they did this, they created an exposure for these systems whereby they became available to the indexing community to search and classify. This dependency forced upon development teams a need to leverage the paradigm in order to be better able to compete with other software providers. Organizations needed for these customers to find their products first and thus keep these much coveted dollars from finding a home with other businesses. Organizations needed to win the race of indexing so that they could leverage the World Wide Web and have their customers use these products independently of geographical location. This competition that was forced upon organizations changed the rules of the game and changed how these products needed to be marketed. Today you see this playout when searching for any product or service as you will undoubtedly see the advertisements of companies that are in search of your business. So, lucrative has been the market segment of online advertisement that the social networks followed suit and also began to engage in a similar model, all in search of those much coveted marketing dollars from corporations throughout the world. The rules of engagement changed along the way as did the businesses that made the products because after all there is no corrective factor as great as the influx of capital. These businesses had to survive, they had to compete and as a result they adapted to the change in the landscape. When they did they unknowingly changed the engagement forever and consequently changed the development landscape as well.

The development landscape has changed such that it has strategically altered how products are formatted, displayed, and conveyed because of the internet. This flux has yielded a symbiotic relationship between the patrons of the information highway and the virtual storefronts of the businesses that seek to fulfill a need in these customers. Businesses have pivoted in an effort to find a more favorable station with the search providers as a result of this drive to find these willing patrons, and it has worked, they have seen a direct and tangible benefit for their businesses. Where businesses find themselves now is at a similar junction, where they once stood, they find themselves at a point in time where the applications they develop can be modified to create a tangible benefit with the search providers. Organizations find themselves at a point in time where they can once again turn to technology to help them capitalize on the nature of the game before them. They can leverage the advancements in technology up to now and use what is freely available to them to create the new breed of applications that can be provided to their users to be used directly in their applications. When they do such, it allows them to find life in all the distinct environments that provide these applications with lodging and by doing so these businesses can obtain an additional degree of relevance in the indexing race. The fact that organizations can now create applications that physically live outside of their domain entails that they become the source of authority, they become the expert that must be listened to, and consequently they become the most important amongst their brethren. The fact that their customers select them to live inside their ecosystems means that they are the preferred choice, and this degree of acknowledgement becomes echoed with the search providers as they have to acquiesce to the natural selection process that unfolds before them. The search providers become consumers of this survey and in turn have no choice but to give the creators of such content their rightful place in the hierarchy of relevance. When these organizations become these providers of functionality it entails that they in turn become the beneficiary of the will of the free market, they become the choice in what can only be described as the natural process of selection. It is the affirmation that is seen here of the democratization of business because of the World Wide Web.

The future state of the architectural footprint of any business is being affected by the current state of the indexing effort. Given the degree of clout that the search engine providers have it has entailed a paradigm shift in how web development is viewed and the type of components that need to be built. This paradigm shift is in alignment with the evolution of the space as well because of the advancements that have been made with technologies and utilities that facilitate the development effort. What industry is seeing is the marrying of technological domains where the tools available to create online content have simply become part of the ecosystem that is pertinent to search. This future state while it may be in a constant state of flux it is nevertheless affixed to some datum point that are the ruins from once was known as the status quo. It entails that future state will never see expedience but will rather be evolutionary and be progressive. This incremental advancement has brough development teams to the new breed of applications that are to be built and that can only be termed Micro Distributed Applications (MDAs) as they will be smaller and reside in domains throughout the internet.

REFERENCES

Berry, M., & Browne, M. (2005). *Understanding Search Engines: Mathematical Modeling and Text Retrieval*. Siam. doi:10.1137/1.9780898718164

Clement, J. (2020, February 28). *Global Content Delivery Network Internet Traffic 2020*. Statista. https://www.statista.com/statistics/267184/content-delivery-network-internet-traffic-worldwide/

Graham, M. (2021). *How Google's $150 Billion Advertising Business Works*. CNBC. https://www.cnbc.com/2021/05/18/how-does-google-make-money-advertising-business-breakdown-.html

Johnson, J. (2021, October 8). *Global Market Share of Search Engines 2020-2021*. Statista. https://www.statista.com/statistics/216573/worldwide-market-share-of-search-engines/

Smyth, B., Balfe, E., Freyne, J., Briggs, P., Coyle, M., & Boydell, O. (2004). Exploiting Query Repetition and Regularity in an Adaptive Community-Based Web Search Engine. *User Modelling and User-Adaptive Interaction.*, *14*(5), 383–423. doi:10.100711257-004-5270-4

Chapter 3
System Variables

ABSTRACT

Prediction over the domain stands a greater degree of success if the system variables of the first and second order are identified and encompassed within the system boundary. It is by functioning in this mode that the inherent need of the empiricist can be satisfied, and which is the gateway to understanding that resonates with the audience. It is the means by which curiosity stands to be satisfied. Since the sensory needs of humanity are but the gateway to acceptance, it becomes an essence of the investigative study therefore to proceed from this leverage point that can only be brought forth if the systems doctrine is infused within the endeavor undertaken. It is also the only insurance that may be purchased to offset the influence of chaos and leave human curiosity satisfied.

INTRODUCTION

In software development the class is referred to as the golden grail of the process. This definition is used because it is all encompassing as it is the attributes that define the characteristics of the object, and it is the methods which act upon these attributes that collectively define homeostasis. Modeling behavior is the process of identifying those system attributes that are contained within the class and acted upon by the methods of the parent object. In this chapter the creation of classes or the coding effort will not be undertaken, but this body of work will nevertheless dive into the current literature of the domain which may be used to identify those components or attributes if you will that drive search engine architecture and consequently define its datum point. In this discourse the definition of the search engine formulas for Bing, and Yahoo will be defined through a modeling endeavor for the purpose of determining how page worth may be best understood. While each of the search engines has control over their own search algorithm what is a constant is that the search engines have a constraint to model around - the system. Any system that you look at will have specific characteristics that define its behavior and the difference between similar systems entails a disjoint in the attribute mapping. The current problem frame that is brought to light here deals with a construct that is actually quite simple at an onset – the system is the web page. The variables are an interesting paradigm to understand however as there are many and their underlying focus or contribution factor is undocumented for the most part or at all in the case of Bing and

DOI: 10.4018/978-1-6684-4849-6.ch003

Yahoo. The modeling effort can be obfuscated because variables may be combined in n! ways without taking into consideration variable order. In data science, the grooming of these attributes to derive the best possible model for prediction is referred to as feature engineering, which is a task that is undertaken in later chapters. What the reader will discover in these later chapters is that truth can be found despite the noise that exists in the landscape by being able to correctly identify those base system attributes as is often done in software engineering to model behavior.

The major search engine providers have since the very onset of the internet utilized the page content of the document to determine standing of the page within the greater group of all pages indexed. In the very beginning there existed a project called APRANET which had as a purpose the linking of documents that were related across distributed repositories. The APRANET project linked like documents so that researchers could locate similar content. Fast forward to today and the World Wide Web; the same principles apply; it revolves around the linking of related content through anchor tags or hyperlinks. Hyperlinks are simply links between pages that allow an individual to jump from one page to another and just as a human can so can a computer as the link reference represents content at some other location that may be retrieved programmatically. This retrieval process by the search engine providers was the first algorithm in linking like content. And now the discussion progresses to current times; where the rules of the game have changed dramatically and the conjecture and hypothesis about what is relevant and not relevant is a forum that litters the World Wide Web. This discussion proceeds by identifying those key elements where the general consensus is that they are relevant. Once the key attributes have been identified the discussion will move forward to the derivation of the mathematical model to prove or disprove the conjecture. By following this process, it will be feasible to migrate the discussion from the qualified to the quantified and consequently arrive at a junction point where there can be no debate about truth. This truth is important to understand because it paves the roadway for the architecture of web applications to come. This truth helps to define where the much sought after point lay and consequently helps to clarify the paradigm and the significance of MDAs.

It is by understanding this paradigm of indexing and worth that it becomes feasible to make the linkage with proper web design because after all, the message can only be understood if the interpreting node understands the protocol. It is this protocol that becomes the key to developing content going forward as it is the measuring stick by which the search providers evaluate content. It becomes in essence almost primal to identify this path as it is by it that relevance for the business on the internet can be revealed. Given the degree of capital that is at stake for businesses with electronic commerce it becomes a battlefield that must be contested and won by the business if it is to survive. This is why it can be stated that while this text is technical in nature it is nevertheless a book about business. It is about building the persona of the business in the ever evolving world that is this ubiquitous media that is the internet. Business and conversely the heads of organizations that fail to understand the dynamic at play when creating applications will find that the message created will fall short of expectation because after all their will not be an audience tunning in on the station that they are broadcasting on.

OVERVIEW

While there has been many content published on search engine indexing there are two bodies of work that stand out amongst the rest. The first body of work is that of Jerkovic (2010) and his book SEO Warrior; in this book the author provides a collection of site attributes that determine page rank. The second body of work that stands out is the work of King (2008) and his book titled Website Optimization; in this body of work King (2008) dives into the intricacies of creating online content to organically reach positive results. While the work of the two aforementioned authors does stand out amongst the forest of literature and a solid contribution to the subject matter what is missing and what remains a void to be filled are the facts or the statistical underpinnings for those components. This body of work aims to fill this gap and it begins by first identifying those attributes that are relevant and that will be fed into a statistical model later. This migration to a metric context is fundamentally necessary when understanding truth as it prevents the argument from going astray to the realm of subjectivity. It is for this reason that this body of work stands out as it is the only body of work that lays the statistical underpinnings of worth and develops a search engine formula to reference as a plum line for that argument that is to be made later. Truth and its influence must always part from the lips of that individual that holds the data to support the conjecture because if such is not afforded to the audience then it is simply an opinion. In the current day and time however it becomes almost an illusion that society is plagued with, since opinions can be had by anyone that is willing to register a domain name and create a website to voice an argument. And while the dynamic does point to the democratization of authorship it has regulated humanity to an indefensible corner, as not all voices carry the same weight. Degree of influence must be the domain of that individual that holds papers in hand showing proof for their assertion. This chapter is the beginning of that discourse whereby the data to support the assertion will be brought to bear as it is the only means by which authorship stands a chance to have relevance. Before such an undertaking can be pursued however the discussion must first part from the qualified and the literature that supports such because these types of arguments are but the points where inquisition parts from.

TITLE TAG

The first page attribute that adds value to the search engines and consequently manifesting itself in the search results positively is the title <title></title> tag. The title tag represents the verbiage that is displayed in the browser window for a given page. Systems have a way of telling you or indicating intent and while the indicators may be subtle, they are there for all to see. A simple search of the term 'Search Engine Algorithms' on Google.com shows a list of results, an exert from one such endeavor is given below for the reader.

Search Engine Algorithm Basics - Moz
    https://moz.com/blog/**search-engine-algorithm**-basics

The first line entry from the above exert is the actual title of the page; you can validate this by selecting the link and then when the page renders in the browser window right clicking on the page and choosing 'View Page Source' (at least in the Google Chrome browser). The snippet retrieved from the page source showing the title definition is provided below.

<title>Search Engine Algorithm Basics - Moz</title>

The intent of the search engine is grossly apparent from the above example. You will also notice that the title verbiage in the browser results of Google is accentuated to draw the attention of the reader to the content. In case you are curious Bing showed the exact same content in the first two lines on the same query. One point of interest however is that Bing placed this same entry in second place and placed the Wikipedia page first. The Yahoo search engine showed the exact same results as Bing for the top two entries in the result set, helping to clarify the notion that similarity exists between the search engine providers and while their exact mode of evaluation may vary there are consistencies because after all the system attributes that may be depended upon to draw some inference are finite.

PAGE COPY

Page copy is the second component on a document that has significance to the search engine providers. Page copy up until recently referred to the verbiage contained within paragraph <p></p> tags and header <hX></hX> tags. There currently exists a large dependency on content layout through the use of Cascading Style Sheets (CSS) however and as such this definition of page copy needs to be extended to include the division <div></div> tag and span <span></span> tag. In the case of the header tags the value of 'X' can be any number between one and six inclusive; the smaller the value of 'X' the larger the font on the screen. King (2008) makes the argument that primary keywords should be placed in the first level header tag. The implication here is that the larger the font the greater emphasis the search engines will place on the keywords identified in the page copy. This implication entails that a formula to measure keyword index worth needs to allocate a dimensional component to the header tags. As the reader will discover in a later chapter of the text, this assertion fails to hold weight as the influence factor denoted here is not supported by the metrics derived. This once again highlights the need to migrate an argument from the qualified to the quantified as it is by the metrics that ambiguity diminishes and leads that compass pointing to true north.

A simple query to the search engine purveyors reveals interesting factoids to the astute listener, for example a search on the phrase 'Toronto Ontario' on Google results in the following Wikipedia entry (2nd entry in result set).

Toronto - Wikipedia, the free encyclopedia
    https://en.wikipedia.org/wiki/Toronto Wikipedia
Toronto (/təˈrɒntoʊ/, local /təˈrɒnoʊ/ or /ˈtrɒn-/) is the most populous city in Canada, and the capital of the province of **Ontario**. In 2011, **Toronto** had a ...

The description displayed in the third line is actual page copy. If you follow the link and look at the physical HTML content of the page, you will notice that the description displayed for the reader is contained within a paragraph <p></p> tag; proof that Google does index page copy and utilizes the paragraph tag as a measure of worth. Further inspection of the page copy will also reveal that the first header tag displayed the word 'Toronto' and this header tag preceded the paragraph tag in the layout; why display one over the other then in the search results? The paragraph tag did contain one grossly apparent benefit – more text and more keywords. Did Google prefer to display the paragraph tag in the description because it physically contained more keywords over the alternative tag? By replacing the previous result with the proposed alternative results in the below noted content.

Toronto - Wikipedia, the free encyclopedia
     https://en.wikipedia.org/wiki/Toronto Wikipedia
Toronto

From a visual perspective it becomes trivial to justify the reason why one output was chosen in lieu of the other. Do you think maybe the search engine providers spend time in a boardroom mocking up user interfaces and have individuals that have gone to university to study such subjects to create a cost benefit analysis over layout value? After all user adoption affects the bottom line and the advertisement revenue from keywords that are selected by the community; there is a lot of money at stake, and you can bet they are analyzing the platform to determine the best possible message to convey to an audience. It is also a fact that this degree of engagement that must be derived from an audience is subject to the constraints of the playing field at large – the page content being indexed. There is just no escaping it, it is the system at hand that determines worth irrespective of how this worth is disseminated.

URL

The third component that adds value to the search engine domain is the domain or URL. URL is an acronym for Uniform Resource Locator and essentially means the location of the document on the World Wide Web. What you type into the address bar has a lot to do with search engine indexing and consequently there is a significant amount of money at stake with domain names. Jerkovic (2010) makes the argument that domain names that are smaller in length are preferred, but from the search engine results provided previously it can be seen that this premise is doubtful as search rank was found to be irrespective of length of URL. The Wikipedia page for the search term 'Toronto Ontario' proved to be the second result in the list. The Wikipedia link also had one of the search terms in a secondary position in the URL, i.e., not part of the domain name, but was rather an internal link of the website. An URL has several components in its makeup; take the Wikipedia link placed below.

https://en.wikipedia.org/wiki/Toronto

This link may be broken down further into sections as depicted in Figure 1 below. The letters from below represent zones in the URL, zone 'A' represents the protocol of communication. In this example the mode of communication is the secure hypertext transfer protocol. Zone 'B' represents the subdomain of the website. Subdomains are simple mechanisms which can aid in separating a website with folders and subfolders or even with applications. A subdomain is also a mechanism that may be used to optimize website content for the internet as each subdomain could be created to fit a particular purpose, such as is seen below as the subdomain partition appears to be language centric

Take for example a website about cars, one way to create specific content for a car on the website would be to have the domain:

http://Lamborghini.ExampleOfCarsWebsite.com

Figure 1. URL Structure

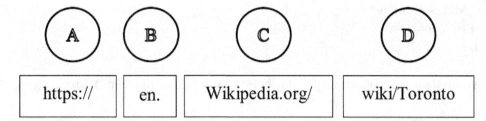

In this scenario zone B is utilized to target each type of a car that is needing to be identified by the search providers and consequently be indexed accordingly. Zone 'C' represents the actual domain name of the website. Zone 'D' is an internal website route that typically points to a subfolder in the application or website. For domains that are easy to remember and tied to a word in the English language such as cars.com it becomes the burden of zone 'D' to function as the second mechanism for search engine optimization in the URL structure, for example the Wikipedia page for the city of Toronto as provided above in Figure 1. This would also explain why it appears to be the case that Google, Bing, and Yahoo did not appear to penalize the site for the rather long verbose URL as was given above. One of the components that you may have noticed from the URL that is missing is the three letters www from the domain name. In the case where a subdomain is used the www prefix to the domain is eliminated and if on the other hand the URL did not have a subdomain then you could have left out the www prefix altogether and would have had the same result. The www prefix stands for World Wide Web, given how the URL is a website the prefix is redundant and a relic of the past.

One of the website optimization techniques that is used by online resellers is to utilize the URL as a mechanism by which to stuff keywords for some product an example of this would be book sellers. The example given below for a hypothetical vendor highlights this URL route strategy.

http://www.MyLittleBookStore.com/The-Hunger-Games

The URL from above would point the reader to the book 'The Hunger Games' at the website 'MyLittleBookStore.com'. As was noted above, the utilization of keywords in the URL plays a role in the indexing effort by the search providers which was seen in practice through the query results obtained in this section. It is important however to make note of this fact with healthy skepticism because it can only be stated as fact if the data supports the argument.

META TAGS

The fourth component that adds value to the search engine domain are the meta tags. Meta tags physically reside within the header section of a web document. The reader should note that the phrase web document was used here as there are a vast number of technologies that may be used to render web content and while the mechanism changes the web browsers will always read a hybrid of XML or HTML. Web pages may have varying extensions such as the ones provided below and each of them supports the embedding of meta tags within their content.

1. asp – Classic Active Server Page
2. apsx - .NET Server Page
3. php – PHP document
4. jsp – JavaServer Page

Meta tags are atomic and contain varying attribute key values. The signature of a meta tag is as follows:

<meta name="" content="">

The key attribute 'name' may contain one of three values 'description', 'keywords' or 'author'. The description designation identifies the meta tag containing a short description of content that resides within the page layout. The keyword designation identifies a meta tag containing the keywords that are pertinent to the document. King (2008) advises on using a limit of less than 20 keywords in the meta tag and whereby applying more results in the search engines deeming this act to be keyword stuffing which may result in possible blacklisting of the entire page. The author designation identifies the meta tag as holding the value of the creator of the document. Jerkovic (2010) states that the description meta tag may be completely ignored by the search engines and instead they may opt to use the description found on Dmoz.org. Dmoz.org is a web directory for site content. This example highlights the extent to which search engine providers are going through in order to validate web content. King (2008) does state however that description meta tags should be used and that the length of the description should be limited to 250 words at most. Meta tags represent a protocol that needs to be adhered to in order to aid the message to find a receptive audience with the search engine purveyors.

Meta tag content can aid in search query results as may be validated through experimentation. A query on Google.com for the phrase 'san jose california plumber' brings up a result with the following description on the first page.

"Sewer and drain cleaning, all **plumbing** repairs, **San Jose**, **California**."

Selection of the link provided brings up the web page where if you look closely, you will find that the description text is nowhere to be found. Using Chrome version 47.0.2526.80 and right clicking on the web page brings up a context menu such as the one below in Figure 2.

Selection of the highlighted option brings up the source code used by the browser to interpret the web page content. In this content you will find in the top section of the page the following.

<meta name="description" content="Sewer and drain cleaning, all plumbing repairs, San Jose, California.">

You will notice that the value used for the content attribute is verbatim what Google chose to use in the search engine results. In the case of Bing the same entry was found in the fourth position as opposed to the position for Google, which happened to be the third position. The description displayed by Bing also differed than that for Google, in the case of Bing the description displayed was as follows.

San Jose Plumbing is a professional company doing plumbing repairs and services with the knowledge to bring you the best.

Figure 2. Chrome Context Menu

Back	Alt+Left Arrow
Forward	Alt+Right Arrow
Reload	Ctrl+R
Save as...	Ctrl+S
Print...	Ctrl+P
Translate to English	
View page source	**Ctrl+U**
Inspect	Ctrl+Shift+I

This description differs from that of Google and if you follow the link you will find that the text from above is displayed prominently towards the top of the page under a paragraph tag. Two distinct philosophies are at work here. Following the same process for the Yahoo search engine yields the same text results as those obtained for Bing with one exception; in the case of Yahoo the search result for the entry in question was found to be in the fifth position.

Google set the position of the entry investigated in the third position, Bing placed the result in the fourth position, and Yahoo placed the result in the fifth position. The same query with varying results was determined for each of the search engine providers and two of which also used the same display content. In the case of the Google search engine, they opted for the meta tag details in lieu of the web document content. This alludes to the subtle differences that are at work between each of the search engine providers, but nevertheless does show that the system doctrine remains intact, i.e., the page is the point of relevance.

KEYWORD PROXIMITY

The fifth component that adds value to the search engine optimization domain is keyword proximity. Keyword proximity refers to the physical distance between keywords found in page copy. Physical distance may be measured in bytes or words. The dimensionality of measurement is inconsequential as the degree of importance lays with consistency. A common practice in optimizing web content is the placement of keywords in page copy to coincide with search queries. Take for example the query 'San Jose California', a search engine optimization technique for keyword proximity would be to create page content as follows:

<h1>A vibrant city in Silicon Valley is **San Jose. California** is a state located in the western United States</h1>

The bringing of the search words together as they appear in the page copy results in a direct match to the search query; an optimization over a similar page copy such as.

<h1>**California** is located on the west coast of the United States. A vibrant city in Silicon Valley is **San Jose**</h1>

This example does also give an indication of the algorithm being used by the search engine providers. If you notice in the first example from the previous case, it contains the text 'San Jose. California'. A period is physically present in the verbiage, but the search engine provider (Google in this case) chose to ignore the period and deem the phrase to be significantly relevant to the search string. Does the search engine provider strip out punctuation before carrying forth their analysis of the web content? While answer to this question in the affirmative is a point of contention, what can be stated with certainty is that it does highlight another point of investigation.

KEYWORD PROMINENCE

The sixth component that has significance to the search engine providers is the prominence of the keywords in the document body. Keyword prominence refers to the physical location of keywords with respect to the top of the document and the type of header tag used to display the content. The argument here is that content that is specified towards the top of the document is more relevant than content that is specified towards the bottom of the document. This is one particular area where online resellers have taken advantage of the search engine providers and represents a specific example of the hunter becoming the hunted. Through the use of content formatting with Cascading Style Sheets (CSS) it is possible to alter the appearance of content on a web page while leaving the static text optimized for the search engine providers. Take the example of NewEgg.com; the online reseller of computer equipment has a typical website whereby the web document lists a series of products for sale. Online resellers are highlighting images for patrons in lieu of the alternative, but the search engine providers are specifically targeting text. The website's main page is displayed below in figure 3. If you strip out the inner tags of the header tag, the script tags, and the JavaScript content you end up with the content in Figure 4. The content in bold highlights a description or series of keywords that the online reseller would like the search engines to take note of and index. This same content if searched on the NewEgg.com website is absent. The online reseller has taken the time and effort to place their keywords at the very top of the page while at the same time ignoring the content to the passing user.

The astute reader will also notice that the paragraph tag <p></p> is contained within a division tag <div></div>, the division tag has a unique identifier or 'ID' attribute that has the value 'message2OlderBrowser'. This unique identifier allows the element to be referenced via an external file such as a Cascading Style Sheet (CSS) file and format the display content to suit the needs of the interface layout, i.e., hide the desired content for individuals and show it to the website crawler. By enabling the developer tools in the browser, you can view the actual code to create the content along with the external references such as the Cascading Style Sheet content. If you use Firefox as a browser, then you can install Firebug which may be downloaded from here: https://getfirebug.com; this plugin allows for the enablement of developer debugging features. Chrome was used for this example and the same was achieved by selecting 'More Tools' and then 'Developer Tools' from the context menu.

Doing a quick search for the target text from below you can see that the formatting is defined in a file that is located at the URL http://images10.newegg.com/WebResource/Themes/2005/CSS/USA/W WWShared.Newegg.12709.1.min.css. This file contains the definition for the unique identifier and provides the desired functionality that has been discussed here.

Figure 3. Example of an e-Commerce Website

Figure 4. Page Content

```
<div id="message2OlderBrowser">
<p>Newegg.com - A great place to buy computers, computer parts, electronics, software,
accessories, and DVDs online.  With great prices, fast shipping, and top-rated customer service -
once you know, you Newegg.</p>
<p>If you are reading this message, <b>Please  <a href="http://www.newegg.com/?Local=y">click this
link</a> to reload this page.(Do not use your browser's "Refresh" button).</b> Please <a
href="mailto:webmaster@newegg.com">email us</a> if you're running the latest version of your
browser and you still see this message.</p>
<p><a href="http://www.newegg.com/">Newegg.com - Computer Parts, Laptops, Electronics, HDTVs,
Digital Cameras and More!</a></p>
</div>
```

Figure 5. CSS Attribute

#message2OlderBrowser {display: none;}

The designation 'display' in Cascading Style Sheets denotes the user interface action to take and the 'none' value forces the hiding of the element with the unique identifier, this CSS format syntax is provided in Figure 5. In the version of Chrome used a checkbox was provided next to the display designation. Selection of the checkbox allows you to turn on or off the CSS attribute. If you go through the exercise and enable the display content, you will find that the web page will change dramatically. In Figure 6 below you can see the change that occurs if you select the checkbox or change the visibility to true. The keywords were hidden and now they are visible at the very top of the page once the tag is set to visible. This is your classic example of how you may optimize the content for the web by using the tools available and turn the hunter to the hunted.

Figure 6. Example e-Commerce Website with Visibility Change

King (2008) makes the argument that header tags that display larger font and the text contained within them is deemed more relevant to the search engines as opposed to the same content in a less prominent tag. In the example given previously this means that NewEgg.com would have benefited from simply changing the division tag to a header one tag <h1></h1>. As you will see in the data analyzed and the formulas derived, the header tag content was evaluated to be similarly in weight. This highlights the necessity to gravitate towards a metrics driven doctrine as opposed to a qualified centric mode, whereby doing so facilitates the derivation of the facts that drive the truth proposition.

To build on the previous example you could display a product listing matrix at the top of the page in code and then change the location to the bottom of the page through CSS to help further optimize the page. The CSS could be as follows for example.

```
.showBottom{
position: absolute;
left: 0px;
top: 300px;
}
```

The ability to optimize the page content via a formatting paradigm such as CSS can be a helpful tool and should be part of your search engine optimization (SEO) repertoire.

ANCHOR TEXT

The seventh component that conveys page relevance is keywords within anchor text. Anchor tags refer to the elements on a page that facilitate the reference to some external document. Anchor tags were the basis for the creation of the web by Lawrence G. Roberts. Roberts initially wanted to create a linked repository of like documents where you would be able to jump from one document to another through this reference. Anchor text is relevant to the search engine purveyors because the anchor text conveys meaning. The keywords in the anchor text allow the search engines to qualify the significance of the link and provide the search engine purveyors a mechanism by which they may index like content. When performing a search today with the search engine providers such as Google, Bing or Yahoo you will find that they make a concerted effort to highlight this relationship in the search findings. Yahoo and Google both highlight the searched words in the URL displayed in the search engine results page while Bing highlights the keywords searched in both the URL and the Title displayed in the search results page. This is an indication of intent by the search purveyors as they are explicitly indicating worth to the end user in a visual form.

The largest utilizers of this paradigm as a search engine optimization tool are the online resellers. A search for the book 'The Hunger Games Book' results in a top five entry on each of the search engine providers Google, Yahoo, and Bing for the Amazon domain. The result for Amazon.com as provided by the search purveyors is displayed below.

Bing
Amazon.com: the hunger games: Books
www.amazon.com › Search › the hunger games
See All Books in The Hunger Games Series. The Hunger Games #2: Catching Fire(Discussion Guide)
    ... by Suzanne Collins

Google
The Hunger Games (Hunger Games Trilogy, Book 1)
www.amazon.com › ... › Self Esteem & Reliance
Amazon.com, Inc.
Frequently Bought Together. **The Hunger Games (Book** 1). +. **Catching Fire** (The Second **Book** of **the**
    Hunger Games). +. **Mockingjay (The Hunger Games)**.

Yahoo
The Hunger Games (Hunger Games Trilogy, Book 1) -...
http://www.amazon.com/The-Hunger-Games-Book-1/dp/0439023521
Amazon.com: The Hunger Games (Book 1) (9780439023528): Suzanne Collins: Books.

If you follow the links provided by each of the search purveyors, you will find that they all terminate in the desired endpoint as provided in the link detail. On inspection of the link detail however through the developer tools that browsers make available you will find that each of the search purveyors is in fact processing the request distinctly. One of the purveyors is redirecting the traffic to their own domain prior to routing the request to its final destination point. It is for a reason that some of the search providers are taking it upon themselves to carry out an extra burden and it is to facilitate their own endeavors. It should also be mentioned that this dynamic was not always the case. This highlights the ever changing dynamic that is present in search engine relevance as factors of importance become a moving target over time. The search indexes and the attributes that determine worth become relative to time and as a result it becomes imperative to be able to create a model that accommodates this flux factor, which becomes feasible through an equation.

SITE ICON

A site icon represents an ico file on the website. The icon file is found on the website in the upper left hand corner of the navigation URL as is displayed below in Figure 7.

Figure 7. Website Icon Example

The file is named the same for each icon to be used on a site and is named 'favicon.ico'. The file is referenced in the header section of the HTML page by using the tag displayed below.

<link rel="shortcut icon" href="/favicon.ico" type="image/x-icon" />

The favicon image from a meta data perspective has no value and the search engines are only interested in indexing page content not the site icon detail. Some SEO enthusiasts believe that the favicon.ico file helps to build the brand image and as such should be used when optimizing search engine content. While the direct tangible benefit might not be immediately present, please do remember that some of the search purveyors referenced in this body of work track page clicks and just as importantly the search bars from the same big search providers, which translates to a direct impact to their model potentially. In general, any value that you can add to the user experience through the website should be leveraged because it could lead to tangible benefits down the line.

GEO LOCATION

Site content is specific to region, the assertion of which can be proved empirically. Every website URL is bound to a specific region on the planet, so when you think of http://www.MyURL.com you can alternatively think of an IP address of the form ###.###.###.### such as 10.100.100.100. Every computer connected to a network has an IP address. You can find your current IP address in Windows by simply opening up the command prompt and typing the words 'ipconfig /all' as is displayed in Figure 8. The point of interest from Figure 8 is the line that reads 'IPv4 Address', this represents the physical address of the computer. Servers function in a similar way, each machine may have an external or internal IP address, but an IP address, nonetheless. This external IP address of the machine is tied to a geographical location and as such the search engine providers can take the geographical location of the domain into account when serving up content to the visitor. The rational for the decision being that users are interested in content that is geographically relevant to them. A user searching for Sushi Restaurant in Des Moines, Iowa is probably interested in a restaurant in Des Moines Iowa and not in a Sushi restaurant in Saskatchewan, Canada. Mimicking the behavior of a user in another place is quite simple nowadays, you simply need a proxy server that serves up the content for you from the desired region. A proxy server is simply a substitute for you, and it becomes the requestor of the content. Figure 9 illustrates the process; a query is sent to the proxy server, which then sends the request to the search engine provider. The search provider utilizes the proxy server address as the point of invocation and consequently replies in kind with what it deems to be relevant to the geographical local.

Geographical location inherently implies a relationship between worth and the individual. While it may be true that the internet has enabled the connection of the disconnected, when it comes to search and relevance, these same individuals are interested in finding content that is regional to them. An individual that is interested in making a purchase may be most interested in finding the product that is closest to them. An individual that is interested in finding a restaurant will be most interested in finding that local which is close enough to walk or drive to. The internet in essence has replaced the yellow pages of days gone by and has become the new mode by which humanity is able to locate that which it needs. There is a reason why you will find that when conducting a search on Google.com for example you will find the map to a location that fits the inquiry. The search purveyors have come to understand this dynamic and as a consequence have adapted their systems to facilitate this need of the masses because after all it is the customer that mandates the course of action that is to be taken.

In order to change the browser settings to function through a proxy server you need to enable the proxy. In Internet Explorer version eleven the process is quite simple. In IE v11 simply left click with the mouse on the gear icon in the upper right hand corner; a context menu will appear as seen in Figure 10. From the context window that appears select the 'Internet options' entry.

The 'Internet options' dialog box has a tab labeled 'Connections'; the connections tab window has a button labeled 'LAN settings'. The selection of the 'LAN settings' button brings up the 'Local Area Network (LAN) Settings' window. At the bottom of the LAN Settings window is a section to enter a proxy address; please refer to Figure 11 below. This is where you will need to enter the IP address of your proxy server that will in turn take it upon itself to transfer all your requests to the desired target. Proxy servers enable the masking of the requestor and allow connections to function in a clandestine manner whereby the particulars of the requesting party are hidden from the host providing the response to the request.

Figure 8. Example of a Local Network Configuration

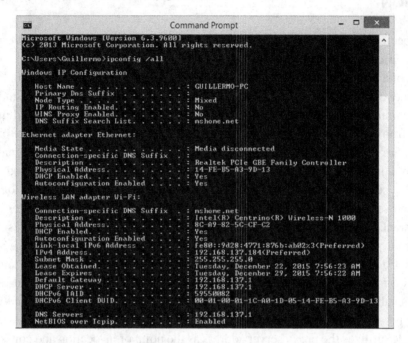

Figure 9. HTTP Web Request Route Using a Proxy Configuration

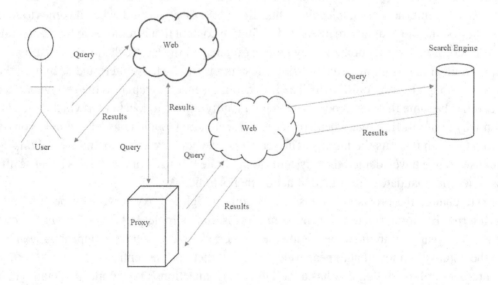

If you search for 'proxy server' through any of the search providers, you will end up with a list of available proxy servers ready for utilization. The results obtained by searching Bing.com for a proxy server using 'proxy server Canada' as the search string brings up the partial list of entries displayed in Figure 12. From the list generated below a random IP address was selected. The IP address 198.169.246.30 resides in Regina, Canada, but any other entry would suffice. Placing this IP address in the 'Local Area Network (LAN) Settings' window to change the browser settings to use the designated proxy will result in all traffic to appear as originating from Regina, Canada. What you will notice by adding a proxy server to the Internet Options pane is that content becomes tailored by the search providers to local. While society has become distributed and less connected, search relevance has not been such as each individual will likely be more interested in a destination point that is closest to them in lieu of the alternative, at least this is the message that is being conveyed by the major search purveyors and which may be validated through the utilization of a proxy server that resides in a distinct region from that of the original request. The search purveyors have simply become a proxy themselves for the needs of the masses and as such have created solutions that echo this sentiment.

Figure 10. Internet Explorer Context Menu

Without the proxy connection configured the URLs for the major search purveyors Google, Bing, and Yahoo are listed below (Table 1) as are their respective endpoints when a Canadian proxy server is utilized. In the case of Bing and Yahoo both are the same, but in the case of Google it is different. Google is specifically serving up Canadian content from a Canadian domain.

If a search for 'sushi restaurant' with no proxy server is conducted, then the following data for the top 5 results for each of the three search engines is displayed below in tables 2-4.

Figure 11. Internet Explorer Options

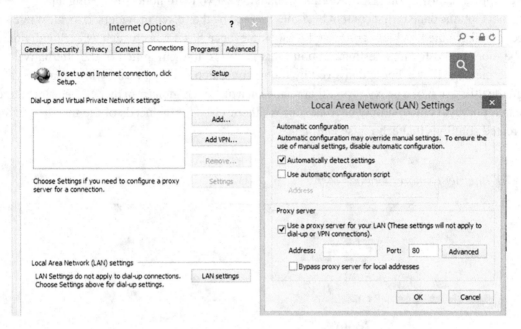

Figure 12. Sample Proxies

616,000 RESULTS   Any time ▾

Canada Proxy Server List - **Canadian** Proxies

www.proxynova.com/proxy-server-list/country-ca ▾
22 rows · Canadian Proxy List - Proxies from Canada. **Proxy Server List** - this page
provides and maintains the largest and the most up-to-date list of working **proxy servers**
...

Proxy IP	Proxy Port	Uptime	Proxy Country
131.161.124.22	3128	56%	Canada - Wolfville
131.161.175.250	8080	53%	Canada - Wolfville
198.169.246.30	80	98%	Canada - Regina
68.171.65.230	8081	64%	Canada - Thurso

See all 22 rows on www.proxynova.com

Table 1. URL Translations by Search Purveyor

Search Purveyor	URL Translation	
	With Proxy	**Without Proxy**
Google.com	https://www.google.ca/?gws_rd=cr,ssl&ei=5bt5VpD8FsHIerW4osgC	https://www.google.com/?gws_rd=ssl
Bing.com	http://www.bing.com/	http://www.bing.com
Yahoo.com	https://www.yahoo.com/	https://www.yahoo.com

Table 2. Top 5 Google.com Results

Rank	Result
1	10 Best Sushi Restaurants in Los Angeles I L.A. Weekly
2	2015 Best – tope 10 Sushi Restaurants LA Los Angeles Area
3	Kabuki Japanese Restaurants
4	Sushi Food Delivery I Sushi Restaurant Delivery GrubHub
5	The Essentials Los Angeles Sushi Restaurants – Eater LA

Table 3. Top 5 Bing.com Results

Rank	Result
1	Top 10 BEST Sushi Restaurants I TheSushiCritic.com
2	Top 10 Ten Best Sushi Restaurants Los Angeles
3	Sushi Bars in Los Angeles – Yelp
4	Best sushi restaurant Los Angeles, CA – Yelp
5	RA Sushi Bar Restaurant, Sushi, Sake & Japanese Fusion

Table 4. Top 5 Yahoo.com Results

Rank	Result
1	Osushi Cambridge O Sushi Cambridge I Premiere Sushi
2	RA Sushi Bar Restaurant, Sushi, Sake & Japanese
3	Sushi Food Delivery I Sushi Restaurant Delivery
4	Sushi Delivery I Sushi Restaurant Delivery I Eat24
5	Kabuki Japanese Restaurants

When the process is repeated with the utilization of a proxy server in Internet Explorer version eleven whereby the proxy server in Regina Canada is utilized it yields the results displayed in tables 5-7. The apparent difference between the two data sets that are derived through the use of a proxy server and through the exclusion of one demonstrates the regionality of search and the burden that each of the search engines has taken upon themselves to craft the necessary message for its audience. Relevance has subsequently been proven to be regional much like the language construct is because after all search departs from a grammar. The search providers are but simply the manifestation of the reality that humanity subscribes to and consequently must be made to conform to this dialect. This factoid brings to light the essence of this body of work and this being that language is central to search and as such it becomes those applications that become infused with the language construct that stand a statistically more likely chance of becoming relevant because after all these endpoints will only be found if they can be indexed.

Table 5. Top 5 Google.com Results with Proxy

Rank	Result
1	Montreal Sushi Restaurants I RestoMontreal
2	Toronto.com – Top 10 Sushi Places in Toronto
3	Sushi Village – Japanese Cuisine and Sushi
4	Ki modern Japanese + bar I - Toronto
5	Miku Restaurant

Table 6. Top 5 Bing.com Results with Proxy

Rank	Result
1	Top 10 BEST Sushi Restaurants	TheSushiCritic.com
2	RA Sushi Bar Restaurant, Sushi, Sake & Japanese Fusion
3	Fuki Sushi :: Japanese Restaurant
4	Best Sushi Restaurants, Best Sushi Rolls, Sushi Online
5	Sushi & Sushi – Anchorage Alaska's Premiere Fine Sushi

Table 7. Top 5 Yahoo.com Results with Proxy

Rank	Result
1	Montreal Sushi Restaurants	RestoMontreal
2	Toronto.com – Top 10 Sushi Places in Toronto
3	Sushi Village – Japanese Cuisine and Sushi
4	Ki modern Japanese + bar	- Toronto
5	Miku Restaurant

The geographical region from where a domain resides plays a vital role in the indexing of the content by the search engine providers. The search engine providers are trying to serve up content that is not only relevant, but also specific to user and the region that the user is from. They are taking great pains to ensure that they provide the best possible experience to the customer because after all what is at stake is significant – advertising dollars.

If you have an issue connecting by way of the proxy server to the search engine providers you could simply use the link to the search provider's regional domain such as google.ca, bing.com/?cc=ca, or ca.search.yahoo.com. The astute reader will notice that the search results for both Google and Yahoo in Canada are identical for the search term 'sushi restaurant', Bing does differ dramatically, however. The results for Canada from above point to the clear case that there are parallels between the two search providers in their Canadian algorithm for search indexing. This preliminary result is one reason why the argument was made previously that while the Google search engine did not allow for the mining of data through their website that nevertheless part of the secrete sauce has been leaked as the quantitative formula for the Yahoo search engine that is derived would have to have parity with that of a Google search engine formula given the similarity of resultant datasets, which is seen here.

LINK EQUITY

The final component that is significant to the search engine providers is the quality and quantity of back links to the page or as is commonly referred to - link equity. Links to a page on the internet represent a voting share to the destination site from the originating node. Each time a link is placed on a site to another node the site containing the destination link(s) is voting the destination page(s) as being relevant. Back links to the page are related to the infamous metric of PageRank and the basis for the popular ranking algorithm of Google. Sun and Wei (2014) defined the PageRank algorithm as:

"...[a] link structure-based algorithm, which gives a rank of importance of all the pages crawled in the internet by the Google's web crawler."

PageRank is the original mechanism which Google used to index the World Wide Web. Jerkovic (2010) makes the argument that back links from pages that have a PageRank value of at least 4 yield the best results. The result of this assertion by Jerkovic (2010) is that linking to some site from just any site is fruitless or less than optimal unless the source site has a positive PageRank. PageRank was defined in equation 3 of previous chapter and for which a simplified variant form is given below in equation 1.

$$PR(u) = \sum_{v \in Bu} \frac{PR(v)}{L(v)} \tag{1}$$

The PageRank for an individual page is tabulated as being the sum of the PageRank of each linking page divided by the outbound links from the same page. The end result of the equation is that each contributing link adds to a site's presence on the search engines but does so on an incremental scale that is directly proportional to the PageRank of the contributing site. A search engine optimization technique could then be to go through sites that allow an individual to place comments and then proceed to create links back to some desired site. The HTML markup contains an attribute to the anchor tag called 'rel' that when set to 'nofollow' informs the crawlers to not consider the target URL in the PageRank algorithm; once again an example of the evolving search indexing paradigm and the cat and mouse game that is played between the search engine providers and the would be high indexed aspirers. King (2008) brings to light an interesting aspect of the PageRank algorithm and this being that internal links will dilute the PageRank algorithm, i.e., it elevates the denominator $L(v)$ of equation 1. There are some individuals that believe you can go aimlessly through blogs and social media sites posting comments that link back to their desired site creating link equity and while these links might get you better results with the search engines there is no guarantee of this given the available attribute of 'rel' that can be attached to some link element. The other point to note as well is that if the link source comes by way of some entity that contains a plethora of outbound links it entails that the benefit derived will become diluted due to the nature of the algorithm implemented.

The ramifications of equation 1 entails that by simply posting comments on twitter or some other website and referencing some external site it will not necessarily catapult the desired web document to the top of the heap and the reason why is that twitter for example has disabled the transfer of their link equity to some target sink node. If you go to the URL: https://twitter.com/chromaticcoffee you will find a link to an external document at some URL. If you look behind the covers and find the actual HTML code that generates the link tag you will find that the link tag has a definition similarly to what you will find below. The point of interest is the text in bold; the Twitter algorithm is such that each external link has the 'rel' attribute defined and has it set to 'nofollow'

<a title="https://instagram.com/p/1ep79-K6jJ/" class="twitter-timeline-link" dir="ltr" href="https://t.co/DPLIbK5vx0" target="_blank" **rel="nofollow"** *data-expanded-url="https://instagram.com/p/1ep79-K6jJ/"><span class="tco-ellipsis"></span><span class="invisible">https://</span><span class="js-display-url">instagram.com/p/1ep79-K6jJ/</span><span class="invisible"></span><span class="tco-ellipsis"><span class="invisible"> </span></span></a>*

The manner by which websites can obtain a benefit through the creation of link referrals has been constrained through the use of the available link attributes that may be utilized by the source applications. What remains therefore is the creation of relevant content that will organically see the gradual accumulation of link equity. This has been the general premise from the onset of the indexing space as what has been sought has been the promotion to the top of the heap that which is deemed important to the community at large. This paradigm is seen in practice outside of the internet with the determination of relevance in publications by way of referencing articles. The determination of worth whether it be in academia, or the World Wide Web takes on a similar prescription and that being that relevance can be derived by way of quantity of referring entities. This discourse is what has led to the content of this body of work in that the paradigm has shifted the development space and it will be those businesses that are able to obtain clout through the utilization of prescribed applications that will be able to reap the benefit of the masses and by doing so be able to catapult their respective domains to the top of the heap. The prescription is not new but has taken on a distinct dynamic from what has been seen and as such represents an opportunity for businesses. It will be those mortgage companies for example that facilitate mortgage applications through widgets that may be consumed by the masses that will see their traffic increase and consequently see their mortgage applications also increase. It will be those businesses that facilitate function across the internet in general that will stand to benefit most because after all the internet has simply become an election and the electees will be those businesses that are able to provide the greatest degree of benefit across the internet.

SUMMARY

The purpose of this chapter in part has been to aid the user in understanding those components of the system that are relevant and as such may be utilized in a predictive formula of worth that may be evaluated to determine the value of each page. Below in Table 8 are the attributes that are significant to the search engines in classifying content as has been determined here through the research literature, qualitatively. It will be through this qualitive context that the quantitative context will be developed and that will allow for the determination of what truth actually is, but this argument could not have been made without first understanding the problem frame from a macro level or a qualified perspective. The reason why this argument may be made is because in order to be able to begin the feature engineering process what first must exist are the features to investigate.

To find relevance with the search providers entails the migration to a new development paradigm whereby functionality becomes the equity in the market. It will be through the creation of needed functionality that consumers will provide those applications with a place to reside and serve to help those domains to obtain positive link equity. It is for this reason that Micro Distributed Applications will come to resonate with many; it will be because they capitalize on the leverage that already exists with the search providers. Building a positive marketing presence online is not simply a matter of utilizing the correct indices to create content but it is also a function of creating relevant utility for the masses to consume. This functionality will need to be such that the subscribing clients will render their page to the service provider and by doing so allow the content creator to craft their desired message as they see fit. By doing this it becomes feasible to forgo the burden of losing clout through the structuring of the link tags as the content provider is afforded stewardship of the entire web document. It is a message that supersedes what has been seen with iframes because MDAs become physical applications that fulfill a function for the subscribing client and as such can become indispensable to the point that they become a need, such as a table reservation system on a restauranteurs website for example. This need is symbiotic as it is the subscribing client that comes to have a dependency in terms of utility and the creator of said utility for the leverage that is created by the subscribing clients in terms of indexing relevance. This protocol that is created between client and service provider becomes the new mode of currency whereby it will become the mode by which commerce is done. This protocol that is spoken of is the domain of a new breed of applications that have been termed Micro Distributed Applications or MDAs.

Table 8. Search Engine Indexing Attributes Summary

Attribute
Page Copy
URL
Meta Tags
Keyword Proximity
Keyword Prominence
Anchor Text
GEO Location
Link Equity

REFERENCES

Jerkovic, J. (2010). *SEO Warrior*. O'Reilly Media Inc.

King, A. (2008). *Website Optimization*. O'Reilly Media Inc.

Wei, Z., Zhao, P., & Zhang, L. (2014). Design and Implementation of Image Search Algorithm. *American Journal of Software Engineering and Applications*, *3*(6), 90–94. doi:10.11648/j.ajsea.20140306.14

Chapter 4
Prescriptions

ABSTRACT

The data points that are afforded freely and may be utilized as factors to a decision become tributes that can never be repaid as their benefits are a gift from a benefactor that has no agenda to bear. It becomes these data points that become the leverage that comes to resonate the loudest because it is through them that efficiencies may be obtained. Life at times seeks an all too familiar prescription, but unfortunately, that detail becomes much like an old family recipe that has been misplaced. For progress to happen then it becomes a matter of gleaming insight from that which is present, but yet often overlooked because disruption at times can only take root when the trivial is looked upon with a different lens and through which a yield may be obtained that is simple and efficient because the data mandates so.

INTRODUCTION

The search engine provider Google has given their input as to what can be done to find prominence with the indexing domain. Bing and Yahoo have opted to not put forth any sort of guidance that would aid in the understanding of their particular indexing effort. Google on the other hand has taken a stab at answering the question but has done so in such a generic and basic manner that it simply amounts to a common doctrine that is deemed to be more or less common knowledge by the profession. The placing of relevant descriptions and keywords in meta tags is what the W3C consortium specifies in their online literature for the proper use of the tags, which coincidently enough is equivalent to what is provided as guidance by Google. The regurgitation of this verbiage cannot be made and pointed to as providing insight over the domain and much less be deemed to provide special insight into creating relevant content. It is understandable why the search provider of choice chooses to obfuscate their true intent as doing so would affirm for the masses the direction that would need to be followed. To ask the search purveyors to relinquish the magic formula would be like asking the chef for the recipe to their special dish, it is but a request that is never answered with anything but a passing nod.

In this section the discussion proceeds by looking at the prescriptions from Google as to what they suggest should be done to create content that can be indexed in a positive manner. This chapter also discusses some utilities that are made available by the search providers to be able to gain further insight

DOI: 10.4018/978-1-6684-4849-6.ch004

into the paradigm and be able to decipher the truth that is masked. The exercise with Google is taken even though it is not one of the search engines for which a model is created because even though the team is different, the playing field is the same and consequently it helps to further the claim of the parallel that exists with the search engine providers. As was also seen in the previous chapter, the query outputs can be found to be similar between Google and its competitors. The work of Jerkovic (2010) and King (2008) point to search engines in general and whose body of work coincides with the content found here, their work helps to further clarify that a degree of congruency does exist between the search engine providers irrespective of their specific methodology with the indexing domain. As an exercise this chapter will look at the Google search engine results and compare them to the style guide to validate the guidance provided by the search vendor, which helps to further reinforce the notion of what true north is for the other counterparts given the data points that have been made available so far.

The doctrine of search and its evolution has resulted in the current state of software products where a primary factor of importance of web applications has become their ability to find a receptive audience. This doctrine has been exploited by domains such as yelp (www.yelp.com), PayPal (www.paypal.com), DOORDASH (www.doordash.com), and OpenTable (www.opentable.com) to name but a few. The websites listed here have been able to capitalize on the link equity factor with varying degrees of success. They have all come to understand the importance of equity on the internet given their concentrated effort to capitalize on the prescription. The fact that Google has physically come forth and been explicit in their intent as to what constitutes worth simply helps to reinforce the mandate that some website owners have come to adhere to and as a result have come to invest in. In the case of the domains given previously some of them have implemented simple HTML elements that may be incorporated by website owners to leverage their functionality via linking structures while in other cases the domains have created physical artifacts to embed themselves directly into the webpage of clients. Technology has actually been on this migration path from the inception of the qualification of search given the base elements of HTML, specifically linkage tags as they have become an essential element of dictating who the prom king will turn out to be. PayPal was an early adopter of the linkage structure paradigm with buy now buttons that allowed website owners to embed directly in their applications. In prior days when shopping cart technology was not where it is now it became a necessity to be able to embed buy now buttons on webpages because of their ability to enable selling online, which invariably helped to create equity for the target domain. Today, SaaS organizations have become more sophisticated and have created physical widgets at times where some basic functionality becomes immediately available to subscribing users. This has become feasible because of JavaScript libraries, and theme layouts that can be embedded on any HTTP enabled application through a CDN. While these widgets have been an incremental and positive factor in the usability race they are not full fledged applications as of yet. The profession is still stuck in the paradigm of large websites that drive functionality and have not migrated quite yet to the doctrine of small applications that may be consumed as needed by clients. The new breed of applications that will drive the functionality of the internet will come through these small components that will adhere to the style guide of the search providers. These applications will need to adhere to this doctrine because it will be imperative to continue to fit the content to the template of the indexers because after all it is by their scorecard that all content is judged by.

By understanding in finer detail, the prescription that Google lays out for web content it will facilitate the discussion that is to come. In chapter six a supervised learning model will be shown to bare parity with the content provided here and consequently it will demonstrate the physical influence of each of the attributes on the evaluation of the model. While the content in this chapter and the detail provided by Google is welcome news it does fail in a significant regard and this being on the actual measurements of the attributes. While the style guide does give a sense of right and wrong it does not give a true north bearing. It deprives its audience from being able to make the quantitative argument and leaves the reader with an inferior version for discussion, it leaves the would be marketers with a qualified argument that simply functions to keep the masses from truly understanding the subject matter. The prescription provided is simply but a pill that can be taken and if it is consumed in the right doses and at the correct times it should help the patient to feel better about the ailment. It is imperative to look at life with healthy skepticism and let the numbers tell where truth lay. This chapter does not delve into the creation of elaborate calculations but what is performed here is rather the investigative process of the outlined content by the search engine vendor of choice to formally decipher what they have provided. This allows for at a very minimum to be able to state that what is being argued is plausible or alternatively that the observations made do not align with the narrative that is provided. Society cannot simply just swallow the pill provided without first looking at what is being given at a very minimum. To meet this endeavor the discussion proceeds through the style guide and compares what has been provided as guidance and compares it to what can be found directly via the search engine vendor's own search utility. To provide further clarity basic metrics are derived to gauge the plausibility of the argument made in the style guide by the search purveyor. When this process is followed it will allow for the removal of part of the haze that obscures the view of the landscape that currently exists.

There is great parity between each of the search providers from the standpoint of intent as should be the case given that all businesses subscribe to the basic tenants of economics. While it was Google that took it upon itself to map the world, they did so for the explicit purpose of being able to facilitate search. If an individual is in need of a restaurant currently, they are not simply provided with the link of the restaurant, but they are provided with the map and the reviews to the restaurant as well. Bing and Yahoo may have been laggards in the paradigm but nevertheless took it upon themselves to perform a similar body of work to facilitate search for their audience. The economics of the matter dictated that they needed to do such because otherwise they would be willingly forfeiting the race before them. The endeavor of search has been a paradigm that has been under a constant flux of innovation and evolution because the demand has been there. Humanity collectively wanted to see the map to the restaurant that was searched for and because of this the search providers yielded to their customers and provided what was expected free of charge. It was because of demand that they took it upon themselves to map the world, as difficult of a task as this was, they still did it because capitalism mandated it. It was then not simply enough for users to see where the physical restaurant resided, but they also wanted to see the reviews of the restaurant in the search results, so the search purveyors once again yielded to the customer's whim and provided this detail. Search has evolved and has along the way transformed the lives of everyone to something that was wanted and was yet unknown. Society did not have the courage or the imagination to ask for the utilities that are afforded by the search purveyors and yet the search providers created solutions to create engagement. This constant challenge that the search providers are all under will not end but will simply continue at infinitum because the economics of the equation mandate it. It has not been enough for the search purveyors to help locate what is desired, but they also provide the route to go to get it and they also denote the degree of suitability of the destination. It is because of the search providers that society can now translate whatever text is needed to whatever target language is desired. They have even taken it upon themselves to translate the queries posed to them to help society find the answers to their questions. This is the extent that the search providers have gone to in order to maintain engagement by the populous. Search has become such a fundamental aspect of life that now the namesake of one organization has become a verb, which means to query. The leveraging of this dynamic has consequently become an essential endeavor for businesses and as such the understanding of the architectural components of search systems has become essential to conducting business. These facets of leverage have consequently been the focal point of much study much as the pages that you find before you now. This point of leverage has to be capitalized on by businesses going forward because the economics of the dynamic are skewed to such an extent now that businesses that do not utilize it risk the condition of extinction. This discourse is important for such a reason because it is only by understanding what is relevant that a proper message will be able to be crafted that not only resonates with an audience but with the search engines themselves. It is paramount therefore to understand what is deemed to be proper by them and use it as a datum point for further study. By doing such it becomes feasible to pay the minimum bounty to play the game and forgo the painful process of learning from experience.

This bounty that is sought must be obtained because of the nature of competition now. Foot traffic at the mall has been replaced in part with traffic on the information highway and customers will only become available if storefronts are created that can leverage the doctrine of search. Traditional storefronts suffer from the constraint of regionality while electronic merchants have freed themselves from this burden because after all products can be exchanged for currency as long as an address exists. Commerce has transformed because of the domain of search, and it will become those organizations that are best able to leverage the doctrine of search in their applications that will become the rest stop for all that traffic on the information highway. What is at stake is nothing short of extraordinary for businesses that are able to leverage the search paradigm and it will be those businesses that are best able to understand the search domain and the manner by which applications need to be developed that will see their revenue grow, while those other businesses that are not able to do such will become much like those traditional storefronts in small towns all over the country that have seen the only large employer in the area close their doors. Viability for commerce has become a function of the customers that cannot be seen and yet be heard by the digital footprints that they leave on the servers that house those applications and websites that they visit. The survival of the organization has become directly dependent on electronic prowess and the leverage that may be generated with the populous through their engagement. It is for this reason that it becomes imperative for organizations to understand how to best be able to create these new breed of applications that will be able to create this leverage and this will be the domain of the MDA. But in order to be able to create these MDAs it becomes imperative to gleam what is already present and decipher the message that is inherently there as this mode of behavior is the greatest assurance for success that can be obtained given that the alternative has been historically erroneous. It is the cheapest route that is sought because after all who ever seeks to pay a greater bounty than is needed? It is best to part from a purview that rests on solid footing and can there be any stronger bedrock than what comes from the mouth of the largest search purveyor in the world? Of course they will not disclose their formula, but truth does lay in the message conveyed if it can only be deciphered and understood and this is what is sought in this chapter, to understand the inherent message that has been provided because it is this prescription that is the gateway for the molding of the message that is to be built through MDAs.

STYLE GUIDE

What is certain is that while the style guide by Google is a generalized prescription over pertinence on the internet, this relevance that is sought has evolved and will continue to evolve in order for the search providers to keep their following and in turn to also remain relevant. The degree of success of the search providers is directly tied to their determination of relevance because they are but a proxy for what society deems to be pertinent and while this degree of pertinence is bound to change and evolve over time the metrics of the first and second order are bound to remain influential. This prescription that is temporal can be adaptive to change given that metrics may always be derived to determine equilibrium. By understanding these factors of influence and helping them to guide the discussion is the only manner by which applications that are to be built stand a chance to remain influential. This is why understanding the style guide by Google is important, as it is a window to this desired state that all applications need to strive towards, irrespective of how small that window actually is.

Google has become part of the vernacular and as such it infers a dependency and consequently a degree of trust in that the needs of the populous will be met when engaged. And much like Google tries to fulfill the needs of the masses it is up to corporations to create this dependency between client and offering whereby the indexing effort by the search providers becomes but an existential point of leverage. It will become the burden of development teams to harness this leverage point through the creation of small applications that will be JavaScript laden, and which will be distributed throughout the internet. These applications represent the temporal state of matters currently because they tap into the dynamic of the ecosystem. Relevance is tied to link equity, and each node that provides lodging for these micro distributed applications in essence is providing a clear vote to the provider of the utility. These applications leverage the hardware of the client executing the application and free the creators of which from the excess burden of having to incur excessive capital outlays to keep them operational. MDAs represent an optimum point in the development effort, which is validated by Google and their style guide as presented here.

The Google guide provides a general reference to follow when creating page content for the web. While the guide identifies some of the attributes that are deemed significant by Google it does not disclose the complete algorithm. The style guide is but simply a small window to provide the development community with some degree of information about how their ranking algorithm functions and what it deems to be pertinent. The Google style guide may be found at the following link: https://developers.google.com/search/docs/beginner/seo-start er-guide. To the astute reader however the style guide does provide detail with regards to what may be done at a high level to create relevant content for the web. This degree of attribute relevance is important because it helps to clarify how Micro Distributed Applications (MDAs) may be structured to help create significance. The style guide also provides guidance as to how routes may be structured in MVC applications to facilitate their content indexing. So, while the style guide may be brief what is quite contrary are the ramifications for what it entails for the systems that are to be built. In essence the style guide provides a prescription or formula that needs to be followed in order to find alignment with the search doctrine. By following this path it therefore becomes feasible to find favor with the indexing algorithm of not simply Google, but for each of the search engine providers.

While the style guide may be specific to the Google search engine there is a great degree of similitude between the search engine providers due to the manner by which they determine relevance of online content. It should come as no surprise then that the content provided by Google is also relevant to the Yahoo and Bing search engines. While the manner in which the field may be navigated may be distinct the truth remains that the playing field and consequently the players on said field remain the same and as such there must be some degree of similitude between each of the search engine providers. Further proof of this parity lays in the aforementioned examples that have been presented as the search results by the search purveyors have shown a degree of similitude. The results presented in the previous chapter allude to this parity as it was shown in a direct example that the query results between Google.com and Yahoo.com were identical, using a Canadian proxy. The choreography between companies definitely takes on a distinct flavor, but in the end, it is but a dance that unfolds before an audience that may be understood and embraced, especially when variables of the first and second order are made to bear upon the problem frame.

The reader should note that in determining the indices in the tables given below what was utilized was not an exact word match, but rather a fuzzy match where words deemed to be equivalent were credited for in the calculation. For example, if the word 'car' was sought then the equivalents to this would be considered, such as 'van', 'automobile', and 'vehicle' for example. This facilitates the calculation of the index factors in a similar manner to that of the search engines as they find relevance based upon the language context of the word and not the exact ASCII character match. As you will see in the chapter to follow, the use of the NLTK was incorporated into the search algorithm for the explicit purpose of being able to search for relevant content based upon the lexical context of the search term as by doing so it facilitates overcoming the challenge with performing a simple textual match and are consequently able to perform an impression match based upon the true intent of the word(s) sought.

It is because of the evolution of the tools that are available to the computer scientist that in part this particular body of work was feasible, and it is because of this progression and the merging with the data science domain that a new understanding unfolds. Through this dynamic it becomes feasible to leverage data science to infer context from a horizon that was once blurry and help to reach conclusions that help guide the enterprise towards that same horizon. So, no matter how small that window may be, it is feasible to infer a simple premise and utilize that fact as a steppingstone towards the next stage of the process, such as is found in academia, whereby discovery is possible because of the labor of others. This progressive doctrine is what led to the understanding of what is before the reader and should be considered significant, as it denotes a change to how development needs to occur going forward, and for which the result becomes a product that takes a different tone. This product is smaller, distributed, more economically efficient, aligned with the indexing endeavor of the search purveyors, and it is an elegant solution to the problem frame. This simplicity that MDAs represent functions as a metric itself to denote the degree of sophistication that the profession has matured to since simplicity is the hallmark of good design or elegance rather. Complexity is but the domain of the ill equipped because after all that is the mental model that they subscribe to, while simplicity denotes a higher class since it strips away the excess to leave only the essential. MDAs make sense because of their simplicity, and it just so happens to be that their architecture coincides with that one metric of value that all deem to be pertinent – search relevance. The style guide helps to reinforce this design patter that must be adhered to and the fundamental reason why this chapter exists. It behooves all to come to understand the message that is conveyed irrespective of the noise surrounding it since there can be no better data point than that which is derived directly from the horse's mouth.

TITLE TAG

The first component that Google identifies as being significant to their crawler is the title tag <title></title>. The title tag is displayed for users by Google in the search results at times depending on the textual match to the query string. Google makes the argument that each page created should have a unique title tag, which is understandable given that each page should be dedicated to a specific message. An arbitrary search will return a series of entries for which their inspection provides some insight into the indexing paradigm. Indexing prowess is not necessarily directly proportional to length of text and keywords in title tags as may be validated by the text provided in the results below, thus suggesting an indexing dynamic that is not solely tied to the title tag. A query string of 'electric vehicle range' was submitted to the search provider and upon which the results provided below were returned.

1. New EVs with the Longest Driving Range Ranked - Car ...
    https://www.caranddriver.com›shopping-advice›ev-1...
    Nov 19, 2021 — Power is supplied by two **electric** motors with total outputs ranging between 469 and 750 horsepower. Both the Taycan Cross Turismo 4 and 4S share ..

2. Electric Vehicle Range – Plug'n Drive
    https://www.plugndrive.ca > electric-vehicle-range
    Electric Vehicle Range ... "Range Anxiety" is the number one concern potential EV buyers have; the fear that they will run out of electricity half way and get ...

While it was the second result that showed to have the shorter verbiage on the first line it was the alternative that had the higher ranking, thus pointing to an indexing dynamic that is composed only in part with the verbiage identified on the first line of the result set. Upon inspection of the physical page content what was determined was that the verbiage from the first entry was in fact not the title of the page, but it was rather page copy that was displayed. This case shows an example of the extent that Google is now going to in order to tailor the content to the request of the user. In this particular case the title of the page was found to be 'Which EVs Have the Longest Driving Range?'. In the second case a different dynamic was shown to be present where the title of the page was what was displayed in the search results output. Google took it upon itself to display for the user the text in the first place that it deemed to be the most pertinent for the query specified, thus trying to entice the user to selecting the link. The implications to the matter at hand are significant as it can now be stated that while document title text is indexed, it is also indexed and compared for relevance given the additional verbiage that is available for indexing in the document.

The style guide specifically makes note that title tags should be descriptive, but as short as possible because only a portion of the text will be displayed in the search results, which is precisely what was seen here as part of the verbiage was cutoff in the first case. What is also apparent here however is that what is more important is the matching of the search query to the physical content of the document as this is the basis for determining worth independent of tag attribute, at least in terms of the results that are displayed for the user. To further highlight the inconsistency with the length argument an exercise can be performed whereby both examples can have their keyword index derived through equation 1.

$$\text{Keyword Index} = \frac{\text{Words identified from query term}}{\sum \text{Words in target text}} \tag{1}$$

Using equation 1 and equating 'electric vehicle' to 'ev', the values in table 1 were derived. From the calculations it can be seen that the keyword index for the URL in the first position obtained a lower score than the URL in the second position. This leaves to conclude once again that the categorizing of worth is not simply tied to the density of the keywords in the title or verbiage of the document. What is important however when determining relevance is the degree of significance that the query term has to the content in either the title or page copy of the document indexed. It becomes quite a different argument that can be made when the qualitative sentiment acquiesces to the quantitative doctrine. It behooves the individual therefore to take that healthy skepticism on any investigative study in order to be able to determine quantitively where truth resides as blindly following what is dictated has the potential to burden the individual with ambiguity as is seen in this direct case. The literature that has been referenced has specifically denoted the sentiment that has been echoed by the Google style guide, which in both cases was the qualitative mandate. After inspection and the application of a derived index it was shown that the argument that has been posed cannot be taken simply at face value as the data does not quite support that narrative. Google has provided a window into their domain, but it appears that they have done so by placing a tint on that windowpane in order to keep their secrete sauce just that, a mystery to the masses.

From what can be gleamed from the simple analysis conducted here is that the indexing effort is complex and not the domain of simply one factor in determining worth. Search relevance is in fact a multifaceted component that is not unary and it cannot be because the search purveyor of choice has confessed to such as the style guide contains six factors of relevance and not simply just one. This is in part what complicates the determination of truth, it is that truth is being conveyed in parts by the search purveyor and they are leaving part of the picture blank to operate in a clandestine manner.

Table 1. Page Rank Compared to Keyword Index

Rank	Keyword Index
1	0.33
2	0.6

Meta Tags

The second component that Google identifies as having significance to their algorithm is the description meta tag. The description meta tag contains the key value pair of name and description. Google also makes note that the description text may be used by Google in the search engine results. Page content that is displayed for the user on the search engine results page is significant because keywords found can be shown in bold text, which are more likely to catch the eye of a normal reader and consequently be clicked on. Google may opt to use content from the Open Directory Project in lieu of the meta tag description as an alternative. The specification also states that they might use page content in lieu of the meta tag content if a better match is found for the users' query much as was seen for the title tag.

Using equation 1 and determining the keyword index for the two URLs identified from above it becomes possible to create the content of table 2 for the description meta tag. In the case of URL 2 the description meta tag was not present in the source file and yet the page was able to find favor with the search engine provider to the point that it was able to achieve a second place ranking. As can be validated through this case, the search guide by Google is simply just that, a suggestion over the domain in how HTML content may be structured to facilitate the indexing of the page. This indexing doctrine that is of interest to the search purveyor serves the purpose of facilitating their work effort and may in actuality have less to do with creating relevant content for viewers, it is after all their style template. The argument could very well be made that given what has been seen so far that the style guide is but the preferences to structure that the search engine desires in the content, but yet the indexing of the page content is determined by them independently of this suggestion that is referred to as the style guide. To be perfectly frank they have stated just that as they went as far as to name their document a guide.

Table 2. Page Rank Compared to Meta Keyword Index

Rank	Keyword Index
1	0.118
2	0

URL

The third component that is identified by Google as having significance to their search engine is the URL. The URL is displayed prominently as the first entry of the search results. Google also makes noted that small URLs are preferred over large ones and that a consistent directory structure should be used to display content. Take for example the case of an online retailer selling shoes; a directory structure and consequently a URL structure such as that given below would be preferred.

/shoes/men/nike/1890.html
/shoes/women/Adidas/1890.html

The above is the preferred method by Google to structure content as opposed to some URL structure such as the following:

/mens_shoes_nike_1890.html
http://www.somesite.com?id=18902569775

Does the above point to an indicator of what Google is doing internally to evaluate worth? A string of text separated by some specific character can be split into an array at which point the specific keywords associated with the URL become clear. This structure also alludes to an internal directory structure which facilitates the indexing paradigm as in such a dynamic it becomes easy to identify the top node of the structure, i.e., the main page of the website. The argument posed by Google also strengthens the argument for search trees being part of the search algorithm as a hierarchical directory structure can be represented as tree structures easily.

The keyword index is tabulated for the two domains under study using equation 1 as given above. The derived values for the index factors are displayed in table 3 below. In the determination of the keyword index for the URL, the strings were split on the '-' character to be able to separate the words within the URL. With regards to the domain name, it was simply used as a substring match to identify the relevant words from the URL. From the calculations it can be seen that the second URL has the better quantified index and yet is listed second. Another point of interest is that the search provider defines length of the

URL as having importance where shorter length URLs are deemed to be favored and as can be seen this factor was not sufficient to overcome the placement of the entry in the search results. This helps in understanding that the dynamic at hand is more complex than has been outlined by the style guide and as such it entails that there are further factors that provide the degree of differentiation that is witnessed.

Table 3. URL Keyword Index

Rank	URL	Keyword Index
1	https://www.caranddriver.com/shopping-advice/g32634624/ev-longest-driving-range/	0.375
2	https://www.plugndrive.ca/electric-vehicle-range/	0.75

Model View Controller

The Model View Controller (MVC) design pattern facilitates the segregation of the development effort between the client side and the server side, which also facilitates the formatting of the URLs of the domain. There can be no doubt that the style guide as provided by Google is just that, a guide, which does entail that the suggestions provided in the document cannot be discounted even though the immediate data points derived highlight the subjectivity of the matter. Any indexing strategy needs to strive to keep the datum point lest it forfeit that additional equity that can come about because the specification is not adhered to. The search providers do a good job of indexing content, but they do so to the specification of their template to align with their world view, they have simply not disclosed to the masses what the complete picture is, but they have given an overarching guide by which to operate under either explicitly or implicitly by the results they generate. It behooves you therefore to consider the utilization of the MVC framework in your development efforts as it reinforces the doctrine of segregation and of the explicit mapping between business objects and function, which is what the guideline specifically alludes to. The utilization of the MVC framework provides the implementor with another great benefit, it allows for the segregation of user interface functionality with back office business logic and by doing such it means that the application can then implement the client side language of JavaScript. This first step is the beginning of Micro Distributed Applications (MDAs) where there is but only one client initially and that would be the specific domain of the implementor. It becomes feasible therefore to leverage the prescription dictated by Google and leverage it to create the footprint that is much needed for the initialization of MDAs if the leverage of the MVC design pattern is utilized. This is where alignment begins to be found between a product and the viability of said product on the World Wide Web; it is because the ecosystem for the products existence must be such that first and foremost the application must be found and indexed by the search purveyors which inherently leads to lift. The products that teams are to build need to first be planted in the appropriate soil for growth to occur because otherwise the business places itself in a position whereby viability becomes a precarious proposition.

By understanding the intent of the message, it becomes feasible to understand how the process must proceed forth with the application development of future offerings. These applications will need to adhere to the doctrine expected and the segregation of structures in their configuration through the use of URL structures which are facilitated through the MVC design pattern. The additional benefit that is also derived through this implementation is that the structure of MDAs begins to take root. With this structure in place, it then becomes a more viable proposition to distribute the functionality to clients without having to change the paradigm at hand and by doing so organically begin to reap the benefits of the link equity that becomes accumulated over time by way of these micro applications. This dynamic represents the acceptance and the embracement of a protocol which inherently leads to that message that is accepted and rewarded for by the search purveyors not just simply Google. The creation of this alignment is what will lead the business forward to be better able to compete with its adversaries because after all customers buy from who they know, and this argument will default to that one domain that resonates with them the most.

Anchor Text

The fourth component that Google identifies as having value to its search engine is navigation text or anchor text if you will. Google states that anchor text should be simple text and as short as possible. Google has directly stated in this case that length does matter. Does length matter because it entails a smaller byte array to store internally in their system or does it matter because an index is calculated for each anchor text component based upon length of text string or phrase? The argument here is suspect given the indexes that have been tabulated already. As you will see in a later chapter of the book, indexing attributes will be derived for each of the system attributes of the page much as was started here, which will provide additional insight over the domain at hand and help to further clarify the argument that is posed here by the search engine purveyor. What will be seen when this process is carried out is that there is a complex dynamic at hand that supersedes the simple arguments that are made here by the popular search engine purveyor.

In the case of the MDA, it becomes important to understand that link structures created need to show relevance to the sink node of the network structure and as such a framework for the creation of this link structure will need to be derived so that the leverage point sought may be capitalized on through Micro Distributed Applications. MDAs will need to ensure that the physical verbiage in the links created accurately defines the target node and helps to create a correlation between source and sink for the search providers so that the maximum benefit in the dynamic may be leveraged.

Alternate Tag

The fifth component that Google identifies as having value to their search engine is the alternate attribute of the image tag. The 'alt' component identifies a text string to associate with each image or meta text of the object. For the visually impaired the text component of the image tag has significant meaning and a clear indicator of how Google is tailoring content to their audience. This point of interest also highlights the process being undertaken by the search purveyor whereby non textual object references are being converted to verbiage which may then be indexed. It is a proposition that is consistent with the message of the search purveyor and an indication of the extent that the organization is going to in order to understand web content at a granular level.

In order for MDAs to be sensitive to the needs of those that require assistance in viewing content it will be imperative for the creation of alternative tag structures that adequately define any relevant content that is placed on the hosting node by the MDAs. It is not simply a matter of adhering to the style guide that is the reason why the claim is made here, but it is to be sensitive to the needs of the users of these applications, which ultimately will only result in a better adoption rate for these applications. This point also elucidates the parallel that exists between traditional business and electronic commerce as online retailers are but the same businesses that were once known with a new storefront to accommodate the whim of the clientele. Online commerce is much like traditional business and as such it entails that the standard protocols for decorum between client and business must be preserved.

Header Tags

The sixth element that Google identifies as having value to their search engine are the header tags <hx></hx>, where 'x' is an integer and a value between one and six. This assertion by Google is consistent with King (2008) and Jerkovic (2010) and a strong indicator that header tags need to be encompassed in a predictive model. When you look at the case of the URLs provided above however a different story arises, as each of the links noted showed to have keywords in diverse locations as given in table 4. Given the flexibility that Cascading Style Sheets (CSS) provide it stands to reason that relevant content cannot simply be a matter of parsing header tags since Cascading Style Sheets provide the ability to completely change the layout structure of content inclusive of font size. The detail of table 4 gives further evidence that this is actually the case as keyword relevance was found outside of simply the header one tag.

Table 4. Keywords by Tag Type

Rank	Tags
1	Paragraph
2	Header One and Paragraph

The sophistication of the search paradigm has evolved over time and a fundamental reason why the student of the subject needs to keep an open mind as to how it actually functions and to the factors affecting homeostasis. The data shown above helps to depict this fact and helps to further clarify that in order to build relevant MDAs what will be needed is the creation of relevant content for online users because doing so will enable the search engines to find the content and consequently allow tertiary domains to provide this benefit back to the original content creator. This relevant content that is spoken of is distinct from what it was once known to be as this degree of relevance will cease to be simply static content, but will rather transform to functionality that also meets the needs outlined in the style guide. It is a problem frame that has metamorphized and become something similar to what it was in the past, but at the same time something different and evolved because evolution is the constant flux that technology is always burdened with.

Robots File

The robots.txt file informs the search providers of the individual links that need to be indexed or alternatively which URLs do not need to be indexed. The file is a suggestion because after all the search providers are free to crawl a particular node as they deem fit. The format of the file is provided below.

User-agent: [Name of crawler or * to designate all crawlers]

Allow | Disallow: [The relative path that should either be crawled or ignored]
Sitemap: [The URL of the site map, such as https://www.MyWebsite.com/sitemap.xml]

In the definitions given above, the 'User-agent' and 'Allow' keys may be repeated in an effort to provide granularity for the search engines. In the case of Google, the site map document may be created in a PDF or HTML format and not simply be a text file. A sample set of some common web crawlers is provided below.

- Google: Googlebot
- Bing: Bingbot
- Yahoo: Slurp
- DuckDuckGo: DuckDuckBot
- Facebook: facebot

In the case of MDAs the subscribing nodes will need to have a clear sink node that they will need to designate as the container for the application. The application however will be able to function autonomously and will be independent of its creator as the MDA will execute directly within the confines of the browser window of each user. By creating such an environment, it will be feasible for the subscribing clients to alter their robots.txt file and see minimal disruption to their own domain. Take the example of the restaurant (Sam's Pie Shoppe), which could have an URL such as follows:

www.SamsPieShoppe.com/order

By physically creating the corresponding entry in the robots.txt file and formatting the URL such that it denotes scope of intent it facilitates the discovery process for the search purveyors. In this paradigm it becomes feasible to associate an act of ordering with the list of items that would reside on the target page housing the MDA. MDAs therefore fit into the mold that fits the expectation from the search purveyors. Under this dynamic it becomes feasible to attenuate the friction to the adoption of the technology that are micro distributed functions.

Link Equity

In reading through the style guide an interesting factoid emerges and this being that they do not discuss link equity, the complete style guide by Google does not mention the phrase 'link equity'. No great chef tells the judges exactly what is in the secrete sauce of course, the evaluators simply have to infer from what they can sense. There is a reason why the tabulations presented here show inconsistency with the paradigm that unfolds, it is because truth is such and it is so because the metrics can gauge it. This truth is also such because cause and affect can be linked through a quantitative context, all of which was left void from the argument posed by the search purveyor of choice here.

The component that was suspiciously missing from the style guide is what will be investigated further in this section and in later sections of the text. The data provided in table 5 was obtained through the Yahoo search engine and the use of the link attribute in the search string. As you can see from the data given, there is a clear winner in the indexing race and the reason why the URL for Car and Driver was ranked first. There was also a clear factor that determined the exclusion of the link equity from the style guide, it could even be argued that the name of the document is as such to exclude network structures from entering the discourse. The data in table 5 is clear and helps to clarify the inconsistency that were identified with the formatting between the two websites considered. There was an additional factor of importance in the equation, and it was a significant factor in the determination of worth with online content. The argument becomes different when the data is laid bare for all to see and in this case the delta is significant and consequently helps to clarify why one entry is deemed to be more important than the other.

Table 5. Backlinks to Page Rank

Rank	Links
1	65,200
2	2,360

While it has been an interesting exercise to investigate the significance of the protocol that the search vendor has provided it is yet more enlightening to be better able to understand firsthand where true north lay. In the next chapter the discourse will dive further into the granular detail of search and a supervised learning model will be derived that will help further in understanding the indexing paradigm from a quantified perspective. By following this process, it will be feasible to come to appreciate the ramifications of the content on worth, which helps to translate the doctrine of MDAs to an applicable context. It will be at this junction where this argument is embraced that it will allow the discourse to proceed forth to define the architectural framework for MDAs.

SUMMARY

While the Google specification only alludes to six components driving search relevance the investigative study undertaken in this chapter clearly indicates a more complex model at work. The predictive model to be built must not only incorporate the six components defined by Google, but it must also encompass a larger framework as has been identified in previous chapters and further validated here.

While search engine providers cannot be counted on to disclose the magic sauce to their recipe, there can be another leverage that is harnessed and this being data science. Google has been the most transparent of the group as they have come out and disclosed some of the attributes that they deem important as displayed in the table below, but from previous chapters it can be stated however that this attempt has been but a vague attempt to appease the masses and keep questions at bay. If you look closely at the list below you will notice one attribute is missing and this being link equity. Why would Google not disclose this small caveat about their search paradigm? Both King (2008) and Jerkovic (2010) denote this attribute as having significance to the indexing domain, but yet the Google style guide makes no mention of this attribute. For further clarification one only need to take into account the PageRank algorithm, which specifically designates link structure as a fundamental tenant of significance and yet this was missing from the style guide, which only leaves the question as to why?

Table 6. Relevant Google Style Guide Tags

Rank	Tag Element
1	Title
2	Meta
3	URL
4	Anchor
5	Alternate
6	Header

In the following section the discussion proceeds to the physical algorithm to extract the hard metrics from physical domains. Through this data mining algorithm, it becomes feasible to create indexes for each of the attributes that have been deemed to be important. This process moves the discourse formally to the realm of the quantitative from the qualitative. Under this condition it becomes impossible to argue with true north because after all the numbers will point to where it stands. The search indexing landscape is changing and will continue to change this is why the algorithm has been made available along with the data extracted in a GitHub repository. It is because of the data that an affinity for true north can be disclosed and this point of truth helps to further clarify the development landscape. Up until this body of work the realm of online relevance had been qualified and now it is quantified. This quantification leads to the realization that software development has changed and has done so dramatically. Gone will be the days when large servers will house large applications. Industry has migrated to smaller units of function that are distributed and operate within the confines of the hardware of the clients that utilize them. This doctrine represents an optimization to current practice and shows elegance in the process.

Microsoft has invested in a company by the name of Foursquare and a major reason for having done so was to acquire user data to feed into their search engine algorithm. Take for example the case where 'X' amount of people have checked into some location and since 'X' is greater than 'Y' (an alternate location where people have checked in) then it stands to reason that location 'X' is more popular than location 'Y'. It therefore also stands to reason that location 'X' will be ranked prior to location 'Y'. For the sake of an exercise replace 'X' with 'the restaurant chain Subway' and 'Y' with 'Billy's Sandwich Hut'. It is quite brilliant if you think about it, they have invested in a model similar to what Yelp is. For which coincidently enough the search results on Bing (04/29/2019 at 4:40 PM PDT) came up first when issuing the query 'Mountain House CA Burger Restaurant'. This dynamic represents the evolution of the web and the fundamental reason why the discourse must part from a truth, otherwise the argument will veer off course and lead to something other than desired.

Truth as has been seen in this chapter may be obfuscated for some reason and the only mechanism by which this haze will be removed will be if the discussion migrates to a metrics driven context which forces the discussion to alleviate itself of the burden of falsehood that is prevalent in the qualified. Everyone has some form of bias, and it is these biases that keep society from seeing the world in its true form. It changed the dynamic of the discussion when the discussion migrated from simply accepting that which was dictated by the style guide and proceeded to attach numbers to the discussion. When this occurred it allowed the argument to come to a new reality, which is metric induced and void of the I that too many arguments are infused with. Healthy skepticism should not be frowned upon but should be embraced because it is impossible for society to be correct all the time, humanity errors and consequently fails, but yet humanity prior to having the blindfold removed was certain about what was before it. It is part of humanity and part of this experience that is life, society will never be correct 100% of the time, but if the discussion departs with 'the numbers state X' then it is more difficult to lose the footing by which the argument is supported by. Truth is much like that child that is upset because they need a nap, and it is only the open arms of that parent that will suffice. Will you be able to embrace your truth? Will you be able to be receptive to it when it comes to you because when it does it might not sound as you might want it to? Take comfort in knowing however that what you will experience when expectations do not meet reality is that it is a feeling that all of humanity has felt, and the feeling needs to be embraced because to embrace that child means that you are closer to finding true north. Prescriptions are for those that are asleep at the wheel and are willing to accept without questioning and humanity must question, and it was because of that questioning that you find this text before you. It was because of this questioning that it can now be stated that the search paradigm can be modeled through a supervised learning context. And to live in this mode of being a metrics driven individual it entails that you have the opportunity to live your life by adhering to the observations that are before you and thus alleviating yourself from paying that expensive bounty that at times can only be paid through experience, failure.

REFERENCES

Google. (n.d.). *Search Engine Optimization Starter Guide*. Retrieved July 15, 2015, from http://static.googleusercontent.com/media/www.google.com/en/us/webmasters/docs/search-engine-optimization-starter-guide.pdf

Jerkovic, J. (2010). *SEO Warrior*. O'Reilly Media Inc.

King, A. (2008). *Website Optimization*. O'Reilly Media Inc.

Chapter 5
Search

ABSTRACT

Even though the term "search" is a small word, it denotes an endeavor that occupies the time of many in diverse organizations. It is a work effort that is ambiguous and often plagued with consternation since it denotes discovery of that which is unknown. Search may be a pastime or an arduous process depending on the actor that has embraced the endeavor. Searching for truth has been aided in recent times through the use of mathematical models that have been applied through a computational context, but in order to be effective in this manner, it mandates that the individual first understand not only the nature of said data, but also the mathematical context that applies to the dataset. If this data can be converted to information, then what results is nothing short of extraordinary as it leads the discourse to a better state.

INTRODUCTION

Searching is an endeavor that humanity has gravitated to seamlessly; search is performed endlessly for answers to questions that need to be satisfied. The search space has simply become an extension to humanities inquisitive nature. It is used throughout the daily working day to find answers to questions that arise randomly. It has become such a paradigm shift that there are phrases that have become commonplace such as 'Google it'. The company namesake has now become a verb in the English vernacular. The correctly answering of the questions posed to the search engines has become the golden formula for each of the providers. In this section of the book, a search algorithm is explored and while searching is rather simple in the form of English phrases it does highlight the base working structure of the paradigm under investigation. This study will utilize the same search engines that are harnessed by the masses to help shed light on the base functionality in a quantified context, which facilitates the escape from the qualitative context of the subject and enables the understanding of the domain in a metrics manner. The result of this process will then be used as the input to the model that will be evaluated in a following chapter of this book to derive the actual formulas for indexing by Bing and Yahoo. The algorithm that is used for this section of the book is displayed in the back of the book for your review. The algorithm in its entirety has been uploaded to GitHub as well (https://github.com/guillermorodriguez/Dissertation) where the code may be freely download and used for your own purposes without limitation and guarantee

DOI: 10.4018/978-1-6684-4849-6.ch005

of course. The algorithm was written in the Python (https://www.python.org/) programming language, which is free to utilize and may be coded with a product such as NetBeans (https://www.netbeans.org) or Eclipse (https://eclipse.org/ide/) both of which are free to harness for your own development efforts. The algorithm is provided for your viewing and utilization for two purposes the first being for full disclosure and the second being to allow you to use it for your own needs. If you do pull down the codebase, please note that the project is a NetBeans project and may be directly loaded to the environment bearing its name. The only issue that might arise through this effort is the resolution of dependencies, which may be overcome by simply invoking a dependency resolution tool such as pip (https://pypi.org/project/pip/).

The version of Python that was used for this project was 3.4.3 and may be downloaded here https://www.python.org/downloads/release/python-343/. The Python programming language is dynamic, free to use, and also features diverse opensource libraries that can be used to facilitate development. This dynamic allows for the creation of solutions that can be shared easily given the economics, adoption, and richness of the construct. The lack of a cost barrier and the richness of the toolsets that are available for its development is the primary reason why the Python programming language was chosen as the implementation mechanism. The other benefit that arises with the use of the Python programming language is that there exist components that may be leveraged directly through the programming language that facilitate the analysis of data. Through the use of packages such as Scikit (https://scikit-learn.org/) or pandas (https://pandas.pydata.org) you can within the Python programming language leverage mathematical and data science constructs. This is one avenue that is pending development directly within the GitHub repository provided and a prime candidate for the forking of the project. Through the use of Scikit the possibility exists to understand the data further such as through the use of alternate classifications, regressions, and clustering studies. These avenues for further study highlight the degree of clout that can now be harnessed by development teams through the implementation of mathematical constructs directly within a programming language. This condition of enablement relates to the direct influence that developers, organizations, and teams have been infused with. It is through this enablement that previous datasets can be altered to become information that only leads to new realizations about the physical and metaphysical world that surrounds all. This book is a prime example of this enablement taking root since because of it a truth was able to be derived whereby the creation of an approximation model that showed almost an 80% parity with the indexing results of the Yahoo search engine were found. Given the availability of data and the openness that is the internet it became feasible to utilize the same search engines to validate the derived models. In essence it was because of the behavior of the system under study and the cause and effect relationship that results because of said system that it became possible to derive a mathematical context for its behavior and for which the effort undertaken was performed exclusively outside the boundaries of search system.

Development teams are no longer living in a day and time where the point of friction to innovation is due to the lack of avenues that are available to pursue, but rather the point of stagnation is a result of all the possibilities that exists to innovate. There are more avenues to investigate than there is time to perform the needed body of work; teams are living under a condition whereby they are only limited by their ingenuity since the possibilities for discovery are bountiful given the sophistication of the profession. Gone are the days when large capital outlays are needed to create product lines as lines of business can now be created by teams that are dispersed, culturally diverse, and nimble. Add to this fact that these teams are capable of performing this needed body of work because they have been empowered to build better and bigger only leads to ripe conditions for business to reap benefits as have never been afforded prior. This empowerment has only been fueled through the ability to leverage large datasets as has been done directly in the pages that unfold before the reader, which leads to the realization that development teams sit at a junction in time whereby their physical work products stand to create a benefit for society as has never been seen prior.

In this study the statistical programming package R (https://www.r-project.org) was selected for the analysis of the data for the specific reason of segregation between the codebase and the computation endeavor. R also provides a great degree of flexibility given its formal programming structure as well as the development environment that it has at its disposal. It was through R that the calculations were performed and that you will formally be exposed to in the next chapter. The attribute of relevance was also studied using the random forest package that is available through R natively. A subsequent chapter is specifically dedicated to the studying of the relevance of the attributes identified using machine learning and data science methodologies.

R has been made available through the GNU General Public License which gives the user the right to us the software without any out of pocket expense, which represents a significant benefit to other alternatives such as MATLAB (https://www.mathworks.com) or SAS (https://www.sas.com) where the expense could run several hundred dollars at a minimum. With the removal of the entry point barrier and the fact that R allows you to create your own packages that may be distributed through the main project website makes for compelling reasons to use R for all your statistical analysis needs. Today you have many options available to you for your statistical analysis including Python and R with their available packages, rich development environments, and rich syntax.

The degree to which software can be leveraged to consume and categorize data has empowered everyone to investigate the world before them as the heavy lifting can now be done through a component that does not tire and is willing to perform the same task repeatedly. There is also a vast amount of data at everyone's disposal as can be seen directly in this study. The data that was used to determine the supervised learning model was made possible by the same search engines that were used to understand the paradigm. The data that the same search engines made available freely was utilized to validate their own model. There was never a need to store the plethora of data that is indexed by the search engines themselves as they made it available at no cost and on demand. It became simply a matter of turning loose the algorithm and letting it run its course and having the search engines reply in kind. Even though the search engines did not provide a physical API to extract the needed data from their datastores it still became possible to interact with their search systems and leverage the same HTML constructs that they use to extract relevant content. This data that is littered throughout the internet and is ready to be leveraged can be consumed directly by applications through the use of libraries that are available in various programming languages such as the HTMLParser package in Python. Even in R there exists the possibility to consume web resources through the use of the httr and jsonlite packages. The ability to consume the data that is freely available and accessible via the internet has become feasible because of the opensource community and the packages that they build. It is a great time to dedicate one's labor to this type of effort given the possibilities that exist for further understanding of variant domains and for which this particular effort is but one such example of what may be accomplished.

SEARCH TERMS

The individual search terms posed to the search engine providers were generated through a randomization process where the file words.txt was used as the potential source of query terms, which is given in part below and which may be viewed in its entirety via the GitHub.com repository (https://raw.githubusercontent.com/guillermorodriguez/Dissert ation/master/src/words.txt). The file was downloaded from a free online resource and was utilized as such in this effort. From this set of words, a randomization process was followed where 100 words were chosen at random and placed in the file named words_chosen.txt. This file was created through the Python script named words_set.py. The script utilized for this random word generation is provided below. The Python script ingested the words.txt file and placed its contents in an array, which was later parsed in a loop that iterated 100 times and where a random word was chosen through the use of the random.choice() function that selected a random word from the array of available words. This selected term that was placed into the _term variable which was then written to the words_chosen.txt file. The words_chosen.txt file is given in part below for the user and which may be viewed online in its entirety here: https://github.com/guillermorodriguez/Dissertation/blob/mast er/src/words_chosen.txt.

The randomization of the query terms allowed for the process to follow an unbiased procedure where the human element of the word selection was removed. It was this random set of words that was fed into the search algorithm and allowed for the process to continue in a lexically sensitive manner by way of the NLTK library. This step in the process was important as it allowed for the removal of the human element, which preserved the integrity of the process from the onset. The reader should note that execution of the script would entail a different set of data elements as the random function in Python is tied to a time context, which denotes that even physical computer systems cannot themselves currently remove the bias constraint from their own undertakings. The reader should also note that these search terms that were derived from the script were fed into the search systems as selected and as such represent simple search endeavors that lack the complexity of multiple search terms. This also represents another avenue for further investigation and an enhancement of the model that is presented here. Alternatively, what could have been done was that the algorithm presented below could have been enhanced whereby for each line entry two separate word entries could have been derived to model a search query in a more realistic manner. This point of contention highlights the argument that was made prior in that currently the point of consternation is not the lack of avenues to pursue, but it is rather the plethora of undertakings that exists which leads the argument to a stagnation point.

```
# Script to select 100 words at random from repository of English words.

import sys
import os
import random

print("Started ....")

# Get dataset file path
_source = os.getcwd()+'\\words.txt'
_words = []

# Set words selection file particulars
_archive = os.getcwd()+'\\words_chosen.txt'
```

```
if not os.path.isfile(_archive):
    # Create Query History File
    _queries = open(_archive, 'w')
    _queries.close()

# Read dictionary – add word to dictrionary
with open(_source, 'r') as _file:
    for _line in _file:
        if len(_line.strip()) > 1:
            _words.append(_line.strip())
    _file.close()

# Select 100 random words and append to destination file
for iteration in range(100):
    _term = random.choice(_words)
    with open(_archive, 'a') as _file:
        _file.write(_term)
        _file.write('\n')
        _file.close()
```

PERSPECTIVE

A limitation of the exercise undertaken was that the search terms created were singular in nature and did not represent search instances whereby a series of words were searched for in unison. While this argument might lead credence to the argument that the task undertaken was simplistic in nature, the alternative argument could also be made that this simplicity is but the first step in the understanding of the paradigm. Before a second level argument can be made it is this first level argument that must be undertaken so that a decision may be made as to whether further study is warranted. To also be clear this second step that is sought, whereby a series of words are brought together to form a more complex query is but the first step taken with a further level of complexity applied, but nevertheless it is a problem frame that is rooted in the first step undertaken. What the reader will find in the reading of the pages that are to follow is that this need for further study is warranted, but what is also warranted is to take note of the findings that are brought to bear by first undertaking this initial step. It is this first step that is the crucible to any argument that is to follow since the assertion of some future premise must first part from a rudimentary premise that lays the groundwork for any future assertions that are to come. What the reader will also find is that this need for greater complexity is greatly diminished by the factors of relevance that are found.

Words.txt File Extract

```
# http://www-01.sil.org/linguistics/wordlists/english/wordlist/wordsEn.txt
a
aah
```

aahed
aahing
aahs
aardvark
aardvarks
aardwolf
ab
abaci
aback
abacus
abacuses
abaft
abalone
abalones
abandon
abandoned
abandonedly
abandonee
abandoner
abandoners
abandoning
abandonment
abandonments
abandons
abase
abased
abasedly
abasement
abaser
abasers

Words_chosen.txt File Extract

vanilla
crazes
planetoid
reassess
ungraciously
diametrically
extroverts
fluctuating
truces
dies
stereotype

manrope
trussed
plutons
shies
weaker
hemiolas
animus
nuttier
unbiasedly
revivalism
before
reinflaming
misinterpretation
expurgators
cracklier
musket
likenesses
bloodshot
xenogamy
cyclones
swamper

NATURAL LANUGAGE TOOLKIT (NLTK)

The major search engines provide search results not simply on a textual representation of the query, but provide output based upon the context of the search query. Take for example the querying of the term 'The Big Apple', which returns results for the city in New York state in the top ten results for each of the search engines Bing, Yahoo, and Google. Understanding search context is of the utmost paramount in the search space as language has an inference and to void the search paradigm from it means to be out of synchronization with the intent of the audience. It is the marrying of this context with true intent where the paradigm takes root as this is the means by which viability can be determined. The search community at large has gone to a great extent to manage user expectations and they have been able to do such because of the leveraging of utilities such as the Natural Language Toolkit (NLTK). The NLTK is a platform that addresses the lexical context of language by matching up words to their equivalent counterparts, which is how understanding functions across individuals with varying modes of fluency. For example, a car is a form of a 'vehicle' or as a mode of transportation and using such does not diminish the expectation of what should be displayed to the user via the search providers. Users have come to expect search engines to understand intent and they can because of the context of search that can be managed through coding constructs such as the NLTK. It was because of the NLTK library that drove the decision to utilize the Python programming language for this particular effort. The NLTK may be downloaded from the URL here: https://www.nltk.org/. The library is written for the Python programming language and allows the incorporation of it through the standard pip install command, which is given below.

pip install -U nltk

If you are running through the codebase you will need to install the NLTK prior to executing the code as the Python package is a dependency to the codebase. Once the Python package is installed you can incorporate its functionality by simply importing the functionality through a formal import statement in the Python code and use the library reference to derive the language context for alternative words to match the particular word sought.

To be able to obtain the lexical context within a Python program you must first download the corpus dependencies, which may be done through the Python programming language itself via the script given below. The nltk.download() function will give a separate popup window that is shown in figure 1 below. The issuing of the brown.words() function call will display a partial list of the words in the Brown Corpus. Further details of the nltk.corpus package may be found here: https://www.nltk.org/api/nltk.corpus. html. Once the dependencies are downloaded and available on the machine it will become possible to leverage the full toolset of the NLTK library and all of its dependent packages.

```
# First execute the command line
# pip install -U nltk
# or
# pip3 install -U nltk

import nltk

# Generates popup window for package dependency download
nltk.download()

# Physical importation of functionality
from nltk.corpus import brown
brown.words()
# Keywords
_keywords = []

# Retrieval of synonyms based on query term
for _synonyms in wordnet.synsets(query):

# Lemmas from individual synonym for _s in _synonyms.lemmas(): _s = _s.name().replace('_',
' ') if _s not in _keywords: _keywords.append(_s) # Append to keyword array to search
if len(_keywords) == 0: _keywords.append(query)
```

The incorporation of the NLTK package within the solution created was paramount as each word searched upon was first put through the NLTK library to derive its lexical meaning and it was this grouping of words that were searched within the target documents to derive the metrics used in the computational formula. This paradigm allowed for the alignment between the solution created and the functionality of the actual search engine providers, thus ensuring parity and allowing the mimicking of the mode of operandi of the search purveyors. The search algorithm took as ingestion the series of ran-

Figure 1. NLTK Packages

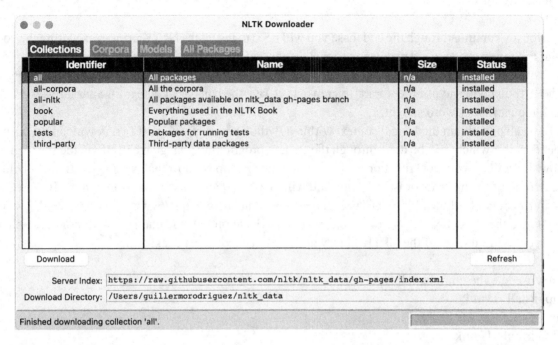

dom words that were created and consumed via the words_chosen.txt file as was created in the Python script provided previously and used those words as the input for the derivation of the lexical context. The NLTK package was imported and given the alias wordnet in the partial script given below and which may be viewed in its entirety here: https://github.com/guillermorodriguez/Dissertation/blob/master/src/pyBing.py. The partial script fragment that was used to create the lexical context for the words searched is for the Bing search engine but it is identical to what was used for the Yahoo search engine as well. The query term was passed through as a function parameter and represents the individual word that was sought, and which was obtained from the random words generated file that was discussed previously named words_chosen.txt. By calling the synsets() function it became possible to retrieve the set of synonyms for the individual word. This combined with the use of the lemmas() function enabled the determination of all the possible alternative dictionary representations of the given word. With this code fragment it allowed for the creation of a similar system to what the search engines utilize in their indexing endeavors as they do not simply index given keywords based upon their ASCII representation, but they rather index content based upon the lexical context, which is mimicked with the code fragment from below.

ALGORITHM

The HTML utility that was utilized in the data mining algorithm is part of the Python language and for which the documentation may be found here: https://docs.python.org/3/library/html.parser.html. The fact that this library is part of the Python programming language simply lends credence to its utilization for projects such as the one that you find here. The library is robust and readily available for utilization without the need to have to import third party components. Through this utility it becomes feasible to inspect and extract content from HTML pages readily. The richness of the available utilities that are accessible within the Python programming language simply help to reiterate the argument for the utilization of Python in development endeavors. Yet another argument that may be made in favor of the Python programming language is also the fact that it is a loosely typed language, thus alleviating the programmer from having to worry about memory contentions as Python scripts are interpreted and not compiled, thus removing the burden from the developer of having to understand the intricacies of traditional programming languages such as C or C++.

The search algorithm takes as input one of the search engine providers – Bing or Yahoo which in turn defines the search engine that is targeted in the data mining process. The algorithm then ingests the contents of the words_chosen.txt file which become the individual entries that are searched upon using the NLTK library. Once each of the individual words and their corresponding context are found the algorithm reaches out to the search engine provider of choice and retrieves a series of links. The links that are retrieved are the search results by the provider in the order that they deem most important first. This essentially becomes the indexing hierarchy and the groundwork for the investigative study. The program can be initiated from the command line by typing the following (assuming you have Python installed):

python pySearch.py -engine [BING|YAHOO]

The program pySearch.py takes a command line argument named 'engine' that may hold the value of either 'BING' or 'YAHOO'. The engine type determines the folder that will be used as the container for the data results. In the code repository you will find two folders each named after its search engine namesake that contains a sub folder named data, this is where the results of the execution of the search algorithm were placed.

In a sub folder of the data folder, you will find a folder named Source that contains a series of files where each file is named after the query term used and a timestamp showing when it was created; the files all have the .data extension. Within these files you will find a header row detailing the points of significance for each end point that are defined as follows.

- Index value
- URL
- Description index
- Content tag (DIV, H<X>, P, SPAN) index
- Total links inbound and outbound
- Meta keyword index
- URL index
- Tag title index

In each of the attributes given above the index designation denotes where an index was calculated. In each of these cases the index is tabulated by the formula given below in equation 1. The word length in the numerator denotes the sum of the length for each instance of the lexically relevant word found. The word length of the denominator denotes the length of the content for the given attribute such as the length of the content in the division tag for example.

$$\text{Index} = \frac{\sum_i^n \text{Word Length}}{\text{Text Length}} \tag{1}$$

The search algorithm served the purpose of searching through each data set returned by the search provider and performing the calculations on each of the links found that were not of an advertisement nature. For each result set returned the algorithm traversed through the next sequence of entries by following the corresponding link given by the search engine provider in the HTML document returned. By following this process, it was possible to index the search results for any query posed to the search engine providers.

The base entry of the data mining algorithm is the pySearch.py file, whose invocation initiates the whole data ingestion process for each of the search engine providers of choice. The algorithm in part is provided below for the reader. If the command sequence is given as needed then the application proceeds with the data ingestion process and if the input does not adhere to the specification the command line help is provided to the user via the print_help() command. If the command sequence is as expected then the algorithm proceeds by parsing the ingestion file line by line and invoking the corresponding search engine class, which would be either pyBing() or pyYahoo(). Once the correct object is determined then the getLinks() function is called on the corresponding object which takes as a parameter the individual word sought with the search engine. This separation of functionality is possible due to the implementation of objects as they facilitate the work effort by compartmentalizing the coding structures. This division of labor was needed as each of the search engine provider's output a specific version of HTML that is specific to their engine and consequently it entailed that a specific parser be utilized to accommodate the ingestion variance.

```
if parse.engine:
    if _MODE == "DEBUG":
        print("Engine: %s" % parse.engine)

    with open(_source, 'r') as _file:
        for _line in _file:
            _term = _line.strip()
            if _term[0:1] != "#":
                print("Searching: %s" % _term)

                if parse.engine.upper() == 'BING':
                    # Bing search
                    _bing = pyBing()
                    _bing.getLinks(_term)
                elif parse.engine.upper() == 'YAHOO':
                    # Bing search
                    _yahoo = pyYahoo()
                    _yahoo.getLinks(_term)
else:
    # Display script utilization for user
```

```
parser.print_help()
```

```
print("Ending Search ......")
```

Each of the classes pyBing and pyYahoo has three functions defined, the constructor, getLinks(), and getBackLinks(). The purpose of the getLinks() function is to act as a gateway for the retrieval of each of the links from the search engine results and then to facilitate the classification of the content within that target link for the needed metrics that are under consideration, which were defined previously in this chapter. The getLinks() function is discussed next for the pyYahoo class and which is displayed in part below. The function defines the name of the output file as being composed of the search term and a timestamp. This is the output file where the output metric content is ultimately sent to. The function loops through the HTML found until it determines that a next page is not available from the search provider at which point it terminates the parsing of the content. The individual links are extracted from the HTML content of the output from the search provider by calling the extract_links() function that may be found in the Extract class via the extract.py file. The Extract class contains four methods, the constructor, extract_links(), extract_indexes(), and external_links(). The content of the extract_links() function is provided next. The function leverages the HTMLhelper() method which is in turn used to override the functionality of the HTMLParser object in order to parse the needed content by search provider and which is discuss next. The extract_links() function facilitates the retrieval of the needed page content by physically making the request to the search engine with the search term as a parameter in the query string. The algorithm then leverages the helper method to physically extract the needed content of the page retrieved.

```
# Extract Link Attributes for a Given Search
def getLinks(self, query):
    # Obtain API Settings
    _config = config()
    _config.yahoo()

    try:
        # Set Repository Structure
        _name = os.getcwd()+'\\YAHOO\\'+query+'_'+time.strftime("%Y%m%d%H%M%S")+".data"
        _file = open(_name, "w")
        _file.write('index\turl\tdescription\tdiv\th1\th2\th3\th4\th5\th6\tinbound_links\tkeywords\toutbound_links\tp\troot\tspan\ttitle\n')
        _file.close()
        # Direct Call
        _html = self.extract_links(_config.yahoo_settings['url'] + query, 'YAHOO')
        _indexValue = 0
        _page = 1
        _maxPages = 6
        while _html.next != '' and _page < _maxPages:
            for _entry in _html.links:
```

```
                _indexValue += 1
            if '.pdf' not in _entry:
                print("Searching: %s" % _entry['url'])
                _indexes = sorted(self.extract_indexes(_entry['url'], _keywords).items())
                if _indexes:
                    _file = open(_name, 'a')
                    _file.write(str(_indexValue) + '\t' + _entry['url'])
                    for _index in _indexes:
                        _file.write('\t'+str(_index[1]))
                    _file.write('\n')
                    _file.close()

        if _html.next != '':
            print("Next: %s" % _html.next)
            _html = self.extract_links(_html.next, 'YAHOO')
            print("Pausing for 3 seconds")
            time.sleep(3)

        _page += 1

    except urllib.request.URLError as e:
        print("Error: %s" % e.reason)
    except ValueError as v:
        print("Non urllib Error: %s" % v)

# Retrieve series of links from search engine query
def extract_links(self, url, engine, use_proxy = False):

    # Invoke HTML helper utility
    _html = HTMLhelper()
    _html.search_engine(engine, 'URLS')

    try:
        if len(self._agents) == 0:
            _source = os.path.dirname(os.path.abspath(__file__)) + '\\' + 'agents.txt'
            _file = open(_source, 'r')
            _agent = _file.readline().strip()
            while _agent:
                self._agents.append(_agent)
                _agent = _file.readline().strip()
            _file.close()

        _request = None
        url = url.replace(' ', '%20')
```

```
        if use_proxy:
            if len(self._proxies) == 0:
                _source = os.path.dirname(os.path.realpath(__file__)) + '\\proxies.txt'
                with open(_source, 'r') as _file:
                    for _line in _file:
                        self._proxies.append(_line.strip())

            _prox = random.choice(self._proxies)
            print("Using Proxy: %s" % _prox)

            proxies = { 'http': 'http://'+_prox}
            opener = urllib.request.FancyURLopener(proxies)
            with opener.open(url) as f:
                print(f.read().decode('utf-8'))
        else:
            _request = urllib.request.Request(url)
            if engine.upper() == 'YAHOO' or engine.upper() == 'GOOGLE':
                # Set header detail
                _request.add_header('User-agent', 'Mozilla/5.0 (Windows NT 6.3; WOW64) AppleWeb-
Kit/537.36 (KHTML, like Gecko) Chrome/53.0.2785.116 Safari/537.36')
            else:
                _request.add_header('User-Agent', random.choice(self._agents))
                _response = urllib.request.urlopen(_request)
                _html.feed(_response.read().decode('utf-8'))
    except ValueError as v:
        print("Error: %s" % v)
        exit()

    return _html

indexes = { 'description': 0, 'div': 0, 'outbound_links': 0, 'h1': 0, 'h2': 0, 'h3': 0, 'h4': 0, 'h5': 0, 'h6':
0, 'inbound_links': 0, 'keywords': 0, 'p': 0, 'span': 0, 'title': 0, 'root': 0 }
links = []
operation = ''
next = ''
root_url = ''
tag = ''
type = ''
url = ''
words = {}
backlinks = []
```

The HTMLhelper class inherits from the HTMLParser class which allows for the overriding of the needed functions of the HTMLParser class. The methods that were overridden were handle_starttag(), handle_endtag(), and handle_data(). The HTMLhelper class defines a series of attributes for data capture which are provided below. The individual page element indexes are tracked by way of the indexes dictionary. The links variable tracks the list of links found on the page, similarly to the backlinks variable which tracks the list of backlinks to the URL. The operation variable can have the value of URLS, KEYS or INDEX, which determines the operation point of focus such as determining the backlinks to the main URL for example. The next variable determines if another page is available in the search results and if so, it sets the variable to the corresponding URL. The root_url strips away the excess content such as 'http' and '//' from the url variable which is simply the link being inspected. The tag variable identifies the current tag being evaluated when parsing the HTML content of the page. The type variable identifies the search engine type which will be either BING or YAHOO. The final variable tracked is the words variable which contains the instance of the keywords found to match via the NLTK library. The main functions used in the HTMLhelper class to identify the individual indexes by page attribute are the handle_starttag() function which enables the codebase to determine the entry point of each tag element such as header tags for example and the handle_data() function which allows for the parsing of the individual data within a particular tag. A partial extract of the handle_data() method is provide below for the reader. If the particular operation is set to KEYS then the data content is parsed to determine the ratio between keyword to content that is found and this is added to the running total for the attribute type. This is the mechanism by which the individual page element attributes are determined to have weight in the overall parsing of the documents as there can be a multitude of paragraph tags for example and each paragraph tag may or may not contain keywords.

The culmination of these keywords by content length is what was sought to be determined and for which the corresponding index values were to be tabulated. The handle_data() function is what facilitated the derivation of the metrics sought. In a similar manner the meta tag and title tags were parsed to determine their corresponding index values. The utilization of the HTMLParser object that is native to the Python programming language facilitated the data collection and dissemination of the content in order to be able to process the needed indexes by page attribute in the HTMLhelper class and all of which was feasible in part through a utility that is found natively in the Python programming language.

```
def handle_data(self, data):

    if self.operation.upper() == 'URLS':
        # Parse individual search engine links

    elif self.operation.upper() == 'KEYS':
        # Keywords in Text Tag Elements - div, h1, h2, h3, h4, h5, h6, p, span, title
        for _key in self.indexes:
            if _key == self.tag:
                for _word in self.words:
                    if len(data.strip()) > 0:
                        self.indexes[_key] += (data.lower().count(_word.lower()) *len(_word)) / len(data.
strip())
```

DATA

The data files that were created by the algorithm provided were placed in folders from the root of the solution under the name of the search engine. For each of the search engine results, the files may contain instances where the index value is not an integer. The reason for this is that in some cases the query results returned the URL in random order. Both of the search engines mined are using the user as a validation instrument to their own search engine indexing effort.

The data files were created in a tab delimited format that could be read by some external modeling utility such as R for example and the reason why this file format was chosen. Each row of the data files represents a specific link that was extracted from a result set of some query, which is given as the first part of the file name. The first entry in each of the data files is the header that details the attributes that are modelled. This again helps facilitate the importation of the data into a third party tool for later processing.

Two sample data sets are provided next, they are the partial content for the indexing of the adheres word for both the Yahoo and Bing search engines. For the sake of brevity only a partial set is provided here, the full dataset may be found in the GitHub repository.

The data mined was sent to the corresponding file through the code fragment given below and which may be found in the getLinks() function of either the pyYahoo.py file or the pyBing.py file. This code fragment leverages the Extract class and which in turn leverages the HTMLhelper class. The data retrieved is sorted for the entries by directly appending to the needed files. The attribute set was placed in alphabetical order for this purpose as it allowed for the sorting of the data collected and consequently the dumping of the data directly to some data store.

It was through this data mining endeavor that it become feasible to collect a series of data points that could later be studied and understood, but this study of the data would never have been feasible if the protocol for the data extraction had not been available, if the programming language and its corresponding utilities had not been developed, and if the data had not been made available by the search providers. This points to the evolution of the web and what the web has been able to extend to the masses freely and openly. It is because of this evolution that now industry finds itself at a junction point in the development profession that denotes change. This change that is forthcoming is such because it is the data that points to this point in the horizon, but it is the burden of all to understand what the data entails.

```
_indexes = sorted(self.extract_indexes(_entry['url'], _keywords).items())
if _indexes:
    _file = open(_name, 'a')
    _file.write(str(_indexValue) + '\t' + _entry['url'])
    for _index in _indexes:
        _file.write('\t'+str(_index[1]))
        _file.write('\n')
        _file.close()
```

Bing Sample Data Extract - Adheres

index	url	description	div	h1	h2	h3	h4	h5	h6	inbound_
links	keywords	outbound_links	p	root	span	title				
1	http://www.oxforddictionaries.com/us/		0.0	0	0.0	0.0	0	0.0	0	

0　0　0.0　14　0.0　0.0　0.0　0.0

2　http://www.thefreedictionary.com/adheres　0.8458781362007167　3.0263273893007403
6.0　48.0　0　0　0　0　0　0.6033519553072626　171　0.0
1.2413793103448276　84.79654875000406　1.3333333333333335

3　http://legal-dictionary.thefreedictionary.com/adheres
0.7868852459016394　0.6792452830188679　24.0　0　0　0　0　0
0　0.6033519553072626　266　0.0　0.782608695652174　68.5714285714285
2.0571428571428574

4　http://medical-dictionary.thefreedictionary.com/adheres
1.0778443113772456　0.6545454545454545　6.0　0　0　0　0　0　0
0.6033519553072626　173　0.0　0.75　71.99999999999994　1.3584905660377358

5　http://www.thesaurus.com/browse/adheres　0.2903225806451613　2.7714285714285714　6.0
0.0　0　0　0　0　2.4406779661016946　14　0.7982062780269057
1.2857142857142856　23.454978354978348　1.44

6　http://www.dictionary.com/browse/adhere　0.8046875　2.290826612903226　0　0
1.565217391304348　0　0　0　0　1.5999999999999999　27　0.0
1.2857142857142856　89.08416810050211　1.8

7　http://www.macmillandictionary.com/dictionary/british/adhere-to　0.6585365853658537
0.0　0　0　0　0　0　0　0.5373134328358209　3　0.0
0.6923076923076924　22.800000000000008　0.5070422535211268

8　http://www.adherishealth.com/　0　0.0　0.8181818181818181　0　0　0.0
0.0　0　0　0　7　0.3176672384219553　0.0　0.13584905660377358　0.0

9　https://www.merriam-webster.com/dictionary/adhere 1.0989010989010988　0.0　6.0
41.251970638057564　0　0.0　0.0　0.0　0　0.6390532544378699　42　0.0
0.9729729729729273　0.0　1.5

10　https://en.m.wiktionary.org/wiki/adheres　0　0.0　5.142857142857142　0.0　0
0　0　0　0　0　2　0　1.125　0.0　1.8

11　https://en.m.wikipedia.org/wiki/Adhesion　0　0.8695652173913043　0.0　0.0　0
0　0　0　0　0　5　0.34441164527323836 0.0　0.0　0.0

12　https://en.wikipedia.org/wiki/Adhesion#Surface_energy　0　0.0　0.0　0.0　0.0
0　0　0　0　0　56　0.34441164527323836 0.0　0.0　0.0

13　https://en.wikipedia.org/wiki/Adhesion#Mechanisms_of_adhesion　0　0.0　0.0　0.0
0.0　0　0　0　0　0　56　0.34441164527323836 0.0　0.0　0.0

14　https://en.wikipedia.org/wiki/Adhesion#Strength　0　0.0　0.0　0.0　0.0　0
0　0　0　0　56　0.34441164527323836 0.0　0.0　0.0

15　https://en.wikipedia.org/wiki/Adhesion#Other_effects　0　0.0　0.0　0.0　0.0
0　0　0　0　0　56　0.34441164527323836 0.0　0.0　0.0

16　http://www.adherishealth.com/　0　0.0　0.8181818181818181　0　0　0.0
0.0　0　0　0　7　0.3176672384219553　0.0　0.13584905660377358　0.0

17　http://sentence.yourdictionary.com/adhere　1.0799999999999998
0.0　0　2.4230769230769225　0.0　1.0285714285714287　0　0　0
1.0799999999999998　92　0.0　1.0588235294117647　6.0　1.411764705882353

18　http://www.definitions.net/definition/adheres　0.6857142857142857　0　0.0
0.0　0.0　0.0　0.0　0　0　1.7560975609756098　88　1.231578947368421

1.0588235294117647   0.0   1.565217391304348
19 https://en.wiktionary.org/wiki/adheres   0   0.0   5.142857142857142   0.0   0.0
0 0 0   0   0   20   0   1.2   0.0   1.8
20 https://phys.org/news/2016-10-superomniphobic-tape-adheres-surface.html   0   0.45
0.8372093023255814   0.0   0   0   0.0   0   0   0   53
0.245748987854251   0.5714285714285714   0.0   0.8372093023255814
21 https://phys.org/chemistry-news/   0   0.0   0.0   0   0   0   0.0   0
0 0 28   0.11335138316523685   0.0   0.0   0.0
22 http://atherys.com/   0   0   0   0.0   0   0   0   0   0   0
2 0.0 0.0   0   0.0
23 https://quizlet.com/1781827/excretory-system-flash-cards/   0.0   0.0   0.0   0   0
0 0 0.0   0   0   2   0.0   0.0   0.36   0.0
24 https://en.wikipedia.org/wiki/Anders_Behring_Breivik   0   0.0   0.0   0.0   0.0
0 0 0   0   0   446   0.08955223880597014   0.0   0.0   0.0
25 http://crosswordtracker.com/answer/adheres/ 0.9999999999999999   0.0   0   2.4
0.0 0.0 0   0   0   0   2   0   0.9999999999999999   0
1.090909090909091

Yahoo Sample Data Extract - Adheres

index	url	description	div	h1	h2	h3	h4	h5	h6	inbound_links	keywords	outbound_links	p	root	span	title

1   http://www.thefreedictionary.com/adheres   0.8458781362007167   3.0263273893007403
6.0 48.0   0   0   0   0   0   0.6033519553072626   171   0.0
1.2413793103448276   84.79654875000406   1.3333333333333335
2   http://www.thesaurus.com/browse/adheres   0.2903225806451613   2.7714285714285714   6.0
0.0 0   0   0   0   0   2.4406779661016946   14   0.7982062780269057
1.2857142857142856   23.454978354978348   1.44
3   https://en.wiktionary.org/wiki/adheres   0   0.0   5.142857142857142   0.0   0.0
0 0 0   0   0   20   0   1.2   0.0   1.8
4   http://www.macmillandictionary.com/dictionary/british/adhere-to   0.6585365853658537
0.0 0   0   0   0   0   0   0.5373134328358209   3   0.0
0.6923076923076924   22.800000000000008   0.5070422535211268
5   http://legal-dictionary.thefreedictionary.com/adhere
0.8044692737430167   0.6923076923076924   24.0   0   0   0   0   0
0   0.6136363636363636   270   0.0   0.7999999999999999   75.42857142857143
2.181818181818182
6   http://www.dictionary.com/browse/adhere   0.8046875   2.290826612903226   0   0
1.565217391304348   0   0   0   0   1.5999999999999999   27   0.0
1.2857142857142856   89.08416810050211   1.8
7   https://www.merriam-webster.com/dictionary/adhere 1.0989010989010988   0.0   6.0
41.251970638057564   0   0.0   0.0   0.0   0   0.6390532544378699   42   0.0
0.972972972972973   0.0   1.5
8   http://www.thesaurus.com/browse/adhere   0.2926829268292683   2.7714285714285714   6.0

0.0 0   0   0   0   0   2.618181818181818   14   0.7982062780269057
1.3333333333333335   24.109523809523804   1.5
9   http://www.adherishealth.com/   0   0.0   0.8181818181818181   0   0   0.0
0.0 0   0   0   7   0.3176672384219553   0.0   0.13584905660377358   0.0
10   https://en.wikipedia.org/wiki/Adhesion   0   0.0   0.0   0.0   0.0   0   0
0   0   0   56   0.34441164527323836   0.0   0.0   0.0
11   http://www.adherishealth.com/   0   0.0   0.8181818181818181   0   0   0.0
0.0 0   0   0   7   0.3176672384219553   0.0   0.13584905660377358   0.0
12   http://www.macmillandictionary.com/dictionary/british/adhere-to   0.6585365853658537
0.0 0   0   0   0   0   0   0.5373134328358209   3   0.0
0.6923076923076924   22.800000000000008   0.5070422535211268
13   https://phys.org/news/2016-10-superomniphobic-tape-adheres-surface.html   0   0.45
0.8372093023255814   0.0   0   0   0.0   0   0   0   53
0.2628430049482681   0.5714285714285714   0.0   0.8372093023255814
14   https://phys.org/chemistry-news/   0   0.0   0.0   0   0   0   0.0   0
0   0   29   0.09139616426604512   0.0   0.0   0.0
15   https://phys.org/chemistry-news/materials-science/   0   0.0   0.0   0   0   0
0   0   0   0   29   0.1501781624982447   0.0   0.0   0.0
16   http://www.definitions.net/definition/adheres   0.6857142857142857   0   0.0
0.0 0.0 0.0   0.0   0   0   1.7560975609756098   88   1.231578947368421
1.0588235294117647   0.0   1.565217391304348
17   http://www.foxsports.com/nfl/story/cam-newton-adheres-ron-riveras-dress-code-two-weeks-tie-
gate-121916   0.0   0   1.125   0   0   0   0   0   0   0   52
0.0 0.39999999999999997   0.0   1.125
18   https://www.collinsdictionary.com/dictionary/english/adhere   0.49999999999999994
8.733742682406312   1.6363636363636362   9.043407755581669   0   0   0   0
0   0   1   0.0   0.7659574468085105   67.10874200426434   1.2857142857142856
19   https://en.wikipedia.org/wiki/Adhesion   0   0.0   0.0   0.0   0.0   0   0
0   0   0   56   0.34441164527323836   0.0   0.0   0.0
20   http://atherys.com/   0   0   0   0.0   0   0   0   0   0   0
2   0.0 0.0   0   0.0
21   https://energy.gov/energysaver/caulking   0.0   0   0   0.0   0   0.0   0
0   0   0   5   0.935861729312612   0.0   0.0   0.0
22   https://en.wikipedia.org/wiki/Anders_Behring_Breivik   0   0.0   0.0   0.0   0.0
0   0   0   0   0   446   0.08955223880597014   0.0   0.0   0.0
23   http://www.adhereinc.com/   0.0   0   0   0.0   0   0   0   0   0
0   3   0.0   2.571428571428571   0.21951219512195122   0.0
24   http://www.freethesaurus.com/adheres   0.8047808764940239   1.0357142857142856
6.0 3.789473684210527   2.6166666666666663   0.0   0   0   0
0.9350649350649352   289   0.0   1.44   86.5714285714286   1.3333333333333335

SUMMARY

The creation of a data mining tool with the Python programming language was possible because of the rich utilities that are available. The incorporation of the NLTK library as well as the HTMLParser package was a tremendous help in creating the data files. This exercise was an example of the power that can be harnessed through opensource solutions and some elbow grease by way of a self-guided development effort. This effort highlights the possibilities that have become available to everyone through a simple protocol that from an onset had but a simple premise and which yet functioned to change humanity forever. The categorization of data has become such a driver for change that an entire profession now dedicates itself to it. Data science and data scientists have come to be because of the shear benefit that may be derived by understanding the hidden truth in the data if it can only be converted to information.

The solution presented here in Python allowed for the utilization of an external datastore, the search engine providers themselves as the repository for the source of the metrics needed. Given the open nature of the web and the ability to communicate with endpoints through simple coding constructs it allowed for the creation of a solution without the need to have painstakingly collected all the data manually. It should be noted that the same process was followed for the Google search engine, but different results were obtained as the search engine provider did a much better job to filter query requests. This is bound to be a paradigm that will be adopted by other search providers in the future, but until then the data is there for all to see and use. It should also be noted that the data output that was extracted for the Google search engine showed some level of consistency with the data of another search engine provider, which simply entails that part of the formula may already be inferred if not fully disclosed.

The creation of the solution presented here has specifically been made available for all to view for the purpose of complete disclosure. As has been stated previously, what truth mandates is that data be brought to the forefront for a discussion to part from. This is the narrative that science mandates because truth is independent of consequence or discussions that are to follow. In doing so it also facilitates the communication going forward as the central theme that was parted from is unbiased and clean in nature. This in part is the environment that all humanity currently subscribes to, a forum that is free and liberated from the confines of class or exclusion because all are free to take note of and leverage that which is before them. This point of leverage is exposed in the next chapter where it will be shown that the application of data science constructs to a data infused pipeline can have impactful results. Humanity is fortunate to live in a time and place whereby discovery is possible to all with a simple internet connection and a laptop to do the data collection, curating, and distilling. This is an age where discovery is to occur, and it is so because humanity has been empowered to drive change through the availability of data and the means by which said data may be harnessed.

These points that have been noted however dictate a reality that is external to the discussion of search and relates to development for the web, as by understanding what denotes significance for search systems translates to points of focus for development teams. It is not enough to collect the data and draw conclusions from said data, what is actually needed is the ability to extract meaning outside of the numeric entries tabulated. The data tells a story that invariably helps to paint a picture for what web development needs to migrate to, which is the essence of the message here. Web development will change to something different from what it is today because the data infers that it be such. Web development has been on an evolutionary path and the data disseminated here simply supports the argument for what future state appears to be headed to. It is a station whereby web development will become woven with the fabric that is ever present in the data that was collected as part of this endeavor in this chapter, which entails that development teams will need to come to appreciate what it means for the applications that are currently being developed and consequently for what it means for them and the applications that need to be developed in the years to come. Change is coming because the data mandates such and because search systems have become the measuring stick by which effective software systems are being judged by.

While the work of Jerkovic (2010) and King (2008) denoted the attributes of worth, what has been needed are the ramifications of the attributes of worth, which has been an unexplored dynamic because the data has been lacking. With data in hand however the arguments that may be made change since each assertion made can be supported by the metrics that may be called upon. In the next two chapters to follow the arguments by King (2008) and Jerkovic (2010) will be tested against that much needed plumb line. It will be this mechanism that will allow for the true story to be told and whereby through it will it become possible to definitively state how software solutions are to change.

REFERENCES

Jerkovic, J. (2010). *SEO Warrior*. O'Reilly Media Inc.

King, A. (2008). *Website Optimization*. O'Reilly Media Inc.

Chapter 6
Formulas

ABSTRACT

The formula is the golden grail that is sought by all, but in order to determine such, the protagonist must first set course on a journey that is void of a blueprint or a prescription that may be followed that will lead to such. This endeavor to find this path however is the burden of the investigator and the reason why much consternation arises, but when epiphany hits, life becomes altered and can never be understood quite the same from that moment forward. Society seeks this recourse to its ailments in different forms, but they are nevertheless just that, similar propositions in variant presentations, whether it be to map the course to the new world for Columbus or to understand motion as Newton; the challenge undertaken is all too similar, the answering of a question whose tribulation is but time away from extinction.

INTRODUCTION

Being able to predict behavior is the ultimate goal of management over any domain for which stewardship is given and as a consequence it should be a formula that is sought to facilitate determining order. Through such an endeavor it becomes feasible to manage because future state can be determined from present state. If a formula to eradicate cancer for example could be determined, then the rest would be a matter of details. In this scenario it would be that overarching process flow that humanity would simply interact with to manage future state. In this endeavor it has been the formula of worth that has been sought to help better understand how value of some node may be tabulated because in doing such it helps to understand how the message may be crafted to find favor with the search purveyors. In order to understand this formula, it has been necessary to have delved into the essence of what search is because by understanding it in its primitive form it facilitated being better able to understand how those base attributes of the class may be invoked by the encompassing functions to drive behavior. When such detail may be identified then it facilitates being able to understand how the practice of development needs to function to accommodate the sensitivity of the indexing domain. To understand relevance means to understand what is supposed to go where on a webpage without the subjectivity around it because by being able to follow a prescription the argument migrates to conform to the world view which is held by the search purveyors themselves. Being able to do this entails that applications built stand a higher

DOI: 10.4018/978-1-6684-4849-6.ch006

probability of wining the indexing race by way of the message that is crafted for consumption. The search providers are not going to broadcast what prescription needs to be followed because it goes against their proprietary magic sauce that makes them relevant and keeps their customers coming back to use their search system. In essence all the would be marketers need to change the discussion from one of "how can the search providers deem this application relevant" to "the application developed aligns with the prescription set forth by the search engines". Communication is much like tuning that old car radio where the knobs are turned to move across the stations and where at some point the static ceases to burden the ears of the listener and at which point harmony hits its audience. It is at this point that the volume needs to be adjusted upwards to drown out all else but the desired melody. The correct message needs to be crafted for the search purveyors to help them drown out the noise and by doing so letting them hear the music. This chapter is here to help clarify where that station resides to help all those would be marketers turn the dial to the correct frequency so that a better message may be conveyed to each of those search purveyors.

When a system definition is taken, and then raw computation power is applied to it the end result can be nothing less than spectacular at times. Computation power can solve a lot of issues, but without the adequate parameters for the investigative study the process is futile. There is a distinct difference between data and information. Data is verbiage, text that does not lead one towards any relevant conclusions. Information on the other hand is the organized data that leads one to be able to make sound decisions. The labyrinth of web documents and their indexing placement amount to nothing less than data. To the search providers it is information nevertheless because they understand how to decipher what is before them. This chapter seeks to turn this data into information and to do so what needs to occur is that a qualifiable premise migrate to a quantified doctrine. It is the indexing formula that is sought because by being able to understand how the data is transformed to information that it enables the deciphering of the landscape.

There is a great bounty that is made available to humanity when it migrates to a quantified mode of operandi, where the system attributes help to determine where homeostasis lay. The path from the qualifiable to the quantifiable is a mystery to humanity at times however because humanity fails to fully appreciate the attributes at hand and the magnitude of their influence on one another that ultimately leads to a perception that the behavior witnessed is simply chaos. Can you state why your competitors' application is ranked more favorably than your own? As was witnessed firsthand in the chapter on 'Prescriptions', following the style guide simply leads to points of confusion and contradiction because the domain has not been quantified by the search vendors. Society lives in this world of the maybes and the likely, which is void of control and assurance because the alternative has not been put forth. This discourse is the migration from the speculative to the quantifiable, to help shed light on the matter at hand. To meet this objective in this chapter the equations that predict search are formulated. Under this guise it becomes easier to understand cause and effect and as such facilitates the understanding of the datum point that is relevance.

It was Albert Einstein that said, "God does not play dice", the father of modern day physics believed one fundamental truism about life – all was deterministic. This chapter of the book utilizes regression modeling to derive the approximation equation for the indexing of two search engine providers – Bing and Yahoo. The regression formula created is a logistic regression that encompasses the systems perspective as it encompasses the page attributes, where the page is the system boundary. The index paradigm that is sought is such that given some index then there exists a functional definition that encompasses the system attributes that allows for the modeling of the behavior witnessed. The relationship given below depicts this definition that is sought, where the functional space is composed of a series of attributes x_1 to x_n and the index of the page is determined based upon some function governing the attributes of said system. And if this function governs the base attributes of the domain, it entails that its tabulation mandate that the dependent variable be deterministic.

Index $\rightarrow f(x_1, x_2, ..., x_n)$

The realm of the web is semi structured data where the structure of the documents is flexible and open to interpretation. HTML, the language of content formatting for the web is flexible to such a degree that it allows different views given the device that is being used. Given the content flux and the objective of the task at hand it then becomes a complex task to decipher relevance. Relevance is framed in the form of the systems perspective in this body of work where the playing field or domain is the page and the attributes that define the behavior of the entity or its index position if you will are directly proportional to the behavior of the attributes or the system variables as they have been defined in this body of work. In the sections to follow an approximation formula is derived for the search engine index values for both the Bing and Yahoo search engines. The formula that is derived in the first phase is consequently taken and an additional component is applied this being the link equity by node. It will be shown in this manner that the significance of link equity in a quantified manner is a clear differentiator to the value of relevance for web documents. This process takes the argument full circle form the qualified mode of operandi that has been constructed by the search purveyors to a quantified doctrine that formally discloses with impunity the significance of that which is indexed by the search purveyors. This enables the migration of the discussion from the I believe prefix to the data states prescription, which entails that from a data science perspective the argument has migrated to solid footing. This entails that the journey to the realm of the predictable and where business decisions can part from has been identified and consequently future discussions may part from.

The significance of the prescription that is being described here transcends the web development paradigm as it leads to the realization of the transformation that must occur within business itself. The mode by which relevance is deemed is in terms of clout and as such the intent of the business in their development efforts must change to create alignment with this mandate and as a consequence of which it will be those businesses that are able to harness this dynamic that will become the new bastions of relevance. This message that must be crafted will be receptive to an audience because of the derived benefit which it will afford. Businesses that are able to leverage this dynamic will in turn find themselves having clout because the masses will deem this to be so. This is the prescription that has befallen the profession and the development space, which is presented in this chapter through a mathematical study.

PARAMATERIZATION

The first set of formulas that will be derived are the index approximations to the search space for both Bing and Yahoo. These functions are void of the link equity attribute and as such the attributes implemented include those defined below where the page index (I) is a function of the five attributes as defined in equation 1. The boundary constraint that is defined here is void of the link equity to help facilitate the investigative process purely and simply. It helps to proceed in an incremental fashion by first determining if viability can be reached without further complication and as such helps to determine if alignment can be found with the style guide from Google from an onset. There can be no need to complicate the problem frame if a simplistic model will suffice, which is investigated first here.

Let

A = Anchor Text
C = Page Copy
I = Search Index
M = Meta Tags
T = Title Tag
U = URL

Where:

I= f(A, C, M, T, U)   (1)

The relationship defined above entails that index value is a function of content copy, anchor text, meta tags, the title tag, and node URL. What you will notice from the above relationship is that the definition is qualified, it is void of a numerical context. What is sought is a computational framework where each attribute is measurable. This may be achieved by an enhancement to the model defined previously and which equation 2 below depicts.

Let

S = Search Engine Index
B_n = Slope of Component 'n'
D = Keywords / Total Words in Description
I = Inbound Links
K = Keywords / Total Words in Keywords
O = Outbound Links
P = Keywords / Total Words in Page Copy
T = Keywords / Total Words in Title
U = Keywords / Total Words in URL

Where:

$S = B_1 D * B_2 I * B_3 K * B_4 O * B_5 P * B_6 T * B_7 U + \mu$ (2)

In the model definition from above the variable 'P' for example is a composite variable where page copy is defined as the summation of the copy tags, which include the header tags, paragraph tags, division tags, and span tags. This can be stated formally as follows below in equation 3.

Let

P = Page Copy Index
DI = Division Tag Copy Index
H1 = Header Tag One Index

H2 = Header Tag Two Index
H3 = Header Tag Three Index
H4 = Header Tag Four Index
H5 = Header Tag Five Index
H6 = Header Tag Six Index
PA = Paragraph Tag Index
SP = Span Tag Index

Where:

$$P = DI + H_1 + H_2 + H_3 + H_4 + H_5 + H_6 + PA + SP$$

Giving:

$$P = B_{51}DI + B_{52}H_1 + B_{53}H_2 + B_{54}H_3 + B_{55}H_4 + B_{56}H_5 + B_{57}H_6 + B_{58}PA + B_{59}SP \tag{3}$$

The page copy content is the amalgamation of all content tag elements. This allows the derivation of the complete indexing formula that is given next in equation 4. Table 1 below summarizes the attribute system relationship. Given the flexibility that is afforded to manipulate page content it becomes imperative to be able to combine the copy text together into one all encompassing component as has been done here. The remaining attributes have been segregated because of the clear lines of partition that exists amongst them.

$$S = B_1D * B_2I * B_3K * B_4O * (B_{51}DI + B_{52}H_1 + B_{53}H_2 + B_{54}H_3 + B_{55}H_4 + B_{56}H_5 + B_{57}H_6 + B_{58}PA + B_{59}SP) * B_6T * B_7U + \mu \tag{4}$$

Table 1. Attribute to Model Mapping

Attribute	Model
Index	S – Search Engine Index
URL	U – URL Index
Meta Tag Description	D – Meta Tag Description Index
Division Tag	P – Page Copy Index
Header One – Header Six Tag	
Paragraph Tag	
Span Tag	
Inbound Links	I – Inbound Links
Meta Tag Keywords	K – Meta Tag Keywords Index
Outbound Links	O – Outbound Links
Title Tag	T – Title Index

Given the data collected data plots were created to determine if a linear relationship existed between the dependent variable – page index and the independent variables as defined in the table from above. The plots are shown in figures 1 and 2; the R statistical modeling tool was utilized for the creation of these graphs. The significance of the data plots cannot be understated as it is a direct indication that the relationship between search index and system variables is complex. There does not exist one factor of influence that determines the value of the dependent variable. This does lead the discussion to the realization that system state will not be able to be mapped by way of a singular parameter constraint such as would be found in the relationship $y = mx + b$. This is concrete proof that shows that the search engine providers are using a non-trivial proposition when determining worth. Equation 4 highlights this complex dynamic as it is a composite of the system attributes that have been identified. You will also find that like attributes are combined in the formula; content tags are brought together under one umbrella to create a unified dynamic over the document space. As was pointed out in previous chapters the creation of content is dynamic given the availability of cascading style sheets (CSS) and JavaScript. With the aid of the styling libraries, it is completely possible to modify layout content so that the textual version of the document is completely distinct from the visual representation of the HTML definition. This is the reason why equation 4 shows the content elements grouped together, thus giving each parity in the encompassing formula.

The ability to create a deterministic model whereby understanding can be translated to a metrics context from a qualified context represents a progression in the paradigm whereby prediction starts to peak over the horizon and transitions to a norm. The understanding of the paradigm at hand has been an elusive prize however given the dynamic nature of the factors that bear influence upon the page. This understanding has also been hampered by the commingling of attributes within the system boundary, which has simply worked to confound the problem frame even further. Added to this punchbowl is the fact that the argument has been void of a metrics doctrine simply helps to clarify the magnitude of the disjoint that has existed between truly understanding and being forced to accept blindly what has been conveyed to be. The work of Jerkovic (2010) and King (2008) allowed for the argument to be understood in a better light, whereby this truth that was sought could be categorized so that the relationship of worth could be understood better. The problem however lay in the argument itself and which may be verified by the plots in figures 1 and 2, there does not exist a driving relationship for worth from any one of the attributes that has been categorized up to now. The problem frame has in fact been more complex than could be understood from a basic cause and effect dynamic. Each of the attributes of the page have in fact acted in such a manner that their influence on page index has been but a zero sum game. The elevation of one factor of influence simply works to deteriorate the benefit of another. The relationship between the system variables is in fact dynamic with search indexing that can only be understood if the parameters that govern behavior are amalgamated in just the right manner. The deciphering of this dynamic is no easy task to say the least, but as was stated previously it is that road that is perilous and plagued with strife, which can lead to an epiphany if the correct combination can be found.

It was because of this apparent complexity of the problem frame that led to the determination that a type of regression needed to be embraced, whereby the variables of influence could be amalgamated into a model that would facilitate the determination of the dependent variable. Given the availability of statistical modeling tools such as R however the process of discovery becomes facilitated and helps to lead the discovery process forward whereby it becomes as little of a burden as it can possibly be given the computational power that is now afforded through a personal computer. It was because of this dynamic that it become possible to leverage the data under different scenarios that allowed for the clearing of the path forward whereby solutions could be investigated and help the data disclose the secret it held tightly to its breast pocket. Discovery at times becomes much like the deciphering of an encrypted message and when it does occur it becomes just cause for celebration. It was because of this process that a road was found, and it was found to have been lit and paved for the comfort of all those who care to travel down its path. It was through this process, and which will be demonstrated in the pages to follow that indexing clout can be determined by a formula, to a high degree.

It might be just the case that Einstein was correct in his assertion of truth, and it is simply humanities fallibility that leads to alternative recourses whereby being in error is diminished by the subjectivity of the argument that is put forth. To reinforce this notion let the argument proceed by putting the possibility forward that the search engine providers might in fact be using a deterministic model to determine page worth.

Figure 1. Bing Pair Relationship Plots in R

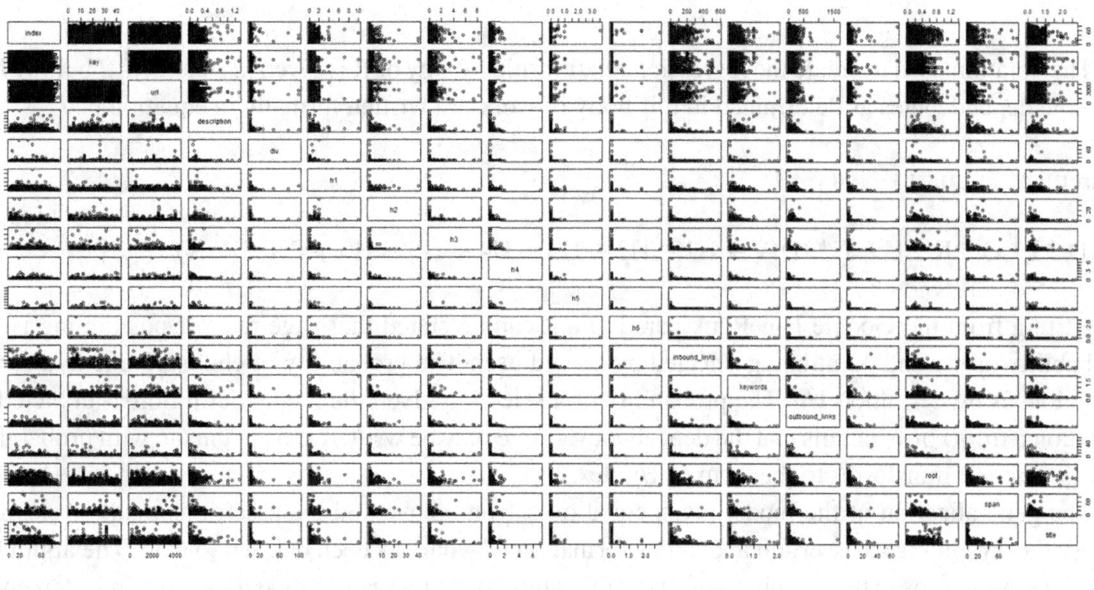

REGRESSION

The data that was fed into the R statistical tool can be found for each of the Bing and Yahoo search engines in folders named by engine type and in files named _complete_r.dat, the partial content of these files may be found below for both the Yahoo and Bing search engines respectively. The R syntax used to import that dataset into R is shown below in statement 1. The 'FILE' parameter represents the file to import including the file path, SEPERATOR designates the data character that separates content, and the header attribute is set to T for true, which designates the import file as having a header line.

Statement 1: lm.data → read.table('FILE', sep = 'SEPERATOR', header = 'T')

Figure 2. Yahoo Pair Relationship Plots in R

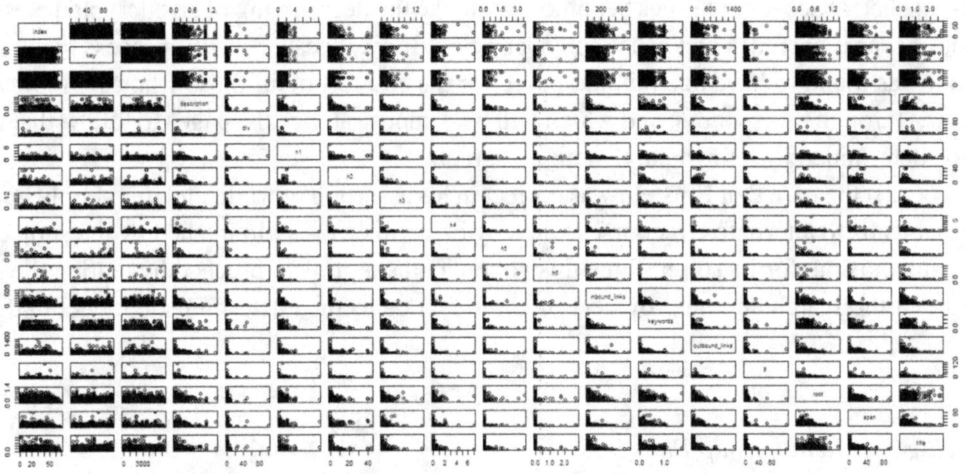

The notation used to create the regression relationship by way of R is given in statement 2 below. The variable dependencies as determined in this body of work are written formally in equation 5.

Statement 2: lm.fit ← lm(y~x)

$$S = D * I * O * K * U * T * (DIV + H1 + H2 + H3 + H4 + H5 + H6 + P + SPAN) \tag{5}$$

Parting from the Google PageRank paradigm, it can be stated that page rank or positioning is the probability of the end point being selected by an end user. The probability of choosing one in a series of options is by definition 1/n. The probability of a selection given the model definition as depicted in equation 5 from above entails that the dependent variable may be written to be in unison with probability theory where it transforms to the form of 1/index.

The generalization of the model given equation 5 from above and the assertions made over probability theory entails an assertion and a transformation of what has been defined to date. The argument therefore transforms to the definition of a generalization to the regression model as given in statement 3.

Statement 3:

$$\text{lm.fit} \leftarrow \text{lm}\left(\frac{1}{S} \sim D*I*O*K*U*T*(DIV + H1 + H2 + H3 + H4 + H5 + H6 + P + SPAN)\right)$$

There is a point of interest in the model defined in statement 3 above and that being that some of the attributes are added while others are multiplied, which by definition implies that some variables experience an interaction while others do not. Variables that are multiplied as opposed to summed entails that these variables experience a more complex dynamic than they would otherwise. Another point of interest in the above equation is that the textual attributes as they relate to page content which is physically viewed by an audience are grouped together which entails that these variables form a singular synergy upon the statement expression and in a manner act in unison to affect homeostasis. The charts depicted in figures 1 and 2 signaled that a more complex cause and effect relationship was seen in the system that could not simply be modeled in a unitary manner. The argument presented in statement 3 also allows for the realization of the systems context to come through as it is the complete set of system attributes that are made to bear upon prediction and whereby cause and effect becomes a manifestation of the inherent underlying attributes of the system.

The exercise that was performed here highlights the integration of the systems doctrine with the quantitative doctrine whereby it is because of the base elements of the attributes that worth may be able to be determined. The R statistical package simply functions as the vehicle to be able to validate the initial premise that is undertaken. Much as the argument was made at the onset that it is because of the base elements of the class that drive worth, so too can the argument be mad here that the base case persists whereby each of the variables depicted in statement 3 are but these class level attributes. In a similar manner the regression calculation can be viewed as that function call within the encompassing class definition that is the container for those variables identified. It is an argument that facilitates the return to an all too familiar paradigm that is well understood and embraced by the development community and which should facilitate the discourse.

Yahoo Search Engine Sample Data

index   key   url   description   div   h1   h2   h3   h4   h5   h6   inbound_links   keywords   outbound_links   p   root   span   title

8.0   adheres   http://www.thefreedictionary.com/adheres   0.14695340501792115   0.5685033059507112   1.0   8.0   0   0   0   0   0   0.1005586592178771   171   0.0   0.20689655172413793   14.317943310185873   0.2222222222222222

9.166666666666666   adheres   http://www.thesaurus.com/browse/adheres   0.04838709677419355   1.5571428571428572   1.0   0.0   0   0   0   0   0   0.4067796610169492   14   0.19282511210762332   0.21428571428571427   8.286147186147186   0.24

6.5   adheres   https://en.wiktionary.org/wiki/adheres   0   0.0   0.8571428571428571   0.0   0.0   0   0   0   0   0   20   0   0.2   0.0   0.3

6.666666666666667   adheres   http://www.macmillandictionary.com/dictionary/british/adhere-to   0.10975609756097561   0.0   0   0   0   0   0   0   0   0.08955223880597014   3   0.0   0.11538461538461539   3.8   0.08450704225352113

6.4   adheres   http://legal-dictionary.thefreedictionary.com/adhere   0.1340782122905028   0.11538461538461539   4.0   0   0   0   0   0   0   0.10227272727272728   270   0.0   0.13333333333333333   12.571428571428571   0.36363636363636365

11.5   adheres   http://www.dictionary.com/browse/adhere   0.21875   0.6048387096774194   0   0   0.2608695652173913   0   0   0   0   0.26666666666666666   27   0.0   0.21428571428571427   14.847361350083672   0.3

12.666666666666666   adheres   https://www.merriam-webster.com/dictionary/adhere   0.27472527472527475   0.0   1.0   6.875328439676265   0   0.0   0.0   0.0   0   0   42   0.0   0.16216216216216217   0.0   0.25

8.2   adheres   http://www.thesaurus.com/browse/adhere   0.04878048780487805   1.5571428571428572   1.0   0.0   0   0   0   0   0   0.43636363636363634   14   0.19282511210762332   0.2222222222222222   8.395238095238096   0.25

9.571428571428571   adheres   http://www.adherishealth.com/   0   0.0   0.13636363636363635

0   0   0.0   0.0   0   5   0   7   0.05294453973699256   0.0   0.022641509433962263   0.0
12.666666666666666   adheres   https://en.wikipedia.org/wiki/Adhesion   0   0.0   0.0   0.0
0.0   0   0   0   5   0   56   0.18143798379105275   0.0   0.0   0.0
13.6   adheres   https://phys.org/news/2016-10-superomniphobic-tape-adheres-surface.html   0
0.075   0.13953488372093023   0.0   0   0   0.0   0   0   0   53   0.049291497975708504
0.09523809523809523   0.0   0.13953488372093023
14.6   adheres   https://phys.org/chemistry-news/   0   0.0   0.0   0   0   0   0.0   0   1   0
28   0.07361838648826734   0.0   0.0   0.0
15.6   adheres   https://phys.org/chemistry-news/materials-science/   0   0.0   0.0   0   0   0
0   0   0   28   0.1326343028491219   0.0   0.0   0.0
16.8   adheres   http://www.definitions.net/definition/adheres   0.11428571428571428   0
0.0   0.0   0.0   0.0   0.0   0   0   0.2926829268292683   88   0.20526315789473684
0.17647058823529413   0.0   0.2608695652173913
18.0   adheres   http://www.foxsports.com/nfl/story/cam-newton-adheres-ron-riveras-dress-code-two-weeks-tiegate-121916   0.0   0   0.1875   0   0   0   0   0   0   0   52   0.0
0.06666666666666667   0.0   0.1875
16.75   adheres   https://www.collinsdictionary.com/dictionary/english/adhere
0.08333333333333333   1.637416497487887   0.2727272727272727   1.507234625930278
0   0   0   0   0   0   1   0.0   0.1276595744680851   11.184790334044065
0.21428571428571427
19.25   adheres   http://atherys.com/   0   0   0   0.0   0   0   0   0   62   0   2   0.0   0.0
0   0.0
24.2   adheres   https://energy.gov/energysaver/caulking   0.0   0   0   0.0   0   0.0   0   0
0   0   5   0.24465284307920215   0.0   0.0   0.0
22.0   adheres   https://en.wikipedia.org/wiki/Anders_Behring_Breivik   0   0.0   0.0   0.0
0.0   0   0   0   50   0   446   0.08955223880597014   0.0   0.0   0.0
21.2   adheres   http://www.adhereinc.com/   0.0   0   0   0.0   0   0   0   0   2   0   3
0.0   0.42857142857142855   0.036585365853658534   0.0
32.42857142857143   adheres   http://www.freethesaurus.com/adheres   0.26693227091633465
0.20238095238095238   1.0   0.631578947368421   1.6166666666666667   0.0   0   0   0
0.15584415584415584   289   0.0   0.24   14.428571428571432   0.2222222222222222
23.75   adheres   http://idioms.thefreedictionary.com/adhere+to   0.12080536912751678
0.20353037766830867   0.6666666666666666   2.0   0   0   0   0   77   0.0972972972972973
162   0.0   0.15789473684210525   11.297323317867562   0.14634146341463414
24.5   adheres   http://www.spanishdict.com/translate/adhere   0.05172413793103448   2.0   1.0
0   0   0.0   0   0   0   0   12   0   0.1875   5.133941532217395   0.12
27.0   adheres   http://www.startribune.com/body-shop-kyle-rudolph-adheres-to-strict-regimen-to-get-from-game-to-game/407159016/   0.0   0.0   0.08108108108108109   0   0.0   0.0   0   0
3   0   28   0.0   0.06   0.0   0.07058823529411765
28.0   adheres   http://www.yourdictionary.com/adhere   0.15677966101694915
0.5732295142751205   0   4.111111111111111   0.0   0.17142857142857143   0   0   0
0.16759776536312848   7   0.75   0.24   1.0   0.26666666666666666
31.0   adheres   http://www.wilsonart.com/adhesives-products   0.029411764705882353   0.0
0.0   0.0   0   0.0   0   0   1   0.04597701149425287   23   0.0   0.0   0.0   0.0

32.0 adheres http://www.dictionary.com/browse/adhered 0.21705426356589147 0.6048387096774194 0 0 0.25 0 0 0 0 0.2553191489361702 27 0.0 0.20689655172413793 15.2759327786551 0.2857142857142857

32.333333333333336 adheres http://www.krylon.com/products/fusion-for-plastic/ 0 0.0 0 0.0 0.0 0.0 0 0.0 137 0 13 0.07407407407407407 0.0 0.06908300860600691 0.0

32.42857142857143 adheres https://quizlet.com/18261529/chapter-13-dental-caries-flash-cards/ 0.0 0.0 0.0 0 0 0 0 0.0 0 0 2 0.0 0.0 0.34383394383394383 0.0

36.0 adheres https://www.muslima.com/ 0.0 0.0 0.0 0.0 0.0 0.0 0 0 27 0.0 51 0.022304832713754646 0.0 0.0 0.0

33.333333333333336 adheres https://www.rackspace.com/security/global-enterprise 0.0 0.0 0.0 0.0 0.0 0.0 0.0 0.0 1 0 11 0.069110809915992471 0.0 0.0 0.0

40.42857142857143 adheres http://www.colliervilleschools.org/ 0.0 0.024793388429752067 0 0 0 0 0 0 19 0.0 18 0.0 0.0 0.0 0.0

Bing Search Engine Sample Data

index key url description div h1 h2 h3 h4 h5 h6 inbound_links key-words outbound_links p root span title

1.0 adheres http://www.oxforddictionaries.com/us/ 0.0 0 0.0 0.0 0 0.0 0 0 498 0.0 14 0.0 0.0 0.0 0.0

17.181818181818183 adheres http://www.thefreedictionary.com/adheres 0.14695340501792115 0.5685033059507112 1.0 8.0 0 0 0 0 0 0.1005586592178771 171 0.0 0.20689655172413793 14.317943310185873 0.2222222222222222

14.285714285714286 adheres http://legal-dictionary.thefreedictionary.com/adheres 0.13114754098360656 0.11320754716981132 4.0 0 0 0 0 0 0 0.1005586592178771 266 0.0 0.13043478260869565 11.428571428571429 0.34285714285714286

15.88888888888889 adheres http://medical-dictionary.thefreedictionary.com/adheres 0.17964071856287425 0.10909090909090909 1.0 0 0 0 0 0 0 0.1005586592178771 173 0.0 0.125 12.000000000000002 0.22641509433962265

16.333333333333332 adheres http://www.thesaurus.com/browse/adheres 0.04838709677419355 1.5571428571428572 1.0 0.0 0 0 0 0 0 0.4067796610169492 14 0.19282511210762332 0.21428571428571427 8.286147186147186 0.24

19.90909090909091 adheres http://www.dictionary.com/browse/adhere 0.21875 0.6048387096774194 0 0 0.2608695652173913 0 0 0 0 0.26666666666666666 27 0.0 0.21428571428571427 14.847361350083672 0.3

9.666666666666666 adheres http://www.macmillandictionary.com/dictionary/british/adhere-to 0.10975609756097561 0.0 0 0 0 0 0 0 0 0.08955223880597014 3 0.0 0.11538461538461539 3.8 0.08450704225352113

10.333333333333334 adheres http://www.adherishealth.com/ 0 0.0 0.13636363636363635 0 0 0.0 0.0 0 5 0 7 0.05294453973699256 0.0

0.022641509433962263   0.0

24.1   adheres   https://www.merriam-webster.com/dictionary/adhere   0.27472527472527475
0.0   1.0   6.875328439676265   0   0.0   0.0   0.0   0   0   42   0.0
0.16216216216216217   0.0   0.25

10.0   adheres   https://en.m.wiktionary.org/wiki/adheres   0   0.0   0.8571428571428571   0.0
0   0   0   0   1   0   2   0   0.1875   0.0   0.3

11.0   adheres   https://en.m.wikipedia.org/wiki/Adhesion   0   0.21739130434782608   0.0
0.0   0   0   0   0   1   0   5   0.18143798379105275   0.0   0.0   0.0

12.0   adheres   https://en.wikipedia.org/wiki/Adhesion_Surface_energy   0   0.0   0.0   0.0
0.0   0   0   0   9   0   56   0.18143798379105275   0.0   0.0   0.0

13.0   adheres   https://en.wikipedia.org/wiki/Adhesion_Mechanisms_of_adhesion   0   0.0   0.0
0.0   0.0   0   0   0   9   0   56   0.18143798379105275   0.0   0.0   0.0

14.0   adheres   https://en.wikipedia.org/wiki/Adhesion_Strength   0   0.0   0.0   0.0   0.0   0
0   0   6   0   56   0.18143798379105275   0.0   0.0   0.0

15.0   adheres   https://en.wikipedia.org/wiki/Adhesion_Other_effects   0   0.0   0.0   0.0   0.0
0   0   0   9   0   56   0.18143798379105275   0.0   0.0   0.0

12.75   adheres   http://sentence.yourdictionary.com/adhere   0.18   0.0   0
0.40384615384615385   0.0   0.17142857142857143   0   0   0   0.18   92   0.0
0.17647058823529413   1.0   0.23529411764705882

24.5   adheres   http://www.definitions.net/definition/adheres   0.11428571428571428   0
0.0   0.0   0.0   0.0   0.0   0   0   0.2926829268292683   88   0.20526315789473684
0.17647058823529413   0.0   0.2608695652173913

13.666666666666666   adheres   https://en.wiktionary.org/wiki/adheres   0   0.0
0.8571428571428571   0.0   0.0   0   0   0   0   0   20   0   0.2   0.0   0.3

19.2   adheres   https://phys.org/news/2016-10-superomniphobic-tape-adheres-surface.html   0
0.075   0.13953488372093023   0.0   0   0   0.0   0   0   0   53   0.0492914979759708504
0.09523809523809523   0.0   0.13953488372093023

20.2   adheres   https://phys.org/chemistry-news/   0   0.0   0.0   0   0   0   0.0   0   2   0
28   0.07361838648826734   0.0   0.0   0.0

21.666666666666668   adheres   http://atherys.com/   0   0   0   0.0   0   0   0   0   76   0
2   0.0   0.0   0   0.0

26.333333333333332   adheres   https://quizlet.com/1781827/excretory-system-flash-cards/   0.0
0.0   0.0   0   0   0   0   0.0   0   0   2   0.0   0.0   0.06   0.0

23.333333333333332   adheres   https://en.wikipedia.org/wiki/Anders_Behring_Breivik   0   0.0
0.0   0.0   0.0   0   0   0   60   0   446   0.08955223880597014   0.0   0.0   0.0

26.666666666666668   adheres   http://crosswordtracker.com/answer/ad-
heres/   0.16666666666666666   0.0   0   0.4   0.0   0.0   0   0   0   0   2   0
0.16666666666666666   0   0.18181818181818182

26.333333333333332   adheres   http://idioms.thefreedictionary.com/adhere+to
0.12080536912751678   0.20353037766830867   0.6666666666666666   2.0   0   0   0
0   83   0.09729729729729730   162   0.0   0.15789473684210525   11.297323317867562
0.14634146341463414

27.0   adheres   http://www.adhereinc.com/   0.0   0   0   0.0   0   0   0   0   2   0   3
0.0   0.42857142857142855   0.036585365853658534   0.0

32.0 adheres http://www.freethesaurus.com/adheres 0.26693227091633465 0.20238095238095238 1.0 0.631578947368421 1.6166666666666667 0.0 0 0 0 0.15584415584415584 289 0.0 0.24 14.428571428571432 0.2222222222222222 29.0 adheres https://quizlet.com/9557650/serous-membranes-flash-cards/ 0.0 0.0 0.0 0 0 0 0 0.0 0 0 2 0.0 0.0 0.22022955523672882 0.0 35.142857142857146 adheres http://www.audioenglish.org/dictionary/adhere.htm 0.11494252873563218 1.0 1.0 0 0 0 0 0 0 0.06666666666666667 0 4.061009973961781 0.15789473684210525 1.8571428571428572 0.06315789473684211 29.5 adheres http://www.foxsports.com/nfl/story/cam-newton-adheres-ron-riveras-dress-code-two-weeks-tiegate-121916 0.0 0 0.1875 0 0 0 0 0 0 0 52 0.0 0.06666666666666667 0.0 0.1875 28.833333333333332 adheres http://www.spanishdict.com/translate/adhere 0.05172413793103448 2.0 1.0 0 0 0.0 0 0 0 0 12 0 0.1875 5.133941532217395 0.12

QUALITY METRIC

The metrics that have been identified and placed into a modeling paradigm up to now are page centric. It is with an additional element that the paradigm is enhanced to yield a new derivative. This paradigm shift is to serve the purpose of utilizing a quality metric of the nodes that point to the sink. The quality metric is defined here as follows.

The quality aspect of the nodes that point to some sink can be measured by way of the system attributes of the source documents, whereby the source documents are compared to the query to derive a measured value of the relative impact of the query term for the source.

The quality metric of the nodes that point to the sink are calculated by equation 6 as given below. Let

c = Copy index which is the sum of the query terms copy text divided by the sum of the words in page copy
d = Description index which is equal to the sum of the description query terms divided by the sum of the words in the description
k = Keywords index which is the sum of keywords in the keyword attribute divided by the sum of the words in the attribute
t = Title index which is the sum of the keywords in the title attribute divided by the sum of the words in the title
u = URL index which is the sum of keywords in the URL divided by the sum of words in the URL
w = Weighted index

Where:

$$w_i = \sum c_i + \sum d_i + \sum k_i + \sum t_i + \sum u_i \tag{6}$$

In the above noted equation (6) the weighted index is a measure of the relative impact of the query term(s) on the nodes that point to the sink. Equation 6 can be used to create a total weight index that may be defined by equation 7 as given below.

Let

N = Number of sources
SS_T = Source to sink ratio

Where:

$$SS_T = \left(\sum c + \sum d + \sum k + \sum t + \sum u \right) / n \tag{7}$$

Equation 7 when combined with equation 2 results in the definition of equation 8 as given below. This new definition for index value is comprised of the same attributes previously defined with one addendum and this being the relative worthiness of the inbound links to the sink relative to the query term(s).

$$S = B_1 D * B_2 I * B_3 K * B_4 O * B_5 P * B_6 T * B_7 U + B_8 SS_T + \mu \tag{8}$$

Equation 8 will be evaluated for each of the search engine providers to determine goodness of fit for the paradigm shift that was presented here. This paradigm shift essentially serves the purpose of weighing the quality of the inbound links relative to the query term(s) provided. This delta when added to the original indexing formula 2 yields an enhanced model that as will be shown produces positive results for the approximation formula of Yahoo specifically. The incorporation of the quality of inbound links places the paradigm under study in a consistent state with the work of King (2008) and Jerkovic (2010) and helps to create alignment with the factor of relevance that has been termed link equity. With this iteration of the regression formula, it helps to create consistency across all system variables that have been identified from the research literature and helps to put the context under study with what has been deemed to be proper and sound with search engine indexing prominence.

BING

The utilization of equation 8 over the data set collected for the Bing search engine allowed for an optimization to be identified; this optimization was a direct result of raising the index variable to an exponent, which was determined to be the quantity of independent variables in the equation. The transformation that resulted as a consequence of this is give in statement 4 below.

Statement 4:

$$\text{lm.fit} \leftarrow \text{lm}\left(\frac{1}{s^{15}} \sim D*I*O*K*U*T*(DIV + H1 + H2 + H3 + H4 + H5 + H6 + P + SPAN) \right)$$

Taking statement 4 and applying the paradigm given by the PageRank formula where inbound and outbound links are placed in relationship to one another allows for another transformation to occur. The variable set defined in statement 4 however encompasses more than two simple components, taking these remaining attributes and binding them to the page or the outbound link component allows for the definition of the R proposition that is made in statement 5. You will notice in this definition that a binomial distribution is to be utilized in the calculation.

Statement 5:

$$lm.fit \leftarrow lm\left(\frac{1}{S^{15}} \sim \frac{I}{\begin{array}{c} D*O*K*U*T* \\ (DIV+H1+H2+H3+H4+H5+H6+P+SPAN) \end{array}}, family = 'binomial'\right)$$

Statement 5 was implemented in the R statistical tool utilizing the _complete_r.dat file with a total of 7,055 entries that were provided in part for the reader previously. Through the use of the summary function in R it resulted in equation 9 being produced.

$$\log\left(\frac{p}{1-p}\right) = \frac{1}{S^{15}} = 1.198e12 * I / ((-2.88e12)*U*(-3.866e10)*O*(-5.963e12)*T$$
$$*(-1.017e14)*D*(-5.387e14)*K*((-8.851e12)*DIV + (-9.563e13)$$
$$*H1+(3.953e12)*H2+(-6.215e13)*H3+(8.406e13)*H4+(2.060e18)$$
$$*H5+(-2.888e13)*H6+(-2.637e13)*P+(1.522e13)*SPAN)) - 4.069e14$$

(9)

Utilization of the ROC function in R allows for the creation of the ROC plot that is given below in Fig. 3. The area under the curve of the ROC plot shows to be 0.4242. Given that the tabulated value of the ROC plot is below the threshold of 50% it entails that the model created here does not meet the minimum factor for consideration. What this entails is that the dynamic of at hand is more complex or needs to be modeled in another manner in order to be able to find conformance between the theoretical and the actual. This factor of determination was performed without taking into consideration the quality metric however, which is tabulated next. The number determined however is significant since a threshold of 50% is within eyesight of being obtained, so while the model defined here did fall short from what is needed, there can be comfort in understanding that some level of prediction was obtained that is approaching a better scenario than a blindfold test.

It should also be pointed out that while the model created here simulates a dynamic whereby the systems doctrine is taken as the plumb line, it does not entail that the formula being used by the search purveyor is in fact in alignment with this premise. The formula that is being used by the Bing search engine could in fact be void of some of the system attributes that were identified. As an additional investigative study, it would be interesting to part from the premise that the search system is in fact not subscribing to the doctrine of systems theory and if a true representation could be determined then it would help to understand why in fact this particular system is less performant than others.

Figure 3. Bing Receiver Operating Characteristic Curve (ROC)

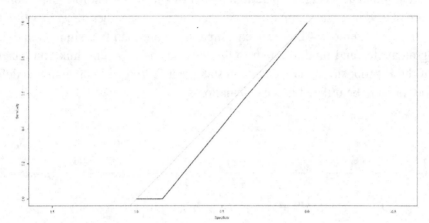

Figure 4. Bing Quality Metric Receiver Operating Characteristic Curve (ROC)

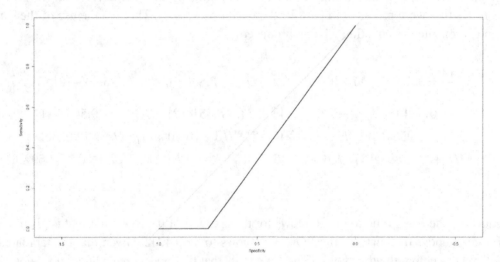

In the data repository you will find a file named _historical_complete_r.dat that contains the quantified quality attribute for the inbound links. You will also find a sample data set from this file at the end of the chapter. The utilization of this data set through the R statistical tool on the regression model is given as statement 6 below and for which it yields the regression formula defined as equation 10 below.

Statement 6:

$$\text{lm.fit} \leftarrow \text{glm}\left(\frac{Inbound\ Links * Quality}{\begin{array}{l} Root * Outbound\ Link * Title * Description * Keywords \\ *(Div + H1 + H2 + H3 + H4 + H5 + H6 + P + Span) \end{array}}, \text{family} = \text{'binomial'}\right)$$

$$\log\left(\frac{p}{1-p}\right) = \frac{1}{\text{index}^{15}}$$

$$= \frac{(1.816e12)*\textit{inboud}*(-2.183e11)*\textit{quality}}{(8.299e10)*\textit{root}*(-6.009e7)*\textit{outbound\_links}} - 4.052e15$$

$$*(-5.643e10)*\textit{title}*(-8.159e11)*\textit{description}$$

$$*(4.966e12)*\textit{keyowrds}*[(1.036e11)*\textit{div}+(-5.951e11)$$

$$*h1+(-8.875e11)*h2+(6.512e9)*h3+(2.281e14)*h5+(1.132e12)$$

$$*h6+(-7.327e9)*p+(-1.695e10)*\textit{span}]$$

$$(10)$$

Figure 4 was derived through the summary function in R which gives an area under the curve of 0.375. This results in a degradation of 5% from the previous model provided. The Bing prediction formula could not account for the quality metric of the inbound links and as a result the prediction factor dropped when this metric was incorporated into the formula. The ramifications of the calculations determined here allude to the possibility that the Bing search engine does not factor into consideration the quality of referrals to a target domain, which is distinct than what is seen with the Yahoo search engine as will be seen in the next section.

The regression to a lower predictive value highlights the degree of skewness that was obtained in the second iteration of the process. The example highlights the fact that while system variables may be available for model utilization, the degree of the variable coefficients and the quantity of attributes incorporated becomes the decision of the implementor.

YAHOO

The Yahoo data may be found in a sub folder of the Yahoo folder named data. Within the data folder there exists a file named _complete_r.dat. The data contained within this folder was imported into the R statistical modeling tool, and for which statement 7 was utilized. The regression model defined below utilized a binomial distribution for its goodness of fit.

Statement 7:

$$lm.fit \leftarrow glm\left(\frac{1}{\text{index}} \sim \textit{keywords} * \textit{root} * \textit{title} * \textit{inbound links} * \textit{outbound links} * \textit{description}\right.$$
$$\left. *(\textit{div} + h1 + h2 + h3 + h4 + h5 + h6 + \textit{paragraph} + \textit{span}), \textit{family} = '\textit{binomial}'\right)$$

As was the case for the Bing data model an iterative process was followed to determine the optimal value of the exponent factor for the index variable and for which the value of 1 was determined. The data summary provided by R for the logistic regression resulted in equation 11 being generated.

$$\log\left(\frac{p}{1-p}\right) = \frac{1}{index} = (1.867e15)*keywords*(2.025e15)*root*(1.88e15)*title$$
$$*(-2.487e12)*inbound\ links*(-1.671e12)*outbound\ links*(2.877e15)*description$$
$$*[(-1.786e14)*div+(7.990e14)*h1+(3.239e14)*h2+(1.692e14)*h3+(-2.83015)$$
$$*h4+(1.001e16)*h5+(3.773e16)*h6+(4.123e13)*p+(2.270e12)*span]-1.272e15$$

(11)

Utilization of the ROC function in R allowed for the derivation of the ROC plot as given in figure 5. The calculation of the area under the curve for the ROC plot was determined to be 0.5333. This value proves to show consistency with that tabulated for the Bing search engine, thus showing parity between the two systems through a supervised learning model.

The incorporation of the quality metric into statement 7 yielded an optimization to the paradigm. Statement 8 defines the regression definition that was utized in R to derive the parameter constraints. Subsequently, applying the summary function resulted in equation 12 being generated in R.

Statement 8:

$$lm.fit \leftarrow glm\left(\frac{1}{index} \sim keywords*root*title*inbound\ links*quality*outbound\ links*description\right.$$
$$\left. *(div+h1+h2+h3+h4+h5+h6+p+span),\ family = 'binomial'\right)$$

$$\frac{1}{index} = (-3.762e25)*K*(-7.973e14)*U*(6.46e15)*T*(2.028e12)*I*(4.150e12)$$
$$*Q*(9.992e12)*O*(-1.662e16)*D*[(1.892e15)*DIV+(2.101e15)$$
$$*H1+(-4.845e14)*H2+(-3.738e15)*H3+(-6.486e19)*H4+(-8.662e19)$$
$$*H5+(-2.983e20)*H6+(8.302e14)*P+(4.086e14)*SPAN]-2.641e15$$

(12)

Utilization of the ROC function generated the ROC plot given in figure 6. The area under the curve was tabulated to be 0.7778, which entails a significant finding for the Yahoo search space. This discourse has shown in a quantitative manner that truth can be determined or at least approximated in this particular case given the system attributes that may be identified and the application of machine learning concepts. The findings here show significance because it is through them that conclusions may be drawn upon that move past the subjective and the qualified to the quantified. It is because of the process undertaken here that it can be stated that it is because of the quality of the link equity that may be derived that page relevance may be elevated, at least through the Yahoo search engine. The findings here let the discourse move forward whereby a truth may be built upon were this truth leads the discussion to further points of relevance because after all the footing that this quantified finding provides is a form of bedrock that cannot be diminished, at least until an alternative model is provided that sheds further light on the dynamic under study.

Figure 5. Yahoo Receiver Operating Characteristic Curve (ROC)

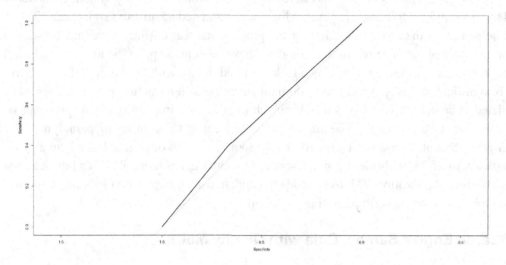

Figure 6. Yahoo Quality Metric Receiver Operating Characteristic Curve (ROC)

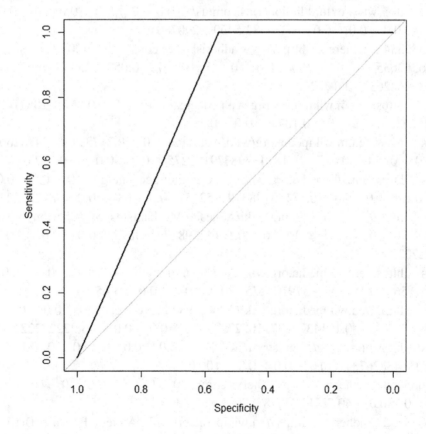

The work of King (2008) and Jerkovic (2010) helped to identify those base system elements that were deemed to be significant to page relevance, which were validated against the style guide. These bodies of work helped to set the course of action for the process that was outlined here and consequently has led to a realization about page worth that could not have been made prior. Search relevance at least as far as the Yahoo search engine is concerned is determined in part with the quality of the referrers. This benefit is significant to the page indexing domain since the differentiation between degrees of worth are tabulated to be 0.7778 - 0.5333 = 0.2445 which implies that link equity in this prescriptive model yielded a benefit in excess of 24%. The importance of link equity to the indexing paradigm of the Yahoo search engine accounted for almost a quarter of the total net worth of page relevance to a given query. The ramifications of this to the development space are significant as it entails that a business that builds Micro Distributed Applications (MDAs) stands to gain almost a quarter of an indexing benefit with the Yahoo search engine by subscribing to this paradigm.

Bing Search Engine Sample Data with Quality Metric

index	key	url	description	div	h1	h2	h3	h4	h5	h6	inbound_links	key-words	outbound_links	p	root	span	title	quality
1.0	adheres	http://www.oxforddictionaries.com/us/	0.0	0	0.0	0.0	0	0.0	0	0	498	0.0	14	0.0	0.0	0.0	0.0	82.54609929078015
10.333333333333334	adheres	http://www.adherishealth.com/	0	0.0	0.13636363636363635	0	0	0.0	0.0	0	5	0	7	0.05294453973699256	0.0	0.022641509433962263	0.0	26.8
10.0	adheres	https://en.m.wiktionary.org/wiki/adheres	0	0.0	0.8571428571428571	0.0	0	0	0	0	1	0	2	0	0.1875	0.0	0.3	20.0
11.0	adheres	https://en.m.wikipedia.org/wiki/Adhesion	0	0.21739130434782608	0.0	0.0	0	0	0	0	1	0	5	0.18143798379105275	0.0	0.0	0.0	7.0
12.0	adheres	https://en.wikipedia.org/wiki/AdhesionSurface_energy	0	0.0	0.0	0.0	0.0	0	0	0	9	0	56	0.18143798379105275	0.0	0.0	0.0	43.22222222222222
13.0	adheres	https://en.wikipedia.org/wiki/AdhesionMechanisms_of_adhesion	0	0.0	0.0	0.0	0.0	0	0	0	9	0	56	0.18143798379105275	0.0	0.0	0.0	43.22222222222222
14.0	adheres	https://en.wikipedia.org/wiki/AdhesionStrength	0	0.0	0.0	0.0	0.0	0	0	0	6	0	56	0.18143798379105275	0.0	0.0	0.0	53.5
15.0	adheres	https://en.wikipedia.org/wiki/AdhesionOther_effects	0	0.0	0.0	0.0	0.0	0	0	0	9	0	56	0.18143798379105275	0.0	0.0	0.0	43.22222222222222
20.2	adheres	https://phys.org/chemistry-news/	0	0.0	0.0	0	0	0	0.0	0	2	0	28	0.07361838648826734	0.0	0.0	0.0	100.0
21.666666666666668	adheres	http://atherys.com/	0	0	0	0.0	0	0	0	0	76	0	2	0.0	0.0	0	0.0	40.78787878787879
23.333333333333332	adheres	https://en.wikipedia.org/wiki/Anders_Behring_Breivik	0	0.0	0.0	0.0	0.0	0	0	0	60	0	446	0.08955223880597014	0.0	0.0	0.0	188.37777777777777
26.333333333333332	adheres	http://idioms.thefreedictionary.com/adhere+to	0.12080536912751678	0.20353037766830867	0.6666666666666666	2.0	0	0	0

0   83   0.0972972972972973   162   0.0   0.15789473684210525   11.297323317867562 0.14634146341463414   142.0

27.0   adheres   http://www.adhereinc.com/   0.0   0   0   0.0   0   0   0   0   2   0   3 0.0   0.42857142857142855   0.036585365853658534   0.0   10.0

43.5   adheres   https://energy.gov/energysaver/caulking   0.0   0   0   0.0   0   0.0   0   0 1   0   5   0.24465284307920215   0.0   0.0   0.0   101.0

Yahoo Search Engine Sample Data with Quality Metric

index   key   url   description   div   h1   h2   h3   h4   h5   h6   inbound_links   keywords   outbound_links   p   root   span   title   quality

9.571428571428571   adheres   http://www.adherishealth.com/   0   0.0   0.13636363636363635 0   0   0.0   0.0   0   5   0   7   0.05294453973699256   0.0   0.022641509433962263   0.0 26.8

12.666666666666666   adheres   https://en.wikipedia.org/wiki/Adhesion   0   0.0   0.0   0.0 0.0   0   0   0   5   0   56   0.18143798379105275   0.0   0.0   0.0   53.2

14.6   adheres   https://phys.org/chemistry-news/   0   0.0   0.0   0   0   0   0.0   0   1   0 28   0.07361838648826734   0.0   0.0   0.0   101.0

19.25   adheres   http://atherys.com/   0   0   0   0.0   0   0   0   0   62   0   2   0.0   0.0 0   0.0   40.69387755102041

22.0   adheres   https://en.wikipedia.org/wiki/Anders_Behring_Breivik   0   0.0   0.0   0.0 0.0   0   0   0   50   0   446   0.08955223880597014   0.0   0.0   0.0   194.1081081081081

21.2   adheres   http://www.adhereinc.com/   0.0   0   0   0.0   0   0   0   0   2   0   3 0.0   0.42857142857142855   0.036585365853658534   0.0   10.0

23.75   adheres   http://idioms.thefreedictionary.com/adhere+to   0.12080536912751678 0.20353037766830867   0.6666666666666666   2.0   0   0   0   0   77   0.0972972972972973 162   0.0   0.15789473684210525   11.297323317867562   0.14634146341463414 158.78947368421052

27.0   adheres   http://www.startribune.com/body-shop-kyle-rudolph-adheres-to-strict-regimen-to-get-from-game-to-game/407159016/   0.0   0.0   0.08108108108108109   0   0.0   0.0   0   0 3   0   28   0.0   0.06   0.0   0.07058823529411765   78.0

31.0   adheres   http://www.wilsonart.com/adhesives-products   0.029411764705882353   0.0 0.0   0.0   0   0.0   0   0   1   0.04597701149425287   23   0.0   0.0   0.0   0.0   38.0

32.333333333333336   adheres   http://www.krylon.com/products/fusion-for-plastic/   0   0.0   0 0.0   0.0   0.0   0   0.0   137   0   13   0.07407407407407407   0.0   0.06908300860600691 0.0   83.31067961165049

36.0   adheres   https://www.muslima.com/   0.0   0.0   0.0   0.0   0.0   0.0   0   0   27 0.0   51   0.022304832713754646   0.0   0.0   0.0   55.68

40.42857142857143   adheres   http://www.colliervilleschools.org/   0.0 0.024793388429752067   0   0   0   0   0   0   19   0.0   18   0.0   0.0   0.0   0.0 35.666666666666664

39.0   adheres   https://safeharbor.export.gov/list.aspx   0   0   0   0   0   0   0   0   204   0 57   0   0.0   0.019736842105263157   0.0   23.511764705882353

43.2   adheres   https://www.law.cornell.edu/uscode/text/18/2381   0   0.0   0.0   0.0   0   0

0   0   55   0   9   0.015625   0.0   0.0   0.0   133.625
43.666666666666664   adheres   http://www.bartlettschools.org/   0.0   0.0   0   0   0.0   0
0   0   22   0.0   27   0.0   0.0   0.0   0.0   26.72222222222222

SUMMARY

What was presented in this chapter lays forth the positive argument that the dynamic for search engine indexing can follow a predictive model given the system attributes of the problem frame. In the case of the Yahoo search engine, it was found that a predictive formula could be derived with an accuracy of 77.78%. Given the argument that Yahoo presents search results in a random format at times it could therefore be argued that the formula derived in this body of work could have an even higher accuracy than was tabulated.

This body of work lays the groundwork for the argument that decision science can be leveraged to create a paradigm for the search space that is void of simple indexing of content as may be found through the use of TF-IDF and thus moves the argument forward in a different direction over search. This argument represents a significant step forward in the search space paradigm as it entails that a predictive model can be defined and followed, thus helping to clarify the previously subjective context of indexing of online content.

The search space can appear to be a complicated domain given the obscurity and vagueness of the search providers, but when systems theory is applied to the problem frame it becomes feasible for understanding to be brought forth. This reality that unfolds leads to better understanding of how content needs to be crafted to have a voice on the internet. The ramifications of what was determined here helps in understanding that content and link equity come together to drive value for the search providers and as such content must be created to leverage this benefit. This realization helps to clarify that there needs to exist a doctrine in web development that must yield a benefit from linkage structures. Web development as a consequence must be such so that it exists outside of the confines of a specific domain. Web applications must become domain agnostic and be distributable to the masses so that applications built can capitalize on the significance of the search engine's algorithm. Web applications need to be able to leverage the rules that all are bound to and that are enforced upon each domain by the search engine providers. Applications built need to take the rules of engagement and harness them for the link equity which entails that a new breed of applications must be developed. This benefit will be brought forth because of Micro Distributed Applications (MDAs). By being able to take these applications and compartmentalize them to small JavaScript entities that may be given to anyone freely on the internet will allow the creators of such to create content on the web that will point to the desired domain and by doing so let the search engines inherently provide the domain with that needed equity that every domain owner covets.

By leveraging the rules of the game that the same search engine providers have set forth and that everyone is bound to will facilitate the creation of domains of authority and it will be these domains that will win the indexing race. By creating these smaller and distributed applications it also allows the authors to leverage the benefit of the internet where these applications can execute by utilizing the resources of the subscribing clients thus alleviating the burden of having to make the investment in large public cloud compute resources. By leveraging the doctrine of indexing and utilizing lightweight

JavaScript components it creates an optimization whereby the economics of the equation become tilted and benefit the creators of MDAs.

Web development has come full circle where it is a simplification of the paradigm that was known previously. The current doctrine as a consequence has become simplified, less expensive to operate, leverages the indexing domain of the search providers, and which may be leveraged to create loosely coupled components. Web development as a consequence of this shift has become more elegant which is the hallmark of good design. The space is shifting organically to a different datum point that has allowed parity to be found with the indexing domain and the development space. Two previously distinct paradigms have merged to coexist in a new reality that stands to be fought over fiercely by the development community because it will be those organizations that are able to create the better applications that will stand to win the embrace of the masses. This voting share that results will be the manner by which the winners will be selected and as such it entails a new wave of development that is to occur because after all it is always the economics of the discussion that mandate momentum. Those businesses that choose to embrace this new doctrine will be the ones that will be able to create the greatest degree of momentum for themselves and as a consequence it will be these businesses that will come to reap the monetary gains that will result.

This chapter has helped to bridge the discussion from the qualitative to the quantitative and by doing such it has become feasible to understand the degree of significance that link equity places on the indexing effort of the Yahoo search engine. It is because of this assertion that it now becomes feasible to state the benefit that may be derived by businesses that migrate their applications to MDAs. The argument for this change to occur has ceased to be qualitative and subjective as now it can be shown why change is mandated. Teams can now go to management and make the case for why an investment in the retrofitting of applications needs to occur because after all, businesses that cannot be located on the internet are but those same businesses that litter malls throughout the country that have little to no foot traffic. The migration to MDAs is warranted because the migration to these applications entails an economic benefit to the business that cannot be ignored and must be leveraged if the business is to compete on the digital highway where foot traffic is plentiful, and economies of scale are at an optimum.

The Bing attribute statistics are summarized in table 2 as provided below, and which are also plotted in figure 7. From the data collected and as processed through the study it can be seen that what is prevalent to the attribute set may not necessarily be relevant. From the data depicted in the charts of figure 7 and 8 it can be seen that outbound and inbound links are outliers. This is but an indicator of the degree of prevalence that is found in the parsing of the pages indexed.

In the comparison of the two data sets what can been seen is that the two data pools mined show a consistency across the indexing dynamic, which points to the fact that while the subtleties of the model may be distinct, the playing field is nevertheless the same. The graphs noted below also reinforce the need to understand the systems dynamic to be able to model problem frames as the boundary constraint that exists because of this reality forces a constraint upon the modeling effort that is inescapable and subsequently must be accommodated for in the derivation of a prescriptive model. Given that the two systems did not find conformity with the equations derived simply reaffirms the reality that the prescription being utilized by one vendor is distinct from that of the other vendor. It is once again a challenge that is not of depth or complexity but rather of avenues that must be pursued in order to be able to arrive at a truth proposition. The proof of this assertion lays in the realization that for one of the search engine vendors this prescription with a great degree of certainty was able to be derived.

Table 2. Bing Attribute Statistics

Attribute	Maximum	Average
Description	1.3	0.0
DIV	100.0	0.1838
H1	10	0.2072
H2	40.0	0.2106
H3	14.0	0.0490
H4	7.0	0.0128
H5	3.5455	0.0022
H6	2.8138	0.0013
Inbound Links	582.0	14.890
Keywords	2.0	0.0425
Outbound Links	1643.0	35.4746
Paragraph	66.0172	0.2388
URL	1.3571	0.1220
Span	93.012	1.1249
Title	2.7238	0.1606

Figure 7. Bing Average Attribute Plot

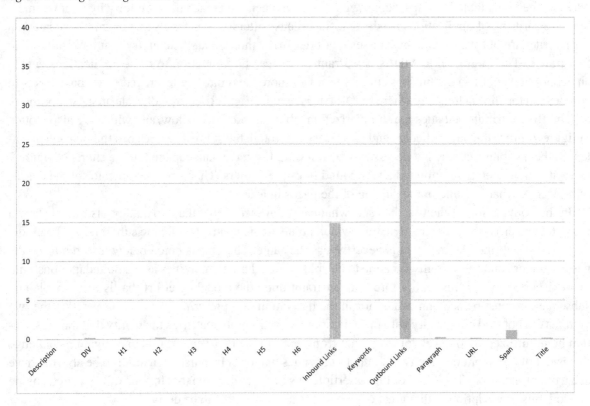

Figure 8. Yahoo Average Attribute Plot

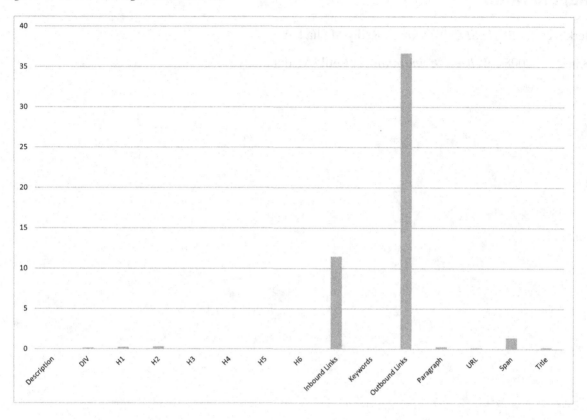

Table 3. Yahoo Attribute Statistics

Attribute	Maximum	Average
Description	1.3	0.0
DIV	100.0	0.1604
H1	10.0	0.2421
H2	43.3288	0.3338
H3	14.0	0.0595
H4	7.0	0.0167
H5	3.5455	0.0041
H6	2.8138	0.0029
Inbound Links	582.0	11.4794
Keywords	1.667	0.0529
Outbound Links	1389.0	36.6681
Paragraph	124.588	0.2639
URL	1.3571	0.1357
Span	93.0122	1.4084
Title	2.7238	0.1755

REFERENCES

Jerkovic, J. (2010). *SEO Warrior*. O'Reilly Media Inc.

King, A. (2008). *Website Optimization*. O'Reilly Media Inc.

Chapter 7
Attribute Relevance

ABSTRACT

A random forest study can help the investigator determine the degree of relevance of some attribute set that is under scrutiny, thus leaving the investigative study with a greater degree of insight into where ultimately that compass actually points towards. This chapter performs a random forest study with the data sets that were derived in previous chapters, and they are leveraged so that under a supervised learning model a degree of relevance over the attribute set may be ascertained. By following this process, it becomes feasible to determine the similitude that may exist with additional bodies of work and to ultimately be able to ascertain a goodness of fit for posterior models. This process of affirmation helps to guide the discussion to an ultimate state of truth, which is what is the only matter of concern for the scientist.

INTRODUCTION

In the previous chapter an approximation formula to the Yahoo search engine was created, which resulted in an almost 80% parity with the search results that were derived from the search provider. What the previous chapter did not disclose however was the degree of significance of the independent variables to the dependent variable. In order to be able to determine the degree of significance of each element on the system it becomes imperative to be able to perform a different type of study, which is what is undertaken in this chapter. This degree of feature relevance may be determined through a random forest study which is facilitated through the statistical programming software package R. The previous chapter was a solid first step to understanding the indexing paradigm that is subscribed to by two of the major search engines, but it left a void in the focus with regards to the development of software for the web, this chapter seeks to close this gap by helping to shed light on how to quantify the indexing domain from a development context. While you may understand that link equity for example is relevant, how relevant is it compared to title tags? Where does the focus need to be when designing searchable applications? How exactly is HTML supposed to be structured to facilitate the indexing of the applications that are to be built? These are the questions that are sought to be answered in this chapter. What is sought in this chapter is the structure of web content for Micro Distributed Applications to enable a web presence to be enhanced and in doing so help the business win the indexing race. Ultimately what is sought here is to determine

DOI: 10.4018/978-1-6684-4849-6.ch007

the focal point of web development; how specifically can MDAs be structured to find alignment with the search purveyors given their focus of the system attributes. What is currently understood between the relationship of indexing and development is the semblance of truth, the development community perceives the silhouette to be actually the person because of the outline but cannot identify the person from this shadow because truth is in fact hidden. This chapter is important because it leads the discussion forward to the identification of the architectural framework underpinnings by which development needs to adhere to in order to be able to create those small JavaScript components that will lead domains to win the indexing race. There can be no doubt that what has been done until now is significant as the disclosing of a supervised learning model allowed for the approximation of search engine relevance of one of the major search purveyors with an almost 80% degree of accuracy, but unfortunately this is not quite enough because it does not afford that blueprint that needs to be followed by development teams in general in order to be able to create systems of subsistence. These systems of relevance will only ever come to fruition if the silhouette of truth will simply not suffice.

The content of this chapter is an alternative paradigm to what was presented in the previous chapter as in this chapter an alternative view of the reality is brought forth. This chapter utilizes a mathematical model through the use of R to help understand how the data collected may be categorized in terms of relevance. Random forest and Support Vector Machine are two forms of supervised learning algorithms that facilitate classification of which in this chapter the study will utilize the former to help determine the degree of relevance for the attributes collected previously. The attribute sets that were discussed in the previous chapter can be categorized using this mode of classification to help in the understanding of their respective degree of relevance or the degree of their influence over the behavior of the model. Being able to do such will allow for the creation of a mathematical paradigm that can then be translated to the individual tag elements of HTML documents where a developer can then infer from the element underpinnings how best to present content to the search purveyors. From this station it becomes feasible to understand how to structure that much needed JavaScript content with MDAs that will adhere to that much expected protocol by which content is being judged by the search purveyors. If for example it is determined that header five <h5></h5> tags are more significant than header one tags <h1></h1> then it would behoove the developer to model layout content accordingly where the correct header tags are utilized to facilitate their indexing by the search purveyors. It is not enough to simply state a supposition and follow blindly to the slaughterhouse, the process needs to be justifiable and void of that silhouette if the course of action is to show worth and it is through a metrics approach that a quantifiable context may be placed around the problem frame, which is void of that shadow. This is the reason why this particular investigative study has taken root here, it has been to validate the cardinality of relevance. Once the mathematical context to prove relevance has been performed then the process can proceed to define the architectural framework by which online content needs to be modelled after, which is the task of the subsequent chapter.

This chapter serves to also highlight the benefit that may be derived through the segregation of the development effort with a statistical modeling effort as all the calculations that were performed in this chapter were done so through the R statistical modeling package which in turn did not require the creation of any additional code in Python to be written. The data files that were identified in previous chapters and that may be found in the GitHub repository were utilized in the manner in which they were initially created. By following this process, it was possible to perform all the needed data scrubbing, analysis, and output generation exclusively through the R interface and its native programming language. The degree of flexibility that R affords cannot be understated as the software affords alternative approaches to understanding the data that may be ingested such as through the use of Naïve Bayes or K-Nearest Neighbor (KNN) for example. It is important to understand that the data that was collected is probabilistic in nature given the time dependence or the staleness of the data and the state of the search engine algorithm when the data was extracted and as such what is of interest is not necessarily the exact degree of importance found through a computational effort, but rather the relative nature of this significance. This relativity alludes to the degree of importance between the factors of consideration and consequently helps to further shed light on the focal points that need attention in the predictive model. The fact that a random forest study deems header one tags to have an importance of 8.12980 and that of header six tags to be of 1.090782 for example depicts the relative focus of where the interest needs to lay in the crafting of the message for the audience. By understanding this degree of relativity, it helps to further understand how the architectural framework needs to function in order to create the best possible outcome for the consumers of the message. While the numbers are important, what is even more significant is the degree of disparity between the attributes as this helps to refine the final message and consequently helps to be better able to understand how Micro Distributed Applications (MDAs) may be leveraged in the development doctrine to provide the creators of MDAs the greatest degree of lift possible with the search engines. This is the reason why this chapter was needed, this is the reason why a random forest study needed to be done, it was for the attainment of a firm handle on the degree of relativity of the factors of influence.

RANDOM FOREST STUDY

Random forest is a supervised learning model that is utilized to categorize based upon the wisdom of the many, which functions in a similar manner to the search paradigm in general as it is the many that help differentiate the few. In the random forest algorithm what is sought is the bagging of constraints which occurs through the grouping of similarity as dictated by the dataset. The function of the trees in random forest is to work as the mode of filtering where this process of filtering aids in the ultimate determination of like sets, much as when water is filtered through a thin membrane, random forest does a similar task and helps to remove the waste that surrounds what is sought. By being able to accumulate these data structures into points of commonality what is ultimately sought is that by doing so that they in turn reveal a truth proposition in the underlying data collected as classified through the random forest construct. The availability of the random forest library in R facilitates the complete process of this grouping directly, which is performed next. What follows is the complete random forest study in R with the collected data that has been identified previously. With this aim in mind, it will become possible to identify all those components that are truly relevant in the modeling effort of a search system where the end result is a physical determinant of worth by way of the random forest algorithm where each attribute of the model becomes associated with a level of worth or importance.

In order to be able to utilize the random forest package in R you must first install it, which can be accomplished through the invocation of statement 1 as given below. Once the random forest package becomes available in R you can utilize it to import data through the generic expression provided in statement 2, where formula designates the expression to evaluate, and data represents the dataset being consumed. The data that will be consumed in this exercise may be found in the data folders respectively for both the Yahoo and Bing search engines as was presented in a previous chapter. It should be noted that the reader does have an option currently of utilizing R in the cloud through R studio online (https://

rstudio.cloud/). Through the use of R studio online it becomes feasible to avoid the complete installation of R directly on a personal computer. You are also afforded the ability to utilize R in the cloud for free as long as your utilization is minor, i.e., requires minimal computational resources.

Statement 1: install.packages(randomForest)
Statement 2: randomForest(formula,data)

In order to be able to work with the random forest utility there are additional libraries that need to be imported and are given as statements 4 and 5 below. Statement 3 is required to enable the random forest package in R. The random forest library documentation for R may be found here: https://cran.r-project.org/web/packages/randomForest/randomForest.pdf. The caret package in R serves the purpose of facilitating model training, the documentation of which may be found here: https://cran.r-project.org/web/packages/caret/vignettes/caret.html. The e1071 R package serves the purpose of facilitating statistical operations, the documentation of which may be found here: https://cran.r-project.org/web/packages/e1071/e1071.pdf. It is through the use of the denoted imports given below that random forest operations are facilitated in R, the specific operations of which are detailed next.

Statement 3: library(randomForest)
Statement 4: library(caret)
Statement 5: library(e1071)

With the above noted packages installed and imported it becomes feasible to then utilize the random forest functionality directly in R, to be specific the first step in the process is to utilize the trainControl function that becomes available through statement 6 as given below. The trainControl function in R can take as input as many as twenty seven parameters, but for this case it will simply be utilizing three parameters as provided in the signature below. The documentation particulars for the trainControl library may be found at the link here: https://www.rdocumentation.org/packages/caret/versions/6.0-90/topics/trainControl. The method attribute designates the type of re-sampling type that is to occur for which this study will be utilizing the 'CV' value. The number designation denotes the folds being utilized in the K-fold cross validation, which in this case will be set to 10. The search designation denotes the mode by which the tuning parameter is implemented which will be set to "grid" in this implementation. In the case of the train function, the form attribute denotes the particular equation to fit the data to. The data attribute denotes the particular dataset being utilized in the model training process. The method designation denotes the classification model to use. The final parameter utilized has the train control designation which denotes the train control object to use as input. The full documentation of the train function may be found here: https://www.rdocumentation.org/packages/caret/versions/4.47/topics/train.

Statement 6: trainControl(method, number, search)
Statement 7: train(form, data, method, trControl)

Sample commands for the trainControl and the train function are provided below as statements 8 and 9. The variable that is created in statement 8 is later fed into the train function as the input value to the trControl key.

Statement 8: train_control ← trainControl(method='cv', number=10, search='grid')
Statement 9: index_train ← train(index~., data=input_data, method='rf', trControl=train_control)

The data designation as denoted in statement 9 needs to be partitioned into two separate segments, the first being the training set and the second being the validation set. For the purposes of this endeavor the data will be portioned into a 30/70 split where 30% of the data set is utilized for the model training. The data partition commands are provided in statements 10 through 12 as given below. Statement 10 utilizes the sample function of R whose documentation may be found here: https://www.rdocumentation.org/packages/base/versions/3.6.2/topics/sample. The sample function serves the purpose of extracting a partial data set from a superset where the second parameter is the size of the dataset to choose from, i.e., 30% of the total dataset in this case. In statement 11 what is physically achieved is the extraction of the subset based upon the partition chosen from the sample function as provided in statement 10. The validation partition is provided in statement 12 where the partition occurs over the negation of the partition variable, thus giving the complimentary dataset from that derived in statement 11.

Statement 10: partitions ← sample(nrow(input_data), 0.3*nrow(input_date), replace = FALSE)
Statement 11: train_partition ← input_data[partitions]
Statement 12: validate_partition ← input_data[-partitions]

The economies of scale that may be achieved because of the inherent module definitions that are made available from R cannot be understated. The physical importation of three libraries as defined in statements 3 through 5 allowed for the utilization of statistical functions that culminated in the utilization of the random forest function directly in R. It should also be noted that this mode of operandi was accomplished with a minimal amount of coding structures, which only serves to highlight the benefit that is afforded via R as opposed to other popular programming languages such as Python for example. Through the utilization of the statements given above and the data repository that is accessible through an HTTP protocol it becomes feasible to perform all the needed calculations directly via R studio (https://www.rstudio.com/), which is performed next for both the Yahoo and Bing search engines. The version of R studio that was utilized for the exercises to follow was 1.2.5019. You do however have the option to utilize R studio online as was stated previously if you do not want to install R studio locally. The process depicted below was also tested by way of R studio online without alteration to the commands provided below, you are free to proceed in the manner which is best suited to you without having to worry about the integrity of the process to follow.

Bing Search Engine

The dataset for Bing is imported through the use of statement 13 as provided below for the reader. The read.csv command of R allows for the importation of the data directly from the GitHub repository, which is then assigned to the 'bing_data' variable. Validation of the assignment to the variable can be assessed by simply typing the name of the variable with an enter key proceeding, which will provide you with the details of the assignment performed. Next the data is partitioned based upon the 30% threshold as given in statement 14 below. Subsequently the data is divided into a training set and a validation set through statements 15 and 16 as provided below.

Statement 13: bring_data ← read.csv('https://raw.githubusercontent.com/guillermorodriguez/dissert ation/master/src/BING/data/_historical_complete_r.dat',header = TRUE, sep='\t')

Statement 14: partition ← sample(nrow(bing_data), 0.3*nrow(bing_data), replace-FALSE)

Statement 15: partition_train ← bing_data[partition]

Statement 16: partition_validate ← bing_data[-partition]

From statement 6 of the previous chapter, the formula in equation 1 is derived, which is utilized as the basis for validation of the attribute set. The formula as defined in equation 1 was fed into the R state-ment defined as 17, which functioned as the basis for the training of the model. Execution of statement 17 yielded the result of table 1 as provided below, from this output it can be seen that the optimum value of mtry is 2 given the minimal value derived for RMSE. This detail was fed into statement 18, which computed the random forest attribute levels of significance. These levels of priority are provided for the reader in table 2 as they were generated using statement 19 as provided below.

$$\frac{1}{index^{15}} = \frac{inbound\_links*quality}{root*outboud\_links*title*description*keywords} \qquad (1)$$
$$*(div + h1 + h2 + h3 + h4 + h5 + h6 + p + span)$$

Statement 17:

$$bing\_train \leftarrow train(\frac{1}{index^{15}} \sim \frac{inbound\_links*quality}{root*outboud\_links*title*description*keywords},$$
$$*(div + h1 + h2 + h3 + h4 + h5 + h6 + p + span)$$
$$data = partition\_train\left[c(1,4:19)\right], \ method = 'rf', \ trControl = train\_control)$$

Statement 18:

$$bing\_model \leftarrow randomForest(\frac{1}{index^{15}} \sim \frac{inbound_{links}*quality}{root*outboud_{links}*title*description*keywords},$$
$$*(div + h1 + h2 + h3 + h4 + h5 + h6 + p + span)$$
$$data = partition\_validate\left[c(1,4:19)\right], \ importance = TRUE, \ mtry = 2)$$

Statement 19: varImp(bing_model)

The data tabulated below provides interesting insight into the degree of relevance of the attribute set as can be determined by simple inspection. The most relevant attributes are respectively header two, description, inbound links, keywords, and the header three tags. The remaining attributes outside of the

URL proved to be non influential to the determination of worth for the dependent variable. While the reader needs to be cautioned with the results derived given the predictability of the model as determined in the previous chapter of this book, it is nevertheless interesting to note where the perceived datum point lay in the overall determination of worth. The data derived in this study points to an alternative proposition whereby a simplified form of the model could be considered, a model by which the feature set could be narrowed to create a greater focus on the positive feature values derived in table 2.

Table 1. Bing Statistical Factors

mtry	RMSE	R Squared	MAE
2	0.01298550	0.0044712543	0.002526619
162	0.01793185	0.0004770602	0.002232776
322	0.01798214	0.0004596956	0.002248556

Table 2. Bing Attribute Averages

Attribute	Average
Description	4.14787289
Division	-3.05828326
Header One	-4.14356169
Header Two	6.18891938
Header Three	1.31899473
Header Four	-0.09817419
Header Five	-0.98950346
Header Six	-1.12672017
Inbound Links	3.47496751
Keywords	2.50056934
Outbound Links	-0.87075937
Paragraph	-3.02187608
Root	0.45565955
Span	-2.25143046
Title	-3.29162974
Quality	-2.21172061

Yahoo Search Engine

Following a similar process as was adhered to for the consumption and dissemination of the Bing data it was possible to consume and decipher the Yahoo dataset. Statement 20 as provided below is what was used to ingest the raw Yahoo data directly into the 'yahoo_data' variable in R studio. Once again, the data was portioned on a 30/70-fold where 30% of the data was used to train the model and the remaining data was used for the random forest validation, again similar to what was done previously for the Bing search engine calculations. Statements 21 through 23 provide the details used for the data partitioning into train and validation groupings.

Figure 1. Bing Attribute Plot

Statement 20: yahoo_data ← read.csv('https://raw.githubusercontent.com/guillermorodiguez/Dissertation/master/src/YAHOO/data/_historical_complete_r.dat',header=TRUE,sep='\t')
Statement 21: partition ← sample(nrow(yahoo_data), 0.3*nrow(yahoo_data), replace=FALSE)
Statement 22: partition_train ← yahoo_data[partition]
Statement 23: partition_validate ← yahoo_data[-partition]

From statement 7 of the previous chapter it leads to the utilization of equation 2 as given below as the resultant formula for the determination of attribute relevance. This leads to the utilization of statement 24 as given below in order to train the model and assign it to the 'yahoo_train' variable. The printing of the variable results in table 3 being generated in R studio, which discloses the optimal mtry value of 2 given the minimal value of RMSE that is associated with this value. This results in the use of statement 25 as provided below for the reader. The application of the random forest function across the validation partition set is assigned to the 'yahoo_model' variable in R studio, which allows the utilization of statement 26 to display the attribute significance that is tabulated by way of the random forest function. This process leads to the derived output of table 4 as provided below for the reader.

$$\frac{1}{\text{index}} = \text{keywords*root*title*inbound links*quality*outbound links}$$
$$\text{*description*}\left(\text{div} + \text{h1} + \text{h2} + \text{h3} + \text{h4} + \text{h5} + \text{h6} + \text{p} + \text{span}\right) \tag{2}$$

$$\text{yahoo}\_\text{train} \leftarrow \text{train}(\frac{1}{\text{index}} \sim \text{keywords*rootitle*inbound links*quality}$$

Statement 24: $\text{*outbound links*description*}\left(\text{div} + \text{h1} + \text{h2} + \text{h3} + \text{h4} + \text{h5} + \text{h6} + \text{p} + \text{span}\right),$
$$\text{data} = \text{partition}\_\text{train}\left[\text{c}\left(1, 4 : 19\right)\right], \text{ method} = \text{'rf'}, \text{ trControl} = \text{train}\_\text{control})$$

Statement 25:

$$\text{yahoo}\_\text{model} \leftarrow \text{randomForest}(\frac{1}{\text{index}} \sim \text{keywords*root*title*inbound links*quality}$$
$$\text{*outbound links*description*}\left(\text{div} + \text{h1} + \text{h2} + \text{h3} + \text{h4} + \text{h5} + \text{h6} + \text{p} + \text{span}\right),$$
$$\text{data} = \text{partition}\_\text{validate}\left[\text{c}\left(1, 4 : 19\right)\right], \text{ importance} = \text{TRUE}, \text{ mtry} = 2)$$

Statement 26: varImp(yahoo_model)

From the variable qualifications that are provided in table 4 below it can be seen that an alternative hypothesis comes forth, one in which model significance is composed of thirteen factors and whereby the remaining features of the model are but excess. This explains why the derived Yahoo formula of the previous chapter proved to be significant, the model incorporated the totality of the system attributes and for which using a random forest study it is shown that the majority of these independent variables are pertinent. Truth was feasible because of the degree of parity that was found between variable relevance and model adoption. The argument could very well be made after the random forest study that the model derived in the previous chapter could be improved upon if the variables utilized found alignment with this study.

Table 3. Yahoo Statistical Factors

mtry	RMSE	R Squared	MAE
2	0.09939361	0.05810243	0.04782494
50	0.10567087	0.04406592	0.05075685
1279	0.11281871	0.03807242	0.05392833

Table 4. Yahoo Attribute Averages

Attribute	Average
Description	8.6324595
Division	3.4556776
Header One	5.4902766
Header Two	6.3692140
Header Three	2.3433891
Header Four	0.5506063
Header Five	-1.8719347
Header Six	1.3110729
Inbound Links	4.1463020
Keywords	6.0161746
Outbound Links	5.2923387
Paragraph	2.8934412
Root	3097442
Span	-1.3300545
Title	9.5220903
Quality	1.5678853

Figure 2. Yahoo Attribute Plot

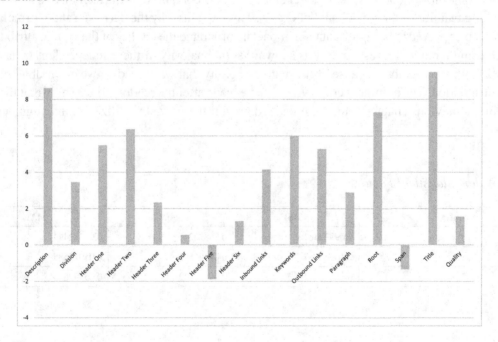

From the data made available in table 4 it can be seen that the top five attributes showing relevance in the model are found to be title, description, URL, header two, and keywords. The quality attribute showed to have a positive relationship with relevance, but it did not account for a significant level of worth in the random forest study, which does contrast the supervised learning model that was derived in the previous chapter. This study nevertheless does help in the understanding of the degree of relevance of the attribute sets that were captured via the data mining exercise and helps to put context around attribute importance. Attribute relevance derivations put into context the degree of benefit that may be derived by their appropriate utilization in the creation of content and consequently helps to shed light on how Micro Distributed Applications (MDAs) may be further enhanced through their use. It can be seen from the data in table 4 for example that using small header tags should be avoided in the creation of content as the largest benefit may be derived from the utilization of the larger tags, i.e., header one and header two tags. It is because of this study that the understanding of the relevance of tag attributes in the creation of online content can be understood to capitalize on the worth that the search engines place on the styling of online content. It is because of this understanding that consequently a framework for the development of this media can be crafted which is the discussion of the following chapter.

RELEVANCE

Given the results that were tabulated for attribute relevance through the use of a random forest study implies that the degree of importance of attributes in the classification of web content can be stated in a quantitative manner. This study has helped to further migrate from the qualitative manner by which previous studies have taken root and helped to migrate the discussion to a quantitative context that has helped to only decipher truth. Though the work of Jerkovic (2010) and King (2008) helped to put a boundary around the notion of web page relevance as did the style guide by Google, there still remained a gap, an unknown, the arguments put forth just simply did not extend to the reaches that were needed of them. This gap was a result of relying on the subjectivity of the underlying premise because in such cases what was claimed was relative to that element that has that inherent property of bias that can never be removed, the human element. This attribute that humanity is laden with is the cause of much consternation as each individual sees the world before them under that light which is all too convenient for them. This is the reason why the indexing domain has been in flux, it has been because the authors of the stories that have been told have been infused with a degree of inspiration that all arguments would be best left without, the bias of self. To confound matters further it has been difficult to have made progress in the understanding of the domain because after all it has been but the shadow or semblance of truth that has been witnessed. This figure or semblance of truth has been held onto by the masses because it was all that was known, there was no alternative proposition to where truth lay. This study however has helped to guide the discussion of relevance to a better state since the argument was made here through the utilization of data science, which becomes a stance that is difficult to oppose and even harder to tumble given that it is void of that element that humanity cannot escape, the bias of self.

Relevance of online content and its inherent underpinnings can be gauged, and assertions may be made as to what relevance entails given the data that has been made accessible by the search engine providers. No longer does the community need to sit in obscurity and claim something to be true without having the data to support the argument as the quantifiable argument can now be made given the generosity that was afforded by the search engine providers. Truth can be determined and quantified because of the openness that is the World Wide Web and the tools that are available and made freely accessible to everyone such as R studio and Python. All that is required is an understanding of how these tools may be leveraged along with the data that may be collected by way of them. It is a leverage point that has been bestowed upon all and whereby this leverage requires very little from its steward. The consequence of which is that this truth that is sought is decipherable if the needed effort to consume and disseminate the data is performed. The exercise in this chapter proves the power that is afforded to each and every one if the effort is undertaken to transform the data to information. It is this actionable data that allows inferences about the physical world to be made, which in turn functions as a gateway to conclusions that lead to discourses that were not in the purview prior. This new view that is afforded through this discovery process is what can force innovation to sprout and help to lead to a better world than was once known. In terms of the development domain for example it has led to the understanding that the economics of the dynamic have been altered for the betterment of the business, and that development has become easier to perform given the utilization of smaller components. It has also led to the realization that the focus of the marketing teams needs to shift to one whereby the utility for the masses is the point of focus in lieu of a personal benefit. Think about the ramifications of it all, it means that the dynamic has been altered to other than self first and a society that places others prior to self will always be a better version than the alternative.

In a sense the indexing domain has become an irony as the same companies that have bound humanity to the constraint that is search relevance through the magic formula that is their indexing algorithm have in turn disclosed it through search results. It is the case of the message the speaks the least that resonates the most, the secrete sauce has been leaked at least in part and through the utilization of data science and computer science, this reality can be gauged quantitatively, as has been seen in this study and prior studies. This once unknown formula that kept intent from showing her profile and which bound everyone to supposition can be eliminated through the migration of the perspective. The migration of this perspective mandates that a transition occur from the silhouette of that shadow to a firm assertion of the person that creates that projection or alternatively in this case for the attributes of worth to make themselves known. It was because of this journey that a supervised learning model for the Yahoo search engine was able to be determined with an almost 80% accuracy. There was a reason why Google went through the painstaking task of ensuring that their search engine could not be mined, it was because they understood that this reality that is sought can be determined, after all they much like Yahoo and Bing are bound to the same particulars in the equation, the system attributes, i.e., the page elements.

Relevance is subjective as it is the determination of the search engine companies that determine this reality. But this reality that is bounding can be understood by the outsider given the degree of data that is available. Much as the search purveyors have the ability to understand quantitatively what is before them, so too does the rest of humanity because mathematics after all knows not an owner. The indexing domain has proven to be a moving target as the level of sophistication of online content has evolved with time. Technological progress aids to this flux and as such the search purveyor's determination of worth will evolve with time as must the understanding of those that are external to the business as well, but what is certain is that this degree of relevance can and will be understood given studies such as this and the work of others to come. Relevance is time dependent and much as humanity finds itself, it persists in a constant flux because after all change is one of the only guarantees that life affords. You can be sure that relevance will change as does technology and humanities want, but with this change will also come the need to build better models to help to understand the reality that is to be experienced. The development community will need to continue to further its understanding of the playing field in order to be able to stay in tune with the message that is needed to be conveyed by the web applications that the search purveyors crawl. With the migration of organizations such as Facebook to place an emphasis on a virtual world it is bound to become the next frontier of classification and sure enough of the indexing domain. This metaphysical world that is experienced through the internet will evolve to encompass a virtual component that will further push the boundaries of the indexing space and along with it the need for its understanding and consequently this will lead to the re-evaluation of the applications that will reside in this frontier, which simply implies the re-engineering of that message to better fit the protocol that is expected by the search purveyors. In essence it becomes but another cycle of the wheel that is innovation and progress.

Online relevance is important because of the economic proposition that it entails and given the high degree of electronic commerce that currently occurs, and which will likely increase in years to come it has become a necessity to be relevant online. This is the reason why the subject matter before you is so important, it is because it is tied to an economic proposition that all businesses are all too eager to capitalize on. This journey has however taken on a different connotation given the degree of relevance of the web development space. It is because of the development community at large that build these online applications and the degree of benefit that may be afforded to the creating domains that online relevance will take on a distinct mold from what is known currently. It will become these MDAs that will drive relevance because they will push the frontier. Organizations that take it upon themselves to embrace the dichotomy that currently persists will be able to reap that link equity bounty that is all too coveted. It will be these businesses that will be able to craft a targeted message based upon quantifiable evidence that will be able to present a favorable face to the search purveyors and by doing so will be able to find favor with them, which will lead to a high ranking domain. Gone will be the days when SaaS applications will be created and placed online in a hope that customers will stumble across them. The proposed paradigm is different; in the proposed paradigm the same technologists that build this online presence will need to take a front seat and help maneuver the business forward because such is the degree of relevance that technology has imparted on business. It is now the burden of the technical personnel to drive value for the business through applications that are built to help these businesses win this much needed indexing race. Given the migration to the cloud and given the need of customers for instant gratification it will be those businesses that are located first that will stand the best chance to stay relevant. Customers have changed much like search has changed over time, they have become transactional in nature, they no longer want to log into some website and trade their stocks for example, they want to do so from a mobile application that they use as a game. It is this need for instant gratification that businesses must fulfill if they are to stay relevant and in order to do so they must become relevant to the search engines because after all before a transaction is undertaken what is sure to happen first is that these customers will perform some sort of search. To remain or become relevant entails that your business must be found and in order to be found you have to come to the realization that what is needed is for your business to evolve. You will need to become that business that is relevant because the masses have deemed you to be, and they will only do so if you come to have a digital presence that makes you such. To be this new type of business means that you will need to create those tools and utilities that the masses use and by doing so give your business this degree of relevance that you so desperately need to have.

Now that relevance has been further clarified it entails that certain conditions have been identified which means that a framework by which relevance will be obtained needs to be created. In the chapters to follow the discussion will dig further into what it means to build relevance through the use of Micro Distributed Applications (MDAs). This degree of relevance that you and all businesses are after can be had if you build those applications that the masses will adopt. You will need to evolve and come to understand that every business is a technology business in this day and age and as such it is paramount for your business to create those tools and utilities that the masses will embrace, thus giving you the degree of relevance that you are after. It will be by winning this race that your business will have a chance to either become or remain relevant in the years to come, at least until the indexing space changes again and the community at large is forced to adapt to the new reality. Do take some comfort however in knowing that the current state of matters has been in the making for years and it is only now that a migration needs to occur with web applications where this software will need to become smaller and containerized which will then facilitate it being consumed by the populous in mass. Society does not get to some junction point overnight, but rather migrates to this new datum point over an extended period of time. Do take note however that the race has begun, and it will only be those businesses that invest in the right technology that will be relevant and as such it behooves each and everyone at your organization to embrace the change and become a leader in the new paradigm that is proposed in this body of work.

SUMMARY

This chapter has afforded the benefit to unequivocally state in a metrics manner the degree of significance for the attribute set for each of the search engines Yahoo and Bing. No longer does the argument need to grasp in the dark hoping to at some point be able to find the light switch as the derived metrics for each of the search purveyors point to the latitude and longitude of where the target lay. It is with a degree of certainty that the argument in a quantitative manner for all to bear witness to can be made now, as the indicators that show clout have been determined. The argument has migrated from the domain of the subjective and the qualified to that of the quantified. It is no longer a matter of believing what the style guide suggests as to what truth is, but it is rather a matter of understanding the numerical context that is derived mathematically. The community at large does not have to settle anymore for viewing the semblance of truth by seeing the shadow on the ground and making the assertion that a person must be there, but rather it can now be stated that the person is in fact there unequivocally because the numbers dictate so. This journey has already been in excess of 100 pages, but it was needed because there was no shortcut to understanding, the discourse had to embark on the journey that has been seen in order to arrive on footing that could bear the weight of the argument that was made. It is an argument that can only come about in a data infused manner and to short circuit the process simply entails the relegation to other than truth or at an optimum to subjectivity. Let this be part of the lesson to the reader in that what was important was not necessarily the endpoint, but what was the most important was the enlightenment that was achieved because of the journey that was embarked upon. What was discovered because of the journey that was undertaken was actually quite significant as the journey helped to shed light on the domain and the understanding of the indexing space in a metrics context. This helped to shed further light as to how the domain of web development in general needs to change to leverage the search purveyors.

Unknowingly with each click of the mouse by the internet community it has affirmed a reality that is being forced upon it at large because of its own actions. Much like that random forest algorithm that is pertinent because it is based upon the decisions of the collective that make it pertinent so too is the reality that the search purveyors enforce upon the masses. The search community inherently voted for the reality that persists because of its actions and the search purveyors simply acquiesced. Search has taken on such a significance in the world that it now mandates what it expects of the applications that it indexes. Gone will be the days when the development community creates monstrosities of SaaS applications and unleashes them on an audience as the masses have voted and they have rejected this paradigm for what are simple and dynamic JavaScript based applications that can be consumed by any website that deems them to be worthy. The indexing race has mandated this paradigm shift, and it is now upon the development community at large to pivot and change how these applications are built.

The evolution of web development did not occur in a silo or through a cosmic bang, but rather happened over decades whereby the masses affirmed what was pertinent through the slew of opensource projects that were created and consumed in mass. This journey began by facilitating dynamic web content through the infusion of dynamic HTML via JavaScript and as small and rudimentary as those applications where they did initiate the winds of change to come given the nature of the web were content can be fluid because of the of the Hypertext Transfer Protocol (HTTP). By making this implicit commitment to change the development community unknowingly stumbled upon pandora's box and unleashed this change that was bound to take flight because of the significance that indexing was to hold. Indexing has not only changed the lives of the development community, but it has also changed the mode of marketing forever as audiences now live glued to their mobile devices. This change that now persists has happened because of the economics of the game, Google and the other search providers invest and dedicate their resources to the search domain because they have an affinity for capital. They function in a particular mode because of the monetary gains that are to be made, much as Facebook is able to capitalize on their ecosystem through targeted advertisements so too do all of the search providers, and this is why they dedicate their resources to this labor. Humanity collectively has built the reality that now enslaves it and will continue to live in it until the world of virtual reality is thrust upon the masses but rest assure that even then the domain of classification will still persist it will simply take upon itself a new dialect and when it does arrive you can guarantee yourself that so too will web applications change. This flux that is being seen is but simply part of the momentum that will keep leading humanity to new modes of existence. Just as humanity ushered in the day of developing applications for personal computers to see it end to cloud based applications, so too will the day come when the current mode of development will change to some variant of what currently exists. This variant now however is the Micro Distributed Application (MDA) where it will be these JavaScript infused fragments of function that will exist in disparate environments that will come to dominant the world that is currently known because the economics mandate it. The development community will need to build this new wave of applications because of the need to remain relevant to its audience and the only manner by which that will occur will be by winning the indexing race. The next chapter provides for the reader the architectural framework by which this new breed of web applications are to be built. It is a blueprint that may be followed by the reader to create this new class of lightweight JavaScript infused applications. In subsequent chapters practical examples are undertaken where MDAs for real world business cases are undertaken, thus giving the reader direct examples of how the architectural framework may be leveraged to create this benefit of relevance for the business. These examples that have been created for the reader reference coding artifacts in GitHub repositories so the reader may be able to download the artifacts and consequently have an initial point of reference for future endeavors.

This chapter has been the glue to the content that was presented prior and also serves as a gateway to what web development has become. This chapter provided the direct numbers that speak for themselves as to what is important in the web development landscape when it comes to indexing. So important has become the indexing space that it now dictates the manner by which applications are built and those businesses that do not come to understand the significance of this and its direct bearing on current web development only stand to lose the indexing race and become regulated to obscurity. It will be those businesses that stand to pivot and change that will stand to be pertinent to the masses and stand a chance to remain or become digitally relevant. It is the burden of the technical personnel however at the businesses that they work at to sound the trumpet and let their colleagues understand the paradigm that is here and that all must adhere to. You can also take comfort in knowing that you can make your argument with numbers in hand and avoid the subjectivity of the matter altogether. You can now go into your meetings and tell them that change is here and place those hard numbers before them to help them understand why change is mandated. Gone are the days when claims of subjectivity can be made with regards to the indexing domain because now the hard numbers have been derived. It may be easy for two people to argue over a matter that is subjective, but it is quite another to argue against the numbers that are laid bare as that type of argument can only be made by the irrational. There is no need to go there and there is no need to have friction as the numbers have stated where true north resides. This new truth is significant as it entails that the mode by which applications need to be created has changed and as such so too must the mode of operandi change. This change that is spoken about however is already being seen within the development community with frameworks such as React (https://reactjs.org). The momentum of the migration to MDAs is already here, but until now the connection between the development domain and the indexing space has not been made. This text is here to tell you that this marriage has already happened, and it has happened because the collective of the internet users have voted for such.

This journey that the development domain has been under has been a long journey and not recent by any means as current state is such because of the evolution of the technological domain. The migration of content to the web entailed that entities such as Google, Yahoo, and Bing could come to fruition. For this existence to have come to fruition entailed that a pre-existing condition existed, i.e., the web content to index. It was because of this need to classify web content that it entailed that another change needed occur and that was the alignment of the development paradigm with the indexing domain. It is not the case that Google for example does an inadequate job of classifying content, but it is rather that the content provider is not fitting the message to the protocol and hence the disjoint. This point of friction has now taken on a distinct flavor because the protocol has evolved as has the technologies around the creation of content on the web. This synergy that is sought is feasible because of the symbiotic relationship the exists between the classification domain and the development effort. One entity depends on the other, and each is in desperate need of its brethren. Solutions that exist on the web need the search engines in order for customers to find them and the search engines are in need of these applications so that the masses may gravitate towards their domains in order to find an answer to their questions. Society has in fact been on this course since the very beginning because in the beginning what was sought was the linking of like memos, it just so happens that now the players have changed, but yet the game is all too familiar as are the names on the back of the jerseys at times.

The new architectural framework by which web development going forward will need to adhere to is such because the metrics support the argument, and the metrics consequently define the pillars by which this architectural framework is to be composed of. The development community will need to refactor its philosophical outlook on web development not simply because an individual or group of people state so, but because the numbers dictate this paradigm shift to be warranted. So important is the need to be relevant in the new economy that it mandates that a change occur, and this change needs to find alignment with the data derived in this chapter and previous chapters since it is the numbers that dictate the course of action that is to be taken. If this paradigm is adopted, then it entails that applications developed will find the embrace of the search purveyors in general because the message conveyed will resonate with them. If you simply follow what the data dictates it can be seen that for the Yahoo search engine forgoing the pillar of referral link quality entails that applications developed will forfeit that benefit that is being afforded by the search purveyor. In this random forest study this benefit was deemed to be of a particular magnitude and in a previous study it was deemed to be another, but irrespective of position taken, the benefit cannot be ignored as the data states what the benefit afforded is. Gone are the days whereby an argument and a mode of implementation could be undertaken because the software engineer deemed it to be such as now the argument in favor of one stance or another can be quantified, which leaves little room for debate given that the truth is plain and visible to all that care to take note. Page relevance has brought about a new mode by which applications will be developed, which implies that the web development domain is now under a new steward that mandates a new modern web architecture.

REFERENCES

Jerkovic, J. (2010). *SEO Warrior*. O'Reilly Media Inc.

King, A. (2008). *Website Optimization*. O'Reilly Media Inc.

Chapter 8
A Modern Web Architecture

ABSTRACT

The degree of influence that the search purveyors have imposed on the development landscape has been significant given that the search engines have become the proxy for the will of humanity. It is the masses that dictate relevance through their interaction with online content that places this flux upon this voting system that all subscribe to and must subsequently abide by. This flux that has been placed on online content entails that the manner by which web content is to be built in the future must change given technological progress and the fact that it must conform to this voting power of the masses that is held in stewardship by the search purveyors. It will subsequently be the burden of development teams to embrace a new doctrine to their development effort whereby this leverage that was previously not harnessed can now be wielded to create value.

INTRODUCTION

Now that it can formally be stated what constitutes relevance in the search space it leads the discussion of the current development paradigm in a new direction. In the current day and time Software as a Service (SaaS) and the public cloud are significant technological leverages, but what does the data convey about where the indexing space is pulling software solutions of the future? Indexing relevance is tied to the roots of web scraping, PageRank and the HITS algorithm. It was from these simple beginnings and the need to classify content that the domain has evolved to its current state that has become the reality of the development effort. It was the same systems that facilitated the deciphering of truth that is inherent in each node of the web that worked to bind society to the constraint that is prevalent currently and which has functioned to simply redefine development. The work of the previous chapters was much like the skeletal structure of those same search engines where truth was deterministic because of the system attributes. The data tabulated in previous chapters helped to facilitate the understanding of the significance of link equity and quality of referral. The previous chapter specifically helped to further refine the world view where it became feasible to come to understand the degree of relevance of each of the attributes that the system incorporated. This reality that can now be deemed a constrained has forced a paradigm shift on the development community and is physically forcing development teams to have to adopt a new

DOI: 10.4018/978-1-6684-4849-6.ch008

mode of operandi where development will remain in part the semblance of the past but will pivot to take a new mold. Development teams seek to create worth for the businesses that employ them through the creation of the systems that will provide a tangible benefit to the organization and to such a degree now that what is sought is for the organization to be named prom king no less. Web solutions not only seek the embrace of users, but they also seek the acceptance of the search providers as their embrace is what greases the wheels for the acceptance by the masses. As a result of this dynamic the rules of engagement that dominate how the game is to be played and how applications are to be built needs to embrace a new mode of existence which facilitates the pairing of the expectation of the search purveyors with that of the inner workings of the applications built. In essence the development community has become slaves to those systems that are a dependency since they represent the gateway to that much needed infusion of subsistence. The prison guards in this penitentiary are the Google, Bing, and Yahoo's of the world to name but three and it is in vain for the captives to try to escape as the dependency created has been such that it equates to nothing short of gravity. Businesses must play the game and excel at the game because it is the manner by which they can hope to leverage the economics at play. It is almost a game of musical chairs where the chairs have the names of the businesses carved into them and those that refuse to acknowledge and play by the rules are left to sit on the floor.

The constraint of search engine indexing mandates that modern web development along with the modern web architecture adapt and change to the new constructs at play. The ability to sell or become relevant on the internet entails that your product, service or offering have alignment to your online architecture. Gone are the days were technical execution and the business mandate were separate domains. Given the relevance of the web and the fact that being found online can play a pivotal part in the survival of the business it means that it is paramount that a service or product offering contribute to your search prominence. This search presence is directly tied to the attributes of relevance that have been identified in previous chapters. It has therefore become paramount for each unit of development endeavor to take on a twist on an old game in order to be able to leverage the rules of the game that the search providers bind the participants to. To be relevant means to adhere to this mode of development where applications need to be sensitive to the constraints that have been placed upon them as this is the mechanism by which clout is determined. Search engine indexing has changed the development space because popularity is directly proportional to the survivability of the business. Being found online is not only important it now drives the technological work effort.

This driver that is relevance is paramount to the economics of the business and to such a degree that search purveyors have brought the development community at large to a junction that has been in the making for quite some time. It has been possible to place content on a page from an external node by way of an iframe and through the iframe it has become possible to distribute desired functionality across domains. With the advent of JavaScript it became possible to program the browser to perform some body of work all without having to execute the code on the server end. Through the creation of cross platform frameworks such as jQuery and Bootstrap it became possible to create dynamic content that could be interacted on by users across devices such as phones, tablets, and computers. This natural progression from iframes to distributed JavaScript was in the making from the onset of the iframe tag in HMTL. The utilization of libraries and programming constructs has simply aided in the migration to where the profession finds itself now of loosely coupled components. This journey in the development space in general is seen in other facets of the software engineering domain for example with thin clients. The profession has migrated to smaller and siloed pieces of code that are more resilient because they are distributed and function with a greater degree of robustness consequently. The current state of web development is such not simply because of the search engine influence as it has been but merely a partial contributor to the datum point as the progress that has been seen has been such because of the evolution of the development space as well that has taken years to occur. Gone are the days when content is forced onto a canvas because it is embedded through an iframe as this functionality can now be created through dynamic content by way of small JavaScript applications that have become autonomous. These small artifacts can be distributed to external users for their own use and consumption because such is the state of matters now. The profession has evolved and it has progressed to the point that now development has been facilitated for the community at large because of the distributed nature of resources and as a consequence this paradigm has been embraced and liters the internet. It is because of this progression that the function that the masses depend on via the internet is in its current state and it is because of this progress that there is the merging of current technology with the indexing space which has entailed a paradigm shift in current doctrine. This shift entails that there is a force that is pushing the development community at large forward in how development is to occur. This is the discussion of this chapter; this chapter seeks to set a framework in place so that future development comes into harmony with the indexing space and thus allows businesses to find a leverage where none existed before. It is this leverage that is spoken of that has become the architectural framework for web development going forward in what yields small distributed JavaScript applications that have been termed Micro Distributed Applications or MDAs. MDAs allow their creators to put into synchronization the indexing domain with the development domain. This synchronization places harmony between the web development domain with the stewards of the web that have become the search engines. It allows for leverage to be reaped through the indexing space and helps organizations to win the popularity race thus giving the business a tactical leverage over the competition. Given the dependency of search by the masses it has become an essential factor of consideration to find clout with the stewards of the indexing space as this is the mechanism by which discovery occurs. This is the mode by which customers may be found expeditiously and in the most cost effective manner. It becomes wasteful to invest capital on marketing campaigns when customers naturally gravitate towards the business because the business is ranked towards the top of some search endeavor. It becomes but a farce to have to play the marketing game in the hope to attract clients to the domain of the business when they can be funneled to the business by the same search purveyors naturally and organically.

If search relevance can be tied to technological prowess, then it entails a leverage over the competition, it means that the business stands to gain financially over other businesses. Take for example the case of an online service let's say a menu ordering service such as OpenTable (http://www.opentable.com) where you can go online and create table reservations and as an alternative a product offering that may be called 'My Table Ordering Service Example, Inc.'. In the case of the former it is an online service that allows you to go to the provider's website and create a table reservation for some restaurant. In the latter it represents a pluggable feature that restauranteurs can place on their website and have patrons create reservations directly on their website. As a restaurant owner would you not prefer to have customers remain on your domain in lieu of the alternative where they could be drawn to a competitor for example? It is this stewardship that is vital to execution that mandates that a paradigm shift occur in part. This stewardship of customer is guaranteed through MDAs because the needed function would reside directly on the owner's domain. This benefit to the restauranteur also extends to the software vendor of the MDA since adoption of utility entails an additional factor of relevance. This benefit to the provider of the utility would come forth because of the inherent mode by which ranking algorithms function as has been determined in this body of work quantitatively. The benefit of rank would come from several factors and these being as follows.

1. Provisioning of link equity directly on customers online presence.
2. Adoption rate given containment of functionality directly on customer's online presence.
3. Availability of consumable libraries by third parties
4. The tailoring of the content to meet the requirements identified in previous chapters

It stands to reason that there is an alternative to the current development doctrine that can be used to gain a competitive advantage. This new breed of applications will need to adhere to an architectural framework that is defined in this chapter where their creation will facilitate the winning of the indexing race and consequently help to propel those businesses that adopt the framework forward. There is much at stake for businesses going forward and it will be those businesses that leverage the framework of MDAs that will stand to win the popularity race and consequently the bulk share of the attention of the masses. Web development has arrived at its current state because of the progress that has been made and when this is aligned with the formula of relevance that the search engine providers utilize to assess worth it only furthers the case for MDAs. It is up to each and every one that works in the development domain however to make the commitment to migrate their applications to this new doctrine of Micro Distributed Applications (MDAs). The argument could very well be made that this new phase of evolution that the web development space is under is similar to the phase that mainframe or installable software was under at one point in time. To cease to progress and adopt the wave of change that unfolds is but to simply die a slow and painful death.

SOFTWARE AS A SERVICE (SAAS)

Software as a Service (SaaS) is a product offering mode by vendors that allows businesses or individuals to use a service such as a web application for a fee that is typically structured to be incurred monthly. In the past businesses would have to acquire hardware and would have done the physical installation of a product on premise much as was the case for individuals with standalone computers and say tax software that would be purchased in a retail store. In the current paradigm however the hardware much like the software is leased and used as needed where virtual machines may be destroyed and created on demand.

The paradigm shift of SaaS applications has had a disruption to the software delivery domain and has had a significant impact especially to the indexing domain because applications now reside in a public forum. Given the argument that has been laid bare to now and the fact that prediction of rank can be affirmatively tied to link equity as has been shown in this body of work then it stands to reason that creating referral links from individual nodes that a business can directly influence has a significant positive impact in the indexing space and consequently on the popularity of applications that reap this indexing benefit. This is precisely what has been occurring within the SaaS domain as businesses have been placing their marketing logo and referral links on their customer's domain. Take the case of a hosting provider that allows you to purchase a domain and host it on their servers, these service providers are providing their product in a variant form of a SaaS offering and they are directly placing their branding on your domain until you physically change the hosting provider or setup a web page for your content overriding their default branding page. The hosting provider has essentially used the domain as free link equity back to their domain, thus creating worth for themselves.

Currently SaaS product offerings function in a similar manner to that of the hosting provider mentioned previously as they are placing their branding on the application you choose to use at some domain. Take the example of a web service product offering for some business domain, it could be any domain as business sector is irrelevant to technology. What is currently being done is that whether the destination node is a domain or a page within some domain the SaaS provider is placing their branding and referral links back to their domain directly on the node that is subscribing to their service. Businesses that are purchasing some SaaS offering and are placing the offering on their publicly available façade are inherently providing value back to the SaaS provider and giving up some of their link equity along the way. The prediction formulas derived previously both utilized outward links as an attribute in the overall result and consequently it can be quantitatively stated that this argument is valid. This framework is seen quite commonly now whether it is business reviews or an applicant tracking system (ATS) that allows individuals to upload their resumes directly on some business' website, the argument is pedestrian. Link equity is being created by these SaaS providers to their benefit by leveraging the link referral of the domain that is purchasing or utilizing their utility.

The current trend with SaaS product offering providers is to have the offering made available through an open cloud service provider such as AWS, Azure or Google Cloud where the bare metal implementation is not administered by the company providing the SaaS product. This is a significant challenge to the new web architecture because it means that the component you are leveraging could reside across the coast from your physical business. The new modern web architecture must be able to account for this and have enough resources available by region to accommodate the demand or better yet remove itself from this paradox. So, how could this happen if the solution is truly agnostic to the requirement? Well, the point becomes mute if the new architecture is simply a component within the grander whole where the application or website could reside at any local provider and the component could be downloaded from there. There is consensus in the research literature that region plays a pivotal role in search result, which may also be validated by way of a proxy configuration. Search results are defined by region by the search providers, consequently failing to accommodate for this dynamic will lead to less than desirable results. The new breed of SaaS applications need to address this requirement and as such align with the dynamic that is present with index-able content. The development context has changed because of the search paradigm such that a new dynamic must be adhered to in order to create relevant content that will allow the business to leverage a mass online audience. SaaS applications are simply part of the evolutionary process that is at play where function resides across domains, and this said function is made available to each subscriber. The next progression in the paradigm however is a different type of application where utility will be provided by smaller distributed JavaScript components that will execute directly within the confines of the subscribing website. The monstrosity of SaaS applications will become part of the history of technology and what will remain will be smaller versions of what was known where the resources of the legacy systems will be replaced by the hardware of the clients themselves. This represents an optimization in the paradigm where solutions will be able to forgo part of the large expense that the public cloud providers charge customers in lieu of the freely available resources that are immediately available to them and provided for free by the users of these systems. Think of an online calculator application that resides in your browser and performs the needed calculations directly within the confines of your own hardware and all without the need to depend on some server that resides in the confines of some rack somewhere in Ohio. The dynamic has now changed where applications can leverage the resources of their clients and shed themselves of the need to have to pay for the heavy lifting that is required by previously developed applications. SaaS has consequently been an intermediary step in the evolutionary process that is web development where it has been supplanted by a variant form of its distant cousin that facilitates not only the development effort but also mitigates the operational cost of these same applications. The development community has achieved progress and has done so because of a new mode of design that is simplistic to its predecessor and consequently affords its implementors the much coveted feature of efficiency which is the hallmark of good design.

IFRAME

An iframe is an embedded container of functionality that allows a sink to consume the resources of a source. In a manner MDAs mimic the relationship of iframes at an abstraction as the container in this case, i.e., the consuming website becomes the housing for the application much as the iframe provides that window by which some desired utility can be imported to a desired node. iframes may be viewed as the predecessors to MDAs at a rudimentary level because MDAs represent an evolution in the landscape whereby functionality becomes dynamic and infused with the hardware leveraged from the client themselves. This factor of differentiation is significant because it means that the burden of work has consequently been removed from the hands of expensive hardware and placed into the hands of that inexpensive hardware that the creators of the functionality do not control or have a vested interest in. This benefit is possible because of the dynamic nature of JavaScript and its rich functionality, which is not a factor of consideration with iframes. The browser has become not simply a collection of windows of functionality but has rather become an ecosystem where diverse functions occur. In this ecosystem there does not exist dictation but what rather exists is autonomy that unlike iframes may be controlled by the client themselves. The syntax of the iframe is defined below and the attribute definitions for the given tag are given in table 1.

<iframe align="" frameborder="" height="" id="" longdesc="" marginheight="" marginwidth="" name="" sandbox="" scrolling="" src="" srcdoc="" width=""></iframe>

From the set of tags presented above it is only six tags according to the HTML 5 specification that are supported, and these are height, name, sandbox, src, srcdoc, and width. The HTML 5 specification as of the writing of this book is the standard for determining valid tag definitions for web browsers and is the plum line that development efforts need to adhere to. The iframe specification is an evolving definition given the inherent change that is web development and the reason why disparity is seen between table 1 and the current specification of the HTML 5 standard.

From its onset the utilization of the iframe tag allowed developers to take already made content and place it directly in their bodies of work all without the need of a laborious work effort, it represented a mechanism by which content could be created by a third party and utilized across the web, freely, openly and accessible via an HTTP call. There was one major problem with this dynamic however and this being that it was consumed without an agreement of service. Developers simply took the content and implemented it directly in their applications. You could for example have a blog on stock investments and then take a stock ticker from a major banking resource and place this content directly in your online presence, the web does not explicitly require consensus by both parties to be consumed it only requires

Table 1. iframe Attribute Detail

Attribute	Description
align	Alignment orientation
frameborder	Visual display status of frame border
height	Frame height
id	Object unique identifier
longdesc	Descriptive text of content
marginheight	Margin height size around frame object
marginwidth	Margin width size around frame object
name	Name designation for object
sandbox	Filter for restrictive functionality
src	Content source
srcdoc	Description of the source content
width	Width size of frame object

the motivation of one party to be implemented as was seen directly in the data mining efforts undertaken in this body of work. As is the economic case with a civilized society, before there can exist prosperity there must exist rules and laws that govern this behavior, which leads the discussion to the next point of interest – JavaScript. JavaScript has become the de facto standard for the building of highly distributable software, but it has also served another purpose, it has given way to a mechanism that allows for order to take shape in the development landscape, which differs from the roots of the iframe. Unlike the iframe component, JavaScript functionality can be versioned and distributed accordingly along with a license agreement no less. The web and its roots have given way to the current state of the domain that has led the industry to a standard client side programming language and a mechanism by which order may be given to the landscape and it is this paradigm that is discussed next.

JAVASCRIPT

JavaScript is a terse programming language that has provided the ability to take a server side component and transform it to the client side thus putting the burden on the browser to perform the work. Development has progressed from the domain of the thick client where artifacts were installed locally to the anonymous whereby clients interact with the software across the internet. This migration to the client browser has consequently infused browsers to become a window of utility that can be linked to the direct functionality of an application. By doing such it has infused the browser to become a rich and interactive playing field for applications. Applications as a consequence have become more in alignment with what use to be the domain of thick clients. JavaScript as a consequence has created ubiquity in the landscape whereby these lightweight applications can reside anywhere there is a browser and often times without the burden of compliance across browser types given the adherence to the W3C standard. Add to this landscape the plethora of opensource projects that have helped to create functionality for JavaScript, and it has simply functioned to create a tidal wave of innovation and product offerings.

JavaScript has no concept of the stack as it binds to resources during the building of the heap. Developers don't declare variable particulars such as type in JavaScript as the language is agnostic to variable class and a burden not worth considering because memory allocation is determined at runtime. Due to this latitude in language construct JavaScript variables are deemed to be objects and as such consume more resources than should be required, but this is a minor burden given all it affords. Even with this latitude in resource consumption JavaScript has one major benefit that cannot be discounted as it is browser based. JavaScript consequently has enabled development teams to create function and place it in front of an audience without the need to have to install the software locally, giving an instant audience to a product. This has resulted in an increase in the popularity of the language and the embrace by the masses of web applications, which has only furthered the argument for JavaScript. It is because of this acceptance by the masses and its functional implementation that has led to the current state of the domain in part. JavaScript has shown such a high versatility that it has become part of the development framework for mobile applications. The language has managed to cross the boundary of mobility and has consequently seen its popularity grow because of it. It is because of this flexibility and viability of the JavaScript language that now MDAs can leverage it and utilize it to gain a further benefit for the would be implementors.

With the advent of HTML 5 also came one remarkable feature of the JavaScript development framework and this was the canvas object. The canvas tag of HTML 5 allows for the creation of graphical content directly within a browser. This now means that you can put images and create text dynamically all through the use of JavaScript. The syntax of the canvas object as defined by the W3C is given below.

```
<canvas height="" id="" width=""></canvas>
```

The attribute definitions are given in table 2 as provided below. The canvas tag was a major achievement for JavaScript as it allowed for the incorporation of dynamic images and image manipulation directly within a browser from code. This enhancement to the language elevated the context of JavaScript as in some languages the generation of images is simply not feasible or implemented through a third party plugin that is external to the language. JavaScript not only managed to get around this hurdle but was also able to expose this dynamic via the World Wide Web.

In JavaScript obtaining a handle to a canvas object can be as simple as the code fragment given below.

Table 2. Canvas Object Attributes

Attribute	Description
height	Canvas vertical size
id	Unique object identifier
width	Canvas horizontal size

With this simple code fragment, it is then possible to completely manage the painting and rendering of content on the canvas object. This paradigm has allowed developers to create greeting cards online with customizable text and family pictures all to be picked up at the local photo shoppe. The ever increasing functionality of JavaScript keeps being augmented with every version that has worked to create a greater following and a better experience for the internet user.

The true power of the JavaScript doctrine however is not in its ability to facilitate the creation of family albums online, but by its distributable nature of the components that can be created and consumed because of it along with its portability between a server side programming context and a browser based paradigm. For the purpose of building distributable web components, it is the prescription needed as it allows for the interconnection between disparate code fragments across the World Wide Web. It allows for the consumption of resources and libraries by importing them dynamically all through a background process that is void of user intervention or awareness. No longer does a developer have to install the needed libraries prior to executing their code as now this happens dynamically and without user interruption, thus helping to only reinforce the enrichment of the user experience.

```
/*
        Canvas object Handle
*/
canvas_reference = document.getElementById('SOME ID');

/*
        Context reference
*/
context_reference = canvas.getContext('2d')
```

EVOLUTION

SaaS product offerings have come about because of a multitude of reasons and represent the evolution of the technological space as well. This evolutionary process has been in the making for quite some time, take for example the fact that J.R. Licklider's initial premise for what is the World Wide Web today was to simply allow communication between computers. Today the internet is utilized to watch live television and for some to do initial research for challenges experienced during the normal workday. While a duality exists today for the utilization of online content and these being functional and entertainment, the argument still remains intact; the online space is evolving and will continue to do so. What is now being experienced is the next phase of the evolutionary process where the indexing space and the online creation space are merging. The creation of online content and its relevance are directly tied to search results. The search results component is directly influenced by link equity as was shown for the supervised learning model created for the Yahoo search engine and as such this link component is what is sought to be leveraged to a maximum in the new breed of web applications. The ability to create online content via a canvas object dynamically for example can lead to a new generation of applications that could potentially be consumed by clients and thus provide a referral back to the creator of the content. It is up to the community at large to create these new breed of applications that will be voted on by the masses for their utility through their adoption on their own websites much as the iframe was adopted earlier.

The new breed of web applications will be smaller and nimble such that they will provide a specific autonomous functional factor when leveraged. This paradigm falls in unison with the development context of microservices where end points are specific to a particular business object and the operations around that business object such as a customer for example. Please do note that what is being said here has already been in place for quite some time as may be validated by looking at the history of Google maps for example, a mapping utility that fits directly on a website that leverages the computation effort of a third party for which the benefit of its utilization may be seen on the implemented domain. Google provides the API, they provide the image library, and they provide the JavaScript code to implement the dynamic nature of the map utility.

The evolution of the domain has been happening and yet the ramifications of which have been left void of discussion. The pieces have been set in motion because of the general evolution of the search domain and the contributing factor that is link equity, which relates back to the base attributes of the general indexing paradigm that the search providers subscribe to. The popularity metric that can be leveraged because of Micro Distributed Applications will be the driver in part for the new paradigm that is the new wave of development that will be seen for web products going forward and that some have already started leveraging in a slightly different flavor of the prescription. MDAs represent an optimization not simply on an indexing front but also from the unit of labor required to build, the economics of their execution, and their openness for distribution. MDAs as a result represent a wave of momentum that is taking the development domain in a new direction whereby this new work effort will become the mode of operandi. This mode of operandi mandates traction because of the simplicity of the design and the elegance of its execution, which history has proven to be a general rule of thumb for change to occur. This is a journey that the industry has been on but has yet to fully appreciate given that final destinations are never fully disclosed until such a time as the train enters the station and when this does occur what is realized is that it is simply a stop along the way.

In the past external functional components were added to a target node through the implementation of iframes or Java Applets, the advent of JavaScript, microservices and jQuery has brought about a paradigm shift however where now the functional code elements may be created in real time through a dynamic coding effort and where applications are initialized across hosts dynamically though the use of modular components. These modular components much like Google maps are simple library references that allow for the creation of content once the browser invokes it. This is a twofold benefit to the content creators as it unloads the computational work effort to the browser, which is external to the server configuration that was utilized previously, and it also affords the content providers the ability to create components that are simple to distribute. In previous days individuals would go to local retail stores and purchase some piece of software to install on their computers, nowadays this functionality is downloaded directly to the machine and going forward this content will load dynamically within a browser independently of where you execute the function, i.e., a phone, tablet, or computer.

The software development domain has changed from its inception to what is now current state. Gone are the days when vendors would distribute fat clients and where vendors would update software on remote servers; in today's paradigm software is delivered on demand. The software is delivered to phones, tablets, PCs or IoT devices dynamically and with a common language such as JavaScript if the offering is browser based. What is new to the architectural context of the web application frameworks is the nature by which the software is built or assembled where this happens at the sink by the same software itself. The dynamic affords great flexibility as it allows a business to pivot and shift with greater agility than was afforded in the past. Changes to offerings can be delivered in real time to customers due to an agile development process and an integrated CI/CD pipeline. Development is currently in a time and age where software changes are pushed to a production environment multiple times a week and at times hourly by development houses. The beneficiaries of all of this are the consumers who now have the ability to be impacted by software development enhancements in real time.

DISTRIBUTED JAVASCRIPT

It was because of JavaScript that static HTML pages took on a dynamic nature and whereby the user experience became enriched. This need for a dynamic experience was the reason why libraries such as jQuery came forth. jQuery (http://www.jquery.com) was a fundamental shift for the web development paradigm as it represented a mechanism by which the dynamic nature of HTML or as it used to be called in days gone by DHTML was elevated. Today however the JavaScript library that is all too commonly relied upon is versioned, which has allowed consumers of the dependency to stay fixed to a specific release of the library. This anchor point has enabled consumers of the library to find assurance with regards to function which has led to derivative products being more robust. jQuery is currently provided under an MIT license and does not require any payment for its use and is also an opensource product that anyone can contribute to. jQuery met the barriers to adoption in the market by its mandate as a product offering and industry overwhelmingly resonated its embrace. By searching for referral links back to jquery.com on Google.com on May 25, 2019, it resulted in 80,200,000 records or referral links back to the domain. In comparison, searching for link referrals back to AngularJS, a more recent UI offering, resulted in 1,470,000 records. jQuery has become the base layer for other libraries; if you implement Bootstrap for example you are required to provide a reference to jQuery for the third party library to function properly. In the development space what is being seeing are products that are being built on top of this base layer, which implicitly mandates confirmation of the artifact. It is this mode of evolution that has been the catalyst for MDAs as it has enabled them to find green pastures in this ecosystem.

Reference to these resources or artifacts has traditionally had a static nature by convention, but it does not need to be this way as JavaScript affords the implementor the ability to circumvent this dynamic. Software can be structured in such a manner that it can take it upon itself to load resources from any connected network node that is deemed to be relevant because such is the nature of the interconnectivity of the internet that this dynamic has become a birthright. Web products can leverage this dynamic because of the very nature of JavaScript since each dependency needed is but simply a network call from being accessed. This process of dynamic loading is malleable and affords a great benefit which is that dependency injection can occur behind the scenes, void of user intervention, and which can result in a continuous product delivery across a diverse client base as will be seen with MDAs. These dependencies become the core appendages that the system requires to function and maintain homeostasis and as such the software could take it upon itself to determine its needs and only load those base components that are critical to function correctly, thus alleviating the runtime environment of the RAM overhead. This is the equivalent of runtime dynamic loading of resources as is seen with more structured programming languages such as Python for example. The world of the fat client has transitioned to the web whereby it has been improved upon because library dependencies are constantly available, at no cost, and versioned to ensure a seamless integration. The distributed nature of JavaScript may be seen in the code snippet provided below where a dependency is retrieved dynamically from some network repository on the internet. This dependency represents a shift in the software development domain whereby distributed software appendages may reside anywhere that an HTTP connection facilitates the dynamic loading of resources, which also means that your specific library that you distribute could be a small file that downloads resources dynamically itself. The code noted below creates a script tag, sets its type definition to be text/javascript and then attaches the content from the URL to the division tag reference. Similarly, the same could also be done for style sheets as the code snippet from below demonstrates for JavaScript. The second code fragment below demonstrates the creation of the base container element as the first entry, it then sets the external dependency link tag along with the corresponding attributes and their values as the second HTML reference, which entails the encapsulation of the functionality from the external node directly in the target document. This dynamic loading of resources is what has laid the path for the wave of distributed web applications and consequently helps reinforce the indexing paradigm as each node that code is distributed to becomes a link referral back to the source. The index paradigm that the search engine providers have implemented to facilitate indexing online content has helped to usher in the era of MDA web development and what may only be categorized as the new web architecture. This architectural footprint will be based upon a common language – JavaScript, it will be based upon small components that will be used to perform a specific function and they will interact with external resources via microservices. These components will also take it upon themselves to structure the HTML content on the page to facilitate the indexing of the document and it will all be done dynamically through JavaScript.

```
<!—
```

Definition of a division container for a Micro Distributed Application. The division container serves as the anchor point for all elements to embed themselves into. The division anchor tag in MDAs parallels the iframe object reference whereby it functions as the housing for external functionality to reside directly in.

```
// -->
<div id="vendorApplication"></div>
```

```
<!—
```

An example of the importation of an MDA library. The reference is used as a bootstrap component whereby all dependencies are subsequently injected into the page through the bootstrap component. Bootstrap components function as the point of invocation for all external dependencies which could be either Cascading Style Sheets or JavaScript entities.

```
// -->
<script type="text/javascript' src="https://SomeVendorsLibrary.com/javascript.js"></script>
```

The distributive nature that JavaScript embodies is quite remarkable as external resources can now be consumed from code and then dynamically loaded to create content on demand and much as was the case for its predecessor the iframe it represents content that may be consumed without the need to invest in the development effort to create the benefit. As a consumer this means that you should be able to create a specific tag on your web document and add a library reference such as given above from which the vendor's code will then be able to be consumed directly in the HTML document and generate the desired application directly where it was told, i.e. at the specified division tag. All of this work will be done dynamically in a plug and play mode as the masses have become accustomed to. Distributed JavaScript is what has led to MDAs in part and this is relevant to software development because micro distributed functionality will be the manner by which the indexing winners will be elected.

SECURITY

With the openness of web content how does it become feasible to secure the same open applications? The encryption of content between nodes is feasible in JavaScript thanks to third party libraries one of which is from Google and may be found here https://code.google.com/archive/p/crypto-js/. The library from Google implements SHA-1, SHA-2, SHA-512, and SHA-3 all of which are standards in the computing security sector for securing content between nodes. The library by Google is by no means unique as there are countless other offerings by organizations such as those given below in table 3, please do note that this list is not exhaustive and simply represents a small subset of that which is available to be used freely and openly for your development needs. The libraries given below have been made available either through a BSD, General Public or MIT license.

```
<!—
    Container element reference
// -->
<div id="vendorApplication"></div>

<!—

    External dependencies added through an external node reference such as a CDN or dedicated web
reference. Dependencies are added individually and each external reference must have a dedicated node
to service the request.

// -->
<link rel="stylesheet' href="https://SomeVendorsLibrary.com/style.css">
```

Table 3. Cryptography Libraries

Library	Reource
WebCryptoAPI	http://www.w3.org/TR/WebCryptoAPI/
Stanford Library	http://bitwiseshiftleft.github.io/sjcl/
Networking and Cryptography	https://github.com/tonyg/js-nacl
OpenPGP Implementation	https://github.com/openpgpjs/openpgpjs

The loading of dynamic content as prescribed in code fragments provided in this chapter denote a simple arrangement where the end node being used as the sink simply renders the JavaScript file content and while this configuration is common it does not imply exclusivity. As such it is completely feasible to load content from an end point that is encrypted by way of say a microservice that requires a user issued key for validation, which is common in business implementations currently. This pre-existing dynamic of distributed resource loading can then be used along with the implementation of a secure key on the server to render secure encrypted content between peers. This security is of the utmost paramount in the new development doctrine that will usher in the new wave of web applications as otherwise you would simply be rendering your codebase for all to see including your competition. Security must be an integral part of an open solution and this security doctrine must be tightly integrated into the development effort.

Securing an application in the new development age will not simply involve encrypting and decrypting of the content transferred across the wire but will also involve the dynamic construction and deconstruction of coding fragments in real time. What this means is that as a component is needed its corresponding codebase will be initialized on the server, downloaded, executed and destroyed as depicted in Fig. 1 below. The new wave of secure JavaScript applications will follow this standard lifecycle, thus ensuring that if someone were to obtain your code segment it would be just that, a piece of the puzzle and not the entire library. It should also be noted that these code fragments will live only in RAM and will be lost once the code fragment is used thus failing to leave a footprint of the artifact on the user's computer.

There is no doubt that the security context around JavaScript is lagging and as a result it represents an opportunity. What the profession may be even seeing is a change to the security around how web browser's function. Current browser content is unencrypted when it is downloaded, but why should this be the case? A web browser is simply a new implementation of an old doctrine – the old personal computer and installed software. There is no doubt that change is coming, and web development architecture will evolve and adopt any new construct that functions better. Going forward however what is certain is that the new wave of distributed web applications will adhere to a new architectural pattern. This code life cycle is currently the burden of the development team and as such it is upon their shoulders that the burden lay for the modularity of functionality and its security. There is a configuration that could be established whereby only identified IP addresses or specific domain names could be given the privilege to download the actual code fragments of MDAs and as such all other requestors would be denied access to the code fragments. The mode by which exclusion occurs could be a matter of a business decision, but regardless of the decision undertaken by the business there needs to be a central focus on the securing of the MDAs and whether this happens through IP address filtering or a shared private key it needs to occur under the guise of maintaining security.

THE PARADIGM

Web development components with MDAs will be smaller, cross functional, distributable, secure, encrypted, JavaScript laden, dynamic, and easily integrated. This entails no short task for a feature set creation as it is a departure from current doctrine. In the case presented previously with the table reservation service, it is an implementation that is quite popular, but allowing a customer to leave the targeted domain to possibly being lost represents a risk to the consumer of the service. It is also a departure from self, which yields to an awkward customer experience. Customers want to perform their body of work in one place, easily, timely, and all of this through the same customer experience or UI representation. The paradigm presented here is just that, granted a departure from current doctrine, but nevertheless it is at a time and place that demands it. The technological tools are there, the architectural requirements are present what is missing is the evolutionary step for who's time it has come. The process flow that will be adhered to in this new doctrine is given in Fig. 2 below and as you will notice all the technologies that are needed to implement the paradigm currently exist.

Figure 2 depicts strictly web technologies that may reside in various states in their evolution such as JavaScript security and HTML, but their synchronization across the web landscape results in a paradigm shift that maintains the world order of code distribution, search relevance, and modularization of functionality. In this paradigm each web site or document would consume a generic JavaScript library that would be vendor specific. This library would bootstrap all subsequent functionality by calling its designated API to retrieve a code fragment that would be relevant to the specific action being requested by the user. This code fragment would arrive at the sink node encrypted and be decrypted accordingly. The unencrypted code fragment would be executed in the browser to create desired functional state and be destroyed completing the process flow.

This new paradigm much like the iframe implementation that has become a common occurrence represents external functionality that is inherited by some target node providing the host with some needed utility. The diversion between doctrines however is significant as the paradigm shift is void of the internal window and represents a physical coding artifact that is distributed across the web. The argument could even be made that this mode of operation could leverage distributed call stacks as you would see in traditional distributed software development that could be executed simultaneously across a series of open browsers. This would elevate the distributed development context to a new level of functionality where each instance of an open browser at some designated page would represent an available node for utilization. Where in a current day and time the norm is big data and the utilization of distributed systems to solve problems for large datasets; the very nature of the web ecosystem could very well be embracing the realization of the largest distributed computing configuration, millions of open browsers all performing some common body of work on a large dataset. The possibility for MDAs to evolve to the de facto standard of distributed computing may be an argument that is premature but is nevertheless within preview given the benefit that the internet has afforded the masses. MDAs in essence could very well simply be part of this step in the evolution of distributed systems.

The paradigm of Micro Distributed Applications will resonate with teams because of the simplification that occurs through the paradigm. Smaller components that cease to be a burden to the business economically because their execution happens on the hardware of the client will be a message that will resonate with the business personnel of the organization because after all, which business is not keen on saving money. Distributed components will make sense to marketing personnel because it will entail a message that will gravitate to a larger audience organically and that will cease to need the previously allocated marketing dollars. Smaller components that are easier to integrate across development efforts entails an engineering benefit that is efficient, and the datum point that technical teams seek to obtain. These are the reasons why MDAs make sense.

SUMMARY

Distributed JavaScript components are a necessity for business viability in a technologically driven economy as it allows vendors or service providers to create clout by their individual services which are consumed by the masses. This doctrine allows for the ever so coveted link equity component to be leveraged and allows the domain performing the implementation to reap the benefits. While this does

Figure 1. Distributed JavaScript Lifecycle

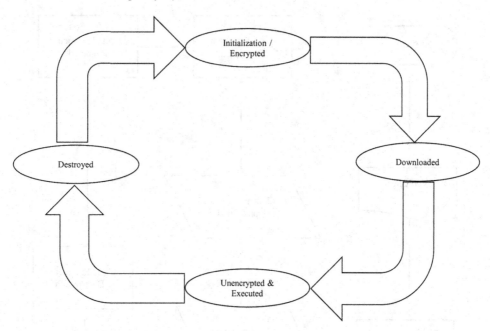

require a paradigm shift and a significant work effort to leverage perhaps the biggest hurdle will be the changing of the guard and the organizational cultural drift that will need to occur in order to leverage the new doctrine. Change is a force that acts counter to friction where in an organization change is a drift in a technological paradigm and the friction is directly related to people, processes and technological debt that will need to be overcome.

The state of the development context has come about because of an evolutionary process that has been driven by the masses. Google and the other search providers only exist because humanity tunes in. For a technological solution to make sense it must fit into an existing paradigm or a paradigm that is prime for disruption, which is where MDAs currently sit within the web landscape and its underlying architectural framework. The framework that is discussed here is a paradigm shift no doubt, but it is an already existing paradigm shift void of the momentum needed to move it to the stature of a norm. This norm is a horizon that is within preview however as the technologies for its implementation already exist, the web indexing landscape demands it, the development context is present, and it all fits into the preexisting paradigm of the computer scientist's desire to solve challenges in a modular fashion. The breaking down of tasks into smaller components that can be bridged together elegantly to solve the general problem frame is the bedrock of computer science. Computer science always migrates to this datum point as it is a leverage that reaps benefits independent of time. Take for example the case of recursion, even though it is computationally expensive it is elegant and succinct, the Fibonacci sequence can be solved through it. With one simple function definition, the Fibonacci sequence can be determined independent of initialization point. Software development at its core is but logic and when a problem frame can be broken down to logical facets it makes for the implementation trivial at times, even though finding this point of triviality can be a challenge. Distributed JavaScript leverages the hallmarks of good design in computer science just like the solution of the Fibonacci sequence, simple components that may be leveraged in a series as needed. If for example you have a distributed JavaScript component that takes

Figure 2. Distributed JavaScript Process Flow

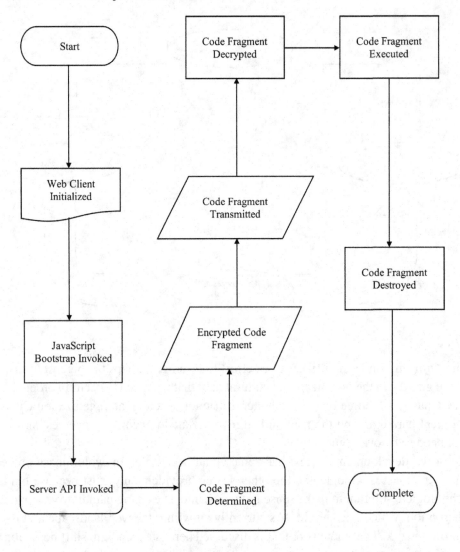

reservations and another that allows menu selection then the world order would be preserved as each would represent distinct components that could be integrated much like APIs, coding libraries, Python packages or a jQuery widget for example. The simplicity of the implementation also represents a hallmark of good design; these are all features that allow for homeostasis to be maintained in the world view of the technologists and scientists that must work with the subject matter.

Even though there exists technological drivers for the migration to occur to Micro Distributed Applications (MDAs) the largest driver of all will always be the economics of the equation and as such the current doctrine that is depicted here will prevail because of the financial ramifications. If development teams are able to make the transition to MDAs it will lead the businesses that adopt them to win the indexing race. The type of business is actually inconsequential because what is sought is to have code function as the gateway to the customer. It is upon each member of the pod to create these much needed MDAs that may be consumed by the masses that will facilitate matters for the business and allow the business to become the voice of authority on the World Wide Web and by doing so, by being this voice of authority the business is guaranteed to win the indexing race and the much coveted funds that customers will spend. The argument here has actually been an economics proposition that cannot be denied and that must be respected by each business that has some sort of online presence.

The profession of building software has been on this path towards MDAs from the very onset that documents were linked and classified, unbeknownst to all, however. Evolution is a dynamic that is never known at the onset and will have no destination point as each stopping point is but simply a pause until an alternative course of action may be determined that is more efficient and serves a better purpose. The indexing effort has imposed such a bounding constraint on development teams that now the dynamic must be afforded its rightful place in the discussion of software engineering. This constraint is such because of the benefit that it affords and it is because of it that now teams must shift and focus on how this constraint may be leveraged to reap as big of a benefit as can be harnessed through it. This is the reason why MDAs will come to be a focal point for development teams. Software teams have always functioned to provide as big of a benefit to the business as possible and there can be no bigger leverage currently than to propel the domain of the business to the top of the search rankings. This is essentially what is at stake and the reason why the argument in favor of MDAs has to be embraced. Businesses that cease to capitalize on the construct will simply become those same businesses that continued to build fat clients when their competitors started offering cloud applications that worked on a subscription basis, i.e., SaaS offerings. Every business is currently a technology company and those businesses that do not realize this fact are but simply walking corpses awaiting their burial. It is a sad proposition, but it is nevertheless the reality that has existed from the beginning of time as evolution is but a bounding constraint that has no escape velocity.

The work of Jerkovic (2010) and King (2008) set the tone for the dialog that needed to occur over the indexing domain, but what was missing was the statistical argument for the discourse. The previous chapters of this text have provided the metrics behind the argument in favor of MDAs, the data is in and now the reality of the new architectural framework for web development must be acknowledged and understood if the business is to remain relevant. While change may be difficult and the argument in favor of an option a point of contention what cannot be argued against are the hard numbers that dictate where true north resides. The development domain is under a new steward and its name is MDA, and for which to argue against it simply means to be contrary to the numbers.

REFERENCES

Jerkovic, J. (2010). *SEO Warrior*. O'Reilly Media Inc.

King, A. (2008). *Website Optimization*. O'Reilly Media Inc.

Chapter 9
Case Study 1:
A Standard Micro-Distributed Application

ABSTRACT

The need of the empiricist will only ever be satisfied if they are able to experience the world visually as this form of validation helps to satisfy that inherent need that they function by. It is the burden of the software engineer however to first define the reality that is coveted by the empiricist because to build to something other than a specification simply means that this experience that is coveted will never truly satisfy the target audience. This case study helps to satisfy the need of that empiricist as it defines the functionality of an MDA in terms of software engineering parlance, which allows for that reality that is coveted by the empiricist to come to existence. While the content here will not provide that complete picture that is desired, what it does provide is the roadmap to be able to obtain such.

INTRODUCTION

In this chapter the constructs defined previously are taken and a practical case study for a business that seeks to create value and consequently generate a business pipeline through a modern web architecture is studied. This case study will highlight the opportunity that exists by first understanding how search engine indexing of web content integrates with a business mandate and secondly by providing a business case for a technological need that leverages a distributable JavaScript laden web architecture. This particular case study will satisfy the paradigm that has been identified as providing worth due to the leveraging of the indexing domain and the page attributes as they were identified in the random forest study that was conducted in a previous chapter, thus showing where value for the business may be generated. The degree of weight of link equity was deemed to have been significant given the supervised learning models that were created in a previous chapter, but what was determined by way of the random forest study was that relevance is tied to the attribute sets of the page and not simply to link equity. To be able to leverage the benefit that may be afforded by way of the attributes it becomes essential to identify those relevant keywords that are deemed to have significance according to the search providers. To this aim the Google trends utility (https://trends.google.com/) was utilized, thus allowing the identification of those perti-

DOI: 10.4018/978-1-6684-4849-6.ch009

nent keywords that will hold the most value to the search provider and consequently search providers in general given the ubiquitous nature of the landscape. Once the pertinent keywords are identified it then becomes feasible to implement those desired textual references directly within the application context, thus facilitating the indexing of the content that is generated directly by way of the Micro Distributed Application (MDA). The case study here will simply serve the purpose of identifying the requirements that will be needed in the physical implementation, which is performed in the proceeding chapter, but which must take a seat to first identifying what needs to be built.

This case study will help to identify all the individual components that will need to be encompassed in the solution that must be implement in the next chapter and by doing so help to create alignment between a business case and the architectural framework that was set forth earlier in this text. This case study is utilized to help bring the concepts developed previously to the physical requirements as would often be found in industry. This chapter helps to bridge the gap between the theoretical underpinnings that have been disclosed to date of MDAs with a practical need of a business. This case study helps to bring the reader forth to understanding the ramifications of what has been discovered and helps to place a focus on the practicality of the theory. What has been determined in this study that you find yourself reading is tangible and immediately applicable to the businesses that have an online presence. What has been brought before you are not abstractions with obscure instances of applicability but are rather tangible constructs that can help you leverage the benefits of the search space and consequently help you enable your business going forward. This text is here to help you migrate your software systems to the new doctrine of development that has been put forth to you and this chapter specifically sets out to help you understand the immediate applicability of the discussions up to now.

In this case study a mock business called the ACME Mortgage Company will be used where this business needs to generate leads for mortgages. The ACME Mortgage Company like many such businesses is seeking to leverage the search engines so that potential customers may reach out to the business for their mortgage needs. The ACME Mortgage Company could be any business that is in need of customers and is willing to utilize some technological work effort to help it meet its business objectives and as such the particulars surrounding this case study could be applicable to a slew of other businesses. In this particular case the ACME Mortgage Company is in need of generating organic leads, thus alleviating itself from the need to invest in costly search advertisements and as such is seeking to benefit from its network of dealers that currently send it leads. The company is hoping to be able to increase its web presence so that it becomes easier for potential customers to find them and thus mitigate the current high expense of new account acquisitions through formal pay per click advertisements. The company up until now much like many organizations in the space understands the significance of having an online presence but has no idea of how to proceed to lower its account acquisition expense to help it become a more viable business. The business understands what it needs but unfortunately much like most businesses that lack technical prowess does not understand how to be able to get from a point of a need to a point of accomplishment where its goals for increased revenue can be met.

The ACME Mortgage Company is much like any business where execution is lacking because of direct knowledge over the development domain. Fortunately for the business a team member has come to understand how to leverage the nature of the indexing space and is able to introduce the business to the notion of MDAs. In this case study a formal draft of the requirements that will be needed for the MDA that will be distributed freely to the masses will be defined. The company is wanting to create a solution that can leverage the prowess of the web in order to be able to capitalize on the increased business from an uptrend in visibility. This application will need to function such that it will facilitate the generation of leads for the business all through the workflow of the application and thus reduce the account acquisition expense that the firm is so desperate to alleviate itself from. This application must fit the mold of being a leverage to the current practice of how business is being performed while at the same time help to automate part of the current process.

The solution that is presented here is free from the constraints of common content management systems such as WordPress, which is addressed in the following chapters. This chapter uses this particular case to highlight the benefits that may be derived by the natural extension of the freely available tools that are utilized on the World Wide Web. This implementation consequently leaves you with the most flexibility going forward as it is generic enough that it could be implement in a similar manner with modifications of course in an array of diverse businesses. This again highlights the tangible benefits that may be derived because of the nature of the tools that are utilized and the flexibility that they afford, all of which are hallmarks of technology that should see a high adoption rate. But as was stated in a previous chapter it is the economics of the discussion that always pave the way for action. Distributed JavaScript applications have come of age because the economics mandate it as will be seen in this case here.

The business is seeking to reduce its economic overhead with its current marketing direction, it is also hoping to utilize technology to create leverage through automation. It is because of the economics of the equation that change is mandated typically and whether you are dealing with a business in a similar light or you are dealing with a business that is trying to find a distinct leverage point the momentum for change is ubiquitous as it is about creating a more resilient organization which leads to a new datum point. Technology is but that leverage point that helps to facilitate where that momentum is to take the business.

PROBLEM STATEMENT

The ACME Mortgage Company is in need of sales leads for its mortgage business, and they want to generate these leads by not having to invest additional capital in pay per click advertisements with search engine providers or with social media platforms. The business has an online presence, but to date does not have very good traction with the major search engine providers and after having spent some financial resources with advertisements via the search engine providers and the social media platforms has not had much success. Management has found that much like their competition they have created a website and created pages to help identify the business, but to date do not see much traffic due to their online presence. The company is at a standstill because they do not know in which direction to proceed to help alleviate the issue with generating qualified leads. The company is hoping to not only be able to generate leads as each lead has an operational expense to the firm because the lead needs to be qualified, but it is hoping to be able to streamline the process of generating qualified leads where the probability of generating revenue from such is heightened. The business keeps track of its competitors and invests in the same manner in which their competitors invest but to date has not been able to crack the code that would allow them to generate that much coveted revenue that they are after.

Management would like to see the ACME Mortgage Company be identified as a leader in their core business and would like to see more business through new customers that may not be linked back to existing customers. The management team understands that their products are equal to that of competitors and that differentiation is a major obstacle in the space as they are selling a common widget comparatively to their competition. Management understands that for the business to grow they must be willing to think creatively and create value where others have not seen it. In order for the business to grow significantly the business understands that growth must be organic and in tune with their user base. Since more people have placed greater utility on their cellphone's functionality in recent years, they understand that a solution must integrate or at a very minimum be operational on mobile devices. Management would like to see an implementation that would eliminate churn and allow for the identification of potential customers that are viable as opposed to spending time with potential customers that will never reach a level of maturity to equate to revenue dollars. The company is searching for more quality leads without the need to increase the expense of internal business processes and consequently incur additional overhead in the acquisition of a larger customer base. The firm understands that the economics of the proposition could be such that even though more work is generated for the firm that they end up not generating more revenue because of the inherent expenses in the process.

The business understands that in order to create greater value for the firm without investing in manual processes or human capital that technology will need to be part of the solution. Management also understands that product differentiation is difficult given the climate of competition and the commonality of the widget being sold, therefore they understand that in order to be able to provide a factor of differentiation for customers for the better that an innovative and user friendly solution must also be implemented. The firm understands that they must be able to think outside the box because to date the solutions that they have put forth have not yielded results that warranted further investment.

The firm works with business partners that funnel traffic to the business in order to process the loan, but currently the process is manual and time laden both of which are factors that need to diminish or be eliminated if economies of scale are to be obtained. This factor has also led the management team to understand that in order to move forward with a viable solution that technology will need to be an answer in the overall arching paradigm that is to be implemented.

The business has identified a series of objectives that they hope to achieve in their investment, and they are as follows.

1. Improve the overall search engine ranking of the corporate website.
2. Facilitate the submission of mortgage requests through their partners and own website.
3. Minimize the capital expenditure that is being consumed through clickthrough advertisement campaigns.
4. Improve team efficiency in the processing of mortgage applications.
5. Minimize time spent in the qualification of loan applications.
6. Identify loan applicants that are to provide the business with revenue as opposed to be an expense of company resources quickly in the process.
7. Provide a differentiation factor to their competition in a market segment that is difficult to find separation in.

The list given above represents desired goals for the business that in essence are common to many businesses and the reason why corporations seek to leverage technology to meet their business objectives. The ACME Mortgage Company's business needs could be interchanged with many likeminded businesses as they all have some attributes to their business that are common. The identification of qualified customers, increasing search engine ranking, and the minimization of internal business processes are objectives that cross organizational boundaries. Problem statements by businesses may deviate from one another in their nuances, but they will share a common thread and this common thread may often find a receptive partner in technology.

The utilization of a software component to create value across partners entails a technological leverage that cannot be denied as technology is void of the burden of humanities labor. Technology is pushing the boundary of how business is being done and the ACME Mortgage Company is but simply another organization that may find its benefit if it is used correctly. Gone are the days when the executive mandate was a subsequent afterthought to technical execution as the two are married now and joined at the hip. In order to be able to execute what is needed as much as the people of the firm is the right technology in such a way so that it solves the general problem frame from the onset.

USE CASES

There exist two distinct actors in the case of the ACME Mortgage Company, the mortgage broker and the mortgage seeker as identified in figures 1 and 2. These two actors are distinct in their nature in how they are to interact with the solution that is needed. The diagrams depicted below are part of the Unified Modeling Language (UML) specification that may found here: https://www.omg.org/spec/UML/2.5.1/ PDF. The purpose of the use case diagram is to depict at a high level how individuals are supposed to interact with the system to be built. The use case diagram will depict an actor and the functions they perform on the system, which is the large bounding rectangular area in which each function resides. Use case diagrams in essence represent the starting point of the discussion that is to proceed. Figures 1 and 2 are simply just that, the high level requirements that will need to be addressed by the Micro Distributed Application that is to be built in the proceeding chapter.

The use cases presented in this chapter should resonate with the reader as the spirit of the endeavor can be extended to domains that are distinct from what is addressed here specifically. Every business needs to be able to create a utility whereby an audience is able to navigate to it via the World Wide Web and be able to fill out some sort of questionnaire. The need to be able to determine loan particulars could be modified for example to be outside of the particular domain being addressed here, such as for users to be able to determine the cost of having their lawn mowed given some preliminary particulars that could be ingested by some utility such as the one that is presented here. So, while the domain in question is specific to a business type, it does not entail exclusivity in the least as technology is domain agnostic. The takeaway for the reader from this chapter should be that there does exist a use case for the particular needs of the organization of the individual and for which a paradigm such as the one undertaken here could also be made to fit those particulars and the nuances of that distinct entity. The architectural framework that was presented in the previous chapter is business domain agnostic and as such could be made to fit a variety of businesses.

The significance of the use cases presented in this chapter are that the need that they exhibit can be linked to an online delivery that could function to elevate the footprint of the business on the web. This footprint can be made to have more impact through the adoption of the new architectural framework that was presented in the previous chapter and that may be leveraged because of the indexing endeavor of the search providers. In the end it is but simply a matter of creating that correct message that may be disseminated by the search engine providers and by the masses so that a lift can occur whereby the bottom line of the business is enhanced. Every use case that interfaces with this online presence can be made to fit this mold that is spoken of with Micro Distributes Applications and as such it becomes a necessity to be able to craft those points of interaction that users will be able to migrate to independent of domain providing the needed housing that will allow the benefit of link equity to be reaped by the business. In this dynamic the input fields or the layout become but details in the grand scheme of things because the leverage that is sought never migrates far from home, a leverage that is JavaScript laden and distributed. It is because of this reason that the argument is made that every business is now a technology business and those businesses that are not ready to embrace this new reality are but some delta of time away from that proverbial end.

The particulars of the business and the need that must be addressed with technology is important, but just as important is the ability to tie this final deliverable to the measuring stick that search prominence is tied to. If this alignment is not created then it simply means that the system is in disharmony from the expectation and a solution that is less than optimal to say the least. The businesses that will survive in the new economy will be those that will be able to create a leverage through their technological investments whereby this hedge that is sought can be taken to the masses and allowed to bloom in this field of opportunity that is the World Wide Web. In doing so the business will be putting itself in the best possible position to be able to reap the largest harvest possible. It is a bounty that only the masses can provide through their collective approval of the applications that are put forth for their consumption and when doing so the proxy for this vote, the search engines will have but little choice but to acquiesce to their demand and afford the creators of these applications their due place on the search rankings no less. Are the use cases presented in this chapter specifically applicable to the reader's own business? Probably not, but what is pertinent is the architectural framework of Micro Distributed Applications that may be leveraged as is presented in this chapter to reap that benefit that only the World Wide Web may afford through its mass foot traffic of customers that ultimately need to have their electronic commerce needs met.

In the new economy it will be organizations such as the ACME Mortgage Company that will be able to create alignment between their particular use cases and the architectural framework of modern web development that will be able to stand a better chance to survive since every business depends on customers and if the business is better able to be found than others than it stands to reason that it has a greater probability of remaining in existence or maybe even thriving. It would behoove the reader therefore to begin to determine how their particular business use cases could be made to have that alignment with MDAs for this benefit that is search prominence to take hold and help to create that leverage that is sought. The digital highway is plentiful of foot traffic and those organizations that are best able to attract these customers will be in the best position possible to either remain viable or better yet to thrive in the new economy irrespective of the particulars of the use case.

Mortgage Broker

The mortgage broker needs to be able to locate qualified leads via the solution provided without the need to invest time in weeding through the applications that will not come to fruition for the mortgage company. The use case for the mortgage broker is given below in Fig. 1. It will be necessary therefore to have an implementation that generates messages or notifications to the internal staff that are to process the loan when a potential loan is identified as being viable to the business. To meet this objective entails the satisfying of items 3, 4, 5, and 6 from the list given previously where item 3 is satisfied by the minimization of advertisement dollars via the search engine providers

The case of the mortgage broker is not unique as most businesses have a deep desire to only invest time in those business relationships that will yield good fruit. With the high degree of speed that is needed in business it becomes paramount to be able to alleviate the mortgage brokers from having to spend their time on cases were a positive outcome is not a reasonable probability. It is argued at times that business boils down to a numbers game and if you are able to tip the cards in your favor then it becomes a potentially lucrative proposition for the business to function in this manner. It is paramount therefore to only have to take up the time of the mortgage brokers with those leads that show a high likelihood of generating income for the business and forgo the time and expense with having to service inquiries that will never become physical accounts for the business. This dynamic also helps the individual submitting the loan application from having a negative experience were their application is denied by a physical person. It stands to reason therefore that for all actors involved it is a better experience to remain in anonymity at the onset. This degree of efficiency that can be derived through the software implementation entails that the solution by way of the MDA can help to facilitate internal operational objectives.

Figure 1. Mortgage Broker Use Case

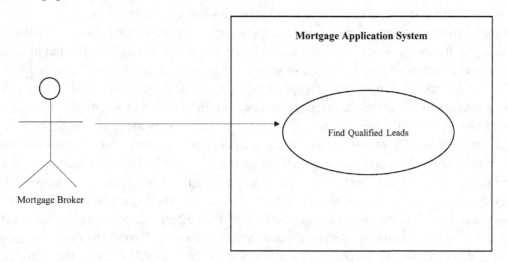

Mortgage Seeker

In the case of the mortgage seeker, their interaction with the proposed solution is given in the use case provided in Fig. 2. The mortgage seeker will need to interact with the application system by first being able to calculate their mortgage detail. In order to calculate the mortgage detail the individual will need to enter simple numerical values onto a form such as the loan period, the amount being requested for the loan, and their down payment amount. The system will then generate for the user their monthly payment amount given the data provided. On the form the user should be able to enter an interest rate amount, but one should be provided by default. This default value could be retrieved from some designated source that is accessible via an HTTP GET request and placed directly onto the form for the user. If the user is then satisfied with the loan payment amount, then they need to be directed to an application that needs to be displayed and submitted from one location easily and efficiently before their interest is lost. The keeping of the individual in one location differs from what is currently experienced with some SaaS solutions as was pointed out in the previous chapter. It is because of the user experience that the user needs to be kept in one location where they can perform all of their needed operations succinctly and void of interruption.

In the spirit of the executive mandate, it will be necessary for any solution implemented to meet objectives 1 through 7 from the list given previously. With the proposed MDA the requirements that were set forth will all be met as they are outlined in the list provided below, where each numeric entry corresponds to the requirements numeric entry that was outlined previously.

1. Overall search relevance of the website would be enhanced because the MDA would provide link equity back to the point of authority, i.e., the business' main website.
2. Mortgage applications would be streamlined because the MDA would be able to be implemented on the website of the business and the corresponding websites of each of the partners.
3. Clickthrough expenditures would be minimized because the current implementation plan would alleviate the need for the same degree of expenditure given the increase in search relevance.
4. Applications would be filtered through the MDA and consequently only qualified leads would be provided to the mortgage brokers.
5. The MDA would alleviate the need to spend excess time in reviewing applications as the application would place the burden unto itself to perform the previous manual work.
6. Only those qualified leads would be forwarded to the business and consequently the mortgage brokers would only invest their time in fruitful applications.
7. The ability to provide a seamless solution to partners and facilitate the mortgage application

Figure 2. Mortgage Seeker Use Case

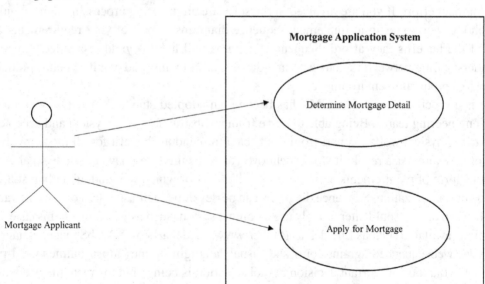

The implementation of an MDA solution would provide the ACME Mortgage Company with a clear technological hedge over the competition as the solution would leverage the network structure of the internet and help propel the business to a higher degree of relevance because of the nature of the MDA. This technological solution would help propel the business forward because it would leverage an existing system that inherently the masses turn in order to locate what they need, and it would allow the business to grow their online presence organically as each MDA distributed to a partner site would yield another degree of relevance to the business from the partner given the inherent structure of link equity. This case represents a clear example of the benefits that may be afforded to a business that chooses to invest in Micro Distributed Applications to achieve overall business relevance and operational economies of scale.

SEQUENCE DIAGRAMS

Sequence diagrams are part of the Unified Modeling Language (UML) specification as are use case diagrams, the general guidelines for which may be located here: https://www.uml.org. The sole purpose of the sequence diagram is for the depicting of the interaction between objects and consequently the particular data that needs to flow between them for this interaction to occur. Sequence diagrams are the next phase of the creation of the requirements specification because it allows for the breakdown of functionality into more granular detail. Sequence diagrams enable the understanding of the particulars of the communication that is to occur and as such it allows developers to begin to understand what data needs to be captured by way of the user interfaces or what type of data detail needs to be accounted for so that the system developed may be able to maintain data integrity.

These physical depictions of data flows between system objects physical or otherwise allows for the understanding of what is needed to be accounted for in the visual interfaces and communication streams such as APIs for example. This is one of the great benefits of the sequence diagram, they allow the discussion to move from the depths of obscurity of what is needed to a tangible artifact that helps to define the development effort. If you are involved in the software engineering process in your organization, it would behoove you to begin to implement sequence diagrams as part of your requirements gathering because of the benefits they afford. Sequence diagrams will help to yield less defects in products, a better understanding between the business and development teams, and result in better products being promoted to a production environment.

There is a specific reason why UML has become an adopted standard in industry and a staple of software engineering teams. Being able to move from an abstraction to a physical and accepted definition of where physical work can part from has been a tremendous benefit for all those involved in the creation of software. As a result, it would behoove you to begin if you have not done so already to migrate to this form of requirements definition as the benefits of which will undoubtedly result in a great benefit to your organization. Sequence diagrams can be developed with standard office software such as Microsoft Visio or you could alternatively use an online system such as was done in this case. There are many options available such as Lucidchart (https://www.lucidchart.com), WebSequenceDiagrams.com (https://www.websequencediagrams.com), and Visual Paradigm Online (https://online.visual-paradigm. com). What is the most important decision in tool selection is being able to create the needed charts in a manner that can be communicated and disseminated throughout the entire organization. So, the focal point should not be the tool utilized but rather on the mechanism that will facilitate information dissemination throughout your team and organization because adoption will only help to further facilitate the conveying of what is needed to be built.

Mortgage Broker

The Sequence diagram for the mortgage broker is depicted below in figure 3. From the sequence diagram it is noted that the data is to be transferred from the mortgage application system directly to the mortgage broker that is in direct need of the qualified mortgage application leads. The arrow denotes that the qualified lead is transmitted to the mortgage broker without having the mortgage broker having to directly request for the new leads as the system is to simply forward the leads to the mortgage broker as they arrive in the system

The physical implementation for the depiction of the sequence diagram is distinct as the sequence diagram is void of technology particulars. In a practical system what could be seen is a queuing system for example, whereby messages would be routed to corresponding parties based upon a predetermined processing order. The sequence diagram is also void of the data structures that are to be used in the implementation such as the use of JSON or XML data. Yet another constraint that is also void from the UML diagram provided here is the protocol to be used for the data transmission. At this level of detail what is important in the specification is the determination of the data needed between the components of the system.

The leverage that is created through UML cannot be understated as it facilitates the pictorial representation of the system and helps to subsequently create avenues for further discussions and possibly enhancements to the system being initially defined. In the case at hand for example it could very well be desired that if a lead is deemed to be unqualified then it could potentially be rerouted to another team that could work with the individual to help them work towards becoming a qualified lead. Alternatively, the business could create relationships with exterior organizations that could then be leveraged whereby the information of the individual could be routed to them for further assistance or subsequent products.

Figure 3. Mortgage Broker Sequence Diagram

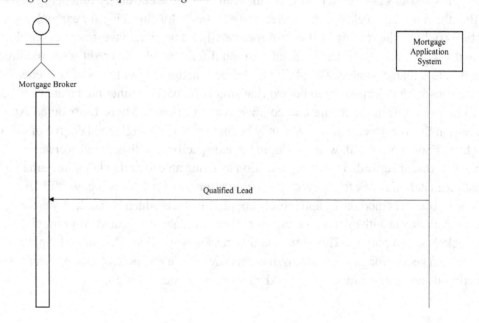

While the sequence diagram for the mortgage broker is simple in nature there becomes a reality immediately apparent, the manner by which communication is to occur is unidirectional. The qualified leads are to be transmitted from the back office system that is the mortgage application system to the brokers directly. In this particular case they will simply be forwarded as email to a target mortgage broker, but in an actual system what would be required would be the determination of this route, i.e., dependent on which state the mortgage broker is licensed in for example. In an actual system you would even be capable of applying data science to the domain where you could determine statistically what person on your team would be best to address the customer, such as the routing of customers to employees based on language preference for example because by doing so you would be able to pair them with the most likely person that they would be able to connect with.

Mortgage Seeker

The sequence diagram for the mortgage seeker is depicted below in figure 4. In the sequence diagram for the mortgage seeker, there are two events that occur. In the first event the user enters mortgage detail and submits it at which point the system replies with the payment detail. In the second event they physically submit their preliminary application, and the system takes this input and replies back with a confirmation message.

In order to maintain the integrity of the requirements the system will need to be able to determine if the loan is viable and this will be done by ensuring that the monthly income of the applicant does not exceed 30% of their monthly payment. Applicants will also be deemed viable for a loan if their physical credit score is above 650. These factors collectively will be used as the determining factors for loan viability by the system. If the loan is determined to be serviceable then and only then will the loan particulars be forwarded to the mortgage broker for processing.

As in the case of the mortgage broker sequence diagram, the mortgage seeker sequence diagram could lead to discussions that could facilitate enhancements to the current system being developed, such as providing the mortgage seeker with an alternative recourse for financing for example. Another alternative action could be the routing of the customer detail to a personal investment counselor that could help guide the individual to a better financial position if for example the credit score required to obtain financing was less than desirable. The ability to define functionality in terms of sequence flows opens the door for subsequent discussions to be had that simply tie back to functional state of the application needing to be built. Given the nature and compartmentalization of Micro Distributed Applications it stands to reason that the development effort may begin to take on a heightened degree of influence from what had been known prior with web development and specifically distributed software.

The benefits that are afforded to the organization by being able to divide labor into smaller functional pieces that ultimately tie back to a physical representation in a browser is a powerful lever in software engineering as it denotes modularity and loosely coupled artifacts which coincidently is the general trend of software development with microservices, micro frontends, object oriented programming, inheritance, libraries, packages, and plugins. This is but another reason why Micro Distributed Applications makes sense for the next generation of applications, it is because they fit the mold of the engineering of software in an expeditious and elegant manner that is the hallmark of sound design.

Figure 4. Mortgage Seeker Sequence Diagram

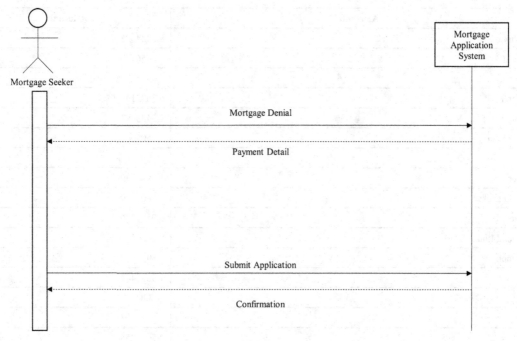

KEYWORDS

Given the particulars that have been determined surrounding indexable content it will be necessary for the system to leverage the appropriate keywords within the confines of the HTML document so that the content can be found by the search engines and consequently by all the patrons that the business hopes to service by way of the MDA. The endeavor will part from the premise that content is being optimized for the Yahoo search engine and as such it will be those factors that will be deemed to be the most important to HTML content creation. The findings of the random forest study that was conducted in a previous chapter are summarized below in table 1.

It will be those attributes that are identified above that will be targeted as the leverage points by way of the derived keywords that will be determined by way of the Google trends utility (https://trends. google.com/). Through the utilization of the Google trends utility, it becomes feasible to determine those particular keywords and phrases that are deemed to be the most relevant under some query context. With the Google trends utility, it becomes feasible to narrow search to the country level and even to the state level if desired. A search was performed under the guise of the continental United States and as such the details determined are applicable under this geographic region as extracted on January 7, 2022. In searching for the term 'mortgage' what was determined was that certain queries proved to have been the most relevant to the inhabitants of the United States, which are depicted in table 2 below. From the query study it can be seen that what was of the most interest related to issues with money flow. It is completely fascinating to come to an understanding of what the data depicts, void of preconceived notions of right and wrong. From the data provided below it can be determined what key phrases need to address the concern of the populous at large for their interest around money flow and a mortgage. To void the targeting of the page attributes from this context entails a departure from the sentiment of the

Table 1. Attribute Relevance Breakdown for the Yahoo Search Engine

Attribute	Relevance
Description	8.6324595
Division	3.4556776
Header One	5.4902766
Header Two	6.3692140
Header Three	2.3433891
Header Four	0.5506063
Header Five	-1.8719347
Header Six	1.3110729
Inbound Links	4.1463020
Keywords	6.0161746
Outbound Links	5.2923387
Paragraph	2.8934412
Root	7.3097442
Span	-1.3300545
Title	9.5220903
Quality	1.5678853

masses. This delta that would result from this disparity would simply entail that the message would be out of synchronization with the querying that is occurring yielding less relevance with the search purveyors. Through the Google trends utility figure 5 was obtained, which conveys the sentiment that the general trend for the search term has been in decline for approximately one year. This data point conveys the message that the population in mass has lost interest in part to obtaining a mortgage and while that may be because of government regulation it could just as likely be because the masses have pre-existing relationships with mortgage providers that are meeting their needs, yet another possible hurdle to the ACME Mortgage Company.

The process of discovery that was followed here simply exemplifies the reason why Micro Distributed Applications must take hold. Given that MDAs can be used to create parity with the search engine providers it entails that search term relevance and as a result the content that may be generated by MDAs for the search engines to consume and index can be harmonized. When this tailored message becomes a focus, it entails that the protocol becomes synchronized. This malleability of the paradigm becomes but another reason why MDAs need to take hold of the web landscape. If for example the content of a mortgage application MDA can be changed to fit query relevance in real time then it means that the particular points of interest of the masses can then be translated to a visual context that the search engines are but simply eager to consume and consequently rank accordingly. With MDAs it becomes feasible to manage this message in one location, i.e., at the controlling node of the MDA and to consequently distribute this message to an audience in mass where it can be indexed and consequently be deemed to be relevant by the search engines themselves.

The ACME Mortgage Company could leverage the data identified and target a particular competitor for example in the message that is disseminated to the audience in mass whereby now the competitor becomes a target across all nodes consuming the application. The synchronization of the message that may be afforded through MDAs with the search engine purveyors can lead to an optimization whereby the creator of the MDA can become but the mirror image of that profile that the search purveyors deem to be truth. The manner by which the message may be controlled through MDAs becomes a powerful leverage for the creators of the functionality as it affords the author of some desired message to find but an attentive and agreeable audience who simply in turn validate the agreeableness of the message by providing an additional factor of relevance to the message received. As the argument that was made prior, it is not in fact that the search engines do a poor job of indexing content, but it is rather that the authors of said message do a poor job of fitting the message to the protocol. This desired message with MDAs can always find that favorable audience and in mass because this message can be crafted given the search interest of the masses and the willing consumption by the search purveyors themselves.

Development must take on a distinct form of its predecessors and it must do so in order to be able to leverage the indexing domain. It must change to leverage the economic efficiencies that result, and it must change because the masses have spoken and currently there does exist an ecosystem that functions in unison to determining worth and if the product developed does not conform to this protocol it will become but simply another artifact that will not find that much needed injection of users that is needed for its subsistence.

Table 2. Query to Relevance

Query	Relevance
rocket mortgage classic 2021	Breakout
mortgage stimulus program 2021	Breakout
marriage or mortgage	+2,100%
congress mortgage stimulus program	+1,000%
reverse mortgage lenders	+500%

Figure 5. Mortgage Search Term Trend

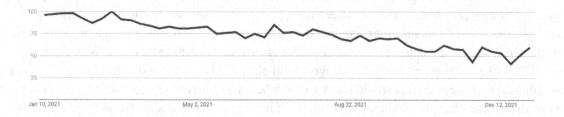

Performing a secondary search for the term 'mortgage application' is just as revealing as was the case for the previous term. There was only one identified term that related to the search term as displayed in table 3 as given below. From this table it can be seen that individual queries with the search term yielded only one fruitful related query, which denotes individuals that are in the process of getting their documentation in order to apply for a loan. The search trend that is provided by Google trends also conveys the message that interest in the search term has had no appreciable uptrend or downtrend and as such there was a consistent outlook in demand over the span of a year. All these factors help clarify that the market sector that the ACME Mortgage Company is vested in has an appreciable degree of supply constraint that further helps clarify why obtaining customers in the sector is especially difficult. It is by understanding this data that facilitates being able to create the needed MDA strategy for the business. As the data obtained denotes, it should be part of the MDA strategy of the business to facilitate a message that resonates with the audience. It would behoove the ACME Mortgage Company for example to create an MDA component that facilitates the collection and tracking of documents to aid in the application of a mortgage loan. This type of development is real time, it is targeted, and it is precise to the needs of the customer which simply helps to facilitate the indexing endeavor by the search providers because a message that resonates with the query needs of the individuals performing a search entails that this message crafted will be indexed according, i.e., with a high degree of relevance.

Yet another indicator that is available by way of Google trends is the regional breakdown of interest over the query term. From this graphic as shown in figure 6 it can be seen that the majority of interest with the term 'mortgage application' comes to by way of the east coast. It can also be seen that within the western central region of the United States there is a remarkable under demand for the query term, which helps to further appreciate where the particular marketing efforts need to be geared towards. With this information in hand it entails that it would behoove the organization to create content within Micro Distributed Applications that would echo this message. A message that would reference the east coast region in general would facilitate the indexing effort of the search engines and help to elevate the message of the organization to find a more favorable audience. In a setting whereby the consumers of these MDAs would reside on the east coast for example the logic of the MDA could be crafted so that the message conveyed would be one of finding financing for a home purchase. In the case whereby the subscribing domain would reside in the Midwest the message would take an alternative tone, one that would resonate with being financially conservative for example. This alignment that can be created with the search engines by way of MDAs represents a paradigm shift in software development, whereby the MDA becomes but the marketing arm of the organization.

The understanding of the interest of the populous is a gateway to being better able to structure the message to the masses and in such a manner so that it may be received favorably or as positively as possible given market conditions. From the preliminary data that was collected however a strategy can begin to be formulated for the message to be crafted through the MDA. This message needs to take a tone of urgency surrounding financial matters whereby refinancing can be used to alleviate cashflow problems and also a message of support of the required documentation needed to apply for a loan. This would be the MDA message that would resonate with potential customers on the east coast. With subscribers of the MDA in the Midwest region the message would alter and be one that denotes being conservative with financing. A message that would speak to the inherent nature of the populous that is conveyed by way of the queries they are conducting. This type of marketing effort is specific and crafted, as well as it could be for the needs of the demographic and simply helps to elevate the business to a better place.

This simple investigation into how to best structure the HTML verbiage to match the interest of the masses has proven to have been insightful and has helped to further create alignment between the MDA and the indexing effort of the search engine providers. It can also be seen that the inherent nature of MDAs facilitates the crafting of this message as each subscribing node by region or IP address can be provided with a message that resonates with the demographics of the region. This type of development is not possible through current SaaS offerings as the focal point with these products is feature set in lieu of alignment between the marketing needs of the business and indexing relevance. In the case of MDAs they are but the vehicle to obtain a marketing benefit, a proposition that escapes current SaaS offerings.

Table 3. Regional Query to Relevance

Query	Relevance
rocket loan application checklist	Breakout

Figure 6. Mortgage Application Regional Search Interest

1	Hawaii	100
2	Rhode Island	95
3	New York	93
4	Florida	93
5	Maryland	89

DUE COURSE

The ACME Mortgage Company would like to minimize the risk of any potential technological solution by first implementing a solution on their website so that they may utilize their own web traffic to determine if any potential problems exist and to also use it as a measuring stick for viability. The solution will be implemented as a JavaScript widget that will allow customers to enter loan relevant information such as the loan amount, the term of the loan, their down payment, and the interest rate, which they will be allowed to change if they choose to do so. The interest rate field will have a default value that will be set to the current market rate. They will also be required to enter their credit score, which helps to further qualify the individual for a potential loan. In practice you would require the individual to enter their social security number which would then be taken, and a credit check would be performed, thus giving the mortgage company a fixed value for their true credit worthiness, but in the case at hand the user will input their credit score detail. Table 4 depicts the fields that will need to be collected by the system initially.

The application will take their information and will provide for them a monthly payment amount and if they agree with the tabulated amount, they will then be able to proceed forward with their application directly on the website. If it is determined that they are not credit worthy, then the application will prevent them from proceeding forward with the loan application and thus help the business to reduce those inquiries from customers that will not yield a capital gain for the business. Table 5 details the fields that will need to be provided in order to formally submit their credit application to the business.

The solution will be implemented as a Micro Distributed Application through the use of JavaScript. This component will then be readily distributed to partners that will be able to place the functionality directly on their own website for the automation of the initialization of the loan application directly with the ACME Mortgage Company. The solution will implement functionality already available by way of common libraries such as jQuery and Bootstrap that will give the solution created a native cross browser look and feel between mobile, desktop, and tablet environments. The interest rate provided by default could be obtained from a third party API that would allow the business to always have a current value, but in this case a fixed value will be provided. Once the loan particulars are submitted by the user the system will either determine the loan as viable and collect their particulars for further processing of the application or simply notify the user that their loan cannot be processed given the details provided by them.

Table 6 as provided below details the keywords that will be targeted given the investigative process that was followed by way of Google. These keywords or phrases will enable the MDA to be consistent with the interest of the masses and thus facilitate the indexing of the individual pages. Given the particulars identified in the random forest study which are displayed in table 1 the business will be targeting those phrases listed below within the confines of page title, keywords meta tag, description met tag, and the header two tag. By following this process, the application will physically be creating the needed alignment between search and content thus helping the search engine of choice find the particular keywords it is in search of and in the manner that it deems them to be pertinent.

An endeavor that could be undertaken for the crafting of a message that would have more impact by the organization with an audience would be to leverage the regionality of search and create dedicated messages for each region. The particular content of the message needed could be identified through a similar process as was carried out here. This would allow for subscribing nodes of the MDA to receive a message that would resonate with their individual customer base. Even though search is global, the needs of the audience of these searches are local as has been identified in prior chapters of this text. It becomes essential therefore to come to understand the regionality of the message that must be crafted by MDAs in order to be able to provide subscribing nodes with the best possible message for their own audience. Gone are the days when a marketing campaign is global in nature as the need of the masses is specific to their particular region and as such it has become the need of the MDA to harness this dynamic and to consequently be able to create alternative messages to particular customers. The benefit of a targeted message that can be crafted by way of MDAs is a benefit that merits attention.

Table 4. Loan Input Fields

Field	Prepopulated
Loan Amount	No
Down Payment	No
Interest	Yes
Credit Score	No
Annual Salary	No

Table 5. Client Input Fields

Field
Name
Email
Phone Number

Table 6. MDA Keywords

Field
Reverse Mortgage
Mortgage Stimulus
Refinance
Mortgage

SUMMARY

Competition in the web space has been a difficult proposition for quite some time now. You only need to look at the current clickthrough advertisement dollars demanded by keyword or phrase to prove this. It is not uncommon for businesses to pay $1, $2 or more for each click on an ad in an effort to try to create value for the firm. There is a reason why Google is able to afford real estate in one of the most expensive property markets in the world. There is a reason why the advertisement methodology implemented by Google has been adopted by other search providers and by businesses such as Facebook and LinkedIn. This mode of advertisement has proven to be effective and lucrative.

Creating value where there was non-previously is the hallmark of capitalism and one of the reasons why distributed JavaScript is here to stay. Being able to create link equity or link value by way of a widget that provides a benefit to the masses across the internet equates to worth, i.e., a translation to monetary terms. Businesses have literary paid individuals to go out onto the internet and create blog posts and user group entries to create this leverage of link equity. This process is greatly facilitated by allowing others to do that for your business – for free through MDAs. Distributed JavaScript has enabled the discussion of an all too ugly a proposition for businesses to be changed. The utilization of the rules of the game to benefit the business at hand is how the game is to be played anyways, so why not leverage that to an optimum? The search providers have created the rules of engagement and distributed JavaScript is the course of action that is to be carried out on the field by the team. Being able to generate link equity and have some specific domain move to the top of the heap has become a marketing mandate and is achievable by way of distributed JavaScript. Much like when the University of Florida's football team started using Gatorade for a competitive advantage, distributed functional components are in the same mold. It is through the elevation of the attributes of the players on the field that competition becomes an easier proposition. To be able to enhance these components that are at play can become the competitive advantage that is sought and in the world of online marketing this can become but that same liquid that infused those same players on the field for the University of Florida.

The direction of web architecture has evolved and has done so in parity with the search engine indexing domain, given how these two are inter-related it becomes a matter of fact now that they influence one another. The scenario given here is just another example of why the datum point lay where it does, and it will be those businesses that are able to capitalize on the advantage that is afforded by way of Micro Distributed Applications that will stand to reap the benefit that only the masses may afford. Businesses can win the indexing race by the applications that they develop, and these applications can create a leverage for these businesses because of the benefit that is link equity to the point that these domains become the voice of authority on the World Wide Web. The conditions surrounding rank have deep ramifications and it will be those businesses that are able to afford utility to the masses through MDAs that stand a chance to win this race. It will be those businesses that are able to create utility to the point that the masses consume this function throughout the internet that will become the means by which the winners will be anointed.

This case study has brought to light the significance that distributed applications can present to business because of the benefit that they afford through the indexing domain. Business has arrived at the destination point it finds itself at because of the importance that humanity has placed on search and what has become the internet and as a consequence it will be those businesses that are best able to leverage the rules of the game that will stand apart from the competition. MDAs have simply become the mechanism by which clout, and authority will be obtained and the manner by which the winners will be elected. There is a race that is underway, and it will be those businesses that are best able to create value for the masses that will be bestowed the crown to wear. It will be those businesses that afford the most that will reap the most because it will be those businesses that will provide value to the masses that they will undoubtedly gravitate towards in an effort to meet some need. It is upon the development teams at the business to help leverage this new paradigm that are MDAs because if they do then they stand a chance at staying relevant. In the next chapter the physically implementation for the requirements created here are undertaken. This proceeding activity brings to life the discussion here and provides for the reader a clear and direct example of how MDAs may be created and leveraged. The next chapter serves as a gateway to subsequent content where another MDA initiative is undertaken. This secondary body of work is performed for the WordPress engine, thus giving another direct example of how MDAs may be implemented. The leverage is there to be created for business irrespective of platform type utilized, this is the message being conveyed. This is the power of the dynamic nature of MDAs that housing is irrelevant to the structure of them.

Through the work of Jerkovic (2010) and King (2008) it became feasible to identify the components of page relevance. This body of work parted from the work of the aforementioned authors and has built upon it whereby the discussion migrated to the quantified context and has now transitioned to practical aspects, this practical context has resulted in MDAs. This chapter has helped to put a practical tone to the discussion whereby a future state of a business system has been able to be defined because of all the prior work. A future state that denotes a paradigm shift to the software engineering domain whereby applications will now show an alignment with the needs of the search purveyors because of the interconnectivity that exists. This interconnectivity that everyone has come to depend on has led to the realization in the software engineering domain that a flux on system state is present and it is a binding constraint that is forcing the profession as a whole to have to rethink the paradigm of software development. This is a paradigm shift that is warranted given humanities need to remain connected as this architectural reality is but a constraint that will become present in future applications. The network structure is a central underpinning that is harnessed by the search purveyors themselves and as consequence will lead to the restructuring of the applications that will operate within these confines. The use cases presented here exude this reality which simply helps to affirm the implications that the metrics resonate.

REFERENCES

Jerkovic, J. (2010). *SEO Warrior*. O'Reilly Media Inc.

King, A. (2008). *Website Optimization*. O'Reilly Media Inc.

Chapter 10
A Modern Distributable Application

ABSTRACT

The process of converting a theoretical construct to physical artifacts helps to win over the empiricist since it is by the physical objects that may be touched and smelled that belief begins to take root. It is this belief that facilitates a transition of the individual that when repeated simply helps to create consensus in the domain. This chapter presents the practical working elements of the requirements that have been defined in the previous chapter and consequently allows the reader to come to appreciate Micro-Distributed Applications through coding artifacts. It is through the content found in this chapter that the reader will be able to come to correlate the theoretical with the practical and be able to understand why change is warranted.

INTRODUCTION

Now that the beacon of light from the lighthouse is within view it is time to create a solution that demonstrates the benefit of the paradigm that has been proposed in this text. In this section of the body of work the case study of the previous chapter will be implemented in a physical artifact demonstrating the paradigm shift of Micro Distributed Applications. The application created in this chapter will demonstrate for the reader the tangible benefits that are provided by a distributed JavaScript architecture that includes factors such as distributable functionality and the creation of content that may be managed from a single source to be rendered dynamically to all subscribing clients directly. This implementation mechanism as alluded to previously allows the business to reap the benefits of better ranking and allows the business to experience a more prominent search presence that results in a potential benefit monetarily with the search providers. The capital investment being expensed by businesses to be relevant is significant as one only need to look at the stock price of a Google or Twitter that as of this writing (01/07/2022) was \$2,740.09 and \$39.67 respectively. What is at stake for the enterprise is significant, it is a marketing strategy, capital, technological leverage, and a competitive advantage to start. The utilization of technology can be either a leverage or an impediment to business viability as may be validated by the constant churn of startups

DOI: 10.4018/978-1-6684-4849-6.ch010

in the bay area alone. Distributed JavaScript is simply one of those technological leverages whose time has come given the landscape and it is on this note that this chapter begins.

The requirements that were provided in the previous chapter of this text gave a clear direction for what is needing to be built in this chapter. The case study identified the actors at play, the individual data flow with its corresponding elements, the marketing strategy needing to be undertaken, and the technologies that were needing to be capitalized on. In this chapter the physical work of creating the solution that was outlined is undertaken and by doing so helps the reader understand how Micro Distributed Applications may physically be created using open source technologies no less. It represents a minimal investment by the business in tools because such is the state of technology now that teams can utilize a slew of open source technologies to accomplish their mandate as was seen firsthand in this text with the data mining program that was written in Python or the statistical models that were created with R. Gone are the days when businesses need to physically spend thousands of dollars on expensive software in order to build the solutions they want. Teams can now create what they need with rudimentary hardware that may be bought locally and through the use of tools that may be downloaded directly to their hardware at zero cost. It is because of this dynamic that teams are now able to leverage the work of others through utilities such as JavaScript, Node.js, Bootstrap, and jQuery to build those software solutions that will give the business that competitive edge.

This chapter will take those utilities that can be obtained at zero expense and use them to create Micro Distributed Applications which can then be taken and distributed to others so that they can in turn reap the benefit of that labor that was unknown to them. By adopting this mold businesses stand to gain that clout that they so desperately covet where it allows the business to become that voice of authority on the web by providing what is built to be used by others. It is because of the benefit that this utility can provide to the masses that they in turn provide to the business a greater benefit, the benefit of preference where this preference results in a tangible benefit and whereby the domain that yielded this benefit becomes the voice of authority. Through the embracing of this utility the masses become the voice that is needed to derive the clout that invariably leads to search prominence. The search engines subsequently come to realize this clout by way of their algorithm that the domain providing the utility has become the voice of authority and as such they must extend that curtesy that must be awarded to the winner. They must extend that benefit to rank the domain at the top of the heap and all because an effort was undertaken to have provided something for free that in the end was all but as the subscribers pay in kind, but not with money. It becomes an irony in that by doing good and providing something for free what turns out is that business stands to benefit financially as good is returned in kind. Organizations have a chance to create this tangible benefit for themselves and in order to do so they must first extend to the masses a benefit that they will embrace and adopt to the point that they do so eagerly because when they do they affirm to the internet crawlers that this domain has become the de facto standard on the matter. As a consequence of this effort the search engines are compelled through the same algorithm that they embrace to come to the realization that this business has become the winner in the game. There is quite a lot at stake if you think about it as this much coveted place on the search engines is an almost guarantee of acclaim and revenue because after all the majority of web searchers simply click on one of the top five results of the page 90% of the time as noted by Smyth et al. (2004), web searchers do not even bother with result six and lower. Such has become the need for society for immediate gratification that they do not scan past the minimal amount of detail needed to make a decision. So, if a business can create this leverage, then it means that it can have a chance to capture that level of attention of the masses that seek to make their purchases online. The business has a chance to become relevant in a world where it seems that it is all that matters.

The argument has been made prior and it is made once again here, this text is a business text under the guise of technology. It is a text about how the leverage that is indexing may be created and as a result it will be those applications that will drive traffic to the target node that will help elevate the business to a new datum point of exclusivity. There was a reason why the original premise took as long as it did to develop, it had to be determined quantitatively what the lay of the land was. The landscape needed to be quantified to be better able to understand what lay ahead and consequently come to a better understanding of the reality that has redefined business. The time had to be taken to formulate the prescription and do so in such a manner so that truth could be extracted and understood from the data available. This is what led the discussion to identify Micro Distributed Applications, this is what led to make the arguments that were made to the reader. It was because the time was taken to understand what the significance of the data was that it was possible to determine what it all meant in the grand scheme of things. It was because of that process that the noise was weeded out and it is because of that process that understanding has become feasible whereby the significance of the JavaScript laden world has become apparent and why its benefit has become essential to the creation of clout on the internet. It is because of the work that was done prior that the argument can now be developed into a physical artifact that allows for further understanding and appreciation for where businesses need to navigate towards. As a result of the work done prior the discussion can now be had at that corporate meeting where strategy and execution are married and whereby this effort can be physically leveraged for the benefit of not just the business but for the masses as well. It is because of what was discovered that the argument can now move on to solid footing and with confidence that the paradigm of Micro Distributed Applications is such because of the indexing domain and because of which business execution needs to adopt a new dialect. The business can now build those applications and distribute them to its clients or users so that they may proceed forward and reap an immediate benefit that in the end simply helps the originating domain find their voice. In order to be able to find that voice is why the endeavor to build Micro Distributed Applications must be undertaken. MDAs represent the synchronization of business clout with the technological effort that together and in unison may be leveraged to create a benefit that extends past the organization. The mode by which software may be shared and used freely and openly is the mode by which open source software has obtained lift and it will be the mode by which the search purveyors will designate those organizations as the winners in the indexing race and coincidently enough who does not like that which comes to bear at a cost of zero.

ENVIRONMENT

The coding effort in this chapter was performed with Visual Studio Code that may be downloaded here https://code.visualstudio.com. The software is an interactive development environment (IDE) that allows for the editing of coding files directly and all with the benefit of IntelliSense whereby the coding effort becomes facilitated. Visual Studio Code is a lightweight version of Visual Studio, but which is free to use and offers the ability to create applications of varying types and for which this endeavor will simply create only JavaScript applications for both the client and server side.

Server side JavaScript is the domain of Node.js and for which its documentation may be found here https://nodejs.org. Node.js allows for the creation of server side applications with the all common client side development language constructs of JavaScript and while the implementation is different as are the libraries utilized what is the same between client and server side are the nuances of the language so that it becomes feasible to translate a client side skillset to the server side almost seamlessly. The progress that has been created through this paradigm has resulted in economies of scale for the development community as development resources can now program the client and server side, a domain that was a dichotomy in the past and a domain that required multiple resources to address properly.

One of the benefits of using an IDE such as Visual Studio Code is that it provides native integration with the command line to facilitate execution of the codebase directly from the IDE. The additional features that are afforded because of IntelliSense can also facilitate the development effort as it affords the developer the ability to locate needed functions directly through the user interface. The Visual Studio Code interactive development environment integrates with code repositories so that the updating of programming archives becomes facilitated and may be done directly from the IDE. The installation of Visual Studio Code can be performed on Windows and Mac OS systems so that development teams are free to use the hardware that they are the most comfortable with. The largest benefit however that is afforded because of a utility such as Visual Studio Code is that it has been made to eliminate the entry barrier given its cost. The ramifications of having an organization such as Microsoft take a position whereby a lightweight version of their flagship product is made available for free and open to the development community has resulted in a tremendous benefit for all parties involved. Making Visual Studio Code open to contribution has enabled developers to created plugins directly for the application which has created a benefit for the business. This scenario that has been created represents a symbiotic relationship between user base and corporation. The argument that is being made here for MDAs whereby functionality is provided to consumers for a benefit that in the end yields a tangible benefit to the creator of the MDA is not a new dynamic as can be seen here and is another indication of why MDAs make sense. The truth of the matter is however that Microsoft had little choice in their decision to make functionality available to the community for free as developers currently have alternative choices such as NetBeans (https://netbeans.apache.org) or eclipse(https://www.eclipse.org/ide/) for their development needs. The argument could also be made in the current theme of search relevance that organizations also do not have an alternative but to provide this functionality to the masses for free or at an economic proposition that resonates with the audience because to negate this benefit would be to forgo the leverage that can only be provided by the masses, an embrace that leads to clout. The argument that is being made here for the creation of functionality that may be distributed takes on a different version from what has been seen with products such as Visual Studio Code, but it is nevertheless equivalent. Microsoft is also not alone in the dynamic described here, RedHat for example provides support for a Unix variant at a cost, but the product itself may be download and installed for free. The notion of utility for a cost does not always apply in corporate America apparently, so it would behoove all parties involved to simply begin to think of software development under a different guise. To further this argument you simply need to turn to the data that has been tabulated in this text for affirmation of this premise.

WEB DOCUMENT

The base platform for the implementation of dynamic JavaScript is basic HTML, which consumes simple references to the desired libraries. These JavaScript libraries are the bootstrap components from which a complete application may be harnessed. The code snippet given below contains two entries a division tag and a script tag of which only one should be required as in the case of an enterprise solution you would simply provide your customer with the JavaScript reference file. The simplicity of the implementation highlights the power of the construct as it would ease its adoption for customers.

```
<!— Bootstrap custom JavaScript library to load functionality of MDA. // --> <script src=" app.js"
type="text/javascript"></script>
 <!— Container element reference to house MDA content. // --> <div>Mortgage Application</div>
```

In current development practice what vendors ask you to do in order to utilize their JavaScript component is to add each reference required for the component to function properly. Given the feasibility of being able to download and create content dynamically it means that what should be specified by the vendors is only one simple file reference. This file as is the case here would bootstrap all functional requirements dynamically. This dynamic loading of library references is shown below for the reader. It is through this basic construct that the application interface elements are created in real time for the user, and it is all done simply through the external JavaScript file reference. It alleviates the implementor from having to perform any effort outside of including the JavaScript file directly on the page where the functionality is desired. The code fragment shown below is the content that may be found in the app.js file referenced in the first code segment given in this section.

```
/*
   Definition of libraries to be utilized by MDA. The final entry provided in the array of JavaScript/
CSS components to utilize is the housing for the application to authenticate through. The array object is
attached to the physical JavaScript function that is to be called in order to parse the content of the array.
*/
[
   'https://code.jquery.com/jquery-3.3.1.slim.min.js',
   'https://cdnjs.cloudflare.com/ajax/libs/crypto-js/3.1.9-1/crypto-js.js',
   'https://cdnjs.cloudflare.com/ajax/libs/popper.js/1.14.7/umd/popper.min.js',
   'https://stackpath.bootstrapcdn.com/bootstrap/4.3.1/css/bootstrap.min.css',
   'https://stackpath.bootstrapcdn.com/bootstrap/4.3.1/js/bootstrap.min.js',
   './authenticate.js'
].forEach(bootstrap_resources);
/*
   Bootstrap function performs the component loading whereby entries that are JavaScript based are
attached to a script tag and components that are visual (CSS) are attached to a link tag. The function-
ality contained in this function entails that a tag of either type is created for each reference type. The
signature of the method takes as input the array of items to load, which are defined in the code fragment
that is given above.
*/
function bootstrap_resources(item, index, array){
   var tag = null;
   var typeOf = item.split('.')[item.split('.').length -1];

   if(typeOf == 'js'){
```

```
    // JavaScript Resource
    tag = document.createElement('script');
    tag.type = 'text/javascript';
    tag.src = item;
    tag.async = false;
  }
  else if(typeOf == 'css'){
    // CSS Resource
    tag = document.createElement('link');
    tag.rel = 'stylesheet';
    tag.href = item;
    tag.async = true;
  }

  // Physically appends object reference to document
  if (tag){ document.getElementsByTagName('head')[0].appendChild(tag); }
}
```

JAVASCRIPT COMPONENTS

The first JavaScript component in the framework is the bootstrap element that functions as the harness to the coding framework. This component places the burden upon itself with the dynamic loading of the external JavaScript files as well as physically executing the designated JavaScript code where the base functionality of the application resides. It is through this mechanism that the software utility is able to load the proprietary code segment into memory where it can remain clandestine from prying eyes. This sequence of steps represents the execution of the process flow that was described in figure 2 of the previous chapter.

The libraries pointed to in the external file referenced are entries in an array definition which contains all of the JavaScript and CSS components that are required. The authenticate.js file contains an API reference that points to an end point where physical JavaScript will be downloaded from. This end point will be the reference to the Node.js application that will send to the client the physical code to execute. This codebase will be the gateway to the application that performs the heaving lifting. It will be through this file that the floodgates open to the proprietary software.

The contents of the authenticate.js file are given below. This file in theory could be created by the server side for each client, thus providing each client with a unique ID that has been set to the 'KEY' variable in the codebase given above. A unique GUID could be used as the private key for decryption of the text content that is retrieved via the GET method.

/*

Contents of the authenticate.js file, where the sole purpose of this file is to call the API designated below as localhost on port 9595 and request the content of the application by performing a GET request. Once the call to the API is deemed to be successfully by way of the call status then the script decrypts the code segment through the use of the KEY provided as a string below. Decryption of the code segment by the script allows for the code block to be read and loaded into RAM at run time, which allows the MDA to be initialized on the client side.

```
*/
var HOST = 'http://localhost:9595/api/v1.0/software';
var KEY = '1234567890';
var request = new XMLHttpRequest();
request.onreadystatechange = function() {
    if (this.readyState == 4 && this.status == 200) {

        // String received is decrypted through the KEY provided above.
        code = CryptoJS.AES.decrypt(request.responseText, KEY).toString(CryptoJS.enc.Utf8);
        window.eval(code)
        code = null
    }
};

/*
    Request is transmitted to API server as a GET request.
*/
request.open("GET", HOST, true);
request.send();
```

There are various options available for data encryption for example, you could use the domain IP address as the public key, thus ensuring content integrity. This dynamic also helps to ensure that data transferred to the server only comes from the unique domain that is paying some monthly fee. Part of the framework that was defined in the distributed JavaScript process flow of figure 2 of the previous chapter was the encryption and decryption of the coding structures to prevent the theft of intellectual property. It becomes imperative for a solution to be able to obfuscate this intellectual property as part of the overall process and the reason why there is a need to go through the arduous work effort detailed here. In a case however where it is simply sought to distribute code to anyone who would make it available on their individual website, you could forgo this process and simply provide the code structures by way of a simple GET.

INTERFACE LAYOUT

The interface layout is the heart of the application and is provided by the ui.js file. This file is JavaScript code that is transmitted via an encrypted mode from server to client. This entails that the codebase is dynamically rendered by the browser for each client. Given that each client in this case could have an assigned key you could manage to create custom user interfaces for each subscribing client with features such as custom headers, page verbiage, and client specific images to name but three. The options that become available to you under this context become bounded only by the limitations of JavaScript and as such it can lead to the creation of progressive customized software solutions.

```
/*
    Generic function to create individual rows of varying types. The type of row elements created are text
fields, buttons, labels, and numeric fields. Function highlights the ability of JavaScript to be leveraged
to solve the general problem frame as this type of function could have been created for each object type,
but instead was created to accommodate all of the field types needed.
*/

function create_row(label, input, caption){
  // Containing division element
  var row = create_element('div', {'class': 'row', 'style': 'padding: 5px 50px 5px 50px;'});

  // Appendage of division element to body of document
  $('body').append(row);
  var outer_div = null;

  // Creation of label object
  if(input == 'label'){ outer_div = create_element('div', {'class': 'alert alert-primary', 'role': 'alert',
'id': input, 'style': 'width: 100%;'}, caption); }
  else{ outer_div = create_element('div', {'class': 'input-group'}, ''); }
  $(row).append(outer_div);
  if(label){
    var inner_div = create_element('div', {'class': 'input-group-append'}, '');
    $(outer_div).append(inner_div);
    $(inner_div).append(create_element('span', {'class': 'input-group-text', 'style': 'width:
150px;'}, label));
  }

  if(input == 'text'){
    // Creation of text field
    $(outer_div).append(create_element('input', {'class': 'form-control', 'type': input, 'id': label,
'value': caption}));
  }else if(input == 'button') {
    // Creation of button object
    if (caption == 'Calculate'){
      $(outer_div).append(create_element('button', {'class': 'btn btn-success', 'type': input, 'on-
click': 'calculate_payment()'}, caption));
    }else if (caption == 'Send') {
      $(outer_div).append(create_element('button', {'class': 'btn btn-success', 'type': input, 'on-
click': 'submit_loan_inquiry()'}, caption));
    }
  }else if(input == 'link'){
    // Creation of link object type
    $(outer_div).append(create_element('a', {'class': 'btn btn-primary stretched-link', 'href': '#', 'on-
click': 'return create_loan_inquiry()'}, caption));
```

```
    }
}
```

By creating dedicated dynamic content for each client through MDAs, it changes the paradigm of JavaScript where the language now surpasses the constraints of the past. It is this migration of the paradigm through MDAs that forces teams to embrace a new mode of development which simply functions to elevate the notion of JavaScript to become a full fledge development paradigm that surpasses a client or server context as now JavaScript has become ubiquitous. This shift is consistent with the migration of the language as currently development is occurring through server side JavaScript via Node.js, but teams are still living in a duality whereby functional libraries are created for either domain. The landscape needs to change to a point where libraries will function across the client and server side constructs for the paradigm to reach its next level of evolution.

Initialization

The ui.js JavaScript file contains code that is specific to the jQuery library, this is the reason why it was paramount for the bootstrap process to load the needed infrastructure frameworks before moving forward with the actual codebase implementation. To adhere to good programming practice a common function called 'create_row' has been created that performs the needed processing work for the creation of the elements that are needed by the application. You can view the end product of this coding effort in Fig. 1, which is built with the bootstrap UI framework and relies on jQuery for its dynamic nature of content rendering for user interaction. The create_row function takes three parameters these being the element label, the element type, and a caption if needed such as is found with the associated text of input boxes.

```
/*
    Bootstrap custom JavaScript code to create base functionality of MDA.
*/
$(document).ready(function() {
    // Creates text field
    create_row('Principal', 'text', '');
    create_row('Payment', 'text', '');
    // Creates numeric field
    create_row('Interest', 'text', '2.5');
    create_row('Credit', 'text', '');
    create_row('Salary', 'text', '');
    // Creates button object
    create_row('', 'button', 'Calculate');
    // Creates a label object
    create_row('', 'label', 'Monthly Payment: $ 0.00');
});
```

The construction mechanism that has been followed in this body of work is common and found in enterprises, it is referred to as a layered framework where a body of work is layered on top of another thus slowly, but surely building the house so to speak, which also allows for the creation of content that has a common point of interaction or interface. The interface in this case are the function definitions that are used to bind the user interface content together, i.e., the content displayed in Fig. 1. The code fragment given above depicts the manner by which teams may proceed to create each of the row elements and as such you could add additional elements by simply creating a new function call with the desired parameters. From the requirements of the previous chapter it will be needed to create five fields as was noted in table 4, these five elements are created in the code fragment given above through the create_row function.

The initialization function highlights a benefit that is afforded through the compartmentalization of coding artifacts by way of the layering design pattern. Leveraging design patterns in software development needs to be a point of focus as they provide a blueprint for the creation of software artifacts in a proven best practice manner. One of the reasons why MDAs will be able to resonate with the software engineer is that they resonate with a mode of software development whereby the end product adheres to the tenants of good design as is witnessed in the above example. The ability to call functions that solve a generic problem frame entails that the coding effort becomes robust in nature especially if these coding structures can be aligned with a test driven development mindset.

Rows

Each row that is implemented is done so with the help of the bootstrap layout framework, which was implemented by way of the app.js file in the first JavaScript file incorporated. The create_row function creates a row element and appends it to the body of the document, please do note that in an enterprise implementation this could just as well be any division tag. Each row here is defined as either a text field input box, a label, or a button that functions to trigger the reconfiguration of the user interface. If a label is given as is the case for text field input then a label is prepended to the element created.

The create_row function serves the purpose of being a common point whereby this common point can be leveraged to create additional rows as needed. The create_row function takes as input in its signature the label, the input type, and the corresponding caption to attach to the corresponding row element to create. The create_row function first creates a new row to function as a container for the input elements that need to be created in the row. The function then proceeds to either create a label division element or the input group division element, which is dependent on the input type. If the input type is deemed to be of a text type, then a physical input type is created for the physical data input by the user.

In this example it was possible to create a basic function to render rows in general where the particulars of the row being created where such that a pivot point was generated that could be leveraged as needed. This generality is the benefit that is afforded to the masses by computer science as these points of commonality can be created and leveraged so that the addendum of additional features is a matter of adapting and extending what is already present all without the need to have to create functionality from scratch. This is the condition that must be present in solutions that are scalable because scalability is not a function of lines of code, but rather is just the opposite, it can be gauged by how little change is needed with code to adapt to a new requirement. You can gauge this degree of correctness in your code because addendums to the initial requirements should require a scalpel to adopt and if you find yourself using a machete instead then you know that the implementation is off, you know that there was an error made in judgement. This is but yet another reason why MDAs makes sense, they make sense because of the scalpel that is needed to create them.

The solving of the general problem frame is a staple of the craftsman which invariably always seems to escape the technician. It becomes but a farce for the technician to understand that higher lever detail that is required of the craftsman as this mode of existence requires the right pedigree, which is not simply experience or education but is rather the domain of both. The ability of MDAs to leverage coding artifacts that have been generalized and built in such a manner so as to be able to accommodate the general problem frame entails that the product can exhibit a degree of resilience that ultimately will be able to become that leverage that the development team seeks. The fact that the product being built here is with JavaScript does not entail that the efficiencies that are normally sought with development efforts are lost as it simply means that the opportunity that has been reaped in the past has but a new stage to be leveraged upon. The creation of the rows function that allowed for diverse HTML object types to have been created exemplifies the versatility that is afforded through coding structures of which JavaScript is part of and a reason why a solution such as the one that is presented here can have influence. The fact that the programming language of JavaScript may execute in a browser and be free of the necessary hardware obligations of traditional programming languages simply speaks to the versatility of the programming language of JavaScript. It is this diversity and robustness of the language that set it apart from others and a reason why MDAs can come to bear weight for the business. The ability of the programming language to be executed across hardware nodes that are external to the business and consequently free the enterprise from the hardware expense of the code execution speaks to the harmony that the programming language of JavaScript exudes with current doctrine. It is an ideal union in fact, a programming language that is robust enough to be able to solve coding challenges as do its counterparts, its ability to execute on borrowed hardware, its ability to facilitate the indexing effort of the search purveyors, and its terse nature are but attributes of the programming language that facilitate its embrace by the development community at large. It is a language that has come to have influence at the called upon hour and does so in spectacular fashion as may be validated by the plethora of dependencies that are tied to it. It is for the reasons noted here that JavaScript has become the domain of the craftsman.

```
/*
    Generic function to create individual elements with desired attributes as passed in the signature of
the method. The third parameter of the function defines the inner text to display in the HTML content
as the innerHTML of the object reference.
*/
function create_element(object_type, attributes, innerText){
    var element = document.createElement(object_type);
    for(var index in attributes){
        element.setAttribute(index, attributes[index]);
    }

    if(innerText){ element.innerHTML = innerText; }
    return element;
}
```

Figure 1. Mortgage Calculator User Interface

Elements

The create_row function relies heavily on another function definition named create_element that takes it upon itself to create the individual user interface element needed. The create_element function has the sole purpose of creating the HTML element and setting its property definitions after which point it appends the created user interface object to the document object model (DOM). The create_element function details are provided for the reader above. You will notice that in the code fragment of the create_element function is native JavaScript, which further facilitates the operability of the code fragment across the browser types. The reason why this was opted for in the code construction decision is that it avoids a point of failure, this being the library addendum of jQuery. By following the general practice of only implementing what is absolutely needed you shield yourself from future code slippage because of a change by a vendor for example. This is the reason why not only the create_element function but the code fragments created are as such, it is to ensure a standard operability. It is by maintaining this level of generality that the solution shows resilience.

What is highlighted in these examples is the true benefit of distributed JavaScript where code fragments are provided to consumers for their utilization, which in turn affords the domain providing the service the benefit of authority by being referenced as has been discussed previously in this body of work. By maintaining this mode of operation where the most generic of implementations are undertaken you are ensuring that you cannot only provide the best possible scalable solution to users, but you are also ensuring that you can obtain the greatest degree of adoption from the user base, which helps to further the claim for becoming a point of authority on the internet through the MDA.

Calculation

The loan calculation function is provider here for your viewing, it simply takes into account the loan amount, the down payment, the interest amount, the credit score of the individual, and their annual income. The function utilizes the user's credit score and determines if this is above the threshold of 650 and if it is deemed not to be such then they are denied the ability to proceed further. The function takes the mortgage amount and subtracts the down payment amount to determine the amount to finance. If the monthly payment amount exceeds 30% of their monthly income, then they are denied a loan. The function also validates the user input to determine if numeric values are entered by the user. The function created is included in the ui.js JavaScript file and which is also provide for the reader below.

```
/*
    Function to calculate mortgage payment amount. The method also functions as a filter point to keep
from requests being submitted that will not be able to be serviced.
*/
function calculate_payment(){
  // Constants
  var  REJECT = 'Thank you for your inquiry, but at this moment we are unable to provide you with
a loan';
  var ACCEPT = 'Congratulations, we can provide you with a loan';
  // Variables
  var loan = $('#Principal').val();
  var down_payment = $('#Payment').val();
  var interest = $('#Interest').val();
  var period = 30
  var credit_score = $('#Credit').val();
  var annual_salary = $('#Salary').val();

  if (credit_score <= 650) {
    $('#label').text('Invalid credit score provided.');
    return;
  }else{credit_score = parseInt(credit_score);}
  if (isNaN(loan) || loan < 1) {
    $('#label').text('Invalid loan amount provided.');
    return;
  }else{ loan = parseFloat(loan); }

  if (isNaN(period) || period < 1){
    $('#label').text('Invalid period value provided.');
    return;
  }else{ period = parseInt(period); }

  if (isNaN(annual_salary) || annual_salary < 1){
    $('#label').text('Invalid annual salary provided.');
    return;
  }else{ annual_salary = parseFloat(annual_salary); }

  interest /= 1200;
  period *= 12;
  payment = 0;
  if(interest == 0){ payment = (loan-down_payment)/(period);
  }else{ payment= (loan-down_payment)*Math.pow(1 + interest, period)*(interest)/[Math.
pow(1+interest, period)-1] }

  if (payment > annual_salary*0.3) {
```

```
        $('#label').text('Salary does not meet the minimum requirement for funding.');
        return;
    }

    $('#label').text('Monthly Payment: $ ' + String(payment.toFixed(2)));
    create_row('', 'link', 'Apply');
}
```

The ability to take a client node and directly inject into it HTML or code that can be executed given input from a client presents a remarkable opportunity to the business not just from an economics perspective, but also from a technological perspective as it is an application that is void of the heavy burden of processing power on some server as the code is executed on the client node, outside of the downloadable content by clients and for which some will be cached by the client browsers. In recent years there has been a gross exodus from racked servers in cold rooms at individual businesses to the cloud where there is no longer the need for the real estate acquisition, the investment in human capital, and the investment in several other components, which has changed the nature of how software is built and sold. Distributed JavaScript is just the next step forward in this journey where it is being injected into the landscape of client browsers all which take on the burden of doing the processing – the electricity needed, the hardware required, and the manpower needed to administer. If you think about it – it makes sense, the hardware used is underutilized by clients and as such is an opportunity to leverage for computational effort and all of this by simply leveraging some simple client side programming language called JavaScript. These Micro Distributed Applications have come of age not simply because of the technology that has become available to create them but because of the economics of the equation, the processing efficiencies that may be achieved, the development benefit that they afford, and of course the need to create clout on the internet with the search engine providers that have been bestowed the burden of electing that prom king.

Loan Application

The loan application window will be displayed for the user if and only if they decide to proceed with the loan application and for which it only becomes available to them if they are deemed to be serviceable. This allows the application to meet one of the original requirements where it was sought to alleviate the internal staff from the burden of dedicating time to potential customers that could not be converted to physical customers. The loan inquiry form is displayed through the use of the create_loan_inquiry function as detailed below. This function becomes invoked once the user has selected the 'Apply' link that becomes visible only upon a viable loan being determined. The create_loan_inquiry function first removes the entire document content and then proceeds to add input rows for the name, email, and telephone number of the perspective and qualified client. The loan inquiry form as displayed for the user is provided in figure 2 below. It is upon submission of this form that the user is presented with a confirmation message. The submission of the loan inquiry form triggers the submit_loan_inquiry form function as detailed in the code fragment that is provided below for the reader. The submit_loan_inquiry function first clears the entire content of the body of the document and then proceeds to create a single row element that contains a label that displays the confirmation message of 'Thank you for your inquiry. We will begin to process your loan!'

```
/*
    Loan inquiry user interface definition function.
*/
function create_loan_inquiry() {
  // Clear document
  $('body').empty();
  //  Create input elements
  create_row(Name, 'text', '');
  create_row('Email, 'text', '');
  create_row('Phone', 'text', '');
  create_row('', 'button', 'Send');
}
/*
    Function to create submission message
*/
function submit_loan_inquiry() {
  // Clear document
  $('body').empty();
  //  Create input elements
  create_row('', 'label', 'Thank you for your inquiry. We will begin to process your loan!');
}
```

The division of the work effort through the creation of individual functions that rely on common logic for the software enabled the streamlining of the process of creating the user interface. This process highlights the economies of scale that may be achieved if a first step in the process is a planning phase whereby the individual functions that are needed are broken up into generic forms so that a future tangible benefit may be achieved. There is absolutely no need to have to re-create the wheel as through the implicit nature of code you can build this layering design pattern and build upon some common functionality much like the baker does with a cake. The real power that this dynamic affords in code however is that it allows you to segregate functionality so that you can leverage common functionality across work efforts and given the nature of the web you can do so while these code fragments are distributed across the World Wide Web. This is the nature of the world that we now live in where work has been facilitated by the inherent nature of the grammar. Developers have in essence created their own dialect to help facilitate the communication of work because by doing so they have alleviated themselves from the nuances that use to plague the work effort. The community has been able to achieve much through code fragments in this manner, you simply need to look at the dependencies that were incorporated directly in the code here to appreciate this fact.

Figure 2. Loan Inquiry Form

Figure 3. Confirmation Message

Thank you for your inquiry. We will begin to process your loan!

SERVER SIDE JAVASCRIPT

JavaScript has long been a client side development programming language that has transitioned into a server side programming language through Node.js (https://nodejs.org). Node.js allows for the installation of packages or modules through the node package manager (npm). The particular instance that was created here as the server component was built with four modules for Node.js and these were http, httpdispatcher, crypto-js, and fs. The http module serves the purpose of creating the listener object on the port that is specified for the server. The httpdispatcher module allows for the creation of a router object for the server instance. The crypto-js module provides the cryptography functionality for the application and for which this exercise simply used the advanced encryption standard (AES). The fs module facilitates file operations. The code fragment below gives the module import definitions that were utilized by the server instance.

```
/*
      Individual module utilities that needed to be initialized
*/

var http = require('http');
var httpDispatch = require('httpdispatcher');
var crypto = require("crypto-js");
var file = require('fs');
```

The Node.js commands required the installation of both the httpdispatcher and crypt-js modules, the commands of which are given below. Once the modules are installed in the environment it becomes possible to invoke them directly within a Node.js file. It should be noted that prior to the utilization of the installed packages you will need to have the needed configuration defined in your package, which comes by way of a package.json file. This file is created when the 'npm init' command is executed and which when invoked instantiates a node.js environment. The particular package.json file that was created for this project given the module imports is given next for your reference, please do note that only a partial listing is provided.

As you can see from the configuration given below the name of the server instance file is 'server.js', it is this file for which the partial content is provided for you in this section next. After the base variable definitions are provided the next part of the server.js file contains some simple constant definitions and object instantiations all of which are given below. The next part of the server instance defines the router configuration object that serves the purpose of enabling route mappings for the given endpoints that are defined next. This functionality is enabled by way of the module import that was defined earlier for 'httpdispatcher'. In this particular instance there was one dispatcher handle created that was for the

JavaScript file end point, i.e., the ui.js file. The content of this file was provided in a previous section of this chapter.

```
npm install httpdispatcher
npm install crypto-js


....
"main": "server.js",
 "dependencies": {
   "crypto-js": "^3.1.9-1",
   "httpdispatcher": "^2.1.2"
 }

/*
    Router map for application. This file defines one GET endpoint that serves the purpose of extracting
the physical code to transmit encrypted given the KEY variable.
*/
dispatch.onGet("/api/v1.0/software", function(request, response) {
   response.writeHead(200, { 'Content-Type': 'text/plain' });

   // Read Code File
   file.readFile('ui.js', 'utf8', function(err, contents){
      var encrypted_text = crypto.AES.encrypt(contents, KEY).toString();
      console.log("File Contents Encrypted ...")
      response.end(encrypted_text);
   });
});
```

The onGet function does the bulk of the work in the implementation. This function has the responsibility of reading the content of the ui.js file and encrypting its content given a presumably unique identifier and then transmits the contents of the encrypted text directly to the calling object, which takes on the burden of decrypting the content and implementing the data as JavaScript code directly on the target page where the content is needing to be rendered.

Below you will find the content of the router function definition. Given the restrictions that exist because of cross origin requests the implementation needed to accommodate the correct header entries. These header entries facilitate the implementation to function across domains whereby the host would be able to disperse the desired functionality to any calling agent.

This implementation utilized a simple key value to encrypt the data, which was consequently decrypted by the client by way of the same key. While this implementation is simple for illustrative purposes it does highlight the ability to transmit encrypted content through the wire, which in an enterprise solution could be done by way of an authentication key or domain name to name just two possible solutions.

This chapter highlights the code migration effort that the development landscape has gone through and for which the development community at large now finds itself burdened with. In days gone by you would physically embed an iframe in a browser window to render the content from some third party provider and now this functionality is being directly injected through reusable code fragments dynamically through JavaScript. While the change in the development landscape has occurred by shear momentum of the paradigm what is important to highlight here is that for the sake of web relevance this paradigm needs to be adopted as each consumer of the service becomes a hard reference to the benefactor. It is because of this pursuit for relevance that it mandates that applications transform and become smaller, and JavaScript infused so that they may be transmitted to all that desire their utility. This mass adoption will become the explicit assertion by the masses that the voice of authority is such and by extension given the formulas adopted by the search purveyors it entails that they will have no choice but to acquiesce. The search providers will have to subsequently afford those domains that provide this utility the benefit of priority as their equations of worth dictate such.

```javascript
// Router Function Definition
function routerEngine(request, response){
   try{
console.log(request.url);
response.header("Access-Control-Allow-Origin", "*")
response.header("Access-Control-Allow-Headers", "Origin, X-Requested-With, Content-Type, Accept");

                dispatch.dispatch(request, response)
  }catch(err){
                console.log(err);
  }
}


// Router Object Instantiation
var server = http.createServer(routerEngine);
// Constants
var HOSTNAME = '127.0.0.1';
var PORT = 9595;
var KEY = '1234567890'


// Variable Instantiation
dispatch = new httpDispatch();
```

SUMMARY

The first factor to human understanding is language and as is seen in this chapter the doctrine applies in the development context as well. The understanding of the message was feasible because of the language construct; in the dynamic at hand JavaScript is the language, and the audience is the web browser. MDAs allow for the dissemination of the solution across audiences or browsers as they understand the language construct of MDAs. JavaScript allows for the physical work product to be crafted and woven into the fabric that is web content, which implicitly dictates an exposure to the domain and in this domain part of the thread that is woven into the fabric is the benefit that is derived by way of the search engines. By creating a solution that is tightly integrated into the fabric of online content it allows for the leveraging of artifacts that are freely available, reusable, distributed, and indexable. This message becomes powerful because the message resonates with the audience, as they are the benefactors of this freely available utility. The socialization of a solution is a fundamental part of its adoption and if you can provide for your customers a solution that tightly integrates with their online presence and can be implemented with minimal disruption to their business then it means that you have a good chance to succeed.

Technological leverage can only be relied upon if the time is right for it and the time¨ has come for Micro Distributed Applications (MDAs) given search prominence, language adoption by browser vendors, and the familiarity of the construct with the development community as a whole. Distributed JavaScript is not a new construct it has been around since the introduction of JavaScript through the use of external fixed references by way of content delivery networks (CDN). The time has just come for a modification to the message as search engine indexing has forced the development community to leverage the paradigm for the benefit of the business. Teams are already developing solutions using client side frameworks that are based on JavaScript such as React (https://reactjs.org/) and AngularJS (https://angularjs.org/). What is simply brought to light here is that this variant of the Reacts of the world can be distributed and be used to create a tangible benefit with the search providers. It is not a paradigm shift necessarily as it is simply the corralling of the message that has already existed and by doing such there becomes a tangible benefit that is afforded. Gone will be the days when businesses invest a high dollar amount on a solution, buy the servers or time on virtual machines to install the solution and then hire personnel to manage the application, as ridiculous as this sounds it is the norm now. It would be much easier and less capital intensive if the virtual machine where the application executed was the user's browsers. The business can fully leverage this hardware and currently it is being laid to waste or at a very minimum being used in a less than optimal manner. What about the personnel resources required to manage the application, monitor it, and so on? These resources would be diminished or would be eliminated as the controller of the domain would be the vendor themselves who would be able to manage the implementation externally. Businesses look to minimize expenditures and create a tangible benefit to the stockholders and what better way could this be accomplished if not by leveraging technology that has already been laid bare? Distributed JavaScript is here to stay or at least until an alternative that offers a better economic proposition comes forth.

Micro Distributed Applications are the new breed of development effort that teams will undertake that will allow businesses to leverage the indexing domain, re-usable code fragments, smaller coding footprints, and client hardware. Gone will be the days when development teams create giant applications that will sit on the hardware of some public cloud provider consuming much needed capital. Development teams will alternatively rely on the already existing infrastructure of clients and for which they are all too willingly to provide the resources to host MDAs. The profession is moving away from the inefficient to the efficient realm by taking an already underutilized resource and harnessing it. In a day and time when distributed systems have taken center stage with cryptocurrencies, it stands to reason that the dynamic is functional and a viable alternative to the course of action of the alternative. This is a story that has been seen in the evolution of the technical domain, whereby deficiencies acquiesce to efficiencies, it is the mode by which the winners and the losers are determined. The particular use cases that were presented here were able to be resolved because of the efficiencies that have been afforded through JavaScript. Distributed JavaScript components are but a force of change that has caused the development landscape to change and which will usher the evolution of applications to come as this mode of development infers a degree of efficiency that cannot be ignored. For validation of this degree of influence one only need to consider that some 95%+ of all websites utilize some form of JavaScript in their solution. It is but a resounding affirmation of the degree of utility that the programming language affords and a reason why the development landscape has arrived at its current junction. Development teams have embraced the development construct of JavaScript and ever so, to the point that it has become part of the fabric of most of the websites that litter the information highway. This degree of alignment has been warranted given the flexibility of the programming language of JavaScript which has simply led to what are now applications of a distinct form, but yet similar to their brethren. Micro Distributed Applications are built on the bedrock that the World Wide Web has embraced and as was seen in this chapter the ramifications of which entail new solutions that have come to have influence because of this bedrock that they sit on top of in part. The material presented in this chapter simply highlights the influence that the development landscape has come to bear on web applications through JavaScript. Given the degree of embrace that web applications have come to show with JavaScript it simply stands to reason that the content presented here will find a receptive audience because in fact the change denoted is not as big as one would think. The essential message of MDAs is but a message that has existed for quite some time even though it is presented in a slightly different light here as websites have ceased to be a collection of hyperlinks and have been transformed to be the new form of the fat client that was once embraced by the masses.

The nature of development is a moving body of work where the collective effort of each helps to transform the world that was once known, much like the body of work here is but simply the manifestation of where the train has stationed on its journey. It is part of the power of code that may be one of the reasons why technology seems to drive society. It is because of the work of many that the collective is in part able to create new entities and new businesses and whereby society reaps the benefit. What remains undisclosed to you however is that you are also a spoke of the wheel, and it is because of you that technology harnesses its momentum. It is a great time to be alive and it is a great time to dedicate one's labor to creating solutions through code.

REFERENCE

Smyth, B., Balfe, E., Freyne, J., Briggs, P., Coyle, M., & Boydell, O. (2004). Exploiting Query Repetition and Regularity in an Adaptive Community-Based Web Search Engine. *User Modelling and User-Adaptive Interaction*, *14*(5), 383–423. doi:10.100711257-004-5270-4

Chapter 11
Case Study 2:
A Micro-Distributed Application in Wordpress

ABSTRACT

The ability to integrate micro-distributed applications into a content management system such as WordPress demonstrates the flexibility that is afforded through MDAs. In this case study, the challenge is undertaken to define the requirements that would be needed in order to create a restaurant table reservation system that would integrate directly into WordPress, thus giving the solution an immediate benefit to existing restaurant websites that utilize the WordPress engine. This case study illustrates the leverage that may be created for the author's of MDAs such as the one undertaken here whereby the benefit of indexing becomes immediately afforded to these creators and whereby the dynamic lends itself to help elevate the status of the authoring domain with the search purveyors. The solution presented here demonstrates a seamless integration that affords a consistent experience to the client, a benefit from current practice.

INTRODUCTION

In this chapter an alternative case study in the form of a Micro Distributed Application that integrates seamlessly into the WordPress framework (http://www.WordPress.com) is addressed. This section defines the requirements for a table reservation system similarly to what you would find with a product offering such as OpenTable (www.OpenTable.com). This endeavor brings to light the flexibility that is afforded to developers through MDAs. MDAs are not simply applications that may be created exclusive of JavaScript but can rather be woven into the fabric of already existing frameworks whereby the benefit afforded through the framework can be leveraged and enhanced. The benefit that is afforded because of JavaScript cannot be understated as it provides the developer the ability to create dynamic content where the remainder simply become the details of the implementation. While it is true that WordPress has its own framework for the development of its plugins, what remains constant in the equation are the JavaScript components that can be utilized and which can continue to function as has been proposed

DOI: 10.4018/978-1-6684-4849-6.ch011

and seen already all without intervention to the base solution. In the case of WordPress however the applications become ingrained within the context of their host, the ecosystem that WordPress has become. A system of this nature that can adapt to its surroundings has an inherent property of malleability that make them desirable, a domain of MDAs as has been seen throughout this text.

As of this writing it is estimated that there are over 455 million websites that utilize WordPress and as such it allows for a large market capitalization. Given that WordPress facilitates the creation of websites without having to know the intricacies of web development it becomes imperative to ensure that the offering created be as simple as possible, with as few configurations and dependencies as needed. Given that MDAs are simple drag and drop utilities that take it upon themselves to download their own dependencies, they facilitate the creation of WordPress plugins. Given the adoption of WordPress, it becomes a potentially lucrative proposition for a business to explore this domain as an avenue for additional link equity. As a side note, there is already an existing WordPress plugin for OpenTable, whereby reservations can be made directly through this plugin. The particular plugin was not created by OpenTable and as such helps to further appreciate the degree of unawareness that there currently is in the space for the utility that may be derived by way of link equity and Distributed Micro Applications. It should also be noted that in this case, the plugin does not necessarily denote an awareness of MDAs as it is created within the confines of the WordPress framework, which typically denotes the utilization of resources directly within the implementation of WordPress, a clear divergence with the ideology of MDAs. The WordPress framework is structured in such a manner that dependencies are created and housed in specific locations within the directory structure of the application, in the case of MDAs however the resources needed are distributed and as such allow the developer to place them as needed throughout the internet. Even though the architectural structure of WordPress is such that resources can be found with minimal network traffic, it is the distributed nature of the dependencies that is sought as these dependencies facilitate a mode of operation where functionality can be enhanced and distributed in real time to facilitate code robustness. This dynamic also allows the creator to keep the WordPress footprint to a minimum whereby the functionality desired is derived in the vast part from the JavaScript files that may be loaded dynamically. This mode of operation helps to further maintain homeostasis with the paradigm of MDAs as it is by way of its distributed nature that the desired benefit of link equity is derived.

The ability of a plugin to dynamically change the message at an end client cannot be understated as this mechanism facilitates a real time and dynamic message that can help fine tune that desired communication to the search purveyors. Traditional JavaScript widgets have been void of this dynamic nature, but in the case of MDAs, this behavior is implied as it is part of the architecture of the platform. This mode of operandi also facilitates a leverage point of commonality whereby the base structure of the function created would be identical irrespective of housing. The MDA would function unaltered irrespective of its implementation as a widget, WordPress plugin, or web page. This entails that the solution outlined here could at the core function across facades. This behavior speaks to the flexibility that is afforded to users through the creation of generic solutions that can take on the persona of the needed actor. You can create these morsels of applications that can take it upon themselves to adapt and therefore create a uniform or dynamic message for subscribers independent of their chosen infrastructure. This mode of development helps to reinforce the nature of the protocol that development has become. Teams can now strive to create functionality through the development of smaller systems that can take it upon themselves to rely on other systems to help create some desired end state. This case study helps to further the message that MDAs are the mechanism by which you will be able to create ubiquitous functionality across clients, irrespective of what their particulars are since it is the actors that capture the attention of the masses irrespective of the stage that they perform on.

PROBLEM STATEMENT

The ACME Table Reservation Company is wanting to compete in a more favorable light with a direct competitor and as such is seeking to leverage the WordPress framework to help individuals with restaurants to provide the needed functionality for their patrons whereby, they are able to reserve tables for meals. The company has hired a new developer that has enlightened them on the benefits that are afforded through Micro Distributed Applications and as such is looking to create a solution that could be distributed to restauranteurs in mass after the viability of the WordPress solution is proven to management. The business would like to be able to create a solution whereby restauranteurs with a website that is WordPress based would be able to download the plugin and install it on their own website without the need to have to program at all. The business would like to have this solution be customizable whereby the restauranteur would be able to specify the days and hours of operation of their business and have these constraints percolate directly to the table reservation options that would be made available to the patrons of the restaurant. It is also important for the business to create an application that is sensitive to the different devices that individuals use such as tablets, phones, and desktop computers. The business would like to have the application be functional across all these different devices where the application would adapt to the platform being used and present an intuitive and aesthetically pleasing facade to clients. It is important for the business to ensure that any possible solution be made such that it minimizes the technical debt of the business while at the same time utilize technology that is current and can consequently function across the needs of clients.

The ACME Table Reservation Company charges $20 per month to the restauranteurs for the ability to have their patrons reserve tables. It is therefore essential for the business to be able to achieve a high adoption rate because each additional business to come onboard would represent $240 per annum in revenue. The business, much like many starting technology companies is seeking to minimize the capital expenditure that would be required to maintain the system being developed and would like to create one whereby the artifacts created could be leveraged in other endeavors that the business has in mind. The business would also like to create a product whereby the code used is common, which would facilitate the hiring of personnel in the future given a common skillset. The business is seeking to create a leverage with the solution implemented to help the business move forward with their business goals. The ACME Table Reservation Company is seeking to create an initial investment that could be capitalized on going forward and built upon so that they are able to compete with companies as theirs but do so by utilizing technology in their favor. The organization is also seeking to leverage the domain of indexing and is hoping to create a solution whereby the search providers are able to index not only the business, but the subscribers to the business. The business is seeking to gain a competitive advantage over the competition where on a given search it would be their customer's website that would be found for some restaurant and not the website of their competitors.

The hurdles being experienced by the business are common in that they seek to gain a foothold where one has been elusive in the past. The ability for customers to find the business and subscribe to their service is paramount and as such they seek to win the indexing race from their competitors. The business is hoping to win the game of clout that has become the indexing domain whereby it is them that are deemed to be the voice of authority, which coincidently facilitates their agenda of gaining market share as it is those business that have clout that stand a chance to have their voice heard by the masses. The degree of relevance that is sought is achieved in part through the linkage structure that external references provide to that voice of authority and as such it would be each of those restauranteurs that take it upon themselves to embed the created plugin directly into their WordPress theme that would confirm that they are in agreement that the ACME Table Reservation Company merits that resounding vote of confidence that it is that voice of authority with regards to table reservations online and consequently it is the competitors of the company that are not. It is this fight for stewardship of the customer that will differentiate the losers from the winners as it will be the winners that will be found by perspective customers first on their searches. This is the benefit that technology affords to the winners as the spoils of battle are always rendered to that entity that does the better job than their competitors and in this battlefield that is the internet what is at stake is nothing less than extraordinary because of the depth of the pockets that the masses.

The desire of the ACME Table Reservation Company to create a component that will be both adaptable to the web and to the WordPress architecture helps to set the stage for the creation of that much needed Micro Distributed Application. This component will need to facilitate the embedding of functionality across platform types and be such that it does not require refactoring to function across domains. Here is where the viability of distributed JavaScript applications becomes apparent as they are malleable to the mold that contains them and as such they afford a great degree of flexibility. It is this degree of flexibility that is a hallmark of a sound technological solution as it bends and yields to varying requirements because its nature is to do such. Micro Distributed Applications make sense for the development of solutions going forward for this reason despite any tertiary considerations. Given advancements in the development space however organizations find themselves at a junction in time when MDAs provide multiple degrees of benefit outside of the programming context as they lend themselves to the paradigm that the search engines subscribe to for one. They also lend themselves to the benefit of dynamic user interaction because of the housing that encapsulates them. The benefit that is afforded by MDAs is plural and as a consequence simply helps to make the case for their utilization. The benefits that are therefore afforded to the ACME Table Reservation Company because of MDAs cannot be ignored and as such MDAs should become the mode of their technological investment. To put matters into perspective it should be pointed out that in prior development efforts an initiative would be undertaken for the explicit purpose of providing the business with an advantage, but in the case of MDAs the benefit is a multiple better, a factor of consideration that has not been seen prior could very well be argued.

USE CASES

The ACME Table Reservation Company is after that much coveted revenue that may be afforded by the masses if adoption of the application finds critical mass. In order to be able to determine what to build however the organization must first part from what is needed to be built and this task is undertaken through the creation of the use cases for both the patron and the restauranteur. You need to ensure that the solution created meets the needs of both parties as it will be those restauranteurs that will provide that acceptance that will afford the application a place to reside, and it will be those patrons that utilize the application that will cause the restauranteurs to acknowledge the benefit that it affords. In the end it is simply an economics proposition that finds root in technology because after all capital is the medium by which society engages and equally prospers.

This section of the text will present the use cases for the restaurant patron and for the restauranteur where it will be shown that each actor has a distinct set of needs for their interaction with the system. The use cases presented here help to define the general system requirements that drive the discussion to how MDAs can aid in the meeting of these needs.

Restaurant Patron

The restaurant visitor will need to be able to get to some website URL and be able to navigate to the MDA application whereby the MDA will display for the user a date entry field which they will use to input a desired date for their reservation. They will also need to be able to enter a time at which they desire their reservation to be set to. The application also needs to provide the user with the ability to enter their name, telephone number, and email address where the confirmation for the reservation could be sent to. In an enterprise application you should be able to communicate with the individual on their preferred mode of communication which they would need to specify on the form such as text, email, or telephone call. For practical purposes this exercise will simply collect the information and process it accordingly. You could at a later point utilize the WordPress framework to save the data to make it available in multiple places for redundancy or utilize the data to implement an additional marketing process for example.

In figure 1 the use case details of the restaurant patron are given, where their interaction with the system is to simply create a table reservation. The use case depicts the simplicity of the interaction between the patron and the needed system whereby the system needed will simply require the creation of a single form for the user to fill out and where on the form the application would collect the date with the time of the reservation, the name of the patron along with their email address and their telephone number. In an enterprise system you would need to validate the details of the user either through the confirmation of their email address or through the generation of a unique code that could be sent to their phone and could subsequently be entered on the form directly. The collection of such data becomes pertinent outside of this use case because it facilitates the communication with the patron whereby future communication could inform them of specials at the restaurant through email or text messages for example. It is by adding this additional mode of functionality that clients become loyal and come to depend on the technology being offered where they come to question how they functioned prior to it. It is this dynamic that affords the business a much coveted prize and that is the patronage of the subscriber, which is directly tied to the viability of the business.

Creating a solution for engagement across platforms types becomes feasible for the author of the MDA given the inherent flexibility they afford. It is a type of leverage that can be dynamic in nature given that MDAs are physical applications that are infused with the full arsenal of the JavaScript language. This in essence means that the subscribing nodes can in fact become those fat clients of the past where functionality was plentiful and engaging. Through this dynamic it becomes feasible for example to be able to integrate a marketing campaign directly onto the table reservation form whereby clients could be further enticed to visit the restaurant through coupons or some other means. While the example presented here is simple in nature given the objectives required for the text it does not entail in the least that functionality should cease at the requirements provided here. It is really up to the teams that implement MDAs to create those fat client experiences that will allow for the best client experience possible. It could very well be the case that the form ceases to be a form in a future release of the MDA being outlined here and rather become a virtual host that is able to communicate with the patron by speech and take the reservation.

Figure 1. Restaurant Patron Use Case

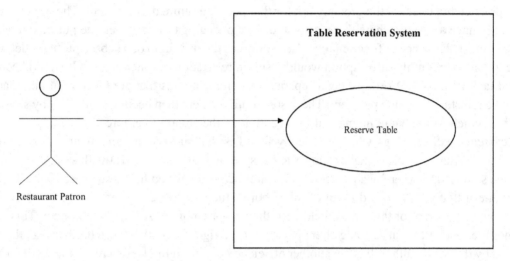

Restauranteur

In the case of the restauranteur their needs for the application are different as they need to be able to specifically define the particulars that surround their business such as being able to define their hours of operation as well as days that the business is open so that individuals would not find themselves in the uncomfortable position where they make a reservation on a date or time when the restaurant is physically closed. It is imperative for the solution crafted to accommodate the intricacies of the businesses that subscribes to its service or else it could find itself in the position of losing its customer share to a competitor that is more sensitive to the needs of its subscribers. The restauranteurs will also need to have a way to be kept up to date of reservations, in the application this will simply be performed through the creation of records in permanent storage for later viewing. In an enterprise application you would not only provide the restauranteur with the ability to log into their application and view their reservations directly but could load the reservation details directly to their Point of Sale (POS) application. Once the reservation has been placed it will be needed to have the application facilitate cancelations, i.e., the restaurant has been overbooked or give them the ability to change the reservation all with the consent of the restaurant patron. The workflow could become immensely complicated in an enterprise solution as the avenues for interjection are plentiful as are the schedules of the patrons and as such the system would need to accommodate for these subtleties to be a viable solution for restauranteurs. In this implementation the application will simply accommodate the ability for the restauranteur to cancel reservations.

Below in figure 2 the details of the use case for the restauranteur are depicted at a high level, this represents the basic interaction with the solution. The restauranteur will need to be able to log into the backend system that only they will be able to access. This private area for the restaurant owner will allow them to define the hours of operation of their restaurant, these hours of operation will trickle down to the reservation form for the patron whereby reservations for valid operation times will only be allowed. The restauranteur will also need to be able to view the current reservations that have been created by patrons and be able to cancel a reservation at which point the individual reservation record will need to be removed from permanent storage.

The use case depicted in figure 2 represents a partial system that you would find as a physical solution in practice but does lay the groundwork for that possible future development. The use case denotes the need to have a system where there is some degree of segregation between the public domain and a private context. This type of functionality also reinforces the paradigm of a subscription model whereby failure to pay the monthly subscription would result in restriction of functionality. It would become but a trivial task with an MDA to display a separate page for accounts that are locked out and that would need to be reinstated through payment. The system outlined here then becomes an MDA by subscription and all of which would entail no manual intervention by the creator to enforce.

In current SaaS offerings what is typically found is that subscribing clients are afforded a portal through which they are able to make changes to the system. In the case of MDAs this back office domain is but the same MDA whereby a particular user interface is displayed for these subscribers. This points to the benefit that MDAs afford as all of this labor of the back office system would be performed on the borrowed hardware of the same client, with the exception of the API calls of course. This scenario becomes the case of the subscribing client paying for the right to use their own hardware in the manner provided by the MDA author. It is but another efficiency that is highlighted here for the reader. Irrespective of functionality needed to be performed, through MDAs this functionality is performed void of the hardware of the MDA creator. The benefit that this affords the creator of the MDA is that an increase in CPU work would cease to be a burden to the financials of the organization as this tax or burden if you will would be the debt of the MDA subscriber and their own hardware. In a time and age when the public cloud providers charge by processing time, it becomes but another benefit that is afforded to those creators of MDAs whereby the burden that was once known changes to be transposed to the beneficiary of the service, the subscriber. MDAs have come to change the dynamic of what was known prior about the economics of software as now the conditions have changed. Now, a point of leverage can be capitalized on that was ignored in the past. It is an efficiency that is of the best kind that is simply a benefit without the drawback given that clients are eager to lend the hardware that they have purchased at their own expense.

SEQUENCE DIAGRAMS

The data flow amongst each of the actors is different as are the use cases for each, given that their needs are distinct. Physically creating the sequence diagrams for each of the actors does allow for the physical validation of the functionality that is required from the MDA. The sequence diagrams depict the information flow that will need to be accounted for by the application and as such what needs to be captured by some relational database system, queued by way of some messaging system, or communicated to an audience such as through a text message. In this simplified scenario the burden of resilience is light, but in an enterprise system you would need to not only account for these data streams but would also need to implement a fallback safe systems to ensure a high degree of quality of service (QoS). You can never ensure that a system will be available 100% of the time and as such must account for periods of degradation so that the application retains homeostasis and all without having to interrupt the users as

Figure 2. Restauranteur Use Case

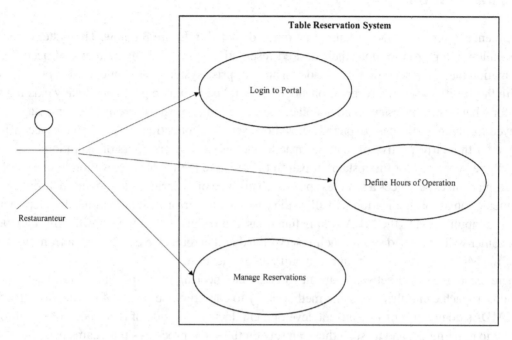

these secondary processes must function in a clandestine manner. Users have become accustomed to a seamless interaction with their applications and if this is not afforded to them then they simply move on to use a competitors' product. There is much effort and planning that is involved in creating these systems that can support this kind of quality of service, so what is depicted here is but simply an introduction to the creation of such a system, but the reality of the matter is that enterprise systems will involve considerably much more labor, capital, and resources.

The sequence diagrams for the restaurant patron and the restauranteur are detailed separately below to help further in the understanding of what will be required by the MDA to provide the needed level of utility sought. In the physical implementation that will be done in the next chapter the process will be further streamlined given the functional requirements defined here but does provide the base functionality to meet the requirements. Following the process that has been outlined here would allow the reader to create a more complicated system whereby all the needed subtleties could be outlined in a physical and visual representation. These artifacts that become the result of this process allow for communication of functionality to a development team that is void of excess jargon and verbiage that often confounds the process. Requirement documents that are void of this excess result in a higher degree of probability of success as gaps have a greater probability of being discovered before the physical implementation is performed. There is a reason why architects communicate in blueprints, but yet in technology teams often miss this benefit because they fail to rely on the standard protocol that is best practice. It is the hope that through the process depicted here it will help to bring the reader to an appreciation of how an UML process may facilitate the general software engineering effort.

Restaurant Patron

The sequence diagram for the restaurant patron is depicted in figure 3 below. The system created will need to allow the patron to input their desired reservation detail and the system will need to provide confirmation that the reservation was made. In an enterprise system you would need to provide the visitor with the ability to select a reservation slot that would be available given an already existing volume and if for whatever reason they could not place their reservation then a corresponding message would be displayed for them. In the case depicted below however the application simply provides a confirmation message for them irrespective of seating capacity and only considers hours of operation.

It will be necessary for the restaurant patron to complete their table reservation in one local so that the customer can experiences a seamless process. This type of experience is supported through an MDA implementation as the application will allow the customer to perform all of their needed steps within the WordPress application as the MDA simply functions as a widget within the website. Through the MDA the customer will be able to submit their reservation detail and receive confirmation from the server by way of the MDA that resides within the WordPress application.

There exists a parallel between current software engineering protocols and Micro Distributed Applications as each can utilize the same methodology to capture the essence of its functionality through UML. MDAs do not differ from current development doctrine outside of their mode of execution, size, dynamic loading mode, and as such they can rely on the same processes that teams have been using to define functionality that needs to be addressed in a physical software artifact.

Figure 3. Restaurant Patron Sequence Diagram

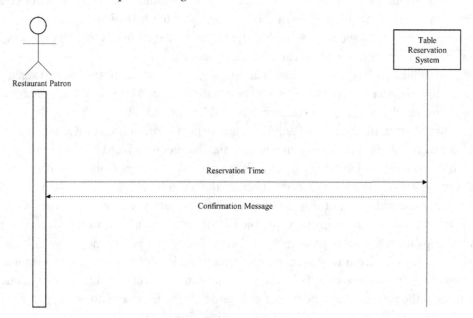

Restauranteur

The restauranteur has divergent needs from the restaurant patron and as such their individual sequence diagrams will differ. The sequence diagram for the restauranteur is provided below in figure 4. The restaurant owner will need to have the ability to obtain the list of reservations that have been made on a given day by submitting a query to the application. Upon submission of the query the application will return to the user the list of reservations that have been made by patrons and that are active. The application must also facilitate the management of the reservations by the restauranteur, where they need to have the ability to cancel a reservation and upon a cancellation have the cancellation trickle through the API to update permanent storage. This entails that the sequence diagram will have two systems, which differs from the previous sequence diagrams that have been created. This particular requirement entails that delete operations will need to be routed through the API to have the data update on the backend system. In the case of the reservations view and the hours view screens it entails that the API will need to return the corresponding list given the request posed as noted in the data flow of the sequence diagram.

The sequence diagram that has been depicted here denotes data flows that need to have a separate area for the restauranteur where only they will be able to manage reservations for their restaurant. This requirement was outlined in the use case for the restauranteur created previously; the requirements outlined here function in conjunction with previously defined needs and as such help to support the narrative of what is needed. While the use case diagram depicts the base system behavior by actor, the sequence diagram denotes the data flow surrounding this functional requirement and, in this case, there are three scenarios where data flows to three separate parties upon one action. The scenarios outlined here speak to the complexity of the software system where there are a multitude of components interacting with one another to create a singular narrative for its audience.

The requirements outlined here denote a need that requires dedicated functions of the MDA, whereby the MDA becomes more complex. The MDA being defined here will need to function in a dual manner whereby in one case it will require the interaction with a patron and and in the other case it requires the interaction with a restauranteur. This duality can be addressed with MDAs as an MDA is but a collection of user interface screens that are linked together though trigger points. These trigger points of MDAs can be created so that they are permissions driven where only certain functionality becomes available if the user is able to authenticate through the system. What would be required of the MDA would be to authenticate through some sort of credential gateway and subsequently have the server return to the MDA a session key that could be used on subsequent requests. In subsequent requests the session key could be taken, validated, and be linked to an individual user account that would signal to the trigger point what sort of screens could be made available to the user. This type of configuration is how web applications function currently and represents parity with MDAs.

The ability of MDAs to create this rich user experience ensures an alignment with existing web development doctrine. In the case outlined here equivalent functionality could be performed with the MDA compared to a SaaS application. This alignment that can be created with what is known to be best practice speaks to the progress that JavaScript has made with user interface functionality. The ability to be able to inject physical user interface elements onto a screen via JavaScript speaks to the flexibility that is now afforded to development teams to be able to create these rich and distributed applications. It is because of this rich functionality that it is feasible to be able to inject a complete user interface screen into the DOM of an HTML page and subsequently allow the user to interact with this user interface while at the same time ensuring that this functionality is tied to a user profile. This type of experience in the past would have been created completely on the server whereby the user interface would have been rendered and processed on some external server and sent subsequently to the client browser with an already defined layout structure. This is but a computational expense that may now be ignored as all of this work can be browser based. This experience also creates another efficiency as subsequent invocation points would reside directly in the RAM of the client machine, thus alleviating the need for the network traffic to satisfy the functional request and just as importantly the latency time for the event to be completed as this would all be performed on the client machine. MDAs are not singular in their derived benefit but are rather multi faceted. It is because of these derived benefits that it stands to reason that Micro Distributed Applications will begin to gain traction.

Figure 4. Restauranteur Sequence Diagram

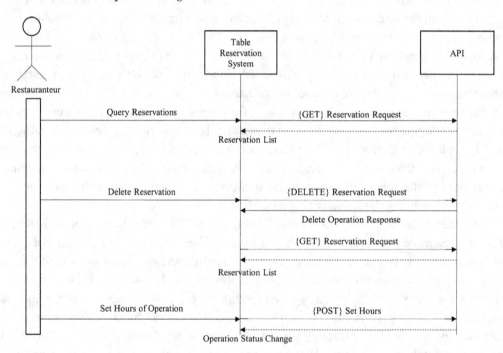

KEYWORDS

In this development effort the solution created will capitalizing on the findings from earlier where a leverage point will be capitalizing on, this hedge being the search purveyors. By crafting the page content to fit the mold expected by the Yahoo search engine the expectation becomes that a lift will occur as the data derived mandates such to be the case. The message will be created to fit the expectations of the Yahoo search engine specifically whereby the tags identified in table 4 of the chapter titled 'Attribute Relevance' will be leveraged and for which the solution will focus on the top five elements. For the readers reference the metrics identified are given in table 1 below. The leverage points that will be harnessed will be those tags that show the greatest degree of relevance as dictated by the numbers in the table. The root tag will be ignored since the solution cannot alter the URL of the website from a JavaScript context.

Outside of these four tags having relevance the application will also rely on the referral links to create relevance for the solution provider of course.

Through the utilization of the relevant tag elements as identified here and through the use of the Google trends utility it will allow for the determination of those relevant components that need to be part of the message to help the solution find acceptance with the indexing engines. Please do remember that the Google trends utility was utilized since Yahoo does not afford the same benefit. This is but a minor inconvenience however as the data extracted elucidates the general consensus of the masses and is not platform specific. Through the utility it is possible to identify the keywords that will allow the message to be indexed better and as such allow for potential subscribers to receive better traction because of this effort. While researching for relevant keywords there emerged an interesting factoid and this being that individuals are actually searching for a restaurant based upon the physically name of the establishment as can be seen from the sample data set that is provide below in table 2. This is the data that is pertinent and linked by association to the search word 'restaurant'. The list shows those search terms that the masses have been submitting to the search provider where the key term was found.

The findings from Google trends gives beneficial insight as to why succeeding in a restaurant can be difficult as the search data helps to clarify that individuals are typically not looking for a particular type of cuisine, but are rather searching for what is familiar to them and an establishment they may have already been a patron of. This factoid helps to clarify that it would be in vain for a marketing strategy to target the type of cuisine or keywords related to a food type as the mode by which a restauranteur would expect to find those elusive customers. The marketing strategy of the organization needs to pivot to one whereby like establishments should be targeted as these are the entities whose customers can be contested. To obtain the lift that is required by the subscriber base to find those customers would require the application to know what are the restaurants that are surrounding this particular establishment that are popular and competitors. Fortunate for the ACME Table Reservation Company there is a service provider that could be counted on to come to the rescue of this challenge, Yelp (www.yelp.com) is a resource that could be relied upon to find local restaurants based upon some search. The ACME Table Reservation Company could rely on the Yelp API to find those neighboring restaurants and tailor the page content so that it could piggyback off of the search behavior of the masses where a particular search for some restaurant would allow for the subscribing client's restaurant page to be found as well, thus giving the potential restaurant patron an alternative option. The ACME Table Reservation Company could even go the extent that reviews are extracted for the non subscribing restaurants, thus allowing for the message to be crafted to attract those customers from the popular eateries.

It is the data that dictates the strategy to implement by way of the MDA and as such it creates a tremendous upside to subscribers of the service because of this doctrine. The indexing domain and conversely the masses have mandated the mode by which a message needs to be crafted in order for it to be received positively. The applications that must be created will need to adapt and fit the mold that is required of them to resonate with the search purveyors. As you can see from this direct example, any utility that needs to be provided to a client base needs to be cognizant of this dynamic to create the greatest degree of benefit. MDAs fit this mold of targeted marketing because they bend and yield to what is required of them. To further highlight the benefit that MDAs provide consider the possibility that marketing sentiment changes, then it would be a matter of adapting the application to fit this new expectation to fit this dynamic. This is a new form of marketing that is timely, flexible, and harmoniously tied to sentiment.

Table 1. Relevance Factors by Attribute

Attribute	Relevance
Title	9.5220903
Description	8.6324595
Root	7.3097442
Header Two	6.3692140
Keywords	6.0161746

Table 2. Keywords Identified

Attribute
mado restaurant
hippos restaurant
aioli restaurant
stillwater restaurant
rosemary and thyme restaurant

For this particular use case the API calls will be mocked to illustrate the data feed from a third party provider. This will help to demonstrate the creation of a marketing advantage for the subscribers of the service as has been discussed. In practice what this would afford would be for subscribing restaurants to be able to compete on a more favorable note with similar establishments when customers would query for a given entity given that searchers would be presented with alternatives in the search results, and for which one such entity would be a subscribing restaurant. This would be the case because of the time and effort placed upon creating a dedicated message for the search purveyors that would subsequently be digested and indexed accordingly. A subsequent result of this type of strategy would be that some competing restaurants that would not subscribe to the services of the ACME Table Reservation Company would lose market share. The marketing strategy described here could subsequently be supported by the ACMA Table Reservation Company through the creation of enhancements to the MDAs created. One such alternative could be to specifically offer a coupon on the table reservation page for example. Another avenue that could also be pursued could be to target keywords in the HTML tag elements to denote a benefit over a competing restaurant such as that same coupon mentioned earlier. The ability for MDAs to create this alignment with the marketing message only helps to further their claim for worth. It is a dynamic marketing initiative that creates alignment with the expected message of the search purveyors and consequently only helps to create a greater degree of leverage.

DUE COURSE

For the application developed to meet the requirements that were defined in this chapter it will need to facilitate the interaction of two distinct actors, the restaurant patron and the restauranteur. Through one common MDA it will be possible to accommodate the needs of both of these parties and all while meeting the requirement that the MDA can be taken and used outside of the WordPress framework. WordPress is an application framework that is written in PHP (www.php.net). PHP is a language that is more than a quarter of a century old and yet it is seen here, it is still relevant and used to such an extent that there are almost half a billion websites powered by it as of this writing. The original version of the Facebook application was actually written in PHP. In the case of JavaScript it is even the older cousin of PHP and yet here it stands building the new wave of applications that can execute in a distributed manner. These relics of the programming landscape have traction in the current day and time because they have utility and in the case of JavaScript its utility has increased with the advent of Node.js. Development teams can now expedite their web service development because of the modules that have been made available through it. It is because of this high degree of adoption, the utilities it affords, and humanities unquenchable need for better that the language has evolved to the point that it resides at the point of becoming the de facto standard for the creation of distributed micro solutions.

It is important to understand that when some argument is posed that the listener must shed the burden of their preconceived notions of right and wrong. They must adopt and immerse themselves in the argument so that it can be appreciated fully. To live in a manner other than this means to forgo the notion of growth as no one individual can always state what truth is given their understanding and life experiences. In technology this is especially so because of the constant flux that technology imposes on all and the constant need for individuals to continually learn, in this dynamic their will always be an individual that understands some facet of landscape better than another. It is futile to believe to know truth because it is relative to the time of the event in technology. It is this type of bias that leads many astray as implementations will vary given the availability of tools. One cannot for example program solutions in PHP as you do so in Java or as you do in C#, but yet many do. Developers strip away the nuances of the paradigm that they subscribe to because it facilitates matters for them and when they do they stumble and fall. Yet this is a common scenario that unfolds itself in offices throughout the world. There was a particular case once when an individual on a mobile initiative for an Android application which utilized the Java programming language exclusively at that time suggested creating a service to listen for a particular event. The disjoint occurred in that the Android framework has a built-in listener that may be leveraged in code known as intents. The individual sought to fit the solution to what they knew and all void to the benefits that were before them. This scenario plays itself out multifold every day because developers do not care to dive any further than is absolutely necessarily into the subject matter at times and when they act in this manner it simply keeps the team from the elegant solution that is present. In another instance one individual remarked to a colleague that they just did not understand the problem and that the system did not work as they believed. It was at this point that the individual retorted and said that they begged to differ as the problem they described was detailed in a book they produced and proceeded to detail the chapter and page where the solution could be found. Some developers fall at times because they cheat themselves from finding the elegant solution that is there for them to discover if they simply took the time to have bothered to have done a little research. It is for the reasons described here that this chapter defines the requirements such that they fit the paradigms that are being implemented. The solution described in the next chapter will be built so that it fits the confines of the framework being utilized and whether that is JavaScript or PHP by way of WordPress is irrelevant as what is sought is to navigate towards that lighthouse since this is the protocol. This is the manner by which the datum point may be preserved and keep the implementation focused on a much needed truth which gives it the best chance to produce good fruit. It is a methodology that keeps the ship from running ashore and keeps the solution on course to a landing spot where the waters are calm and the natives are friendly.

The objective in the next chapter is to merge the PHP construct with the JavaScript construct so that the MDA developed can be made to function under the confines of each language structure. In an enterprise system development teams would be able to leverage the database engine of their individual clients, but in the streamlined solution that is developed next the application will simply place the burden of work on the JavaScript language. The solution will use the WordPress framework as the mode of initialization of the MDA where from this point the solution will find itself in a similar position to what was found in the past. Once invoked it will be feasible for the JavaScript application to fit an all too familiar mold where it can be used to create the user interface much as was done prior. This paradigm allows for the application to remain unaltered if taken outside of the WordPress framework and as such removes the burden of having to refactor code for an alternate implementation. In an enterprise solution the development team would leverage the framework of WordPress further however so that the application would store the data locally instead of having to transfer all the data to a remote location by way of an API call. While the solution provided in the following chapter does give you a base starting point it will be upon you to define your specific business rules that will need to be accommodated with code

In this chapter the discussion outlined a further need of the MDA, the need to adhere to indexing structures to facilitate the creation of a marketing advantage. To this end what was defined was the requirement for a solution that could generate HTML content in a manner that is sensitive to its target audience's need. The discussion expanded on the previous body of work where the discussion transitioned to a new level of sophistication that extended the reach and maturity of the MDA. This type of solution helps to further elucidate the degree of impact that MDAs can have on the business in a technological capacity and in a marketing context. It is because of the requirements outlined in this chapter that a target state was identified for the needed solution whereby this solution helps to create this clout that MDAs create in a more advanced manner. It is because of this degree of influence that MDAs can come to have that facilitates winning the battle. MDAs do not simply represent micro functionality, but they represent a tangible economic benefit to those that adhere to the constructs outlined by them architecturally. The benefits that are afforded by MDAs cross business boundaries because everyone benefits with a targeted micro solution that is index friendly.

SUMMARY

It is an important point to note that the driver for the use of the application outlined here are not the direct customers of the ACME Table Reservation Company but are rather the patrons of the patron. It is the restaurant patrons that will ultimately drive demand because it is they that force the restauranteur to incur the additional expense. It is these individuals that should be kept in mind when designing the solution as it will be the restaurant patrons who by direct engagement through the application inject capital into the restaurant. It is not simply enough when designing solutions to simply consider the base use case but rather it is necessary to understand the system as a whole and the factors that force flux upon that system, much like the page attributes and the indexing domain. It can become a futile exercise to simply create solutions that a developer believes to be great but yet they miss addressing the needs of the audience, which will always lead the discussion to a somber point. It is leverage that is sought through Micro Distributed Applications and as such their development falls under the confines of standard software engineering where their utility must be understood from all of the actors in the play or else the business risks wasting their effort. MDAs are also susceptible to the same constraints that large SaaS applications are impeded by, they need to find the demand that warrants their use and if that demand cannot be found then a re-engineering effort will be warranted. The fact that teams are now developing smaller applications does help however as businesses are now able to turn the ship much easier because as in the case of MDAs the ship is but a canoe while in the case of large monolithic applications what you are dealing with are large battleships. This is yet another reason why the age of MDAs has come to fruition because it allows teams to mitigate that risk that they all incur through technical debt. The technical debt that may be incurred in the case of smaller disjoint applications is actually smaller and as a consequence it makes the business more resilient because missing the target on an initiative simply means that you have to reposition your canoe in another direction, which is a simplified problem from that of changing course on a large cruise liner.

If you think about what has been discussed here it aligns with the manner in which society has progressed. Humanity has streamlined the process of feeding itself as individuals now have their groceries delivered to them where they remove them from their packaging and cook only that which will be consumed. It leaves garbage bins hungry and wanting to be fed as the need to use has been trimmed because the process has been simplified for all. Individuals no longer need to drive themselves as their cars take them to where they need to go by simply entering the address on a tablet that sits next to the steering wheel. Individuals are no longer bothered with the nuances of having to navigate the battlefield that is traffic as vehicles do the labor now. If you look underneath the hood of your car you will find less, the engine is gone now and has been replaced with luggage. Everyone's lives have become simplified because society has demanded such and the development landscape is simply fitting into this doctrine that everyone subscribes to because the alternative will not suffice. MDAs make sense because they fit the ever evolving view of the world where simplicity is mandated and is a hard requirement for products to take flight with customers. Can you imagine meeting a great-great grandchild and telling them on their 16th birthday that you will drive them to the DMV? They will not know what a driver's license is or what DMV refers to. Individuals live in a day and time when they want everything around them to be microwavable, where it will be completed in minutes, not days, and definitely not years. Individuals seek simplicity because it is the destination for gratification specially when it streamlines everyone's life. MDAs have come home to roost because they simplify the development effort where teams can take a common language and use it to create applications that will execute across hardware platforms and all without the need for operational teams to intervene. What would the old guard, the Visual Basic Windows developers have to say about the world now?

The development landscape has evolved over time and this evolution has taken teams to a place where MDAs can be created to simplify product offerings while at the same time help teams capitalize on the search engine indexing domain and as such, they represent a clear direction for the future of web development. The profession has been brought to the junction of where it finds itself at now because of the sheer influence that search engines hold over the populous and because of the leverage that may be created when product offerings are made to align with this technological leverage point. Teams have subsequently been migrating to a station whereby this parity may be obtained, but have been doing so organically and void of the true reason for this. MDAs have come to shed light on this paradigm shift and have consequently been brought to bear because of the inherent benefit that may be derived through them which simply reinforces this alignment that is spoken of.

The ability to be able to craft the needed message so that it can function ubiquitously across housing speaks to the sophistication that development has been able to acquire. This utility can be seen here through the marrying of the requirements laid out and the implementation that will be performed in the next chapter. While WordPress functions to demonstrate the dynamic nature that may be supported by MDAs it does not imply exclusivity as the architectural framework of MDAs is housing agnostic and as such WordPress simply functions as a means to end, to demonstrate this flexibility that is afforded through distributed JavaScript solutions.

One of the components that was left out of the equation in the case studies was the creation of one or more links pointing to some desired target domain that could benefit from the leveraging of the external reference. As was determined by way of the supervised learning model, the link structure plays a critical role in the ranking scheme of the search providers and as such in an enterprise solution the strategy would be to brand the application with a logo that could be tied back to the desired domain thus providing that much needed link equity directly from each website that implemented the solution. The strategy could also be that the solution could forgo this benefit by adding the 'nofollow' value to the 'rel' attribute of the individual anchor tag(s). If it was determined such then the authoring domain would forgo this benefit, which could be a strategy in the case where there are two types of solutions offered, a paid version and a free version for example. It would be up to each MDA author to determine their particular course of action, but it would nevertheless be a decision that would be entirely up to them because the allocation of space to an MDA entails the transfer of control. In the past this control was given up in part through an iframe and today this transfer of control entails that the website becomes the operating system of the past and the MDA becomes the software that was installed on the computer in days gone by.

In the beginning the arguments for relevance were brought forth that were qualitative in nature by individuals such as King (2008) and Jerkovic (2010). This body of work has made the migration to the quantitative realm and by doing so it has been possible to determine where homeostasis lay. It has subsequently been possible to understand what the numbers have spoken and the message that they communicated is that development has changed as it has transitioned to the domain of MDAs. The current trend as of this writing for development are micro front ends, which are just the lower tier of the MDA. Development and consequently technology does not arrive at future state in a cosmic bang, but rather does so through evolution, this body of work has simply put the pages together whereby they are able to tell the story that has always been there, but could not be read because the pages were out of order.

REFERENCES

Jerkovic, J. (2010). *SEO Warrior*. O'Reilly Media Inc.

King, A. (2008). *Website Optimization*. O'Reilly Media Inc.

Chapter 12
A WordPress Micro–Distributed Application

ABSTRACT

This chapter mirrors a previous chapter where a physical implementation of a micro-distributed application was created. The content of this chapter differs from previous work in that what is developed here is more complex because the housing of the MDA is a WordPress application. What the solution presented here will show however is that by leveraging technology in its prescribed mode it becomes feasible to maintain system homeostasis. This system state may be maintained because MDAs function ubiquitously across housing types due to their architectural framework. What this degree of flexibility exemplifies is that an application can be made to function harmoniously across landscape types because of the degree of resilience that the technology affords. This malleability of Micro-Distributed Applications helps to justify why a transition to distributed JavaScript applications needs to occur as it is a step towards resilience and simplicity.

INTRODUCTION

This chapter utilizes the case study from the previous chapter to build a full fledge Micro Distributed Application within the WordPress framework. This distributed JavaScript application will facilitate the reservation of a table at a given restaurant. This solution parallels an offering that is currently available as a WordPress plugin for OpenTable with one major caveat and this being that the solution defined here is a Micro Distributed Application whereby the framework of WordPress is simply implemented as the housing structure for the MDA. This structural configuration of the system created facilitates the creation of the application by leveraging those components of each given domain so that they may fulfill their given intent and thus alleviate the development effort from cross pollinating each domain with excess that they need not be burdened with. Each language construct presents a direct benefit from its implementation and as such it becomes a necessity to be able to enable the construct to function under its primary intended role because to fit the paradigm to anything other than simply implies a farce and the burden of debt that has no place in the discussion. The process outlined here is especially susceptible to this

DOI: 10.4018/978-1-6684-4849-6.ch012

form of egregious act since there is an interaction between two distinct languages, PHP and JavaScript and therefore it becomes a simple act to cross that boundary constraint of functionality where one of the constructs are used in a manner for which a better fit would have been the other. It is this alignment that will allow for the creation of the MDA that will become portable to other landscapes and help diminish that technical debt that is inherently incurred from the onset of any development effort. While the decision for the housing of the MDA was determined to have been WordPress there is no reason why it could not have been an alternative such as Joomla (www.joonla.org) and as such it becomes a matter of scalability to be able to create that boundary constraint for delegation. It becomes imperative to be able to sanction work so that the pivot and shift that is often required by business from technology may be hedged. This hedging will only occur if teams are able to segregate along these fixed lines where the domain in question becomes regulated to a prescribed role and where that role could be replaced if needed by another actor, much like a cast member in a play can have a substitute if needed so too must development teams look at the technological endeavor. Development teams often do not resort to this mode of operandi because of the tax burden that it places on them. Software developers want to dictate and they want to force upon the domain their will at times which diverges from the philosophical outlook that is needed for solutions to remain resilient. Taleb (2014) makes the argument in his book 'Antifragile: Things That Gain from Disorder' that it is those systems that are exposed to flux that become antifragile as opposed to those systems that retain an equilibrium point because of no flux since such systems tend to tumble when the conditions change. This can be see in the world in abundance such as in the stock market with quantitative easing for example, so if teams are to build the best possible software system then they must ensure from the onset that resilience is built into the fabric of the solution. To meet this goal it means that development teams need to place upon their head the hat of the computer scientist where it forces them to think in generics and strip away the triviality. For software systems to have resilience teams need to not only solve the general problem frame, but they must also work within the confines of the doctrine. Development teams must be willing to put aside the shortcut and adhere to that best practice doctrine to infuse that degree of resilience inherently into the systems that they build.

This degree of resilience in applications can be seen with the degree of physical work that is required from the development teams to change the product to adapt to a new change in the discourse. In the case of WordPress for example a developer can add JavaScript code to the plugin by creating a load function such as is defined below. Outside of the comments section the reader can see that the physical code is comprised of four total lines. With these basic elements on the PHP page it is possible to load the complete Micro Distributed Application which would contain the same code that could be distributed to clients that use an alternative choice of Content Management System (CMS), such as Joomla for example. In the case of Joomla, the same functionality could be added to the framework with the code fragment given below. In the case of Joomla it only requires three lines of code to be written in order to be able add the functionality of the MDA to the plugin. This functionality that is contained in the 'table_reservation_app. js' file would also remain unaltered in the implementation for this alternative CMS, thus proving that the solution is resilient and malleable. The MDA referenced through the JavaScript file shows that the much coveted factor of robustness that is sought where the degree of technical debt is diminished because of how the problem frame was accomplished in this case. Finding that generic solution for the challenge that lay before the individual in software development is how you differentiate a great solution from a mediocre one or worse yet a poor one. It was because of the flexibility that MDAs afforded that the challenge was able to be solved in a graceful manner were a pivot point could be endured without having to refactor the application. With seven lines of code you are able to embed the functionality of the table reservation application directly into the framework of two popular content management systems. There is a great advantage that is had by the business when a development effort proves to be as flexible as MDAs, it affords the business the benefit to dedicate resources to creating new functionality and growing the product features, whihc frees the business from having to incur an excess cost operationally to keep the applications that the business relies on functional.

```php
<?php
/*
Plugin Name:
Plugin URI:
Description:
Author:
Author URI:
Version:
*/

add_action('wp_enqueue_scripts', 'table_reservation_init');

function table_reservation_init(){
    wp_enqueue_script('table_reservation_app.js', plugins_url('/js/table_reservation_app.js', __
FILE__));

}
?>
// Joomla as the bootstrap engine
<?php
use Joomla\CMS\Factory;
$document = Factory::getDocument();

$document-> addScript('templates/custom/js/table_reservation_app.js');
?>
```

In the case of Joomla, their market share is much more limited with less than 3 million websites being powered by the framework, which pales in comparison to the market share that WordPress provides. Dedicating resources to be able to create this additional offering is small given what is physically required to be done coding wise to adapt the base system to the Joomla framework. Even if you are able to acquire a 0.025% market share from the populous (assuming 2 million total Joomla websites) it would still represent a market share of 500 websites and at monthly subscription fee of $20 per month it could mean an injection of capital to the business of $10,000 per month or $120,000 annually. The degree of influence in the indexing space was also left out of the monetary gain determined here, which simply implies that this effort, the three additional lines of code could be well in excess of $120,000 of revenue per annum to the organization. To put matters into perspective take the potential annual cash injection and divide that by total number of lines of code, which would mean that each line of code written would represent a cash influx (potentially) of $40,000 per annum. Granted that the discussion is dealing in hypotheticals here, but the argument cannot simply be brushed aside. An organization cannot brush the argument aside because the upside through the MDA is present independently of the target platform. In the case of WordPress for example it was determined that some 455 million websites are powered through the framework and as such the previous discussion would lead the argument here to a similar station. Let the assumption be made that a market capitalization of 0.025 exists which would yield a subscription base of over 11 million, but if you assume for the sake of argument a market capitalization of 1/1000 of that original estimate it would still represent 11,375 subscribers at a monthly subscription fee of $20, which would entail $227,500 per month or $2.73 million per year of revenue dollars. Even if you neglect the capital injection to the business here and assume that you are merely seeking link equity it would mean a positive influx of 11,875 dedicated links from both the WordPress and the Joomla endeavors to the service provider. It means an increase to the link equity of the business to the point that it would create a tangible benefit with the search providers to the point that it could mean a significant number of new customers because the business would become more prominent with the search providers.

The competition for that link equity is fierce as businesses have come to understand that it is a fundamental factor in the ranking scheme of the search providers. If you Google for example link:opentable.com you will find that as of this writing there are more than 20 million links that point to the domain. This is the mountain that needs to be climbed if you are competing with this business for the counterpart business to find a more favorable rank. A business that needs to generate that volume of inbound links will not be able to meet that goal simply by posting on blogs. The competition for link equity mandates that the business leverage whatever avenues are available to it to acquire that much needed clout. This is one of the reasons why relevance objectives needs to be aligned with the doctrine of MDAs as they are a mechanism by which the masses will be able to give the business their vote and consequently name the organization the winner in the race.

DEVELOPMENT ENVIRONMENT

For the development effort in this chapter an alternative to Visual Studio Code will be used. In this chapter the development effort will be performed using the Atom development tool that may be found here: https://atom.io. Atom is a lightweight tool that affords the developer the ability to program in diverse languages such as PHP and JavaScript for example. The environment provides IntelliSense support as long as the corresponding modules have been installed, which you will need to do for Node.js and PHP if you have not already done so. Once the Node.js and PHP packages have been installed you will need to issue the commands provided below in order to initialize the environment and to install the express, body-parser, and crypto-js packages for Node.js. This is the same process that was followed previously where the development environment was Visual Studio Code. The environment initialization as well as the installation of the express, body-parser and crypto-js modules results in the creation of the package.json file as provided below. From the particulars provided below you can see that the functional entry point will be the index.js file this time. This will be the file that will contain the code that will capture the user interaction and will function as the API in the exact same manner as was experienced in a previous chapter.

npm init
npm install express

```
npm install crypto-js
npm install body-parser
```

The primary reason why a distinct development environment was chosen for this chapter was to demonstrate that given a distinct structure of work the physical work effort remains intact. The physical work effort that was performed here was the same as was performed for the MDA that was created to function outside of the WordPress framework and as such it helps to demonstrate the dynamic nature of the paradigm of MDAs. The creation of distributed JavaScript applications has commonality irrespective of the physical working configurations. The creation of MDAs depend on a series of tenants that cross development environment boundaries and for that matter cross implementation boundaries as has been described with WordPress and Joomla. The only factor that is truly important in the domain of MDAs are the feature set and the physical functionality of the application as the remainder are but details that need to be worked out, similarly to the particular development environment as was demonstrated here.

```
{
  "name": "trs",
  "version": "1.0.0",
  "description": "Table reservation system",
  "main": "index.js",
  "scripts": {
    "test": "echo \"Error: no test specified\" && exit 1"
  },
  "author": "Guillermo Rodriguez",
  "license": "ISC",
  "dependencies": {
    "body-parser": "^1.19.1",
    "crypto-js": "^4.1.1",
    "express": "^4.17.2",
  }
}
```

WORDPRESS ENVIRONMENT

The development effort for this chapter was performed under a MAC operating system and as such the utilities used were centric to this environment. In order to be able to create the WordPress application locally the MAMP environment was utilized which may be found here: https://www.mamp.info. MAMP facilitates development as it installs several components, which are MySQL, Apache, Nginx, and PHP to name but the essentials. The reader should note that MAMP can be used for general development in PHP as it is not tied specifically to WordPress development.

Once the MAMP environment has been installed locally then you will need to create the needed structure to support the WordPress environment. In order to have WordPress function correctly locally you will need to create a database to house the WordPress configurations, which is done through the phpMyAdmin console with a database named 'trs' (for this example). The Table Reservation System will not be utilizing the database created in this project as it will simply be using it as the datastore for the WordPress functionality.

The next step in the process is to physically download the WordPress plugin skeleton structure so that it may be loaded to the corresponding directory structure that will allow it to be rendered by the local server. The template file structure may physically be downloaded from the WordPress website and which may be found here: https://wordpress.org/download/. Once the physical files have been downloaded they need to be placed under the physical location where the local web server is able to retrieve them and render them on a physical browser window. For this project WordPress version 5.9 was used, but for your purposes you may download a suitable alternative and follow along with the remainder of the chapter accordingly. The reader should be cautioned however that your WordPress template will need to comply with the physical configuration of your environment, i.e., database engine, server, and PHP versions.

Following the installation, you will need to make some changes to your physical system configuration, the first being an addendum to the hosts file which may be found under /private/etc/hosts on a Mac. The addendum to the file needs to be the local host IP address (127.0.0.1) and the name of the database created earlier, i.e. trs. Following this change you will need to modify the wp-config-sample.php file that may be found under MAMP/htdocs. In this file you will need to assign the correct database connection particulars for the MySQL database connection, which may be found in your MAMP installation if you simply launch the server and navigate to the database header on the page that is rendered. Once the configuration changes have been made you can launch the instance of WordPress by going to the URL that matches the pattern: http://database:port, which allows you to define the configuration for the WordPress instance. The physical administration section will be viewable through the URL that matches the pattern: http://database:port/wp-admin.

With the configuration changes made prior it allows you to have a physical instance of WordPress locally, which you can utilize to test your plugin development. In the steps performed up to now you will notice that no artifacts have been written and the processes followed have been administrative in nature only. These steps have been necessary in order to be able to perform the needed body of work that is to come. The remainder of this chapter will be dedicated to the physical effort of creating that MDA application to fit within the framework of WordPress.

WORDPRESS DOCUMENT

In order to create a WordPress plugin the first order of business is to be able to create the needed file structure and attach them to the base server side files so that the WordPress framework is able to consume the plugin. The development community has contributed to plugin development in order to facilitate their creation and one such utility may be found at the URL: https://pluginplate.com; for the purposes needed here the discussion will only be using the free version of the utility noted above. Once you complete the input form the application creates your plugin shell for download. These generated files are the basic structure that a development team will utilize for the physical plugin development.

```
/**
* Loads the plugin table reservation javascript file.
*
* @access public
```

```
* @since 1.0.0
* @return void
*/
function table_reservation_application_init() {
    wp_enqueue_script( 'table-reservations-js', TRS_PLUGIN_URL . 'js/table_reservations.js', ar-
ray(), 1.0, false);
}
```

The files as were downloaded can be installed to WordPress via the administrator's section of the website upon which the plugin becomes available to you directly via the user interface. The WordPress framework requires that the zipped files conform to a standard doctrine and if they do then the system is able to read and absorb the plugin directly for utilization. From the download files there were some needed addendums that needed to occur in order to be able to structure the solution to what was needed for the Micro Distributed Application of the table reservation application to take hold. The first change that was needed to be made was to the class-table-reservation-system.php file that is located in the core folder of the solution. This file functions as the bootstrap mechanism for the plugin where the individual hooks that are needed for customization for the plugin can be created. It was in this file that a function was created to do the physical loading of the JavaScript file to initialize the complete MDA that was created. The code that was added to the PHP file is provided above for the reader, where you will notice that the specific WordPress framework was leveraged to physically create the ingestion of the JavaScript resources directly into the WordPress domain. It was because of the adhering to the protocol that the MDA construct found a seamless integration with the target host. It is through the leveraging of this dynamic that the degree of technical debt was mitigated as future endeavors would be able to build upon this alignment and consequently help the business stay in tune with future technological mandates that are required of it. The function definition provided above is bound to the WordPress framework through a bridge that is created through the add_action function as provided in the code fragment given above. Exclusive of the comments and the template files as downloaded from the plugin generator the total lines of code that were required in order to bind the needed MDA functionality to the WordPress framework were a total of four lines of PHP code.

```
/**
* Add base hooks for the core functionality
*
* @access private
* @since 1.0.0
* @return void
*/
private function base_hooks() {
    add_action('wp_enqueue_scripts', array( self::$instance, 'table_reservation_application_init' ) );
}
```

The file that is referenced in the PHP code fragment given above is provided for the reader in part below.

```javascript
// JavaScript load event trigger
window.onload = function () {

// API URL
var HOST = 'http://localhost:9595/api/v1.0/software';

// API Key for security
var KEY = '1234567890';

var request = new XMLHttpRequest();
request.onreadystatechange = function() {
   if (this.readyState == 4 && this.status == 200) {
      code = CryptoJS.AES.decrypt(request.responseText, KEY).toString(CryptoJS.enc.Utf8);
      window.eval(code)
      code = null
   }
};
request.open("GET", HOST, true);
request.send();

}
```

This file differs from the previous file utilized on the client side because of the utilization of the window.onload event as opposed to using the jQuery ready function as given the CDN latency, the local JavaScript file was loaded prior to the loading of the external libraries that are referenced, thus causing a reference error due to the unknown object of '$'. This is a subtle change that was required from the previous implementation. Also, to note is that the array of JavaScript files to reference in this implementation excluded the local file that was needed to be included as part of the WordPress plugin and hence there was no need to load it at runtime. This implementation has met the original requirement of being able to create a seamless component that can be used across WordPress and websites that are void of the framework as the local library could be made to function just as it was provided in this chapter in either implementation. In an enterprise solution the KEY variable reference would be removed as you could simply trap for a network request by URL and make it such that the server side code would only function if the requestor IP address matches the domain name for a subscriber. It would make it such that any request that is made from other than a verified client would simply receive a response that informed them of the exception.

With a minor amount of code, it was possible to create a system that calls the MDA application and does so in such a manner that the burden of development is removed from the server side component. This configuration places the burden of functionality squarely on the shoulders of the JavaScript client. This dynamic facilitates the ability of the business to create generic solutions that are able to be rendered across a wide spectrum of hosts such as Joomla for example. It also affords the business the ability to garnish that much needed link equity from a vast array of hosts adding to the degree of authority for the authoring entity of the MDA.

JAVASCRIPT USER INTERFACE COMPONENTS

The physical application is created through a single JavaScript file that is rendered from the Node.js application that is created in the following section. Much as was done in a previous chapter, in this section a generic function is created that can be leveraged across the different user interfaces so that a minimal amount of code is written. What you will also notice is that there is also a great degree of parity with the JavaScript code that was written in a previous chapter. The wheel is not being reinvented here but rather the solution is being aligned with a common doctrine where the semantics of the user interface simply become instances of a configuration. The core functionality is tied to the API layer where data is transferred back to the datastore of the application. In an enterprise system you would want to make the additional effort to store the data locally so that in the case that a service degradation is experienced with the corporate API layer the individual subscribers are still able to function. This discussion is left void from the implementation here as what is of interest is in the building of the MDA to be utilized within the context of the WordPress framework.

As the reader may have noted from the discussion here, the creation of additional tools or user interfaces would be facilitated through the MDA since the core functionality would remain intact and as such could be leveraged in subsequent development efforts. This demonstrates the benefit of economies of scale that MDAs provide to the business since they are software engineering constructs and as such, they follow the same benefit and drawbacks that are seen in more traditional development environments such as Python or C# for example. With the body of work of the table reservation system you will notice that there are parallels that exist with the prior work effort because the task undertaken was to solve the general problem frame, this means that solutions are able to pivot and change since it is a canoe that needs to be repositioned and not a large vessel. Consequently, the pivot and change that was needed to be undertaken here was not as severe as it could have been given how a previous solution had already been defined for the create_row and create_element functions, both of which are leveraged here.

Interface Layout

The interface layout that is required by the table reservation system is slightly more complex than was required by the mortgage MDA that was created prior. In the table reservation system, the solution needs to account for not only input from the user, but it also needs to be able to allow the restauranteur to login to the backend system and view reservations made, at which point they may cancel any given reservation. This particular user interface is slightly more complicated in part because of the data interchange that needs to occur and the ability of the application to not simply track data entry but be able to display input data. In an enterprise system the application would utilize a permanent storage system such as a relational database, but in this case the application will simply use flat files to store reservation detail. The user interface will subsequently make calls to the API to retrieve this information which will be displayed for the restauranteur to view and/or manage.

Initialization

The MDA was bootstrapped to the WordPress template by configuring the application to function on a dedicated page only as would be the case in practice as a customer would dictate some particular page to house the application and as such it would have a fixed website address, thus allowing the application to determine at runtime when to initialize. The code fragment given below demonstrates how this was accomplished in the MDA. Once the application determines that the page URL is as earmarked then the MDA begins the process of creating the user interface to initialize the application. The MDA leverages the framework that was created in a previous chapter, where common functions were created so that they could be leveraged through other functional points. The application created here is more complex than what was created prior and as such some additional functionality was needed to be created to accommodate the requirements that arose, but nevertheless for the most part the theme that was subscribed to previously was maintained.

```
/*
    Function to load MDA within the WordPress template engine. The function is invoked when the
document object is set to a ready state as defined by the browser. The function determines the location
of the current URL and if that matches the targeted endpoint for the invocation of the MDA then the
application is rendered on the screen for the user.
*/

$(document).ready(function() {

  // Target page URL
  var url = "http://trs:8888/book-your-table/";

  if (window.location.href == url){
    // Create base trs_container
    create_container();

    // Login section
    create_row('', 'button', 'Portal');

    // Builds reservation screen
    reservations_make_ui();

    // Creates link equity for the MDA author
    create_row('', 'link', 'www.TableReservationSystem.MDA.com');
  }
});
```

Elements

Given the degree of abstraction that was created through the create_element function it entailed that the application here was able to recycle the logic and implement it out of the box without modification. This function provided the ability to pass into it a series of attributes along with an object and have it cycle through the attribute set and dynamically assign the needed attributes directly to the HTML element. It was because of this function that the work effort here was able to define the interface through a configuration in lieu of having to do so through a physical coding effort. As brief and as simple a function that the create_element code fragment is it does highlight the benefit that may be afforded when building user interface functions that can be leveraged and reused. This being a theme of course of Micro Distributed Applications where that code that is created can be leveraged across domains through a CDN. To put the matter in perspective let it be noted that this simple function was the basis for the creation of two MDAs and was also leveraged without having to have made any modifications to a single part of it. Once you begin to create these reusable functional code fragments in the form of MDA functions you will be able to harness their utility across your applications, thus helping you to build not only smaller physical components, but also modules that may be leveraged as a common core library or component throughout software development initiatives. Much as is seen in traditional development efforts where classes are created that can be used and be extended across the development effort, so too can this courtesy be extended to the smallest of components in JavaScript.

Rows

The individual row elements of the application were created through the create_row function much as how it occurred in a previous chapter, in this chapter however the functionality required a degree of evolution given the complexity of the system at hand as compared to prior efforts. The first part of the create_row function which is displayed above traps for all invocations where the input type is a label. The function creates the corresponding division tag, where the division tag can be either clear, red, blue or green. It is the mechanism by which field labels are created or individual messages such as confirmation messages are provided to the end user. The remaining part of the function determines the type of object to create such as a button or a link and proceeds to create the object by calling the create_element function with the corresponding attributes that are needed. The create_row method functions as the gateway to the creation of the complete user interface for the MDA and as such serves a significant part of the overall utility of the application, this is the reason why it was essential for the MDA to be encrypted between hosts. Failure to have encrypted the codebase would have meant that it could have rendered this proprietary intellectual property directly to prying eyes. MDAs give developers a tremendous advantage by providing them with the ability to create reusable and distributed components, but in doing so exposes them to the loss of intellectual property. In an enterprise solution what you would want to do would be to go a step further and load functionality not only encrypted but in parts where each function could be built at runtime so that at no given time would you be transferring the complete software to the requesting host. If such a transmission could be unencrypted and captured all that would be found would be a partial part of the greater whole, thus giving the business a higher degree of security.

```
/*
    Function to load MDA within the WordPress template engine. The function is invoked when the
document object is set to a ready state as defined by the browser. The function determines the location
of the current URL and if that matches the targeted endpoint for the invocation of the MDA then the
application is rendered on the screen for the user.
*/

$(document).ready(function() {

 // Target page URL
```

```
var url = "http://trs:8888/book-your-table/";

if (window.location.href == url){
  // Create base trs_container
  create_container();

  // Login section
  create_row('', 'button', 'Portal');

  // Builds reservation screen
  reservations_make_ui();

  // Creates link equity for the MDA author
  create_row('', 'link', 'www.TableReservationSystem.MDA.com');
 }
});
```

In the index section of the book you will find the complete source code that was used to create the solution here. You may also find the physical files in the GitHub.com repository that may be found here: https://github.com/guillermorodriguez/Chapter12. You are free to use the code provided through the repository for your own purposes without any obligations, but also without any guarantees. The solution will require the utilization of a development program such as Atom as was discussed previously, but any editor will function as long as you have installed the required dependencies. The solution that has been uploaded to the GitHub repository contains two main folders, these being the WordPress project that you will find under the TRS folder and the JavaScript project which has the Node.js files to execute the server side components.

Reservation

The user interface to capture a reservation is depicted below in figure 1. One of the requirements that was given was to capitalize on the link equity that MDAs provide and to meet this objective is the reason why the link below the 'Reserve' button was added. This is a dead link in the application, but in a commercial solution this link would represent the individual contribution that would be made by each subscriber of the utility to the worth of the author's domain. The input form below accepts the name of the patron, the date of the reservation, the time they wish to start their reservation, their phone number, and email address. Upon selection of the 'Reserve' button the JavaScript application physically calls the Node.js web service to save the reservation and upon a successfully operation the user is provided with a success message. If the time that they require their reservation does not meet the hours of operation of the restaurant, then they are denied the ability to create the reservation. The success message is displayed in figure 2 below.

Each element depicted above relied on the create_row and create_element function, where the function definition to create the user interface component simply called the create_row function with the desired parameters to have the application create and load the element to the browser window.

```
/*
  Function to generate reservation screen.
*/
function reservations_make_ui(){

  create_row('Name', 'text', '');
  create_row('Date', 'text', '');
  create_row('Time', 'text', '')
  create_row('Telephone', 'text', '');
  create_row('Email', 'text', '');

  create_row('', 'button', 'Reserve');

}
```

The user interface displayed in figure 1 was created once the designated page was loaded in the browser as the document ready jQuery function is invoked. The physical code fragment that initiates the user interface depicted here was provided in the 'Initialization' section of this chapter. The code fragment calls the reservations_make_ui function that is provided above for the reader. As can be seen from this function, all that is done is that each desired object is created through a function call to the create_row function. This doctrine of development helped to greatly simply the overall software development effort that was needed to create the MDA.

Figure 1. Table Reservation Form

Figure 2. Table Reservation Confirmation Message

Lubbock Express Cafe

Reservation made successfully.

Login

From the initial table reservation screen the user is able to select the blue portal button that directs them to the login screen that is displayed below in figure 3. This screen acts as the gateway to the administrator's section of the application where the restauranteur is able to administer the table reservation requests or to set their business hours. Upon selection of the 'Login' button the MDA physically makes the outbound call to the API that authenticates the user's credentials. This application simply looks through a flat file to determine if the correct user and password was provided and if they are then it returns a valid authentication message of 'true' otherwise the API returns 'false'. The physical login function is provided above for the reader where it can be seen if the user credentials are provided correctly then the MDA calls the reservations_make_admin_ui function that takes it upon itself create the complete administrators' user interface. This implementation is lacking the needed security token specifics and it is a component that would need to be addressed in a production ready application, but for the purposes of this endeavor, the functionality has been simplified.

```
/*

    Login function of the MDA application that takes it upon itself to extract the entered user name and password data from the corresponding fields and then sends a request to the API endpoint as a GET request. The API responds back with a value of true in the result entry of the data object if the credentials entered are valid for the user. If the credentials are validated, then the function takes it upon itself to call the corresponding function to build the administrators user interface.

*/
function portal_login_action() {

  var request = new XMLHttpRequest();
  request.onreadystatechange = function() {
      if (this.readyState == 4 && this.status == 200) {
        data = JSON.parse(request.responseText)
        // Parse result value to determine login success
```

```
        if(data.result){
         // Build reservation administrators screen
          reservations_make_admin_ui();
        }else{
          create_row('ERROR', 'label', 'Invalid credentials provided.');
        }
      }
  };

  request.open("GET", encodeURI(HOST + 'account?user=' + $('#User').val() +
'&password=' + $('#Password').val()), true);
  request.send();
}
```

Figure 3. Table Reservation MDA Login Screen

Reservations

The reservations screen is provided below in figure 4, where there is simply a single row, i.e., one reservation in the database that is displayed. This screen is generated dynamically given the data that is returned from the API as the MDA loops through the dataset that is returned as an array and for each entry in the array, i.e., each reservation the application calls the create_row function to make a new entry to display on the screen for the user. The list of reservations was extracted from a flat file, but in an actual product offering the data would be extracted from some enterprise system such as SQL Server for example. It should also be noted that the MDA builds each element given the functionality that is afforded through open source libraries such as Bootstrap and jQuery. The screens created are simple interfaces that depend on the base functionality of the libraries used. In a software product offering there would need to be a greater emphasis placed on the refinement of the interface such that a greater degree of parity is achieved through the user interface and the look and feel of the application.

```
/*
    This function serves the purpose of creating the reservation administration screen.
*/
function reservations_make_admin_ui(){
 clear_content();

 portal_admin_make_header();

 var request = new XMLHttpRequest();
 request.onreadystatechange = function() {
    if (this.readyState == 4 && this.status == 200) {
     data = JSON.parse(request.responseText);
     data.result.forEach(function (item, index) {
       create_row(item.name + ',' + item.date + ',' + item.time + ',' + item.telephone + ',' + item.
email, 'button', 'Delete');
       });
     }
 };

 request.open("GET", encodeURI(HOST + 'reservation'), true);
 request.send();

}
```

The selection of the 'Delete' button from the screen shown in figure 4 results in the record being deleted from the database. The delete function of the MDA is given below, the function utilizes the query string displayed next to the delete button as the mechanism for determining which record is being requested to be deleted. The physical fourth entry in this string is used as the determining factor for the record deletion, which in this case is the telephone number. In a product offering you would be using a unique identifier to ensure that only the needed record is deleted as in this example each reservation by an individual with the given telephone number is removed. If a successful message is returned from the API call, then the application simply reloads the reservation list, thus giving the user an up to date list of pending reservations. If the record cannot be deleted, then a corresponding error label is created.

```
/*
    The purpose of this function is to delete a reservation from the administrator's screen. The function
takes the field entry as input in its signature and then proceeds to split the data on a comma character.
The function proceeds to call the API on a DELETE operation with the entry in the fourth position of
the array created from the split operation.
*/
function reservation_delete_action(data) {

 entries = data.split(',')
```

```
var request = new XMLHttpRequest();
request.onreadystatechange = function() {
   if (this.readyState == 4 && this.status == 200) {
    data = JSON.parse(request.responseText)
    if(data.result){
     reservations_make_admin_ui();
    }else{
     create_row('ERROR', 'label', 'Please try again later.')
    }
   }
};

request.open("DELETE", encodeURI(HOST + 'reservation/' + entries[3]), true);
request.setRequestHeader("Accept", "*/*");
request.send();
}
```

Figure 4. Table Reservation Administration Screen

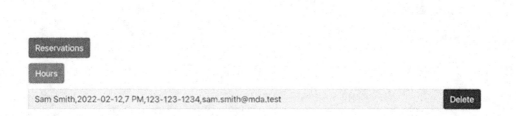

Hours of Operation

The hours of operation screen is displayed below in figure 5, this screen allows the restauranteur to define their hours of operation for each day of the week. These entries help to filter out future reservation requests that do not meet the criteria where the restaurant is not open on a reservation time that is requested. The 'Set' button triggers the call to the API that updates the hours of operation record for the restaurant. The JavaScript function that is triggered through the 'Set' button is provided below for the reader. The hours_make_action function creates a JSON object from the field inputs and sends the data to the API through a POST request upon which either a success or failure message is displayed on the screen letting the user know the status of their request.

What is seen in this example and the previous examples is the direct dependency of a server side component where the user interface is but a mechanism to manage the data stored on the server. The ability to segregate the data domain from the user interface has facilitated the creation of Micro Distributed Applications and has helped to simplify the needs on the client side. The development domain has arrived at a junction in time where the user interface has been enhanced through the use of JavaScript libraries, and style sheets which have helped to further simplify the development domain facilitating the way to Micro Distributed Applications. Applications where data and function are removed by definition implies modularity, the domain of MDAs.

Figure 5. Hours of Operation Administration Screen

Lubbock Express Cafe

Reservations

Hours

Sunday	12 PM - 8 PM
Monday	12 PM - 8 PM
Tuesday	12 PM - 8 PM
Wednesday	12 PM - 8 PM
Thursday	12 PM - 8 PM
Friday	12 PM - 8 PM
Saturday	12 PM - 8 PM

Set

```
/*
    This function takes it upon itself to set the hours of operation for the restaurant. The function takes
the entries provided and calls the API on a POST method.
*/
function hours_make_action() {
```

```
var request = new XMLHttpRequest();
request.onreadystatechange = function() {
   if (this.readyState == 4 && this.status == 200) {
    data = JSON.parse(request.responseText)
    if(data.result){
      create_row('SUCCESS', 'label', 'Hours updated successfully')
    }else{
      create_row('ERROR', 'label', 'Please try again later to update restaurant hours.')
    }
   }
};

request.open("POST", HOST + 'hour', true);
request.setRequestHeader("Content-Type", "application/json;charset=UTF-8");
request.send(JSON.stringify({
   monday: $('#Monday').val(),
   tuesday: $('#Tuesday').val(),
   wednesday: $('#Wednesday').val(),
   thursday: $('#Thursday').val(),
   friday: $('#Friday').val(),
   saturday: $('#Saturday').val(),
   sunday: $('#Sunday').val()
}));

}
```

SERVER SIDE JAVASCRIPT

The server side JavaScript functionality is created through the Node.js framework, whereby functional endpoints are called by the client through an HTTP context. The main body of the application is contained in the file named index.js which is launched utilizing the node command line. Each functional endpoint serves to meet the needs of some user interface or to meet the needs of transferring code dynamically to the user interface as was done in the previous MDA example created.

The creation of the API was facilitated through the express framework that may be found here: https://expressjs.com. This was the mechanism by which it became feasible to create with a high degree of expedience all the needed endpoints to manage the data transfer from the client. Through the express framework you are able to manage POST, GET, and DELETE endpoints, which provides for that alignment that is needed between the client and server side. The discussion next proceeds to those endpoints that were created in order to facilitate the data transfer and storage of input from the client side.

There is one endpoint that was utilized and is not discussed below as it is identical to what was used in the prior example, the physical encryption function that was leveraged to transfer the code from server to the client remains intact and therefore is not addressed below. For your reference the code segment in its entirety was added to the index section, you may also reference the code through the GitHub repository for the chapter.

Account

Account detail was managed through the GET method of the API, which served the purpose of validating the user input for login. The code segment is provided below for the reader. The function extracts the user name and password from the query string as provided through a GET call and then proceeds to validate the input provided. If a corresponding entry is found in the data store where the user and password match what is provided and as long as the account is deemed to be 'active' then the API returns an embedded result of 'true' to the client in the form of a JSON object.

```
// GET
app.get("/api/v1.0/account", (request, response) => {

  var envelope = request.query;
  var outcome = false

  console.log("%s:%s access requested", envelope.user, envelope.password);

  try{
    contents = file.readFileSync('account/account.data', 'utf8');
    contents.split(/\r?\n/).forEach(line => {
      account = line.split(',')

      if (account.length == 3 && !outcome) {
        if(account[0] == envelope.user && account[1] == envelope.password && account[2] ==
'valid'){
          console.log("%s account validated", account[0])
          outcome = true;
        }
      }
    });

  }catch(err){
    response.json({ result: false, exception: err.message });
  }finally{
    response.json({ result: outcome });
  }
});
```

While only flat files were used to store account credentials in this simplified case, in a vendor offering you would implement an interface to a database where the physical user and encrypted password would be stored. Ideally you would also store additional detail such as the IP address from where the call was made, it becomes another mechanism by which authenticity of a request may be made. You could also implement third party validation through a text message confirmation as is currently seen with secure systems. The possibilities to extend the simple example here abound as it is up to you to determine the degree of sophistication that your applications will require, but nevertheless the framework is there to be leveraged through MDAs.

Hours

The physical hours are managed through a GET and POST request in the API where the GET endpoint is used to retrieve the hours of operation of the restaurant and the POST is used to update or create the working hours of the establishment. These are the interface points that allow the MDA to display and update the input from the restauranteur.

Below you will find the GET method that was implemented from which you can infer the simplicity by which the operation unfolds. The data is retrieved from its datastore and transformed to a valid JSON object that is transmitted to the client for viewing. In this simplistic case the application simply retrieved the data from flat file storage, but in a software product offering the data would be retrieved from a database where it would be retrieved based upon some unique identifier that you would pass from the client via the same API as a parameter in the query string much as occurred with the login functionality described prior.

```
// GET
app.get("/api/v1.0/hour", (request, response) => {
  var outcome = {};

  console.log("Hours requested");

  try{
    contents = file.readFileSync('hour/hour.data', 'utf8');
    contents = contents.split(/\r?\n/);

    if (contents.length > 0) {
      data = contents[0].split(',')
      outcome = {
        "Sunday": data[0].split(':')[1],
        "Monday": data[1].split(':')[1],
        "Tuesday": data[2].split(':')[1],
        "Wednesday": data[3].split(':')[1],
        "Thursday": data[4].split(':')[1],
        "Friday": data[5].split(':')[1],
        "Saturday": data[6].split(':')[1],
      }
    }

  }catch(err){
```

```
    response.json({ result: {}, exception: err.message });
  }finally{
    response.json({ result: outcome });
  }
});
```

The operational hours are updated or created through the POST API endpoint that is detailed below for the reader. In the POST endpoint the data is passed in the envelope of the request and consequently the API has to extract this detail where the values attached to each attribute are formatted into a string that is subsequently stored to a flat file. If the operation is successful, then a JSON object is returned to the client whereby the result of the operation is assigned a value of 'true'.

```
// POST
app.post("/api/v1.0/hour", (request, response) => {

  var envelope = request.body;
  var outcome = false

  console.log("Restaurant hours updated");

  try{

    data =  "Sunday:" + envelope.sunday + ',' +
        "Monday:" + envelope.monday + ',' +
        "Tuesday:" + envelope.tuesday + "," +
        "Wednesday:" + envelope.wednesday + ',' +
        "Thursday:" + envelope.thursday + ',' +
        "Friday:" + envelope.friday + ',' +
        "Saturday:" + envelope.saturday + ',' + "\r\n";

    file.unlinkSync("hour/hour.data")
    file.writeFileSync("hour/hour.data", data);
    outcome = true

  }catch(err){
    response.json({ result: false, exception: err.message });
  }finally{
    response.json({ result: outcome });
  }
});
```

The entire operational burden that was placed on the API to be able to retrieve and update hours of operation consisted entirely of two endpoints that collectively amounted to 63 lines of code inclusive of comments and excess formatting to facilitate development. Granted the operations were simplistic in nature in that data was saved and retrieved from flat file storage, however the examples here highlight the simplified process that developers can now subscribe to in the creation of applications that the masses can consume all too willingly.

Reservations

The reservations API required three separate functions to accommodate the needed user interface requirements outlined in the previous chapter. The operations that needed to be accommodated were DELETE, GET, and POST as in this case the application needed to physical be able to delete reservations created by some unique identifier, retrieve the reservations, and create a reservation.. The requirements for the reservations component of the application mirrored those of the other domain endpoints and as such helps to clarify the parity that exists between functional domains of the system. This leads to further understanding of the degree of congruence that must exist with the frontend and its corresponding functionality. This is the reason why it was feasible to create components with a common point of functionality, i.e., the create_row and create_element functions. Developers should not recreate the wheel each time they transition from one functional domain to another, i.e. reservations and account (login) as the elements to capture the detail are uniform. It stands to reason therefore that they should be able to create these functional elements that are simplistic in nature if they simply rely on general abstractions that enforce the integrity of the system.

The DELETE API endpoint is implemented in a similar manner to a GET operation whereby the telephone number of the desired record to be deleted is passed as a parameter to the endpoint. The code fragment of the DELETE API endpoint is provided above for the reader. The endpoint loops through the reservations and finds the particular reservation that was made under the phone number that was passed as a parameter to the DELETE endpoint. The system then proceeds to save to flat file storage all those records that do not include the record attached to the telephone number in question after which the API returns a JSON object to the calling agent with a positive output result.

```
// DELETE
app.delete("/api/v1.0/reservation/:telephone", (request, response) => {

  var outcome = false;

  console.log("Reservation delete requested for telephone: %s", request.params.telephone);

  try{
    data = "";

    contents = file.readFileSync('reservation/reservation.data', 'utf8');
    contents.split(/\r?\n/).forEach(line => {
      reservation = line.split(',')

      if (reservation.length == 5) {
        if (request.params.telephone != reservation[3]){
          data += line + '\r\n';
```

```
          }
        }
    });

    file.unlinkSync("reservation/reservation.data")
    file.writeFileSync("reservation/reservation.data", data);

    outcome = true;

  }catch(err){
    response.json({ result: false, exception: err.message });
  }finally{
    response.json({ result: outcome });
  }
});
```

The GET operation serves the purpose of retrieving all of the reservations that have been saved to record so that they may be displayed for the user in the application portal that they have logged into.

```
// GET
app.get("/api/v1.0/reservation", (request, response) => {

  var outcome = []

  console.log("Reservations requested");

  try{
    contents = file.readFileSync('reservation/reservation.data', 'utf8');
    contents.split(/\r?\n/).forEach(line =>  {
      reservation = line.split(',')

      if (reservation.length == 5) {
        outcome.push({
          "date": reservation[0],
          "time": reservation[1],
          "name": reservation[2],
          "telephone": reservation[3],
          "email": reservation[4]
        });
      }
    });

  }catch(err){
    response.json({ result: [], exception: err.message });
```

```
 }finally{
  response.json({ result: outcome });
 }
});
```

The API function call is provided above for the reader where it can be seen that it simply reads the contents of the data stored in the reservations file line by line. On each line that is consumed the application creates a JSON object that is appended to the outcome array. Once all of the records are processed the API returns to the calling entity a JSON object with the results of each record that was found in storage. The POST method serves the purpose of saving reservation detail to permanent storage where it may be retrieved at a later time by another functional endpoint such as a GET for example. The method implemented to support the POST operation is provided below for the reader.

```
/*
```

The POST method for the reservations serves the purpose of creating a table reservation entry. The method saves the entry submitted to the hour.data file for permanent storage. In an enterprise offering the code segment below would depend on a SQL data structure whereby the data could be held in a manner that would be conducive to a better layout for later querying. The skeletal structure that would be needed by this enterprise system would be in alignment however with the code fragment provided below at a rudimentary level.

```
*/
app.post("/api/v1.0/reservation", (request, response) => {
 var envelope = request.body;
 var outcome = false
 try{
  var availability = file.readFileSync('hour/hour.data', 'utf8');
  availability = availability.split(/\r?\n/)[0].split(',');
  var calendar = envelope.date.split('-')
  var time_given = 0;

  if ((envelope.time).includes('PM')){
   time_given = 12 + parseInt((envelope.time).replace(' PM', ''));
  }else{
   time_given = parseInt((envelope.time).replace(' PM', ''));
  }

  var reservation_date = new Date (parseInt(calendar[0]), parseInt(calendar[1]) -1,
parseInt(calendar[2]), time_given);
  var day_of_week = reservation_date.getDay();
  var open_between = availability[day_of_week].split(':')[1];
  var start_hour = open_between.split('-')[0].trim().split(' ');
  if(start_hour[1] == 'PM'){
   time_given = 12 + parseInt(start_hour[0]);
  }else{
```

```
    time_given = parseInt(start_hour[0]);
  }
  var temp_start = new Date(parseInt(calendar[0]), parseInt(calendar[1]) -1, parseInt(calendar[2]),
time_given);

  var end_hour = open_between.split('-')[1].trim().split(' ');
  if(end_hour[1] == 'PM'){
    time_given = 12 + parseInt(end_hour[0]);
  }else{
    time_given = parseInt(end_hour[0]);
  }


var temp_end = new Date(parseInt(calendar[0]), parseInt(calendar[1]) -1, parseInt(calendar[2]),
time_given);

  if(reservation_date >= temp_start && reservation_date <= temp_end){
      data = envelope.date + ',' + envelope.time + "," + envelope.name + ',' + envelope.telephone
+ ',' + envelope.email + "\r\n";
      // Save reservation to permanent storage
      file.appendFileSync("reservation/reservation.data", data);
      outcome = true
  }else{
    console.log('Restaurant is closed during requested reservation time!')
  }

}catch(err){
  response.json({ result: false, exception: err.message });
}finally{
  response.json({ result: outcome });
}

});
```

SEARCH ENGINE OPTIMIZATION

The requirements outlined the need for the MDA to leverage the indexing domain where there were five components of the physical web document that would need be tailored to fit the narrative outlned. In order to be able to create clout with the search providers it is needed to create relevant content in the tags listed below. This section does not address the anchor tag as it was addressed in a prior section of this chapter.

- Title
- Description

- Header Two
- Keywords

To facilitate the creation of relevant content a function was implemented that could be embedded directly into the current process flow outlined and which is detailed below. The change to the loading of the document consisted of a single function that was named create_seo, which took it upon itself to simply call the needed functions to retrieve the desired content for the page title, the description meta tag, the keyword meta tag, and the header two tag which is physically displayed on the page with the content of 'Faster service than West Lubbock Deli!'. Once the function retrieves the needed content it then proceeds to update or create the tag elements accordingly. It was identified in a previous chapter that customers are searching for restaurants by name and as such the message is physically created on the page to show relevance with a competing and popular restaurant in the area.

The get_title, get_description, get_header_two, and get_keywords functions were stubbed out to return some string representation, but in a physical implementation these functions would call the desired API to retrieve content to show relevance with the search providers. This simple implementation to align the page content with search expectation demonstrates the leverage that may be obtained through the tailoring of the presentation to fit the audience and by doing so create that much needed competitive advantage for the restaurants that choose to subscribe to the service. In this mode of operation, it would be a trivial matter to change doctrine and pivot since the JavaScript code of the MDA is rendered dynamically. It's almost like going to the tailor and being fitted for that suite where the suite expands, and contracts given a daily calory intake. This is the type of message that resonates with an audience because of the malleability of the message where the presentation may be modified with a minor modification of code or maybe none at all. This example demonstrates the viability of code on demand and why MDAs will become the new breed of applications to power the internet.

```
// Mock title data
function get_title() { return "Lubbock Deli Meats"; }

// Mock description tag data
function get_description() { return "Pizza, Pasta, Deli, Restaurant"; }

// Mock header two data
function get_header_two(){ return "Faster service than West Lubbock Deli!"; }

// Mock keyword data
function get_keywords() { return "Pizza, Pasta, Deli, Restaurant"; }

function create_seo(){

 // Title SEO friendly content
 $(document).prop('title', get_title());

 // Page SEO friendly content
 $('#trs_container').append('<h2>' + get_header_two() + '</h2>')
```

```
// Meta tags
$('head')[0].append('<meta name="description" content="' + get_description() + '>');
$('head')[0].append('<meta name="keywords" content="' + get_keywords() + '>');
}


$(document).ready(function() {

var url = "http://trs:8888/book-your-table/";

if (window.location.href == url){
// Create base trs_container
create_container();

// Login section
create_row('', 'button', 'Portal');

// Add SEO
create_seo();

// Build reservation form
reservations_make_ui();

create_row('', 'link', 'www.TableReservationSystem.MDA.com');
 }
});
```

SUMMARY

There was a lot covered in quite a bit of detail in this chapter, from the creation of the WordPress plugin to the development of the client side MDA to the API code needed to support the data needs of the application. It is interesting to note that the MDA required very little physical coding on the WordPress side as the bulk of the code needed was provided by the templating engine that was utilized and the integration of the MDA simply required its bootstrapping to the initialization process of the WordPress plugin. This dynamic speaks to the flexibility and robustness that are MDAs as their implementation is flexible to the needed housing. It is because of the dynamic nature of JavaScript that it was possible to have created this type of solution. It is because of a language that has evolved over time, and it is because of a language that functions across a distributed network that MDAs have taken relevance in part. A solution was created here with a programming construct that is decades in its evolution and as such is able to provide the implementor a certain degree of comfort when used in an implementation. Add to this the fact that the language has not remained stagnant and has evolved to support the needs of the development community the result of which is that you end up with a truly remarkable utility to be leveraged.

The architectural framework of MDAs has led to a new breed of applications that are easier to build and layer upon one another. It is a dynamic that is easy to understand as a computer scientist as a central tenant of problem solving in the space is about creating leverage through artifacts. Add to this dynamic the fact that the creation of these micro JavaScript applications helps to leverage the indexing domain and you end up with a clear decision regarding development going forward. Development teams no longer need to build these overarching all encompassing applications that sit on expensive public cloud provider hardware. Teams no longer need to function under the paradigm of years gone by as they can now be nimble and productive to the point that they create software that is available to the masses through a simple library reference call in one HTML file as was seen directly in the WordPress plugin. Teams can create this functionality to be separated from the data process flows and segregate the core business functionality directly from the user interface particulars. They can create this functionality and let the masses consume it at will and in doing so become that voice of authority that businesses so desperately need to become so that they can take the reins of clout. When businesses do this, they become relevant because the masses will deem it to be so and when they vote the business that proverbial prom king then the indexing engines will have no choice but to concede to the will of the masses and give the business its rightly earned place as the king of the castle, first place on the search ranking algorithm. Businesses seek to become relevant because it is what differentiates the winners from the losers. They seek to have clout because it is the gateway to having their voice heard and when the masses pay attention it means that they will flock to the storefront of the business to buy the products and/or services offered. This relevance that is sought is natural and part of life as a voice is a fundamental need to an existence with individuals and with business as well.

As of this writing, it was Facebook that cried out in agony as their stock price tumbled and it did so because it was in unison with its user base. It turns out that those users do not want to have dialogues with their friends anymore but would rather upload videos to social media platforms an executive at the business said. Translation, humanity does not want to be on equal terms with one another, but rather wants to become the focal point of attention where the masses give this social media content creator relevance because of the attention they garnish. It is no different from what is physically seen in the development context, humanity and the solutions teams build are such because they are infused with the attributes of the creator. It just seems that teams are a little late to the party in software development because after all it is hard for developers to remove themselves from the pages of the books that they read to take note of what unfolds before them but do take note that the two worlds that they subscribe to are definitely in parity, one is simply a laggard to other. The solutions teams build must have relevance as a central tenant of the objective because whether it is people or solutions, those without a voice are but simply irrelevant to the masses and along with them their products and/or services.

REFERENCE

Taleb, N. N. (2014). *Antifragile: Things That Gain from Disorder*. Random House.

Chapter 13
Modeling Search Systems by Composite Inverted Index

ABSTRACT

There tends to be a propensity to utilize search systems that contain a custom software component for the specific purpose of meeting this need of inquiry. What falls through the gap with these systems however is the need of the customer to simultaneously query across datastore types such as web documents, database structures, and flat files. The tenants of indexing as they have been addressed in this body of work help to structure the discussion to one whereby this need to query across data type structures can be facilitated. The essence of search has been identified at the systems level and as such for the construct to carry forward to distinct data types requires the identification of the attributes of these other data structures. This chapter builds a generic construct for search to span repository type through an inverted composite index, which addresses the gap identified.

INTRODUCTION

In computer science computational work is spoken in terms of effort or elegance and to address this a construct was imposed and it is called Big O notation. In Big O notation what is always sought is constant time, so the questions begs to be asked in the search space; how can this be achieved with searching? The profession has come from the days of doing mass searching over some textual domain by looking at the individual word elements and matching them to the required needs and from these humble beginnings teams have moved to the domain of big data and distributed systems where the search domain is simplified and complicated all at the same time. Take the case of HADOOP and the Hadoop distributed file system (HDFS) where work effort is distributed to agent nodes and the search effort is consequently offset from some primary to a series of child nodes. The profession has regressed back to the beginning of time where 16MB machines searched the hard drive one file at a time, but now it happens in the cloud of course so it must be different. Individuals have taken the problem frame and regressed to something that is known and is comfortable with to put the world back into homeostasis, but in doing so teams have not made that large leap forward in the paradigm. What is shown in this body of work is that for search there

DOI: 10.4018/978-1-6684-4849-6.ch013

are some central tenants that hold and whether the domain of inspection is structured, semi-structured or unstructured data there are parallels and rules to adhere to. By following this prescribed doctrine over the domain it becomes possible to approximate O(1), which is achieved by way of a composite inverted index as is defined in this body of work.

The language construct is what governs the search input into some model that has the burden of determining the truth proposition from those inputs. It is the context of the language construct that also places yet another burden on the determination of worth on the system as for example the search term 'Big Apple' will probably refer to the city in the state of New York and would rather not imply a disproportionate fruit. To help alleviate some of the burden of context around these search systems it therefore becomes a necessity to be able to utilize the Natural Language Toolkit (NLTK) that may be viewed here: https://www.nltk.org/. Humanity fundamentally uses language differently to express its thoughts, hence the reason why there exists synonyms, it therefore becomes necessary to incorporate such a component in modeling efforts that compensates for this so that models can be better able to evaluate that truth proposition. The equation developed for the Yahoo search engine proves this point, it's an artifact that helps understand the landscape that is laid bare before all. It is possible to utilize a language construct along with an indexing effort to approximate truth, this was proved. The question now remains, can this go a step further to create generic search systems that allow for the indexing effort to encompass semi-structured, structured, and non-structured data so that a search system can be created over the entire data landscape? The argument of this chapter is that it can be done, you can create search systems that index data lakes for example where there exists flat files (unstructured data), XML documents (semi-structured data), and database files (structured data) to consequently create search systems that go beyond the myopic view of the businesses data. This chapter defines a design pattern that is referred to as a 'Composite Inverted Index' that may be used to create search systems over divergent data store types that when implemented can create solutions to facilitate the search efforts in an efficient and domain specific manner.

The discussion parts by looking at the state of current indexing doctrine that is later expanded on to create a system that can be implemented across industries and businesses. As was the case with the modeling of the Yahoo and Bing search engines, no two are identical; no two business are exactly the same and as such a design pattern must be just that a generic solution that can be implemented across instances as is the case of the interface design pattern for example. The interface design pattern is not programming language specific but is rather indifferent to its implementation. This is the breadth that is needed with solutions, courses of action that surpass the immediate and extend to the generic.

The discussion here takes a look at the Natural Language Toolkit (NLTK) and how it may be used to facilitate the search doctrine. From here the discourse next moves on to examine all the different data storage types that would be affected by the paradigm proposed along with the algorithm that could be used to create an indexing solution under that guise. The next section lays the groundwork for the reader as to how the paradigm may be used in a deterministic model given their own definition of system truths. From here the discourse moves on to define the Composite Inverted Index (CII) where the pieces begin to fit together for the reader as to how the search domain may be governed given the language construct, divergent data source types, and all with a bearing towards efficiency.

Search systems have proliferated the lives all, humanity no longer has to know the answer to the questions that kids pose because they can be Googled. Individuals don't have to look outside to know what the weather is like but can rather look at their phones or ask Alexa for the answer. While search keeps proliferating through the daily lives of everyone what has not occurred is the simplification of this for the development context. Instead of creating search systems specific to the needs of the business teams have rather implemented Google search directly on their own websites to search proprietary content. Teams have fallen to an anti-pattern that may be called mirroring; teams mirror the physical world around them to solve a problem that would be better suited to be answered with just a little more thought. To be fair how many of the individuals reading this text have taken code that was found online and used it, without fully considering the ramifications of the implementation? Developers do this in their daily work efforts when writing code and humanity does it in their physical lives to solve problems because it facilitates moving on. Search has been in this conundrum for far too long and teams need to be better able to create search systems that are specific to their needs and what better way to do this than to define a design pattern that can be leveraged independently of who you may be or what your specific case at hand may be? This is what is done here, the chapter lays forth a design pattern that is independent of self and as the equations for Yahoo and Bing showed earlier, a predictive model over search is possible.

QUERY DOMAIN

The query domain is a complex dynamic that relies on user input to decipher intent and consequently determine truth over some data repository such as URL end points that are indexed. The query submitted to the search provider can be simple or composed of several input phrases all of which must be taken into consideration when evaluating the truth proposition. The query complexity (QC) may therefore be defined as equation 1 as given below, where 'q' refers to the quantity of terms in the query. The work effort required to evaluate the premise given to search upon can be composed of any of the terms given where some of the terms may or may not be found in the documents returned, in the optimal case the documents returned all contain each of the terms provided to search upon.

Query Complexity (QC) = q! (1)

The query complexity (QC) is further complicated because the data sources that are needed to be accommodated are three, semi-structured, structured, and non-structured. The profession currently treats the search domain over non structured data in a rudimentary manner with utilities such as grep and regular expressions. When the discussion transitions to the structured domain the discourse continues as is known best with filters such as 'LIKE' or 'CONTAINS'; SQL Server specifically accommodates searching based upon these two filter types. Developers have simply fit the problem to what is already known and continue without much more concern over the integrity of the search. In the case of semi-structured data the problem becomes different than with structured data as the column sought is now ambiguous and once again individuals are left to their own devices to determine how to derive truth.

In this chapter the architectural foundation is created that may be used to create a search system independent of repository type and independent of query complexity (QC). This framework is such that it may be leveraged to create your own search system for your own specific needs and independently of the type of data you house in say a data lake, it now becomes feasible to classify the query truth proposition through a systematic manner that implements an inverted index paradigm to facilitate search.

TERM FREQUENCY – INVERSE DOCUMENT FREQUENCY

Term Frequency – Inverse Document Frequency (TF-IDF) has been a much-heralded paradigm for indexing content. TF-IDF is composed upon two classifiers, TF and IDF. Term Frequency (TF) refers to the frequency of some token upon some input stream read where the term frequency is simply the ratio of instances found divided by the length of the data stream. Equation 2 given below defines the term frequency (TF) equation.

$$\text{Term Frequency}\left(\text{TF}\right) = \frac{Occurances\ of\ Term}{\sum\ Words\ in\ Document} \tag{2}$$

Inverse document frequency (IDF) is accredited to Karen Sparck Jones who proposed the relationship for the weighing of the terms across some data set. The equation for inverse document frequency (IDF) is given below in equation 3. Determination of the IDF factor is important across some data set because it facilitates the weeding out of popularity of terms.

$$\text{IDF} = log\ \frac{Number\ of\ Documents}{Number\ of\ Doucments\ Containing\ Term} \tag{3}$$

Determination of TF-IDF is simple as it is the product of term frequency and the inverse document frequency, which is defined in equation 4 below. It should be pointed out that classification of document worth by TF-IDF is an issue when the documents have a strong similarity such as is the case with financial documents for example. Balance sheets and accounting metrics in distinct documents will be classified as having the same or similar worth in a TF-IDF calculation.

$$\text{TF} - \text{IDF} = \text{TF} * \text{IDF} \tag{4}$$

TF-IDF becomes a useful tool in the indexing of documents because of its simplicity and its ability to weed out skewness because of common terms. The ability to classify worth given some search term is of the utmost paramount in businesses today and teams have gone as far as implemented search products into the very fabric of business in order to accommodate this effort. Teams currently rely on products such as Elasticsearch (https://www.elastic.co/) and Redis (https://redis.io/) to help cope with the need of data retrieval. Organizations employ dedicated personnel for the management of these systems and others to write the code that interacts with these systems. Being able to classify and categorize proprietary data has become a necessity and in the next section the discussion begins to lay the ground work to show how term frequency can be used to help categorize this data.

INVERTED MATRIX

An inverted matrix is a representation of some token to some location that houses this index. In networking terms the end point is referred to as the sink, so this relationship may therefore be defined between the term to sink as relationship 1 as given below dictates. Each term points to some value that is an element of some sink set. This sink set could comprise files, web pages or database table repositories.

Relationship 1: {key:{value ϵ *Sink*}}

In the case of structured data you would need to go a step further because knowing simply that a table contains the queried terms will not suffice as what is needed for data retrieval purposes is the index that contains the elements or columns that showed the needed data. Relationship 1 may therefore be written as relationship 2 in the case of a structured data source such as a database.

Relationship 2: {key: {value ϵ *Iink*}}

If the data source is semi-structured or structured the determination of worth needs to have an additional component as each of the elements that are searched upon will have an encompassing parent object such as an HTML tag or a table column for example. In relationship three as given below this degree of relativity or impact factor 'f' is specified, where the impact factor is applied to some attribute in the data store searched. The impact factor would be the element showing the relativity of worth in the derivation of the significance of the attribute indexed. Take for example the case of an HTML document, where it was determined that the impact factor for the title tag was twice as significant as that of the URL. In such a case the identification of documents with the query term(s) in the title tag would be viewed as more relevant to those that contained the same verbiage in the URL.

Relationship 3: {key: {value $= \sum f_i * a_i$}}

In the case of relationship 3 as given above each of the attributes is viewed as being independent because they act in isolation to influence the attribute mapping, but you could have the case where they are related and as such it would lead to relationship 4 as given below. This prescription as it will be shown in a later section takes the argument to the realization that determination of worth is either linear or more complex, where the attributes and their influence factors work together to create value.

Relationship 4: {key:{value $= \prod f_i * a_i$}}

The inverted matrix is a powerful tool that allows for the creation of a link between term and repository. This repository must itself be mapped to its corresponding value of worth, where the attributes having influence over the domain could be related or not. Depending on the relationship between these attributes will determine the associative model that needs to be mapped that will be either multiplicative or summative.

NATURAL LANGUAGE TOOLKIT (NLTK)

The natural language toolkit (NLTK) is an open source driven project that is available for the Python programming language. The NLTK allows for the creation of solutions that are language centric; the search space has language as a central tenant, which makes the NLTK an ideal utility. Taking the query terms and being able to stem the words provided to their alternatives is paramount in the search space as individuals express themselves differently. A search system must be able to accommodate this difference in its paradigm to be able to accommodate the masses without exclusion. With the NLTK it becomes possible to obtain the stem of the query terms. Through the use of the NLTK it becomes possible to take some query term and map the query term to its alternate representation, thus allowing for the creation of an alternate mapping between some input and a physical artifact that may or may not contain the exact term provided as input but may contain an alternate representation of the query term, figure 1 below depicts this scenario.

Search systems need to be able to leverage the intricacies that the language construct brings forth and as such the utilization of a utility such as the NLTK becomes a necessity. As shown in figure 1 from below, with the aid of the NLTK you could have several tokens or keys pointing to the same document, URL or row in a database. The manifestation of this would result in one or multiple keys pointing to the same end point, which is what you would need to see in the result set. The NLTK helps to support this key to resource mapping as the language construct affords the searchers the ability to structure their requests in a flexible manner and the mapping of this flexibility must be accounted for in the model, which it does.

By extending the implementation of the NLTK across datastore types it allows for the argument to be extended to previous silos of data that had remained untapped and void of any possible indexing effort. The NLTK naturally extends to material that is unstructured as it is but a simplification to the problem frame of semi-structured data as the former is void of the limitation that is bound to documents of the latter type such as HTML pages for example. Alternatively, you could look at the problem a little different and view the unstructured data as being encompassed by a single hidden tag, which simply helps to facilitate the extension of the paradigm of indexing to this new data structure type. Alternatively, if the argument is extended further to house structured data it is also a simplification to the original challenge that was taken up in this text as this data housing type can be mapped in a more elegant fashion given that this data type may come from SQL database tables for example. In this case each of the columns being targeted become but the same HTML tags in essence. The paradigm being described here that may be extend to previous data stores that had not been considered for indexing across the paradigm opens the realm of search to a higher level of significance. No longer is data in the organization out of the bounds of indexing and as such helps to create an organization that is better suited to locate the data needed by personnel.

The NLTK has opened up the floodgates of the organization to be able to disseminate knowledge across the enterprise and in doing so help the data collected by the business take upon itself a new form of relevance. A benefit that previously could not have been considered because of the simple nature of datastore types and their inherent need to create lines of division. The benefit that may also be derived by the incorporation of an indexing effort by the organization is that it helps to transform the data that is laden throughout the business to information that can help drive the executive mandate. This data becomes a leverage when it is transformed to information, if for example the data once captured is placed through a machine learning algorithm it might just be the case that the business is able to determine simple truths that had previously been hidden. Take the case of a shipping organization that maintains copies of invoices from customers and a database structure with additional detail surrounding shipment entries, it could just well be the case that being able to correlate previous disparate data to understand the general logistics of the business could lead to an understanding surrounding how shipments to invoices to payments maybe better integrated to capitalize on possible discounts that had been written only on the invoices and left void of formal recording. The indexing domain does not simply apply to the search purveyors but has rather become a technological leverage that all organizations must embrace so that the inherent truths that litter the organization may be brought forth and be capitalized on for the benefit of the business. The indexing effort at an organization could help to create outwardly exposed data structures so that this data could be made available by some API for example. If synthesized data is exposed in this manner, then it has the potential to become a point of leverage for the business and maybe even an income stream as customers are all too willingly to pay for information that may be accessed in an expeditious manner. The benefit of being able to transform data to information cannot be discounted and must be sought at every possible opportunity by the organization as it is the manner by which a leverage may be created where one did not exist prior. It is a leverage point that could help to transform the organization to one that is envied for its innovation. The opportunities abound for businesses that are able to create a benefit from a station where one could only have been dreamt of prior.

Figure 1. Keys to Resource Linkage

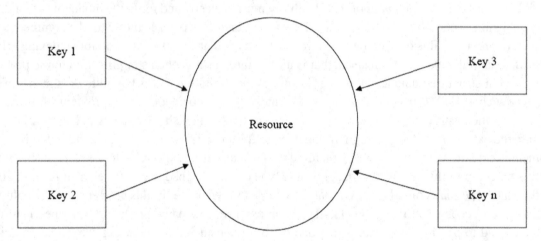

UNSTRUCTURED DATA

Unstructured data represents end point repositories that are of free form and do not follow a standard structure as you would find in a database for example or a semi-structured format as you would find in XML. Unstructured data litters businesses and may be commonly found in data lakes. TF-IDF is well suited for the indexing of this content as long as the content is diverse as pointed out previously. If you currently do a search on one of the popular search engine providers such as Google for example you will find that in the result set, you will find physical documents such as PDF files. Being able to index the unstructured data as well as alternate data formats is pivotal and needs to be a concentrated effort to be able to provide as much coverage as possible over the complete data stores that the business holds.

Indexing unstructured data needs to depend on the ability to account for the language construct in the model. This process of indexing unstructured data represents a first level of complexity over the data set as it is void of data containers such as HTML tags or columns in a database and for which you need to simply accommodate for the language construct; the algorithm that is detailed below takes this into account in the building of the inverted index over the data set.

1. Read nodes N_1 to N_n.
2. Create data set T_0 of tokens for each word found outside of stop words such as 'and', 'or', and 'the' where $T_0 = \{t_1, t_2, ..., t_n\}$ for each node read.
3. Use the NLTK or similar language construct library to discover the additional relationship tokens T_1 to augment original token set T_0, such that T_1 and T_0 are disjoint sets for each node read.
4. Token set T is the set created from the merging of T_0 and T_1.
5. For each node read if there exists the token sought then tabulate the TF for the document and create a mapping between file read to TF factor. For all tokens identified create a mapping M such that $M = \{ T[x] = \{TF_1: file_1, ..., TF_n: file_n\}$ or stated differently for each token or key in the token set T there exists a grouping of associated TF score(s) to file(s).

The creation of a search system over unstructured data follows a simplistic protocol as compared to that for semi-structured or structured data because the term to relevance container is void. Indexing of unstructured data is the easiest of the three indexing endeavors that may be undertaken. The creation of the inverted index over the data nodes allows for the efficient retrieval of the corresponding resources that answer the query posed to the system since the inverted index paradigm contains the answer to the question posed as indexes.

SEMI STRUCTURED DATA

Semi structured data is found most commonly in HTML documents and may generically be found in XML documents as the latter is the superset to the former. As was the case for unstructured data, the incorporation of the language construct is paramount in the evaluation of value in the data elements inspected. With semi-structured data it becomes paramount to be able to not only use a language construct, but it also becomes paramount to be able to associate value to container. Take the case of an HTML document for example, it becomes a necessity in the model to be able to define whether some element is more relevant than another element. HTML web documents have been identified as following this mold as depicted by King (2008) and Jerkovic (2010). This term of significance then needs to be part of the model, which is defined in step three of the algorithm below. As was the case for unstructured data the NLTK is also incorporated in the model. Below you will find detailed the algorithm needed to be able to index semi structured data.

1. Read nodes N_1 to N_n.
2. Identify all of the individual attributes in the data set that make the data partition-able such that there exists P partitions where $P = \{p_1, ..., p_n\}$.
3. Identify the correlating weight factors for each partition such that there exists W weights where $W = \{w_1, ..., w_n\}$ and for each weight there exists only one corresponding partition. For each partition the corresponding weight is determined such that the corresponding total of the impact factors or weights identified sums to one as given in equation 5 below.

$$1 = \sum_{1}^{n} w_i \qquad (5)$$

4. Create data set T_0 of tokens for each word found outside of stop words such as 'and', 'or', and 'the' where $T_0 = \{t_1, t_2, ..., t_n\}$ and where each t element represents the mapping between resource (N) and its tabulated weight factor (TW) by token as given below in relationship 5.

Relationship 5: $t = \{N \rightarrow TW\}$

5. For each node read by partition type 'p' calculate the term frequency in partition (TFIP) as defined in equation 6 below.

$$\text{TFIP} = \frac{length \ of \ term * occurances \ found}{length \ of \ partition} \tag{6}$$

6. For each node by partition type 'p' there exists a boundary constraint such that each term factor tabulated weight (TW) may be defined as given in equation 7 below where the determination is tabulated across all partitions found in at the node.

$$\text{TW} = \sum_{1}^{p} w_i * TFIP_i \tag{7}$$

7. Use the NLTK or similar language construct library to discover the additional relationship tokens T_1 to augment original token set T_0, such that T_1 and T_0 are disjoint sets.
8. Token set T is the set created from the merging of T_0 and T_1.
9. Generate the mapping matrix (M) where each index or term maps to each node traversed, which itself is mapped to its corresponding tabulated weight (TW) such that M = { T[x] = { TW_1: $Node_1$, ..., TW_N: $Node_N$}}.

Creating a search system over semi-structured data represents an increase in the level of complexity over that found for unstructured data because of the points of segregation in the data elements parsed. What you will find however is that the end result as was the case previously terminates in a mapping between tokens to a sequence of dictionary entries that map the node value for the term to the resource that contains the detail. This realization lets the discussion come to the conclusion that the search system could be used to index diverse content types where an index could either point to an URL or flat file definition for example.

STRUCTURED DATA

Structured data represents the third type of data container and the repository type that by definition contains the most stringent factor of segregation on the data layout. Enabling textual search on structured data stores such as SQL Server is possible by enabling full text searching. While this feature is simple to implement in a SQL data store it has a drawback and this being latency as the efficiency of O(1) is void in a textual match. Enabling such a mechanism across columns or tables also represents an option that would not be feasible for most systems to say the least. Being able to create an indexing solution across this paradigm is currently grossly lacking in practice and would be a much welcomed solution. If it would be possible to index text across tables and columns it would also represent an enhancement to current doctrine. Leveraging the language construct in this work effort would represent another benefit that is currently void in practice. If it would be possible to create a search system that could act in almost real time across database tables and columns that was sensitive to the language construct would represent a remarkable improvement over current practice.

In this section the argument leverages the seeds that have already been sowed to show that the argument can be extended to the paradigm of structured data. The paradigm needed could also be leveraged alongside what has already been described for unstructured data and semi-structured data that would allow for the creation of a search system that could span the enterprise or be implemented across a data lake, something that in current practice is but a goal pending to be reached. As was the case previously with regards to the language construct, an algorithm is defined here that takes this component into account to factor in the human element that is part of searching. The steps that would be required to create an inverted index data structure over the data elements is given below.

1. Read rows R_1 to R_n.
2. Identify all of the individual attributes in the data set that make the data partition-able such that there exists P partitions where $P = \{p_1, ..., p_n\}$. The partition set shall occur over the data division boundaries such as columns in a table for example.
3. Identify the correlating weight factors for each partition such that there exists W weights where $W = \{w_1, ..., w_n\}$ and for each weight there exists only one corresponding partition. For each partition the corresponding weight is determined such that the corresponding total of the impact factors or weights identified sums to one as given in equation 5 above.
4. 4. Create data set T_0 of tokens for each word found outside of stop words such as 'and', 'or', and 'the' where $T_0 = \{t_1, t_2, ..., t_n\}$ and where each t element represents the mapping between row read (R) and its tabulated weight factor (TW) by token as given below in relationship 6.

Relationship 6: $t = \{R \rightarrow TW\}$

5. For each row read by partition type 'p' calculate the term frequency in partition (TFIP) as defined in equation 6 as given above.
6. For each row (R) by partition type 'p' there exists a boundary constraint such that each term factor tabulated weight (TW) may be defined as given in equation 7 above where the determination is tabulated across all partitions found in the row (R).
7. Use the NLTK to discover the additional relationship tokens T_1 to augment original token set found in T_0, such that T_1 and T_0 are disjoint sets.
8. Token set T is the set created from the merging of T_0 and T_1.
9. Generate the mapping matrix (M) where each index or term maps to each row (R) traversed, which itself is mapped to its corresponding tabulated weight (TW) such that $M = \{T[x] = \{TW_1: Row_1, ..., TW_N: Row_N \}\}$.

In this section it was shown that indexing structured data is feasible by extending the algorithms developed in the previous sections. Being able to index your content is paramount in order to be able to leverage it through some interface such as an API. The search paradigm can be made to extend over various forms of data stores such as structured data as has been outlined here. With the algorithm defined here it would be possible to create a search system for a blog for example where you could define the fields of relevance to be 'Author', 'Responder', 'Post', and 'Response' and where each field could be weighed at 25% relevance. This would allow your searchers to find articles where the desired query could be found in either column. The ability to index this content across data containers (columns) and also specify the relevance of the container in the total query determination represents a significant upgrade to how search is now handled in current database systems and bound to be a point of discussion for time to come.

ECONOMIC PROPOSITION

The value of searching is in being able to answer a query posed where the content retrieved is deemed to be relevant to the end user. The degree of relevance is a function of the content that is available for indexing. In the case of unstructured data the case is simplified as there does not exist a line of partition between the data elements that are to be read. In the case of semi-structured and structured data what needs to be defined are the tenants of textual relevance so that the answer to some query posed returns the best possible solution to the end user. The case of structured data is similar to that of unstructured data, but there needs to be a relationship created through a unique index that points to the fields of relevance. These partitions that have been identified are the set P such that $P = \{p_1, ..., p_n\}$. Each of these partitions contains one and only one weight w_i factor that represents its relevance in the query response where the weights W are defined as the collection of $\{w_1, ..., w_n\}$ elements. Through the evaluation of the available data then it becomes feasible to create a dictionary that contains relationships by term to datastore relevance which then allows for the execution of queries at runtime and have the system return a response to the query without the need to have to determine at the moment what is relevant. The economics of the discourse have changed in this dynamic as it is no longer required to incur the burden of inquiry at an instance, but it can rather be performed in some background process which allows the user to have a seamless experience. At the moment that they submit their query to the host the host will be able to return a response because the body of work, the heavy lifting to determine relevance would already have been done.

COMPOSITE INVERTED INDEX

In algorithm design you are always after constant time and the reason why an inverse indexing structure makes for a viable option. Below is the formal definition of the composite inverted index (CII).

A composite inverted index (CII) is a mapping between a token set and its corresponding resource to its corresponding index of relevance, such that resources are ordered by index of relevance in descending order.

Relationship 7 given below provides the formal definition for a composite inverted index (CII) in an enhanced dictionary format. Relationship 7 would hold the relationship mapping for all tokens identified through document or resource inspection plus the tokens identified by way of an NLTK library. The composite inverted index (CII) gives an algorithm efficiency of O(1) for a token search because each token is the key of the data structure. The traversing of the values to the token are themselves a dictionary where the key is the index value tabulated and the resource would be the document identified, table row, or URI

Relationship 7: {*token*: {*index*: *resource*}}

The ultimate compliment to intelligent design is simplicity and you cannot obtain a greater degree of efficiency than O(1) in algorithm design as has been done here as each query term maps to a key in a dictionary. In the case where the query term length is greater than one entails an additional step in the evaluation of the response to the end user, but still falls within the domain of the discussion that was laid bare here, this is discussed in the following section.

PROPOSITIONAL CALCULUS

The search space can be plural as each query can contain one or more query terms. Given a series of resources and a series of query terms that map to these resources then what is sought in the optimal response is the series of documents, URIs, and table primary key references that contain all of the query terms posed to the search system. In relationship 8 this optimal relationship is defined where the nodes sought and the tokens provided are found in each of the resources returned.

Relationship 8: $A \cap B \cap ... \cap Z = \{x: x \in A \text{ and } x \in B \text{ and } x \in Z\}$

As the query complexity (QC) increases so does the probability that the documents searched do not contain complete coverage over the query. In the minimal case what will be found is that the evaluation of the query will result in a response where nodes identified as being relevant will contain some share of the query posed. Relationship 9 defines this proposition and is given below. You can see this effect present while conducting a search on Google.com as the missing tokens from the query will display crossed out in a given result entry provided when the token was not found at the node by the search provider.

Relationship 9: $A \cup B \cup ... \cup Z = \{x: x \in A \text{ or } x \in B \text{ or } x \in Z\}$

Mapping the tokens to the resources involved in the search space entails that at any given time the probability of finding a document that provides complete query coverage is inversely proportional to the tabulated composite inverted index (TCII), this probability is expressed as relationship 10 as given below. The reason why it is an inverse relationship is that the factors of relevance in the sinks identified will be fractional and the multiplication of one fraction by another entails an even smaller result. The tabulated composite inverted index in the optimal case is defined as the multiplication for each of the entities indexed by corresponding sink where the target term is identified. The tabulated composite inverted index is defined in equation 8 below where the dependent variable is the degree of relevance and where preference is always conceded to documents that contain the greatest degree of terms from the query posed, i.e., give coverage for the greatest degree of query complexity.

Relationship 10: $P\left(\left\{x_1,\ldots,x_n\right\}\right)\alpha\dfrac{1}{TCII}$

$$TCII = \prod_{i=1}^{n} CII_i \tag{8}$$

In the suboptimal case, the probability of finding relevance across the query space is directly proportional to the tabulated composite inverted index as is defined in relationship 11 as given below. In the suboptimal case or in the case of a union you find the relationship to differ from that of the case of intersection because TCII is derived as a summation exercise across the collective of sinks. In the suboptimal case the TCII is tabulated as defined in equation 9 where summation occurs at sink nodes that show relevance across the query set.

Relationship 11: $P(\{x_1, \ldots, x_n\})\alpha TCII$

$$TCII = \sum_{i=1}^{n} CII_i \tag{9}$$

Propositional calculus may be applied to the search space to help derive a relationship mapping by way of the tabulated inverted index such that a stochastic relationship may be derived. The search domain will need to consider the skeptical and optimal cases for each query posed and evaluate them accordingly. The result set returned will need to list the optimal cases prior to the skeptical scenarios as this entails that more significant results will be provided first. In carrying out this exercise it become feasible to map relevance across previous silos of datasets and help bridge the gap of search across disparate sources of information.

SUMMARY

In this chapter it was shown that the search space can provide coverage to unstructured, semi-structured, and structured data sets. The hurdles with the classification of semi-structured and structured datasets can be overcome by determining boundary points of relevance where each of these boundary points has a corresponding weight factor. By being able to reduce the argument to an all too familiar paradigm entails that an all too familiar prescription may be applied to the classification domain such as term frequency (TF).

Being able to create your own specific search system that meets your specific needs entails that more businesses will be able to index their content and begin to be able to provide it to third parties for consumption or more simply begin to ingest their own data for their own specific needs. Before the argument can move to an action phase it must first be preceded by an understanding phase where the data must first be categorized. Industry has started doing this with the aid of big data tools such as Elasticsearch (https://www.elastic.co/) and all at the expense of an implementation cost, a support cost, personnel development cost, and countless other balance sheet factors. This is all being done in an effort to be able to serve up content to some process, as such is the demand to obtain the needed data in an efficient manner that countless businesses are incurring these expenses. The argument presented here lays bare another paradigm, one that is simple in nature, but at the same time one that is rooted in the garden that has borne good fruit in the past, one based upon principles that have already been identified as being relevant and useful.

Being able to create search system across datastore types presents a significant benefit for businesses as they have data in data lakes already and in the cloud at times ready to be consumed and disseminated across the enterprise for the benefit of the business. It has been from the principles of indexing that the argument has been able to proceed to define a doctrine to facilitate classification for the already existing data that organizations hold. Think about an indexing endeavor for some government body that needs to understand all the data that lay isolated in separate data stores now, by classifying such data they can become better informed and become better able to make decisions for the masses. It might be the case that this degree of data ingestion and further processing through data science tools will allow such organizations to understand and react more efficiently to the demands that lay ahead, such as keeping its citizens better protected. Search is helping organizations convert data to information that can be leveraged and be acted upon to the point that it makes a difference to the businesses that take it upon themselves to utilize this leverage. Think about all the institutional knowledge that lays asleep in repositories all over an organization and with individuals retiring where that knowledge that was once there and ready to be acted upon is lost. Through search systems as outlined here you may be able to retrieve part of that knowledge and make it available to your audience so that they may be better informed and be better equipped to make those needed business decisions. It becomes easy to see under this guise why organizations such as Google, Yahoo, and Microsoft through their search utilities have become relevant, it is because they provided relevance to the data that was once unorganized and by doing such they in turn became relevant and as they did so may your organization or pod become if you can provide a similar degree of relevance to what was once irrelevant.

REFERENCES

Jerkovic, J. (2010). *SEO Warrior*. O'Reilly Media Inc.

King, A. (2008). *Website Optimization*. O'Reilly Media Inc.

Conclusion

The journey that the text takes the reader upon crosses many boundaries as the software engineering domain has a vast reach. By parting the discussion from the roots of search and using it to derive a quantifiable model for the Yahoo search engine it became feasible to have determined the elements of indexing that prove to show clout. The text also provided for the reader a random forest study that utilized the same dataset to tabulate relevance by page attribute. In the case of the supervised learning model, it showed an almost 80% degree of congruency with one of the search purveyor's own search results. It was because of this endeavor that it became possible to have come to understand how development for the internet needed to change from current doctrine. It was because of this effort that Micro Distributed Applications (MDAs) came to be. It was because of what the numbers dictated that it became feasible to understand those factors of influence that web development solutions need to incorporate. It was this process that led to the identification of the architectural framework of Micro Distributed Applications. Under this paradigm it becomes feasible to obtain clout because each subscribing node helps to provide a vote for the authoring domain. Through this development model it becomes feasible to reduce operational expenses because the hardware that MDAs operate under are but the hardware that is used by the user from the comfort of their own local. Gone are the days when software will sit in the cold storage rooms of public cloud providers as now the software can be provided by an API and loaded into the browser window of the user to execute at the expense of the user. It amounts to nothing short than a benefit to the author of the MDA because it is the resources of the client that are consumed by the application and leaves the author of the MDA free of the capital expenditure.

Software today is similar to what it was in the past, but different at the same time. The development domain has reached current state because of the work of others and as such cannot be disparaged but must rather be embraced and leveraged where it is the inefficient components of which that die, and the good parts remain. Software engineering follows but that same process that Darwin himself explained, it just simply occurs in a variant of what he detailed. The evolutionary process in software engineering is real and visible as a matter of fact much as fossils are visible. MDAs were set in motion from the time that dynamic HTML was introduced, where HTML content could be changed by way of JavaScript. It just so happens now that these JavaScript applications are distributed and function across the largest network structure that is known, the internet. MDAs in fact align with the concept of micro front ends, but it just so happens that the technology of the latter stops short of what is needed. It is not simply about creating smaller client side components, but it is about creating alignment between the search purveyors, the economics of software, distributed functionality, and the leveraging of the utility afforded by the masses. This is what the text is about, it is about creating value for the business through an architectural framework that leverages a benefit because the numbers dictate this to be such. The numbers have in fact told the profession in which way it needs to pivot and change, and it is up to development teams to come to appreciate this leverage for what it is, but a whisper, a secret that few are aware of.

The arguments prior to this text regarding relevance where subjective, they were qualifiable. This text moved the discourse from the relative to the quantifiable, whereby it became but a matter at looking at the data to understand what lay bare before all. This facilitated the discourse and allowed for conclusions to be drawn that helped to put into focus the manner by which development came from, where it stands, and most importantly where it is headed. This destination point without question because the numbers state such is towards MDAs. The degree of relevance that businesses will come to enjoy will be tied to the embrace that their products receive by the masses.

Compilation of References

Berry, M., & Browne, M. (2005). *Understanding Search Engines: Mathematical Modeling and Text Retrieval*. Siam. doi:10.1137/1.9780898718164

Clement, J. (2020, February 28). *Global Content Delivery Network Internet Traffic 2020*. Statista. https://www.statista.com/statistics/267184/content-delivery-network-internet-traffic-worldwide/

Google. (n.d.). *Search Engine Optimization Starter Guide*. Retrieved July 15, 2015, from http://static.googleusercontent.com/media/www.google.com/en/us/webmasters/docs/search-engine-optimization-starter-guide.pdf

Graham, M. (2021). *How Google's $150 Billion Advertising Business Works*. CNBC. https://www.cnbc.com/2021/05/18/how-does-google-make-money-advertising-business-breakdown-.html

Jerkovic, J. (2010). *SEO Warrior*. O'Reilly Media Inc.

Johnson, J. (2021, October 8). *Global Market Share of Search Engines 2020-2021*. Statista. https://www.statista.com/statistics/216573/worldwide-market-share-of-search-engines/

King, A. (2008). *Website Optimization*. O'Reilly Media Inc.

Novet, J. (2021). *Amazon Web Services Tops Analysts' Estimates on Profit and Revenue*. CNBC. https://www.cnbc.com/2021/10/28/aws-earnings-q3-2021.html

Smyth, B., Balfe, E., Freyne, J., Briggs, P., Coyle, M., & Boydell, O. (2004). Exploiting Query Repetition and Regularity in an Adaptive Community-Based Web Search Engine. *User Modelling and User-Adaptive Interaction.*, *14*(5), 383–423. doi:10.100711257-004-5270-4

Taleb, N. N. (2014). *Antifragile: Things That Gain from Disorder*. Random House.

Wei, Z., Zhao, P., & Zhang, L. (2014). Design and Implementation of Image Search Algorithm. *American Journal of Software Engineering and Applications*, *3*(6), 90–94. doi:10.11648/j.ajsea.20140306.14

About the Author

Guillermo Rodriguez has dedicated his professional life to working with technology and the management of teams. He holds an undergraduate degree in Computing and Information Systems as well as graduate degrees in Software Engineering & Systems and Engineering Management. When not spending time with his daughters you will find him either working on his next book, working on some startup, or teaching technology related subjects to the next generation.

Index

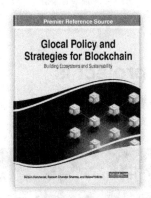

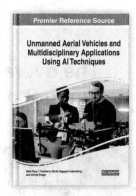

Ensure Quality Research is Introduced to the Academic Community

Become an Evaluator for IGI Global Authored Book Projects

Premier Reference Source

Tax Audit and Taxation in the Paradigm of Sustainable Development

Premier Reference Source

Controlling Epidemics With Mathematical and Machine Learning Models

Premier Reference Source

School-Museum Relationships and Teaching Social Sciences in Formal Education

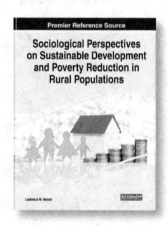

Premier Reference Source

Sociological Perspectives on Sustainable Development and Poverty Reduction in Rural Populations

The overall success of an authored book project is dependent on quality and timely manuscript evaluations.

Applications and Inquiries may be sent to:
development@igi-global.com

Applicants must have a doctorate (or equivalent degree) as well as publishing, research, and reviewing experience. Authored Book Evaluators are appointed for one-year terms and are expected to complete at least three evaluations per term. Upon successful completion of this term, evaluators can be considered for an additional term.

If you have a colleague that may be interested in this opportunity, we encourage you to share this information with them.

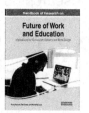

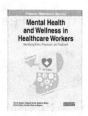

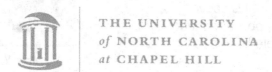

Printed in the United States
by Baker & Taylor Publisher Services